English

Literary Criticism:

RESTORATION

AND

18th CENTURY

GOLDENTREE BOOKS

English
Literary Criticism:
RESTORATION
AND
18TH CENTURY

New York

APPLETON-CENTURY-CROFTS

Division of Meredith Publishing Company

Copyright © 1963 by

MEREDITH PUBLISHING COMPANY

633–1

Library of Congress Card Number: 63–13834

PRINTED IN THE UNITED STATES OF AMERICA
E 47650

PREFACE

THIS BOOK IS THE second of three anthologies of English criticism, covering three general periods of literary history—the Renaissance, the neo-classical age, and the nineteenth century. Of these periods, the neo-classical is the longest and the most homogeneous; the two great English neo-classical critics—Dryden and Johnson —stand at its beginning and its end, defining between them the dominant critical ideas of their age: rules, decorum, the authority of the Ancients, the appeal to nature, reason and "good sense," the proprieties of literary kinds. No critic of the period was unaware of these principles, and all of them can, in one sense or another, be called neo-classical.

But neo-classicism in England was never as rigid as it was in France. From the beginning it showed a flexibility that enabled it, without losing its identity, to assimilate the psychological and emotional bias of the empirical philosophers, and of Longinus— a bias most evident in the criticism of Addison, Burke, and Hume among the critics included here, but evident in nearly all eighteenth-century criticism in England. Reynolds and Johnson, at the threshold of the Romantic Movement, are as neo-classical as Dryden, but neither of them is as thoroughly neo-classical as Rapin or le Bossu.

This series is intended to provide teacher and student with authoritative texts of the most important critical writings in English. All selections are complete unless otherwise indicated; texts are from the best editions, and textual sources are indicated in the headnotes. The spelling, capitalization, and use of italics have been followed as given in the sources cited except for a few cases of archaic typography in which long *s* has regularly been changed to short *s*. Emendation has been kept to a minimum, and the temptation to indulge in profuse annotation has been resisted. Foreign-language quotations have been translated into English and their sources indicated when known and when not clear from the context; also a few obscure terms and illusions have been explained.

v

Brief headnotes provide biographical and critical information, and a selected bibliography of books which treat the authors' critical works; for fuller references consult the *Cambridge Bibliography of English Literature*, 5 vols. (Cambridge, 1940–57). Other useful general works are: George Saintsbury, *A History of Criticism and Literary Taste in Europe*, 3 vols. (Edinburgh, 1900–04); A. Bosker, *Literary Criticism in the Age of Johnson* (The Hague, 1930; new ed., New York, 1953); Samuel Monk, *The Sublime. A Study of Critical Theories in XVIII-Century England* (New York, 1938; new ed., Ann Arbor, 1960); René Wellek, *The Rise of English Literary History* (Chapel Hill, 1941); Walter Jackson Bate, *From Classic to Romantic* (Cambridge, Mass., 1946); J. W. H. Atkins, *English Literary Criticism: 17th and 18th Centuries* (London, 1951); René Wellek, *A History of Modern Criticism 1750–1950*, 4 vols. (New Haven, 1955— [in progress]); William K. Wimsatt, Jr., and Cleanth Brooks, *Literary Criticism: A Short History* (New York, 1957); Walter Jackson Bate, *Prefaces to Criticism* (Garden City, 1959); Scott Elledge, ed., *Eighteenth-Century Critical Essays*, 2 vols. (Ithaca, New York, 1961).

S.H.

Swarthmore, Pennsylvania

CONTENTS

English

Literary Criticism:

RESTORATION

AND

18th CENTURY

John Dryden

[1631–1700]

❦

DRYDEN WAS THE FIRST great English man of letters. Though for a time he enjoyed royal patronage (he was Poet Laureate from 1668 to 1688), he was primarily a professional writer; he wrote verse plays, didactic prose, political satires, and lyrics, and translated Lucretius, Juvenal, Ovid, Horace, and Virgil into English verse. He also wrote, in the critical essays which he often attached as dedications and prefaces to his works, a prose which is remarkable for its clarity and easy, conversational grace.

Dryden's critical importance lies first of all in the fact that he was the first English poet to formulate at length the theories on which his practice was based. His principles, derived mainly from classical and French neo-classical sources, were the critical principles of the century that followed him, and the terms in which he dealt with them—wit, correctness, refinement, propriety, elegancy, good numbers, good sense —are the terms which his critical successors used. His formulations of literary genres were major contributions to the genre criticism which was characteristic of the neo-classical period.

Yet it would be a mistake to take Dryden's neo-classicism in too narrow a sense; if he was a cosmopolitan critic, he was also, as Dr. Johnson said, "the father of *English* criticism," and his appreciation of what was peculiarly English in his national literature (as in his remarks on Shakespeare in the *Essay of Dramatic Poesy,* and on Chaucer in the preface to *Fables Ancient and Modern*) reveal a pragmatic turn of mind, and an historic sense, which was not common in continental neo-classical theorizing. These qualities, derived perhaps in part from Dryden's experience as a poet-dramatist, make his criticism best when it is most particular, and give to his writing as a whole the attractive virtues of generosity, good humor, and good sense.

BIBLIOGRAPHY. *Works,* 18 vols., ed. Walter Scott, rev. George Saintsbury (Edinburgh and London, 1882–93); *Works,* ed. E. N. Hooker and H. T. Swedenberg, Jr. (Berkeley and Los Angeles, 1956—[in progress]); *Essays,* ed. W. P. Ker, 2 vols. (2nd impression, Oxford, 1926).

T. S. Eliot, *Homage to John Dryden* (London, 1924) and *John Dryden: The Poet, The Dramatist, The Critic* (New York, 1932); Louis I. Bredvold, *The Intellectual Milieu of John Dryden* (Ann Arbor, 1934; reprinted 1956); Frank L. Huntley, *On Dryden's "Essay of Dramatic Poesy"* (Ann Arbor, 1951).

TEXT. *An Essay of Dramatick Poesie* (London, 1668); *Fables Ancient and Modern* (London, 1700).

AN ESSAY OF DRAMATIC POESY

[1668]

IT WAS THAT MEMORABLE DAY, in the first Summer of the late War, when our navy ingag'd the Dutch: a day wherein the two most mighty and best appointed Fleets which any age had ever seen, disputed the command of the greater half of the Globe, the commerce of Nations, and the riches of the Universe. While these vast floating bodies, on either side, mov'd against each other in parallel lines, and our Country men, under the happy conduct of his Royal Highness, went breaking, by little and little, into the line of the Enemies; the noise of the Cannon from both Navies reach'd our ears about the City: so that all men being alarm'd with it, and in a dreadful suspense of the event, which we knew was then deciding, every one went following the sound as his fancy led him; and leaving the Town almost empty, some took towards the Park, some cross the River, others down it; all seeking the noise in the depth of silence.

Among the rest, it was the fortune of *Eugenius, Crites, Lisideius,* and *Neander,*[1] to be in company together: three of them persons whom their witt and Quality have made known to all the Town: and whom I have chose to hide under these borrowed names, that they may not suffer by so ill a relation as I am going to make of their discourse.

---

[1] Charles Sackville, later Earl of Dorset; Sir Robert Howard, Dryden's brother-in-law; Sir Charles Sedley; Dryden.

Taking then a Barge which a servant of *Lisideius* had provided for them, they made haste to shoot the Bridge, and left behind them that great fall of waters which hindred them from hearing what they desired: after which, having disingag'd themselves from many Vessels which rode at Anchor in the *Thames*, and almost blockt up the passage towards *Greenwich*, they order'd the Watermen to let fall their Oares more gently; and then every one favouring his own curiosity with a strict silence, it was not long ere they perceiv'd the Air break about them like the noise of distant Thunder, or of Swallows in a Chimney: those little undulations of sound, though almost vanishing before they reach'd them, yet still seeming to retain somewhat of their first horroor which they had betwixt the Fleets: after they had attentively listned till such time as the sound by little and little went from them, *Eugenius*, lifting up his head, and taking notice of it, was the first who congratulated to the rest that happy Omen of our Nations Victory: adding, we had but this to desire in confirmation of it, that we might hear no more of that noise, which was now leaving the English Coast. When the rest had concur'd in the same opinion, *Crites*, a person of a sharp judgment, and somewhat too delicate a taste in wit, which the world have mistaken in him for ill-nature, said, smiling to us, that if the concernment of this battle had not been so exceeding great, he could scarce have wished the victory at the price he knew he must pay for it, in being subject to the reading and hearing of so many ill verses as he was sure would be made upon it; adding, that no Argument could scape some of those eternal Rhimers, who watch a Battel with more diligence then the Ravens and birds of Prey; and the worst of them surest to be first in upon the quarry, while the better able, either out of modesty writ not at all, or set that due value upon their Poems, as to let them be often call'd for and long expected! There are some of those impertinent people you speak of, answered *Lisideius*, who to my knowledge, are already so provided, either way, that they can produce not only a Panegyrick upon the Victory, but, if need be, a funeral elegy upon the Duke; and after they have crown'd his valour with many Lawrels, at last deplore the odds under which he fell, concluding that his courage deserved a better destiny. All the company smil'd at the conceit of *Lisideius*; but *Crites*, more eager than before, began to make particular exceptions against some Writers, and said the publick Magistrate ought to send betimes to forbid them; and that it concern'd the peace and quiet of all honest people, that ill poets should be as well silenced as seditious Preachers. In my opinion, replyed *Eugenius,* you pursue your point too far; for as to my own particular, I am so great a lover of Poesie, that I could wish them all rewarded who attempt but to do well; at least I would not have them worse used then *Sylla* the Dictator did one of their brethren heretofore:—*Quem in concione vidimus* (says *Tully* speaking of him), *cum ei libellum malus poeta de populo subjecisset, quod epigramma in eum fecisset tantummodo alternis versibus longiusculis, statim ex iis rebus qua tunc vendebat jubere ei praemium tribui, sub ea conditione ne quid postea scriberet.* [We saw him in the assembly, when a bad poet from among the people submitted a petition to him on the grounds that he had composed an epigram on him only in rather long, alternating verses. He at once ordered that he should be given a reward from those things that he was offering for sale, on condition that he never write anything thereafter.] I could wish with all my heart, replied Crites, that many whom we know were as bountifully thank'd upon the same condition, that they would never trouble us again. For amongst others, I have a mortal apprehension of two Poets, whom this victory with the help of both her wings will never be able to escape; 'Tis easy to guess whom you intend, said *Lisideius;* and without naming them, I ask you if one of them does not perpetually pay us with clenches upon words and a certain clownish kind of raillery? if now and then he does not offer at a Catachresis or Clevelandism,[2] wresting and torturing a word into another meaning: in fine, if he be not one of those whom the French would call *un mauvais buffon;* one that is so much a well-willer to the Satire, that he spares no man; and though he cannot strike a blow to hurt any, yet ought to be punished for the malice of the action; as our witches are justly hanged, because they think themselves so; and suffer deservedly for believing they did mischief, because they meant it. You have described him, said *Crites,* so exactly, that I am afraid to come after you with my other ex-

---

[2] John Cleveland (1613–58), a satiric poet who affected a metaphysical style.

tremity of Poetry. He is one of those who, having had some advantage of education and converse, knows better than the other what a Poet should be, but puts it into practice more unluckily than any man; his style and matter are every where alike; he is the most calm, peaceable writer you ever read: he never disquiets your passions with the least concernment, but still leaves you in as even a temper as he found you; he is a very Leveller in poetry, he creeps along with ten little words in every line, and helps out his numbers with *For to,* and *Unto,* and all the pretty Expletives he can find, till he draggs them to the end of another line; while the sense is left tired half way behind it: he doubly starves all his verses, first for want of thought, and then of expression; his Poetry neither has wit in it, nor seems to have it; like him in Martial: *Pauper videri Cinna vult, et est pauper.* [Cinna wants to appear poor, and he is poor.]

He affects plainness, to cover his want of imagination: when he writes the serious way, the highest flight of his fancy is some miserable *Antithesis,* or seeming contradiction; and in the comic he is still reaching at some thin conceit, the ghost of a jest, and that too flies before him, never to be caught; these swallows which we see before us on the Thames are the just resemblance of his wit: you may observe how near the water they stoop, how many proffers they make to dip, and yet how seldom they touch it: and when they do, it is but the surface; they skim over it but to catch a gnat, and then mount into the air and leave it.

Well, gentlemen, said *Eugenius,* you may speak your pleasure of these authors; but though I and some few more about the town may give you a peaceable hearing, yet assure yourselves, there are multitudes who would think you malicious and them injured: especially him whom you first described; he is the very *Withers* of the city: they have bought more editions of his works than would serve to lay under all their pies at the Lord Mayor's *Christmass.* When his famous poem first came out in the year 1660, I have seen them reading it in the midst of 'Change-time; nay so vehement they were at it, that they lost their bargain by the Candles ends: but what will you say, if he has been received amongst the great Ones? I can assure you he is, this day, the envy of a great person who is Lord in the Art of Quibbling; and who does not take it well, that any man should intrude so far into his

Province. All I would wish, replied *Crites,* is, that they who love
his writings, may still admire him, and his fellow Poet: *Qui
Bavium non odit, etc.,* [He who does not hate Bavius. . .] is
curse sufficient. And farther, added *Lisideius,* I believe there is
no man who writes well, but would think himself very hardly
dealt with, if their Admirers should praise anything of his: *Nam
quos contemnimus eorum quoque laudes contemnimus.* [We despise the praises of those whom we despise.] There are so few
who write well in this age, said *Crites,* that me-thinks any praises
should be wellcome; they neither rise to the dignity of the last
Age, nor to any of the Ancients; and we may cry out of the
Writers of this time, with more reason than *Petronius* of his, *Pace
vestrâ liceat dixisse, primi omnium eloquentiam perdidistis:* you
have debauched the true old poetry so far, that Nature, which
is the soul of it, is not in any of your Writings.

If your quarrel (said *Eugenius*) to those who now write, be
grounded only on your reverence to Antiquity, there is no man
more ready to adore those great Greeks and Romans than I am:
but on the other side, I cannot think so contemptibly of the Age
I live in, or so dishonourably of my own Countrey, as not to
judge we equal the Ancients in most kinds of Poesie, and in some
surpass them; neither know I any reason why I may not be as
zealous for the Reputation of our Age, as we find the Ancients
themselves in reference to those who lived before them. For you
hear your *Horace* saying,

> *Indignor quidquam reprehendi, non quia crassé
> Compositum, illepidève putetur, sed quia nuper.*

[I get angry when something is criticized, not because it is
crudely composed, or is regarded as lacking charm, but because
it is recent.]
And after:

> *Si meliora dies, ut vina, poemata reddit,
> Scire velim pretim chartis quotus arroget annus?*

[If time enhances my poems as it enhances wine, then I would
liko to know how many years it will take for my writings to bring
a price.]

But I see I am engaging in a wide dispute, where the arguments are not like to reach close on either side; for Poesie is of
so large an extent, and so many both of the Ancients and Moderns

have done well in all kinds of it, that, in citing one against the other, we shall take up more time this Evening than each mans occasions will allow him: therefore I would ask *Crites* to what part of Poesie he would confine his Arguments, and whether he would defend the general cause of the Ancients against the Moderns, or oppose any Age of the Moderns against this of ours?

Crites a little while considering upon this Demand, told *Eugenius* he approv'd his Propositions, and, if he pleased, he would limit their dispute to *Dramatique Poesie;* in which he thought it not difficult to prove, either that the Antients were superiour to the Moderns, or the last age of this of ours.

Eugenius was somewhat surpriz'd, when he heard *Crites* make choice of that Subject; For ought I see, said he, I have undertaken a harder Province than I imagined; for though I never judg'd the plays of the Greek or Roman poets comparable to ours, yet on the other side those we now see acted, come short of many which were written in the last Age: but my comfort is if we are overcome, it will be onely by our own Countreymen: and if we yield to them in this one part of Poesie, we more surpass them in all the other; for in the Epique or Lyrique way, it will be hard for them to show us one such amongst them, as we have many now living, or who lately were so. They can produce nothing so courtly writ, or which expresses so much the Conversation of a Gentleman, as *Sir John Suckling;* nothing so even, sweet, and flowing as Mr. *Waller;* nothing so Majestique, so correct, as Sir *John Denham;* nothing so elevated, so copious, and full of spirit, as Mr. *Cowley;* as for the Italian, French, and Spanish Plays, I can make it evident, that those who now write, surpass them; and that the *Drama* is wholly ours.

All of them were thus far of *Eugenius* his opinion, that the sweetness of English Verse was never understood or practis'd by our Fathers; even *Crites* himself did not much oppose it: and every one was willing to acknowledge how much our Poesie is improv'd by the happiness of some Writers yet living; who first taught us to mould our thoughts into easie and significant words; to retrench the superfluities of expression, and to make our Rime so properly a part of the Verse, that it should never mis-lead the sense, but itself be led and govern'd by it.

Eugenius was going to continue this Discourse, when *Lisi-*

deius told him that it was necessary, before they proceeded further, to take a standing measure of their Controversie; for how was it possible to be decided who writ the best Plays, before we know what a Play should be? but, this once agreed on by both Parties, each might have recourse to it, either to prove his own advantages, or to discover the failings of his Adversary.

He had no sooner said this, but all desir'd the favour of him to give the definition of a Play; and they were the more importunate, because neither *Aristotle,* nor *Horace,* nor any other, who had writ of that Subject, had ever done it.

Lisideius, after some modest denials, at last confess'd he had a rude notion of it; indeed, rather a Description than a Definition; but which serv'd to guide him in his private thoughts, when he was to make a judgment of what others writ: that he conceiv'd a Play ought to be, *A just and lively Image of Human Nature, representing its Passions and Humours, and the Changes of Fortune to which it is subject, for the Delight and Instruction of Mankind.*

This definition, though *Crites* rais'd a Logical Objection against it; that it was only *a genere et fine,* [by general class and by purpose] and so not altogether perfect; was yet well received by the rest: and after they had given order to the Water-men to turn their Barge, and row softly, that they might take the cool of the Evening in their return, *Crites,* being desired by the Company to begin, spoke on behalf of the Ancients, in this manner:

If Confidence presage a Victory, *Eugenius,* in his own opinion, has already triumphed over the Ancients; nothing seems more easie to him, than to overcome those whom it is our greatest praise to have imitated well: for we do not onely build upon their foundation, but by their modells. *Dramatique Poesie* had time enough, reckoning from *Thespis* (who first invented it) to *Aristophanes,* to be born, to grow up, and to flourish in Maturity. It has been observed of Arts and Sciences, that in one and the same Century they have arrived to great perfection; and no wonder, since every Age has a kind of Universal Genius, which inclines those that live in it to some particular Studies: the Work then, being push'd on by many hands, must of necessity go forward.

Is it not evident, in these last hundred years, (when the Study of Philosophy has been the business of all the *Virtuosi* in *Chris-tendome*) that almost a new Nature has been reveal'd to us? That more errours of the school have been detected, more use-ful Experiments in Philosophy have been made, more Noble Secrets in Opticks, Medicine, Anatomy, Astronomy, discovered, than in all those credulous and doting ages from *Aristotle* to us? so true it is, that nothing spreads more fast than Science, when rightly and generally cultivated.

Add to this, the more than common emulation that was in those times of writing well; which though it be found in all Ages and all Persons that pretend to the same Reputation, yet Poesie, being then in more esteem than now it is, had greater honours decreed to the Professors of it, and consequently the Rivalship was more high between them; they had Judges ordain'd to de-cide their Merit, and Prizes to reward it: and Historians have been diligent to record of *Eschylus, Euripides, Sophocles, Lyco-phron,* and the rest of them, both who they were that vanquish'd in these wars of the Theater, and how often they were crowned: while the Asian Kings and Grecian Common-wealths scarce af-forded them a Nobler Subject than the unmanly Luxuries of a Debauch'd Court, or giddy Intrigues of a Factious City: *Alit æmulatio ingenia* (says *Paterculus*), *et nunc invidia, nunc admi-ratio incitationem accendit:* Emulation is the Spur of Wit; and sometimes Envy, sometimes Admiration quickens our Endeav-ours.

But now, since the Rewards of Honour are taken away, that Vertuous Emulation is turn'd into direct Malice; yet so slothful, that it contents itself to condemn and cry down others, without attempting to do better: 'Tis a Reputation too unprofitable, to take the necessary pains for it; yet wishing they had it, is incite-ment enough to hinder others from it. And this, in short, *Eu-genius,* is the reason why you have now so few good poets, and so many severe Judges: Certainly, to imitate the Ancients well, much labour and long study is required; which pains, I have already shown, our Poets would want incouragement to take, if yet they had ability to go through with it. Those Ancients have been faithful Imitators and wise observers of that Nature which is so torn and ill represented in our Plays, they have handed down to us a perfect resemblance of her; which we, like all

Copyers, neglecting to look on, have rendred monstrous and dis-
figur'd. But, that you may know how much you are indebted to
those your Masters, and be ashamed to have so ill requited them:
I must remember you, that all the Rules by which we practise the
Drama at this day, either such as relate to the justness and symmetry of the plot; or the Episodical Ornaments, such as Descriptions, Narrations, and other Beauties, which are not essential to
the Play; were delivered to us from the observations that *Aristotle*
made, of those poets, which either liv'd before him, or were his
Contemporaries: we have added nothing of our own, except we
have the confidence to say our wit is better; of which, none boast
in this our Age, but such as understand not theirs. Of that book
which *Aristotle* has left us, περὶ τῆς Ποιηικῆς. [The Poetics]
Horace his Art of Poetry is an excellent Comment, and, I believe,
restores to us that Second Book of his concerning Comedy, which
is wanting in him.

Out of these two have been extracted the famous Rules, which
the French call *Des Trois Unitez,* or, The Three Unities, which
ought to be observ'd in every Regular Play; namely, of Time,
Place, and Action.

The Unity of Time they comprehend in 24 hours, the compass
of a Natural Day, or as near as it can be contriv'd; and the reason of it is obvious to every one, that the time of the feigned
action, or fable of the Play, should be proportion'd as near as
can be to the duration of that time in which it is represented:
since therefore all plays are acted on the Theater in the space
of time much within the compass of 24 hours, that Play is to be
thought the nearest imitation of Nature, whose Plot or Action is
confin'd within that time; and, by the same Rule which concludes this general proportion of time, it follows, that all the
parts of it are to be equally subdivided; as namely, that one act
take not up the suppos'd time of half a day, which is out of proportion to the rest: since the other four are then to be straitned
within the compass of the remaining half; for it is unnatural that
one Act, which being spoke or written, is not longer than the
rest, should be suppos'd longer by the Audience; 'Tis therefore
the Poets duty, to take care that no Act should be imagin'd to
exceed the time in which it is represented on the Stage; and that

the intervalls and inequalities of time be suppos'd to fall out between the Acts.

This rule of time, how well it has been observed by the Ancients, most of their plays will witness; you see them in their Tragedies (wherein to follow this Rule, is certainly most difficult) from the very beginning of their Playes, falling close into that part of the Story which they intend for the action or principal object of it, leaving the former part to be delivered by Narration: so that they set the Audience, as it were, at the Post where the Race is to be concluded: and, saving them the tedious expectation of seeing the Poet set out and ride the beginning of the Course, you behold him not till he is in sight of the Goal, and just upon you.

For the Second Unity, which is that of place, the Ancients meant by it, That the Scene ought to be continu'd through the Play, in the same place where it was laid in the beginning: for the Stage on which it is represented, being but one and the same place, it is unnatural to conceive it many, and those far distant from one another. I will not deny but by the variation of painted Scenes, the fancy (which in these cases will contribute to its own deceit) may sometimes imagine it several places, with some appearance of probability; yet it still carries the greater likelihood of truth, if those places be suppos'd so near each other as in the same Town or City; which may all be comprehended under the larger Denomination of one place: for a greater distance will bear no proportion to the shortness of time, which is allotted in the acting, to pass from one of them to another; for the Observation of this, next to the Ancients, the French are to be most commended. They tie themselves so strictly to the unity of place, that you never see in any of their Plays, a Scene changed in the middle of an Act: if the Act begins in a Garden, a Street, or Chamber, 'tis ended in the same place; and that you may know it to be the same, the Stage is so supplied with persons that it is never empty all the time: he that enters the second has business with him who was on before; and before the second quits the Stage, a third appears who has business with him.

This *Corneil* calls *La Liaison des Scenes,* the continuity or joyning of the Scenes; and 'tis a good mark of a well contrived play when all the Persons are known to each other, and every one of them has some affairs with all the rest.

As for the third Unity which is that of Action, the Ancients meant no other by it then what the Logicians do by their *Finis*, the end or scope of any action: that which is the first in Intention, and last in Execution: now the Poet is to aim at one great and compleat action, to the carrying on of which all things in his Play, even the very obstacles, are to be subservient; and the reason of this is as evident as any of the former.

For two Actions equally labour'd and driven on by the Writer, would destroy the unity of the Poem; it would be no longer one Play, but two: not but that there may be many actions in a Play, as *Ben. Johnson* has observ'd in his discoveries; but they must be all subservient to the great one, which our language happily expresses in the name of under-plots: such as in *Terences Eunuch* is the difference and reconcilement of *Thais* and *Phædria*, which is not the chief business of the Play, but promotes the marriage of *Chærea* and *Chremes's* Sister, principally intended by the Poet. There ought to be but one action, sayes *Corneile*, that is one compleat action which leaves the mind of the Audience in a full repose: But this cannot be brought to pass but by many other imperfect ones which conduce to it, and hold the Audience in a delightful suspence of what will be.

If by these rules (to omit many other drawn from the Precepts and Practice of the Ancients) we should judge our modern Playes; 'tis probable, that few of them would endure the tryal: that which should be the business of a day, takes up in some of them an age; instead of one action, they are the Epitomes of a mans life; and for one spot of ground (which the stage should represent) we are sometimes in more Countries then the Map can show us.

But if we allow the Ancients to have contriv'd well, we must acknowledge them to have writ better; questionless we are depriv'd of a great stock of wit in the loss of *Menander* among the Greek Poets, and of *Cæcilius, Affranius*, and *Varius*, among the Romans: we may guess at *Menanders* Excellency by the Plays of *Terence*, who translated some of his, and yet wanted so much of him, that he was called by *C. Cæsar* the Half-*Menander*, and of *Varius*, by the Testimonies of *Horace Martial*, and *Velleius*

Paterculus. 'Tis probable that these, could they be recover'd, would decide the controversy; but so long as *Aristophanes* in the old Comedy, and *Plautus* in the new are extent, while the Tragedies of *Eurypides, Sophocles,* and *Seneca* are to be had, I can never see one of those Plays which are now written but it increases my admiration of the Ancients; and yet I must acknowledge further, that to admire them as we ought, we should understand them better then we do. Doubtless many things appear flat to us, whose wit depended on some custom or story which never came to our knowledge, or perhaps on some Criticism in their language, which being so long dead, and onely remaining in their Books, 'tis not possible they should make us know it perfectly. To read *Macrobius,* explaining the propriety and elegancy of many words in Virgil, which I had before passed over without consideration, as common things, is enough to assure me that I ought to think the same of *Terence;* and that in the purity of his style (which *Tully* so much valued that he ever carried his works about him) there is yet left in him great room for admiration, if I knew but where to place it. In the meantime I must desire you to take notice, that the greatest man of the last age (*Ben. Johnson*) was willing to give place to them in all things: he was not only a professed Imitator of *Horace,* but a learned Plagiary of all the others; you track him every where in their Snow: if *Horace, Lucan, Petronius Arbiter, Seneca,* and *Juvenal,* had their own from him, there are few serious thoughts which are new in him; you will pardon me therefore if I presume he lov'd their fashion when he wore their cloaths. But since I have otherwise a great veneration for him, and you, *Eugenius,* prefer him above all other Poets, I will use no farther argument to you then his example: I will produce Father *Ben* to you, dress'd in all the ornaments and colours of the Ancients, you will need no other guide to our Party if you follow him; and whether you consider the bad Plays of our Age, or regard the good ones of the last, both the best and worst of the Modern Poets will equally instruct you to esteem the Ancients.

Crites had no sooner left speaking, but *Eugenius* who had waited with some impatience for it, thus began:

I have observ'd in your Speech that the former part of it is convincing as to what the Moderns have profitted by the rules of the Ancients, but in the latter you are careful to conceal how much they have excell'd them: we own all the helps we have from them, and want neither veneration nor gratitude while we acknowledge that to overcome them we must make use of the advantages we have receiv'd from them; but to these assistances we have joyned our own industry; for (had we sate down with a dull imitation of them) we might then have lost somewhat of the old perfection, but never acquir'd any that was new. We draw not therefore after their lines, but those of Nature; and having the life before us, besides the experience of all they knew, it is no wonder if we hit some airs and features which they have miss'd: I deny not what you urge of arts and sciences, that they have flourish'd in some ages more then others; but your instance in Philosophy makes for me: for if Natural Causes be more known now then in the time of *Aristotle,* because more studied, it follows that Poesie and other Arts may with the same pains arrive still neerer to perfection, and, that granted, it will rest for you to prove that they wrought more perfect images of human life then we; which, seeing in your Discourse you have avoided to make good, it shall now be my task to show you some part of their defects, and some few Excellencies of the Moderns; and I think there is none among us can imagine I do it enviously, or with purpose to detract from them; for what interest of Fame or Profit can the living lose by the reputation of the dead? on the other side, it is a great truth which *Velleius Paterculus* affirms, *Audita visis libentius laudamus; et præsentia invidia, præterita admiratione prosequimur; et his nos obrui, illis instrui credimus:* that praise or censure is certainly the most sincere which un-brib'd posterity shall give us.

Be pleased then in the first place to take notice, that the Greek Poesie, which *Crites* has affirm'd to have arriv'd to perfection in the Reign of the old Comedy, was so far from it, that the distinction of it into Acts was not known to them; or if it were, it is yet so darkly deliver'd to us that we cannot make it out.

All we know of it is from the singing of their Chorus, and that too is so uncertain, that in some of their plays we have reason to conjecture they sung more then five times. *Aristotle* indeed divides the integral parts of a Play into four: First, the *Protasis* or entrance, which gives light onely to the Characters of the persons, and proceeds very little into any part of the action: 2ly, the *Epitasis,* or working up of the Plot where the Play grows warmer: the design or action of it is drawing on, and you see something promising that it will come to pass: Thirdly, the *Catastasis,* or Counter-turn, which destroys that expectation, imbroyls the action in new difficulties, and leaves you far distant from that hope in which it found you, as you may have observ'd in a violent stream resisted by a narrow passage; it runs round to an eddy, and carries back the waters with more swiftness than it brought them on: Lastly, the *Catastrophe,* which the Grecians call'd λύσις, the French *le dénouement,* and we the discovery or unravelling of the Plot: there you see all things settling again upon their first foundations, and the obstacles which hindered the design or action of the Play once remov'd, it ends with that resemblance of truth and nature, that the audience are satisfied with the conduct of it. Thus this great man delivered to us the image of a Play; and I must confess it is so lively, that from thence much light has been deriv'd to the forming it more perfectly into Acts and Scenes; but what Poet first limited to five the number of the Acts I know not; onely we see it so firmly establish'd in the time of *Horace,* that he gives it for a rule in Comedy; *Neu brevior quinto, neu sit productior actu:* [Don't let it be shorter or longer than five acts]. So that you see the Grecians cannot be said to have consummated this Art; writing rather by Entrances then by Acts, and having rather a general indigested notion of a Play, than knowing how and where to bestow the particular graces of it.

But since the Spaniards at this day allow but three Acts, which they call *Jornadas,* to a Play, and the Italians in many of theirs follow them, when I condemn the Antients, I declare it is not altogether because they have not five acts to every play, but because they have not confin'd themselves to one certain number; it is building an House without a Modell; and when they succeeded in such undertakings, they ought to have sacrific'd to Fortune, not to the Muses.

Next, for the plot, which Aristotle called τὸ μῦθος [the story] and often τῶυ πραγμάτων σύνθεσις, [the arrangement of incidents] and from him the Romans *Fabula,* it has already been

judiciously observ'd by a late Writer, that in their Tragedies it
was onely some tale deriv'd from *Thebes* or *Troy,* or at least
something that happened in those two Ages; which was worn
so thred bare by the Pens of all the Epique Poets, and even
by Tradition, itself of the Talkative Greeklings (as *Ben Jonson*
calls them) that before it came upon the Stage it was already
known to all the Audience: and the people, so soon as ever they
heard the Name of *Œdipus,* knew as well as the Poet, that he
had killed his Father by a mistake, and committed Incest with
his Mother, before the Play; that they were now to hear of a
great Plague, an Oracle, and the ghost of *Laius:* so that they
sate with a yawning kind of expectation, till he was to come
with his eyes pull'd out, and speak a hundred or two of Verses
in a Tragick tone, in complaint of his misfortunes. But one
Œdipus, Hercules, or *Medea,* had been tollerable: poor people,
they scap'd not so good cheap; they had still the *Chapon Bouillé*
["Boiled capon" ("tasty dish, luxury")] set before them, till their
appetites were cloy'd with the same dish, and, the Novelty being gone, the pleasure vanish'd; so that one main end of *Dramatique Poesie* in its Definition, which was to cause Delight, was
of consequence destroy'd.

In their Comedies, the Romans generally borrow'd their Plots
from the Greek Poets; and theirs was commonly a little Girle
stollen or wandred from her Parents, brought back unknown to
the same City, there got with child by some lewd young fellow;
who, by the help of his servant, cheats his father, and when
her time comes, to cry *Juno Lucina fer opem,* [Juno, goddess of
childbirth, help.] one or other sees a little Box or Cabinet which
was carried away with her, and so discovers her to her friends,
if some God do not prevent it, by coming down in a Machine,
and take the thanks of it to himself.

By the plot you may guess much of the Characters of the
Persons. An Old Father, that would willingly before he dies,
see his Son well married; his Debauch'd Son, kind in his Nature
to his Wench, but miserably in want of Money; a Servant or
Slave, who has so much wit to strike in with him, and help to
dupe his Father, a Braggadochio Captain, a Parasite, and a Lady
of Pleasure.

As for the poor honest Maid, whom the story is built upon, and who ought to be one of the principal Actors in the Play, she is commonly a Mute in it: she has the breeding of the Old *Elizabeth* way, for Maids to be seen and not to be heard; and it is enough you know she is willing to be married, when the Fifth Act requires it.

These are Plots built after the Italian mode of Houses, you see thorow them all at once; the Characters are indeed the Imitation of Nature, but so narrow as if they had imitated onely an Eye or an Hand, and did not dare to venture on the lines of a Face, or the Proportion of a Body.

But in how strait a compass soever they have bounded their plots and Characters, we will pass it by, if they have regularly pursued them, and perfectly observ'd those three Unities of Time, Place, and Action; the knowledge of which you say is deriv'd to us from them. But in the first place give me leave to tell you, that the Unity of Place, however it might be practised by them, was never any of their Rules: we neither find it in *Aristotle, Horace,* or any who have written of it, till in our age the French Poets first made it a Precept of the Stage. The unity of time, even *Terence* himself (who was the best and most regular of them) has neglected: his *Heautontimoroumenos* or Self-Punisher takes up visibly two dayes; therefore, sayes Scaliger, the two first Acts concluding the first day, were acted over-night; the three last on the ensuing day; and *Euripides,* in tying himself to one day, has committed an absurdity never to be forgiven him: for in one of his Tragedies he has made *Theseus* go from *Athens* to *Thebes,* which was about 40 English miles, under the walls of it to give battel, and appear victorious in the next Act; and yet, from the time of his departure to the return of the *Nuntius,* who gives the relation of his Victory, *Æthra* and the Chorus have but 36 verses; that is not for every Mile a Verse.

The like errour is as evident in *Terence* his *Eunuch,* when *Laches,* the old man, enters in a mistake the house of *Thais,* where betwixt his Exit and the entrance of *Pythias,* who comes to give ample relation of the Garboyles he has rais'd within, *Parmeno* who was left upon the stage, has not above five lines to speak. *C'est bien employé un temps si court,* [It is well to employ a time so short.] sayes the French Poet, who furnish'd me with one of the observations; And almost all their Tragedies will afford us examples of the like nature.

'Tis true, they have kept the continuity, or, as you call'd it, *Liaison des Scenes*, somewhat better: two do not perpetually come in together, talk, and go out together; and other two succeed them, and do the same throughout the Act, which the English call by the name of single Scenes; but the reason is, because they have seldom above two or three Scenes, properly so call'd, in every act; for it is to be accounted a new Scene, not every time the Stage is empty, but every person who enters, though to others, makes it so; because he introduces a new business: Now the Plots of their Plays being narrow, and the persons few, one of their Acts was written in a less compass than one of our well wrought Scenes; and yet they are often deficient even in this: To go no further then *Terence;* you find in the Eunuch, *Antipho* entering single in the midst of the third Act, after *Chremes* and *Pythias* were gone off: in the same Play you have likewise *Dorias* beginning the fourth Act alone; and after she had made a relation of what was done at the Souldiers entertainment (which by the way was very inartificial to do, because she was presum'd to speak directly to the Audience, and to acquaint them with what was necessary to be known, but yet should have been so contriv'd by the Poet as to have been told by persons of the *Drama* to one another, and so by them to have come to the knowledge of the people) she quits the Stage, and *Phædria* enters next, alone likewise: He also gives you an account of himself, and of his returning from the Country in *Monologue,* to which unnatural way of narration *Terence* is subject in all his playes. In his *Adelphi,* or Brothers, *Syrus* and *Demea* enter; after the scene was broken by the departure of *Sostrata, Geta,* and *Canthara;* and indeed you can scarce look into any of his Comedies, where you will not presently discover the same interruption.

But as they have failed both in laying of their Plots, and managing of them, swerving from the Rules of their own Art, by mis-representing Nature to us, in which they have ill satisfied one intention of a Play, which was delight, so in the instructive part they have erred worse: instead of punishing Vice and rewarding Virtue, they have often shown a Prosperous Wickedness, and an Unhappy Piety: they have set before us a bloudy image of revenge in *Medea*, and given her Dragons to convey her safe from punishment. A *Priam* and *Astyanax* murder'd, and *Cassandra* ravished, and the lust and murder ending in the victory of him that acted them: In short, there is no indecorum in any of our modern playes, which if I would excuse, I could not shaddow with some Authority from the Ancients.

And one farther note of them let me leave you: Tragedies and Comedies were not writ then as they are now, promiscuously, by the same person; but he who found his genius bending to the one, never attempted the other way. This is so plain, that I need not instance to you, that *Aristophanes, Plautus, Terence,* never any of them writ a Tragedy; *Æschylus, Euripides, Sophocles,* and *Seneca,* never medled with Comedy; the sock and buskin were not worn by the same Poet: having then so much care to excel in one kind, very little is to be pardon'd them, if they miscarried in it; and this would lead me to the consideration of their wit, had not *Crites* given me sufficient warning not to be too bold in my judgment of it; because, the languages being dead, and many of the Customes and little accidents on which it depended, lost to us, we are not competent judges of it. But though I grant that here and there we may miss the application of a Proverb or a Custom, yet a thing well said will be wit in all languages; and though it may lose something in the Translation, yet, to him who reads it in the Original, 'tis still the same; He has an Idea of its excellency, though it cannot pass from his mind into any other expression or words than those in which he finds it. When *Phædria*—in the Eunuch had a command from his Mistress to be absent two dayes; and encouraging himself to go through with it, said, *Tandem ego non illa care, si opus sit, vel totum triduum?* [Shall I at length not do without her, if necessary, even for three whole days?] *Parmeno* to mock the softness of his Master, lifting up his hands and eyes, cryes out as it were in admiration; *Hui! universum triduum!* [Alas! three whole days!] the elegancy of which *universum,* though it cannot be rendred in our language, yet leaves an impression on our souls: but this happens seldom in him, in *Plautus* oftener; who is infinitely too bold in his Metaphors and

coyning words; out of which many times his wit is nothing,
which questionless was one reason why *Horace* falls upon him
so severely in those Verses:

> *Sed proavi nostri Plautinos et numeros, et*
> *Laudavere sales, nimium patienter utrumque*
> *Ne dicam stolidè.*

[But our ancestors praised both the verses and the wit of Plautus
all too indulgently—not to say stupidly.]

For *Horace* himself was cautious to obtrude a new word on
his Readers, and makes custom and common use the best measure of receiving it into our writings.

> *Multa renascentur quae nunc cecidere, cadentque*
> *Quae nunc sunt in honore vocabula, si volet usus,*
> *Quem penes, arbitrium est, et jus, et norma loquendi.*

[Many words which are now in disuse shall be revived, and
words now held in honor will fall, if that's what usage wants.
With usage rests the decision, the law, and the correct form of
speech.]

The not observing this Rule is that which the world has blam'd
in our Satyrist *Cleveland:* to express a thing hard and unnaturally, is his new way of Elocution: 'Tis true, no Poet but may
sometimes use a *Catachresis; Virgil* does it;

> *Mistaque ridenti Colocasia fundet Acantho—*

[And the colocasia will pour forth, mingled with the laughing
acanthus.]

In his Ecloque of *Pollio;* and in his 7th *Æneid.*

> *. . . mirantur et undae,*
> *Miratur nemus, insuetum fulgentia longe,*
> *Scuta virum fluvio, pictasque innare carinas.*

[Even the waves are surprised, and the grove is surprised, unaccustomed as it is to see the far-flashing shields of men and
painted ships floating in the river.]

And *Ovid* once so modestly, that he asks leave to do it;

> *si verbo audacia detur*
> *Haud metuam summi dixisse Palatia cœli:*

[If I may use bold language, I would not hesitate to call it the
Palace of the highest heaven.]

Calling the Court of *Jupiter* by the name of *Augustus* his Pallace,
though in another place he is more bold, where he sayes, *Et
longas visent Capitolia pompas.* [And the Capitol shall see long

processions.] But to do this alwayes, and never be able to write
a line without it, though it may be admir'd by some few Pedants,
will not pass upon those who know that wit is best convey'd to
us in the most easie language; and is most to be admir'd when
a great thought comes drest in words so commonly receiv'd, that
it is understood by the meanest apprehensions, as the best meat
is the most easily digested: but we cannot read a verse of
Cleveland's without making a face at it, as if every word were
a Pill to swallow: he gives us many times a hard Nut to break
our Teeth, without a Kernel for our pains. So that there is this
difference betwixt his *Satyres* and Doctor Donns, That the one
gives us deep thoughts in common language, though rough ca-
dence; the other gives as common thoughts in abstruse words:
'tis true, in some places his wit is independent of his words,
as in that of the Rebel *Scot:*

Had Cain been Scot God would have chang'd his doom;
Not forc'd him wander, but confin'd him home.

Si sic omnia dixisset! [If only he had said everything this way.]
This is wit in all languages: 'tis like Mercury, never to be lost
or kill'd; and so that other;

For beauty like White-powder makes no noise,
And yet the silent Hypocrite destroyes.

You see the last line is highly Metaphorical, but it is so soft and
gentle, that it does not shock us as we read it.

But, to return from whence I have digress'd, to the consideration of the Ancients Writing and their Wit, (of which by this
time you will grant us in some measure to be fit Judges,) Though
I see many excellent thoughts in *Seneca,* yet he, of them who
had a Genius most proper for the Stage, was *Ovid;* he had a
way of writing so fit to stir up a pleasing admiration and concernment, which are the objects of a Tragedy, and to show the
various movements of a Soul combating betwixt two different
Passions, that, had he liv'd in our age, or in his own could have
writ with our advantages, no man but must have yielded to
him; and therefore I am confident the *Medea* is none of his: for,
though I esteem it for the gravity and sentiousness of it, which
he himself concludes to be suitable to a Tragedy,

Omne genus scripti gravitate Tragædia vincit

[Tragedy excels all other kinds of writing in dignity.]
yet it moves not my soul enough to judge that he, who in the

Epique way wrote things so near the Drama as the story of *Myrrha,* of *Caunus* and *Biblis,* and the rest, should stir up no more concernment where he most endeavour'd it. The master-piece of *Seneca* I hold to be that Scene in the *Troades,* where *Ulysses* is seeking for *Astyanax* to kill him; There you see the tenderness of a Mother, so represented in Andromache, that it raises compassion to a high degree in the Reader, and bears the nearest resemblance of anything in their Tragedies to the excellent Scenes of Passion in *Shakespeare,* or in *Fletcher:* for Love-Scenes, you will find few among them, their Tragique Poets dealt not with that soft passion, but with Lust, Cruelty, Revenge, Ambition, and those bloody actions they produc'd; which were more capable of raising horrour than compassion in an audience: leaving Love untoucht, whose gentleness would have temper'd them, which is the most frequent of all the passions, and which being the private concernment of every person, is sooth'd by viewing its own image in a publick entertainment.

Among their Comedies, we find a Scene or two of tenderness, and that where you would least expect it, in *Plautus;* but to speak generally, their Lovers say little, when they see each other, but *anima mea, vita mea;* Ζωή καὶ ψυχη, [My soul, my life.] as the women in *Juvenal's* time us'd to cry out in the fury of their kindness: then indeed to speak sense were an offence. Any sudden gust of passion (as an ecstasie of love in an unex-pected meeting) cannot better be express'd than in a word and a sigh, breaking one another. Nature is dumb on such occasions, and to make her speak, would be to represent her unlike her-self. But there are a thousand other concernments of Lovers, as jealousies, complaints, contrivances and the like, where not to open their minds at large to each other, were to be wanting to their own love, and to the expectation of the Audience; who watch the movements of their minds, as much as the changes of their fortunes. For the imaging of the first is properly the work of a Poet, the latter he borrows of the Historian.

Eugenius was proceeding in that part of his Discourse, when *Crites* interrupted him. I see, said he, *Eugenius* and I are never like to have this Question decided betwixt us; for he maintains the Moderns have acquir'd a new perfection in writing, I can only grant they have alter'd the mode of it. *Homer* describ'd his

Heroes men of great appetites, lovers of beef broiled upon the coals, and good fellows; contrary to the practice of the French Romances, whose Heroes neither eat, nor drink, nor sleep, for love. *Virgil* makes *Æneas* a bold Avower of his own virtues,

Sum pius Æneas fama super æthera notus;

[I am the dutiful Aeneas, known by a reputation as high as heaven.]

which in the civility of our Poets is the Character of a Fanfaron or Hector: for with us the Knight takes occasion to walk out, or sleep, to avoid the vanity of telling his own Story, which the trusty Squire is ever to perform for him. So in their Love-Scenes, of which *Eugenius* spoke last, the Ancients were more hearty, we more talkative: they writ love as it was then the mode to make it, and I will grant thus much to *Eugenius,* that perhaps one of their Poets, had he lived in our Age,

si fore hoc nostrum fato delapsus in ævum (as *Horace* says of *Lucilius*),

he had alter'd many things; not that they were not as natural before, but that he might accommodate himself to the Age he liv'd in. Yet in the mean time, we are not to conclude anything rashly against those great men, but preserve to them the dignity of Masters, and give that honour to their memories, (*quos Libitina sacravit,*) [which Libitina (goddess of death) has consecrated] part of which we expect may be paid to us in future times.

This moderation of *Crites,* as it was pleasing to all the company, so it put an end to that dispute; which, *Eugenius,* who seem'd to have the better of the Argument, would urge no farther: but *Lisideius,* after he had acknowledg'd himself of *Eugenius* his opinion concerning the Ancients, yet told him he had forborn, till his Discourse were ended, to ask him why he preferr'd the English Plays above those of other Nations? and whether we ought not to submit our Stage to the exactness of our next Neighbours?

Though, said *Eugenius,* I am at all times ready to defend the honour of my Countrey against the French, and to maintain, we are as well able to vanquish them with our Pens, as our Ancestors have been with their swords; yet, if you please, added he, looking upon *Neander,* I will commit this cause to my friend's management; his opinion of our Plays is the same with mine: and besides, there is no reason, that *Crites* and I, who have now left the Stage, should reenter so suddenly upon it; which is against the Laws of Comedie.

If the Question had been stated, replied *Lisideius*, who had writ best, the French or English forty years ago, I should have been of your opinion, and adjudg'd the honour to our own Nation; but since that time, (said he, turning towards *Neander*), we have been so long together bad Englishmen that we had not leisure to be good Poets: *Beaumont, Fletcher*, and *Johnson* (who were onely capable of bringing us to that degree of perfection which we have) were just then leaving the world; as if in an age of so much horror, wit and those milder studies of humanity, had no farther business among us. But the Muses, who ever follow Peace, went to plant in another Countrey: it was then that the great Cardinal of Richelieu began to take them into his protection; and that, by his encouragement, *Corneil* and some other Frenchmen reform'd their Theatre, (which before was as much below ours as it now surpasses it and the rest of Europe;) but because *Crites*, in his Discourse for the Ancients, has prevented me, by touching upon many Rules of the Stage, which the Moderns have borrow'd from them, I shall onely, in short, demand of you, whether you are not convinc'd that of all nations the French have best observ'd them. In the unity of time you find them so scrupulous, that it yet remains a dispute among their Poets, whether the artificial day of twelve hours more or less, be not meant by *Aristotle*, rather than the natural one of twenty-four; and consequently whether all Plays ought not to be reduc'd into that compass. This I can testifie, that in all their Dramas writ within these last 20 years and upwards, I have not observ'd any that have extended the time to thirty hours: in the unity of place they are full as scrupulous, for many of their Criticks limit it to that very spot of ground where the Play is suppos'd to begin; none of them exceed the compass of the same Town or City.

The unity of Action in all plays is yet more conspicuous, for they do not burden them with under-plots, as the English do: which is the reason why many Scenes of our Tragi-comedies carry on a design that is nothing of kinne to the main Plot; and

that we see two distinct webbs in a Play; like those in ill wrought
stuffs; and two actions, that is, two Plays carried on together,
to the confounding of the Audience; who, before they are warm
in their concernments for one part, are diverted to another; and
by that means espouse the interest of neither. From hence likewise it arises that the one half of our Actors are not known to
the other. They keep their distances, as if they were *Montagues*
and *Capulets,* and seldom begin an acquaintance till the last
scene of the Fifth Act, when they are all to meet upon the
Stage. There is no Theatre in the world has anything so absurd
as the English Tragi-comedie; 'tis a *Drama* of our own invention, and the fashion of it is enough to proclaim it so; here
a course of mirth, there another of sadness and passion, a third
of honour, and fourth a Duel: Thus in two hours and a half
we run through all the fits of *Bedlam.* The French affords you
as much variety on the same day, but they do it not so unsea-
sonably, or *mal à propos,* as we: our Poets present you the Play
and the farce together; and our Stages still retain somewhat of
the Original civility of the Red-Bull:
Atque ursum et pugiles media inter carmina poscunt.
[And just as a poem is being recited, they demand a bear and
boxers.]
The end of Tragedies or serious Playes, says *Aristotle,* is to beget admiration, compassion, or concernment; but are not mirth
and compassion things incompatible? and is it not evident that
the Poet must of necessity destroy the former by intermingling
of the latter? that is, he must ruine the sole end and object of
his Tragedy to introduce somewhat that is forced in, and is
not of the body of it. Would you not think that Physician mad,
who, having prescribed a Purge, should immediately order you
to take restringents upon it?

But to leave our Playes, and return to theirs, I have noted
one great advantage they have had in the Plotting of their
Tragedies; that is, they are always grounded upon some known
History: according to that of *Horace, Ex noto fictum carmen
sequar;* [From familiar materials I shall make a poem] and in
that they have so imitated the Ancients that they have surpass'd
them. For the Ancients, as was observ'd before, took for the
foundation of their Playes some Poetical Fiction, such as under

that consideration could move but little concernment in the
Audience, because they already knew the event of it. But the
French goes farther:

Atque ita mentitur; sic veris falsa remiscet,
Primo ne medium, medio ne discrepet imum:
[And he composed fiction in such a way, mixing falsehood with
truth, that the middle is not inconsistent with the beginning,
and the end is not inconsistent with the middle.]

He so interweaves Truth with probable Fiction, that he puts a
pleasing Fallacy upon us; mends the intrigues of Fate, and dis-
penses with the severity of History, to reward that vertue which
has been rendered to us there unfortunate. Sometimes the story
has left the success so doubtful, that the Writer is free, by the
privilege of a Poet, to take that which of two or more relations
will best suit with his design: As for example, the death of
Cyrus, whom *Justin* and some others report to have perish'd in
the *Scythian* war, but *Xenophon* affirms to have died in his bed
of extream old age. Nay more, when the event is past dispute,
even then we are willing to be deceiv'd, and the Poet, if he
contrives it with appearance of truth, has all the audience of
his Party; at least during the time his Play is acting: so naturally
we are kind to vertue, when our own interest is not in question,
that we take it up as the general concernment of Mankind. On
the other side, if you consider the Historical Playes of *Shakespeare*, they are rather so many Chronicles of Kings, or the business many times of thirty or forty years, crampt into a representation of two hours and a half, which is not to imitate or
paint Nature, but rather to draw her in miniature, to take her
in little; to look upon her through the wrong end of a Perspec-
tive, and receive her Images not only much less, but infinitely
more imperfect then the life: this, instead of making a Play
delightful, renders it ridiculous.

Quodcunque ostendis mihi sic, incredulus odi.
[Whatever of this sort you show me, I disbelieve and hate.]
For the spirit of man cannot be satisfied but with truth, or at
least verisimility; and a Poem is to contain, if not τὰ ἔτυμα, [the
truth] yet ἐτύμοισιν ὁμοῖα, [what looks like the truth] as one of
the Greek poets has express'd it.

Another thing in which the French differ from us and from

the Spaniards, is that they do not embarrass, or cumber themselves with too much Plot; they only represent so much of a Story as will constitute one whole and great action sufficient for a Play; we, who undertake more, do but multiply adventures; which, not being produc'd from one another, as effects from causes, but barely following, constitute many actions in the Drama, and consequently make it many Playes.

But by pursuing close one argument, which is not cloy'd with many turns, the French have gain'd more liberty for verse, in which they write; they have leisure to dwell on a subject which deserves it; and to represent the passions (which we have acknowledg'd to be the Poet's work), without being hurried from one thing to another, as we are in the Playes of *Calderon*, which we have seen lately upon our *Theaters* under the name of Spanish Plotts. I have taken notice but of one Tragedy of ours, whose Plot has that uniformity and unity of design in it, which I have commended in the French; and that is *Rollo*, or rather, under the name of *Rollo*, the Story of *Bassianus* and *Geta* in *Herodian*, there indeed the Plot is neither large nor intricate, but just enough to fill the minds of the Audience, not to cloy them. Besides, you see it founded upon the truth of History, onely the time of the action is not reduceable to the strictness of the Rules; and you see in some places a little farce mingled, which is below the dignity of the other parts; and in this all our Poets are extreamly peccant: even *Ben Johnson* himself in *Sejanus* and *Catiline* has given us this Oleo of a play, this unnatural mixture of Comedy and Tragedy, which to me sounds just as ridiculously as the History of *David* with the merry humours of *Golias*. In *Sejanus* you may take notice of the Scene betwixt *Livia* and the Physician, which is a pleasant Satyre upon the artificial helps of beauty: in *Catiline* you may see the Parliament of Women; the little envies of them to one another; and all that passes betwixt *Curio* and *Fulvia*: Scenes admirable in their kind, but of an ill mingle with the rest.

But I return again to the French Writers, who, as I have said, do not burden themselves too much with plot, which has been reproach'd to them by an *ingenious person* of our Nation as a fault; for he says they commonly make but one person considerable in a Play; they dwell on him, and his concernments, while the rest of the persons are only subservient to set him off. If he intends this by it, that there is one person in the Play who is of greater dignity then the rest, he must tax, not onely theirs, but those of the Ancients, and which he would be loth to do, the best of ours; for it is impossible but that one person must be more conspicuous in it then any other, and consequently the greatest share in the action must devolve on him. We see it so in the management of all affairs; even in the most equal Aristocracy, the ballance cannot be so justly poysed but some one will be superiour to the rest; either in parts, fortune, interest, or the consideration of some glorious exploit; which will reduce the greatest part of business into his hands.

But, if he would have us to imagine that in exalting one character the rest of them are neglected, and that all of them have not some share or other in the action of the Play, I desire him to produce any of *Corneilles* tragedies, wherein every person (like so many servants in a well-govern'd family) has not some employment, and who is not necessary to the carrying on of the Plot, or at least to your understanding it.

There are indeed some protatick persons in the Ancients, whom they make use of in their Playes, either to hear or give the Relation: but the French avoid this with great address, making their narrations onely to, or by such who are some way interested in the main design. And now I am speaking of Relations, I cannot take a fitter opportunity to add this in favour of the French, that they often use them with better judgment and more *à propos* then the English do. Not that I commend narrations in general, but there are two sorts of them; one of those things which are antecedent to the Play, and are related to make the conduct of it more clear to us, but 'tis a fault to choose such subjects for the Stage as will inforce us upon that Rock; because we see they are seldom listned to by the Audience, and that is many times the ruin of the Play; for, being once let pass without attention, the Audience can never recover themselves to understand the Plot: and indeed it is somewhat unreasonable that they should be put to so much trouble, as, that to comprehend what passes in their sight, they must have recourse to what was done, perhaps, ten or twenty years ago.

But there is another sort of Relations, that is, of things hap-

ning in the Action of the Play, and suppos'd to be done behind
the Scenes; and this is many times both convenient and beautiful: for, by it, the French avoid the tumult, to which we are
subject in *England,* by representing Duells, Battells and the like;
which renders our Stage too like the Theaters where they fight
Prizes. For what is more ridiculous then to represent an Army
with a Drum and five men behind it; all which, the Heroe of the
other side is to drive in before him, or to see a Duel fought, and
one slain with two or three thrusts of the foyles, which we know
are so blunted, that we might give a man an hour to kill another in good earnest with them.

I have observ'd that in all our Tragedies, the Audience cannot forbear laughing when the Actors are to die; 'tis the most comick part of the whole Play. All *passions* may be lively represented
on the Stage, if to the well-writing of them the Actor supplies
a good commanded voice, and limbs that move easily, and without stiffness; but there are many *actions* which can never be
imitated to a just height: dying especially is a thing which none
but a Roman Gladiator could naturally perform on the Stage,
when he did not imitate or represent, but naturally do it; and
therefore it is better to omit the representation of it.

The words of a good Writer which describe it lively, will
make a deeper impression of belief in us then all the Actor can
perswade us to, when he seems to fall dead before us; as a Poet
in the description of a beautiful Garden, or a Meadow, will
please our imagination more then the place it self can please
our sight. When we see death represented, we are convinc'd it
is but Fiction; but when we hear it related, our eyes (the strongest witnesses) are wanting, which might have undeceiv'd us; and
we are all willing to favour the sleight, when the Poet does not
too grossly impose on us. They therefore who imagine these
relations would make no concernment in the Audience, are deceiv'd, by confounding them with the other, which are of things
antecedent to the Play: those are made often in cold blood (as
I may say), to the audience; but these are warm'd with our concernments, which were before awaken'd in the Play. What the
Philosophers say of motion, that, when it is once begun, it continues of it self, and will do so to Eternity without some stop
put to it, is clearly true on this occasion: the soul being already

mov'd with the Characters and Fortunes of those imaginary persons, continues going of its own accord; and we are no more weary to hear what becomes of them when they are not on the Stage, then we are to listen to the news of an absent Mistress. But it is objected, That if one part of the Play may be related, then why not all? I answer, Some parts of the action are more fit to be represented, some to be related. *Corneille* says judiciously, that the Poet is not oblig'd to expose to view all particular actions which conduce to the principal: he ought to select such of them to be seen which will appear with the greatest beauty, either by the magnificence of the show, or the vehemence of passions which they produce, or some other charm which they have in them; and let the rest arrive to the audience by narration. 'Tis a great mistake in us to believe the French present no part of the action on the Stage; every alteration or crossing of a design, every new-sprung passion, and turn of it, is a part of the action, and much the noblest, except we conceived nothing to be action till they come to blows; as if the painting of the Heroes mind were not more properly the Poets work than the strength of his body. Nor does this anything contradict the opinion of *Horace,* where he tells us,

> *Segnius irritant animos demissa per aurem*
> *Quam quæ sunt oculis subjecta fidelibus.*

[What strikes our ears is slower to stimulate our mind than what our trustworthy eyes have seen.]

For he sayes immediately after,

> *Non tamen intus*
> *Digna geri promes in scenam; multaq; tolles*
> *Ex oculis; quæmox narret facundia præsens.*

[Do not bring out on the stage things which ought to be done inside; you will keep out of sight many things which eloquence will in due course bring before their eyes.]

Among which many he recounts some.

> *Nec pueros coram populo Medea trucidet,*
> *Aut in avem Progne mutetur, Cadmus in anguem, etc.*

[Let not Medea slaughter her children in front of the audience, let Procne not be changed into a bird nor Cadmus into a snake.]

That is, those actions which by reason of their cruelty, will cause aversion in us, or by reason of their impossibility unbelief, ought

either wholly to be avoided by a Poet, or onely deliver'd by narration. To which, we may have leave to add such as to avoid
tumult, (as was before hinted) or to reduce the Plot into a more
reasonable compass of time, or for defect of Beauty in them, are
rather to be related than presented to the eye. Examples of all
these kinds are frequent, not onely among all the Ancients, but
in the best receiv'd of our English poets. We find *Ben. Johnson*
using them in his Magnetick Lady, where one comes out from
Dinner, and relates the quarrels and disorders of it to save the
undecent appearing of them on the Stage, and to abbreviate the
Story; and this in express imitation of *Terence,* who had done
the same before him in his Eunuch, where *Pythias* makes the like
relation of what had happened within at the Souldiers entertainment. The relations likewise of *Sejanus's* death, and the prodigies
before it are remarkable; the one of which was hid from sight
to avoid the horrour and tumult of the representation; the other
to shun the introducing of things impossible to be believ'd. In
that excellent Play, the King and no King, *Fletcher* goes yet
farther; for the whole unravelling of the Plot is done by narration
in the fifth Act, after the manner of the Ancients; and it moves
great concernment in the Audience, though it be onely a relation
of what was done many years before the Play. I could multiply
other instances, but these are sufficient to prove that there is no
errour in choosing a subject which requires this sort of narrations; in the ill managing of them, there may.

But I find I have been too long in this discourse since the
French have many other excellencies not common to us; as that
you never see any of their Playes end with a conversion, or
simple change of will, which is the ordinary way which our Poets
use to end theirs. It shows little art in the conclusion of a Dramatick Poem, when they who have hinder'd the felicity during
the four Acts, desist from it in the fifth without some powerful
cause to take them off; and though I deny not but such reasons
may be found, yet it is a path that is cautiously to be trod, and
the Poet is to be sure he convinces the Audience that the motive
is strong enough. As for example, the conversion of the Usurer
in The Scornful Lady seems to me a little forc'd; for being an
Usurer, which implies a lover of Money to the highest degree of
covetousness (and such the poet has represented him) the ac-

count he gives for the sudden change is, that he has been duped by the wilde young fellow, which in reason might render him more wary another time, and make him punish himself with harder fare and coarser clothes to get it up again: but that he should look on it as a judgment, and so repent, we may expect to hear of in a Sermon, but I should never endure it in a Play.

I pass by this; neither will I insist on the care they take, that no person after his first entrance shall ever appear, but the business which brings him upon the Stage shall be evident; which, if observ'd, must needs render all the events in the Play more natural; for there you see the probability of every accident, in the cause that produc'd it; and that which appears chance in the Play, will seem so reasonable to you, that you will there find it almost necessary; so that in the exits of their Actors you have a clear account of their purpose and design in the next entrance: (though, if the Scene be well wrought, the event will commonly deceive you) for there is nothing so absurd, sayes *Corneille,* as for an Actor to leave the Stage, onely because he has no more to say.

I should now speak of the beauty of their Rhime, and the just reason I have to prefer that way of writing in Tragedies before ours in Blanck-verse; but because it is partly receiv'd by us, and therefore not altogether peculiar to them, I will say no more of it in relation to their Playes. For our own I doubt not but it will exceedingly beautifie them; and I can see but one reason why it should not generally obtain, that is, because our Poets write so ill in it. This indeed may prove a more prevailing argument than all others which are us'd to destroy it, and therefore I am onely troubled when great and judicious poets, and those who are acknowledg'd such, have writ or spoke against it: as for others, they are to be answer'd by that one sentence of an ancient Authour: *Sed ut primo ad consequendos eos quos priores ducimus, accendimur, ita ubi aut proeteriri, aut æquari eos posse desperavimus, studium cum spe senescit: quod, scilicet, assequi non potest, sequi desinit; . . . praeteritoque eo in quo eminere non possumus, aliquid in quo nitamur conquirimus.* [But just as at first we are aroused to follow those whom we consider to be leaders, so, as soon as we despair that they can be surpassed or equalled, our zeal flags, together with our hope; for what it cannot overtake, it stops following; we let pass by that in which we cannot excel, and seek a new field in which to exert our efforts.]

Lisideius concluded in this manner; and *Neander,* after a little pause thus answered him:

I shall grant *Lisideius,* without much dispute, a great part of what he has urg'd against us; for I acknowledge that the French contrive their Plots more regularly, observe the Laws of Comedy, and decorum of the Stage (to speak generally) with more exactness then the English. Farther I deny not but he has tax'd us justly in some irregularities of ours which he has mention'd; yet, after all, I am of opinion that neither our faults nor their virtues are considerable enough to place them above us.

For the lively imitation of Nature being in the definition of a Play, those which best fulfil that law ought to be esteem'd superior to the others. 'Tis true, those beauties of the French-poesie are such as will raise perfection higher where it is, but are not sufficient to give it where it is not: they are indeed the Beauties of a Statue, but not of a Man, because not animated with the Soul of Poesie, which is imitation of humour and passions: and this *Lisideius* himself, or any other, however byassed to their Party, cannot but acknowledge, if he will either compare the humours of our Comedies, or the Characters of our serious Playes with theirs. He that will look upon theirs which have been written till these last ten years or thereabouts, will find it an hard matter to pick out two or three passable humours amongst them. *Corneille* himself, their Arch-Poet, what has he produc'd except *The Lier,* and you know how it was cry'd up in *France;* but when it came upon the English Stage, though well translated, and that part of *Dorant* acted to so much advantage by Mr. *Hart,* as I am confident it never receiv'd in its own Country, the most favourable to it would not put it in competition with many of *Fletchers* or *Ben. Johnson's.* In the rest of *Corneilles* Comedies you have little humour; he tells you himself his way is first to show two Lovers in good intelligence with each other; in the working up of the Play to Embroyle them by some mistake, and in the latter end to clear it up.

But of late years *de Molière,* the younger *Corneille, Quinault,* and some others, have been imitating afar off the quick turns and graces of the English Stage. They have mix'd their serious

Playes with mirth, like our Tragicomedies, since the death of Cardinal *Richelieu;* which *Lisideius* and many others not observing, have commended that in them for a virtue which they themselves no longer practise. Most of their new Playes are, like some of ours, deriv'd from the Spanish Noveles. There is scarce one of them without a veil, and a trusty *Diego,* who drolls much after the rate of the *Adventures.* But their humours, if I may grace them with that name, are so thin-sown, that never above one of them comes up in any Play. I dare take upon me to find more variety of them in some one Play of *Ben. Johnsons* than in all theirs together; as he who has seen the *Alchymist* the silent Woman, or *Bartholomew* Fair, cannot but acknowledge with me.

I grant the French have performed what was possible on the ground-work of the Spanish Playes; what was pleasant before they have made regular: but there is not above one good Play to be writ on all those Plots; they are too much alike to please often; which we need not the experience of our own Stage to justifie. As for their new way of mingling mirth with serious Plot, I do not with *Lisideius* condemn the thing, though I cannot approve their manner of doing it: He tells us, we cannot so speedily recollect ourselves after a scene of great passion and concernment as to pass to another of mirth and humour, and to enjoy it with any relish: but why should he imagine the soul of man more heavy than his Sences? Does not the eye pass from an unpleasant object to a pleasant in a much shorter time than is requir'd to this? and does not the unpleasantness of the first commend the beauty of the latter? The old Rule of Logick might have convinc'd him, that contraries when plac'd near, set off each other. A continued gravity keeps the spirit too much bent; we must refresh it sometimes, as we bait in a journey, that we may go on with greater ease. A Scene of mirth mix'd with Tragedy has the same effect upon us which our musick has betwixt the Acts; and that we find a relief to us from the best Plots and language of the Stage, if the discourses have been long. I must therefore have stronger arguments, ere I am convinc'd that compassion and mirth in the same subject destroy each other; and in the mean time cannot but conclude, to the honour of our Nation, that we have invented, increas'd, and perfected a more pleasant way of writing for the Stage then was ever known to the Ancients or Moderns of any Nation, which is Tragi-comedie.

And this leads me to wonder why *Lisideius* and many others should cry up the barrenness of the French Plots above the variety and copiousness of the English. Their Plots are single; they carry on one design which is push'd forward by all the Actors, every Scene in the Play contributing and moving towards it: Ours besides the main design, have under-plots or by-concernments, of less considerable Persons, and Intrigues, which are carried on with the motion of the main Plot: just as they say the Orb of the fix'd Stars, and those of the Planets, though they have motions of their own, are whirl'd about by the motion of the *primum mobile,* in which they are contain'd: that similitude expresses much of the English Stage: for if contrary motions may be found in Nature to agree; if a Planet can go East and West at the same time; one way by virtue of his own motion, the other by the force of the first mover, it will not be difficult to imagine how the under-Plot, which is onely different, not contrary to the great design, may naturally be conducted along with it.

Eugenius has already shown us, from the confession of the French Poets, that the Unity of Action is sufficiently preserv'd, if all the imperfect actions of the Play are conducing to the main design: but when those petty intrigues of a Play are so ill order'd that they have no coherence with the other, I must grant that *Lisideius* has reason to tax that want of due connexion; for Co-ordination in a Play is as dangerous and unnatural as in a State. In the mean time he must acknowledge our variety, if well order'd, will afford a greater pleasure to the audience.

As for his other argument, that by pursuing one single Theme they gain an advantage to express and work up the passions, I wish any example he could bring from them would make it good; for I confess their verses are to me the coldest I have ever read. Neither indeed is it possible for them, in the way they take, so to express passion, as that the effects of it should appear in the concernment of an Audience: their Speeches being so many declamations, which tire us with the length; so that instead of perswading us to grieve for their imaginary Heroes, we are concern'd for our own trouble, as we are in tedious visits of bad company; we are in pain till they are gone. When the French Stage came to be reform'd by Cardinal *Richelieu,* those long Harangues were introduc'd to comply with the gravity of a Churchman. Look upon the *Cinna* and the *Pompey,* they are not so properly to be called Playes, as long discourses of reason of State; and *Polieucte* in matters of Religion is as solemn as the long stops upon our Organs. Since that time it is grown into a custome, and their Actors speak by the Hour-glass, as our Parsons do; nay, they account it the grace of their parts, and think themselves disparag'd by the Poet, if they may not twice or thrice in a Play entertain the Audience with a Speech of an hundred or two hundred lines. I deny not but this may sute well enough with the French; for as we, who are a more sullen people, come to be diverted at our Playes, so they, who are of an ayery and gay temper come thither to make themselves more serious: And this I conceive to be one reason why Comedy is more pleasing to us, and Tragedies to them. But to speak generally: it cannot be deny'd that short Speeches and Replies are more apt to move the passions and beget concernment in us, then the other; for it is unnatural for any one in a gust of passion to speak long together, or for another in the same condition, to suffer him, without interruption. Grief and Passion are like floods rais'd in little Brooks by a sudden rain; they are quickly up, and if the concernment be powr'd unexpectedly in upon us, it overflows us: but a long sober shower gives them leisure to run out as they came in, without troubling the ordinary current. As for Comedy, Repartee is one of its chiefest graces; the greatest pleasure of the Audience is a chase of wit kept up on both sides, and swiftly managed. And this our forefathers, if not we, have had in *Fletchers* Playes, to a much higher degree of perfection then the French Poets can arrive at.

There is another part of *Lisideius* his Discourse, in which he has rather excus'd our neighbours then commended them; that is, for aiming onely to make one person considerable in their Playes. 'Tis very true what he has urged, that one character in all Playes, even without the Poets care, will have advantage of all the others; and that the design of the whole *Drama* will chiefly depend on it. But this hinders not that there may be more shining characters in the Play: many persons of a second magnitude, nay, some so very near, so almost equal to the first, that greatness may be oppos'd to greatness, and all the persons be made considerable, not onely by their quality, but their action. 'Tis evident that the more the persons are, the greater will be the variety of the Plot. If then the parts are manag'd so regularly that the beauty of the whole be kept intire, and that the variety become not a perplex'd and confus'd mass of accidents, you will find it infinitely pleasing to be led in a labyrinth of design, where you see some of your way before you, yet discern not the end till you arrive at it. And that all this is practicable, I can produce for examples many of our English Playes: as the Maid's Tragedy, the Alchymist, the Silent Woman. I was going to have named the Fox, but that the unity of design seems not exactly observ'd in it; for there appears two actions in the Play; the first naturally ending with the fourth Act; the second forc'd from it in the fifth; which yet is the less to be condemn'd in him, because the disguise of *Volpone*, though it suited not with his character as a crafty or covetous person, agreed well enough with that of a voluptuary; and by it the Poet gain'd the end he aym'd at, the punishment of Vice, and the reward of Virtue, which that disguise produc'd. So that to judge equally of it, it was an excellent fifth Act, but not so naturally proceeding from the former.

But to leave this, and pass to the latter part of *Lisideius* his discourse, which concerns relations, I must acknowledge with him, that the French have reason when they hide that part of the action which would occasion too much tumult on the Stage, and choose rather to have it made known by narration to the Audience. Farther I think it very convenient, for the reasons he has given, that all incredible actions were remov'd; but, whither custome has so insinuated itself into our Country-men, or nature has so form'd them to fierceness, I know not; but they will scarcely suffer combats and other objects of horrour to be taken from them. And indeed, the indecency of tumults is all which can be objected against fighting: For why may not our imagination as well suffer itself to be deluded with the probability of it, as with any other thing in the Play? For my part, I can with as great ease perswade myself that the blowes which are struck, are given in good earnest, as I can, that they who strike them are Kings or Princes, or those persons which they represent. For objects

of incredibility I would be satisfied from *Lisideius*, whether we
have any so remov'd from all appearance of truth as are those
of *Corneilles Andromede?* a Play which has been frequented the
most of any he has writ? If the *Perseus*, or the Son of an Heathen
God, the *Pegasus* and the Monster were not capable to choak a
strong belief, let him blame any representation of ours hereafter.
Those indeed were objects of delight; yet the reason is the same
as to the probability: for he makes it not a Ballette or Masque,
but a Play, which is to resemble truth. But for death, that it
ought not to be represented, I have, besides the Arguments al-
leg'd by *Lisideius*, the authority of *Ben Johnson*, who has forborn
it in his Tragedies; for both the death of *Sejanus* and *Catiline*
are related: though in the latter I cannot but observe one irregularity of that great Poet; he has remov'd the Scene in the same
Act, from *Rome* to *Catiline's* Army, and from thence again to
Rome; and besides, has allow'd a very inconsiderable time, after
Catilines Speech, for the striking of the battle, and the return of
Petreius, who is to relate the event of it to the Senate: which I
should not animadvert on him, who was otherwise a painful observer of τὸ πρέπον, or the *decorum* of the Stage, if he had not
us'd extream severity in his judgment on the incomparable *Shakespeare* for the same fault. To conclude on this subject of Relations, if we are to be blam'd for showing too much of the action,
the French are as faulty for discovering too little of it: a mean
betwixt both should be observed by every judicious Writer, so
as the audience may neither be left unsatisfied by not seeing what
is beautiful, or shock'd by beholding what is either incredible or
undecent. I hope I have already proved in this discourse, that
though we are not altogether so punctual as the French, in observing the lawes of Comedy, yet our errours are so few, and
little, and those things wherein we excel them so considerable,
that we ought of right to be preferr'd before them. But what will
Lisideius say if they themselves acknowledge they are too strictly
ti'd up by those lawes, for breaking which he has blam'd the
English? I will allege *Corneille's* words, as I find them in the end
of his Discourse of the three Unities:—*Il est facile aux spécula-
tifs d'estre sévères, etc.* ' 'Tis easie for speculative persons to
judge severely; but if they would produce to publick view ten or
twelve pieces of this nature, they would perhaps give more lati-

tude to the Rules then I have done, when by experience they had known how much we are bound up and constrain'd by them, and how many beauties of the Stage they banish'd from it.' To illustrate a little what he has said: by their servile observations of the unities of time and place, and integrity of Scenes, they have brought on themselves that dearth of Plot, and narrowness of Imagination, which may be observ'd in all their Playes. How many beautifull accidents might naturally happen in two or three dayes, which cannot arrive with any probability in the compass of 24 hours? There is time to be allowed also for maturity of design, which amongst great and prudent persons, such as are often represented in Tragedy, cannot, with any likelihood of truth, be brought to pass at so short a warning. Farther; by tying themselves strictly to the unity of place, and unbroken Scenes, they are forc'd many times to omit some beauties which cannot be shown where the Act began; but might, if the Scene were interrupted, and the Stage clear'd for the persons to enter in another place; and therefore the French Poets are often forc'd upon absurdities; for if the Act begins in a chamber all the persons in the Play must have some business or other to come thither, or else they are not to be shown that Act, and sometimes their characters are very unfitting to appear there; As, suppose it were the King's Bed-chamber, yet the meanest man in the Tragedy must come and dispatch his business there, rather than in the Lobby or Court-yard (which is fitter for him), for fear the Stage should be clear'd, and the Scenes broken. Many times they fall by it in a greater inconvenience; for they keep their Scenes unbroken, and yet change the place; as in one of their newest Playes, where the Act begins in the Street. There a Gentleman is to meet his Friend; he sees him with his man, coming out from his Fathers house; they talk together, and the first goes out: the second, who is a Lover, has made an appointment with his Mistress; she appears at the window, and then we are to imagine the scene lies under it. This Gentleman is call'd away, and leaves his servant with his Mistress; presently her Father is heard from within; the young Lady is afraid the Servingman should be discover'd, and thrusts him in through a door which is suppos'd to be her Closet. After this, the Father enters to the Daughter, and now the Scene is in a House; for he is seeking from one room to

another for this poor *Philipin,* or French *Diego,* who is heard
from within, drolling and breaking many a miserable conceit
upon his sad condition. In this ridiculous manner the Play goes
on, the Stage being never empty all the while: so that the Street,
the Window, the Houses, and the Closet, are made to walk about,
and the Persons to stand still. Now what I beseech you is more
easy than to write a regular French Play, or more difficult than
to write an irregular English one, like those of *Fletcher,* or of
Shakespeare?

If they content themselves as *Corneille* did, with some flat design, which, like an ill Riddle, is found out e're it be half propos'd; such plots we can make every way regular, as easily as
they; but when e'er they endeavour to rise up to any quick turns
and counterturns of Plot, as some of them have attempted, since
Corneilles Playes have been less in vogue, you see they write as
irregularly as we, though they cover it more speciously. Hence
the reason is perspicuous, why no French Playes, when translated, have, or ever can succeed on the English Stage. For, if you
consider the Plots, our own are fuller of variety, if the writing,
ours are more quick and fuller of spirit; and therefore 'tis a
strange mistake in those who decry the way of writing Playes in
verse, as if the English therein imitated the French. We have
borrow'd nothing from them; our plots are weav'd in English
Loomes: we endeavour therein to follow the variety and greatness of characters which are deriv'd to us from *Shakespeare* and
Fletcher; the copiousness and well-knitting of the intrigues we
have from *Johnson;* and for the Verse it self we have English
Presidents of elder date than any of *Corneille's* Playes: (not to
name our old Comedies before *Shakespeare,* which were all writ
in verse of six feet, or *Alexandrin's,* such as the French now use)
I can show in *Shakespeare,* many Scenes of rhyme together, and
the like in *Ben Johnson's* Tragedies: in *Catiline* and *Sejanus*
sometimes thirty or forty lines; I mean besides the Chorus, or the
Monologues, which, by the way, showed *Ben.* no enemy to this way
of writing, especially if you look upon his sad Shepherd which
goes sometimes on rhyme, sometimes on blanck Verse, like an
Horse who eases himself on Trot and Amble. You find him likewise commending *Fletcher's* Pastoral of the Faithful Shepherdess,
which is for the most part Rhyme, though not refin'd to that

purity to which it hath since been brought: And these examples are enough to clear us from a servile imitation of the French.

But to return from whence I have digress'd: I dare boldly affirm these two things of the English *Drama;* First, that we have many Playes of ours as regular as any of theirs, and which, besides, have more variety of Plot and Characters; And secondly, that in most of the irregular Playes of *Shakespeare* or *Fletcher* (for *Ben Johnson's* are for the most part regular) there is a more masculine fancy and greater spirit in all the writing then there is in any of the French. I could produce even in *Shakespeare's* and *Fletcher's* works, some Playes which are almost exactly form'd; as the Merry Wives of Windsor, and the Scornful Lady: but because (generally speaking) *Shakespeare,* who writ first, did not perfectly observe the Laws of Comedy, and *Fletcher,* who came nearer to perfection, yet through carelessness made many faults; I will take the pattern of a perfect play from *Ben Johnson,* who was a careful and learned observer of the Dramatique Lawes, and from all his Comedies I shall select *The Silent Woman;* of which I will make a short Examen, according to those Rules which the French observe.

As *Neander* was beginning to examine the Silent Woman, *Eugenius,* looking earnestly upon him; I beseech you, *Neander,* said he, gratifie the company and me in particular so far, as before you speak of the Play, to give us a Character of the Authour; and tell us franckly your opinion, whether you do not think all Writers, both French and English, ought to give place to him?

I fear, replied *Neander,* That in obeying your commands I shall draw a little envy on my self. Besides, in performing them, it will be first necessary to speak somewhat of *Shakespeare* and *Fletcher,* his Rivalls in Poesie; and one of them, in my opinion, at least his equal, perhaps his superiour.

To begin then with *Shakespeare.* he was the man who of all Modern, and perhaps Ancient Poets, had the largest and most comprehensive soul. All the Images of Nature were still present to him, and he drew them, not laboriously, but luckily: when he describes any thing, you more than see it, you feel it too. Those who accuse him to have wanted learning, give him the greater commendation: he was naturally learn'd; he needed not the spectacles of Books to read Nature; he look'd inwards, and found her

there. I cannot say he is everywhere alike; were he so, I should
do him injury to compare him with the greatest of Mankind. He
is many times flat, insipid; his Comick wit degenerating into
clenches, his serious swelling into Bombast. But he is always
great, when some great occasion is presented to him: no man can
say he ever had a fit subject for his wit, and did not then raise
himself as high above the rest of Poets,

> *Quantum lenta solent, inter viburna cupressi.*

[As high as cypresses usually tower among pliant shrubs.]

The consideration of this made Mr. *Hales* of *Eaton* say, that there
was no subject of which any Poet ever writ, but he would produce it much better treated of in *Shakespeare;* and however
others are now generally preferr'd before him, yet the Age
wherein he liv'd, which had contemporaries with him, *Fletcher*
and *Johnson,* never equall'd them to him in their esteem: and
in the last Kings Court, when *Ben's* reputation was at highest,
Sir *John Suckling,* and with him the greater part of the Courtiers,
set our *Shakespeare* far above him.

Beaumont and *Fletcher,* of whom I am next to speak, had, with
the advantage of *Shakespeare's* wit, which was their precedent,
great natural gifts, improv'd by study. *Beaumont* especially being so accurate a judge of Playes, that *Ben Johnson,* while he
liv'd, submitted all his Writings to his Censure, and 'tis thought,
used his judgment in correcting, if not contriving all his Plots.
What value he had for him, appears by the Verses he writ to
him; and therefore I need speak no farther of it. The first Play
that brought *Fletcher* and him in esteem was their *Philaster:* for
before that, they had written two or three very unsuccessfully:
as the like is reported of *Ben Johnson,* before he writ *Every Man
in his Humour.* Their Plots were generally more regular than
Shakespeare's, especially those which were made before *Beaumont's* death; and they understood and imitated the conversation of Gentlemen much better; whose wilde debaucheries, and
quickness of wit in reparties, no Poet can ever paint as they have
done. This Humour of which *Ben Johnson* deriv'd from particular persons, they made it not their business to describe: they
represented all the passions very likely, but above all, Love. I
am apt to believe the English Language in them arriv'd to its
highest perfection: what words have since been taken in, are

rather superfluous then necessary. Their Playes are now the most pleasant and frequent entertainments of the Stage; two of theirs being acted through the year for one of *Shakespeare's* or *Johnsons:* the reason is, because there is a certain gayety in their Comedies, and Pathos in their more serious Playes, which suits generally with all mens humours. *Shakespeare's* language is likewise a little obsolete, and *Ben Johnson's* wit comes short of theirs.

As for *Johnson,* to whose Character I am now arriv'd, if we look upon him while he was himself (for his last Playes were but his dotages), I think him the most learned and judicious Writer which any Theater ever had. He was a most severe Judge of himself as well as others. One cannot say he wanted wit, but rather that he was frugal of it. In his works you find little to retrench or alter. Wit and Language, and Humour also in some measure we had before him; but something of Art was wanting to the *Drama* till he came. He manag'd his strength to more advantage then any who preceded him. You seldome find him making Love in any of his Scenes, or endeavouring to move the Passions; his genius was too sullen and saturnine to do it gracefully, especially when he knew he came after those who had performed both to such an height. Humour was his proper Sphere, and in that he delighted most to represent Mechanick people. He was deeply conversant in the Ancients, both Greek and Latine, and he borrowed boldly from them: there is scarce a Poet or Historian among the Roman Authours of those times whom he has not translated in *Sejanus* and *Catiline.* But he has done his Robberies so openly, that one may see he fears not to be taxed by any Law. He invades Authours like a Monarch, and what would be theft in other Poets is onely victory in him. With the spoils of these Writers he so represents old *Rome* to us, in its Rites, Ceremonies, and Customs, that if one of their Poets had written either of his Tragedies, we had seen less of it then in him. If there was any fault in his Language, 'twas that he weav'd it too closely and laboriously, in his serious Playes: perhaps, too, he did a little too much Romanize our Tongue, leaving the words which he translated almost as much Latine as he found them: wherein, though he learnedly followed the Idiom of their language, he did not enough comply with the idiom of ours. If I would compare him with *Shakespeare,* I must acknowledge him the more correct Poet, but *Shakespeare* the greater wit. *Shakespeare* was the *Homer,* or Father of our Dramatick Poets; *Johnson* was the *Virgil,* the pattern of elaborate writing; I admire him, but I love *Shakespeare.* To conclude of him; as he has given us the most correct Playes, so in the precepts which he has laid down in his Discoveries, we have as many and profitable Rules for perfecting the Stage, as any wherewith the French can furnish us.

Having thus spoken of the Authour, I proceed to the examination of his Comedy, *The Silent Woman.*

Examen of The Silent Woman

To begin first with the length of the Action, it is so far from exceeding the compass of a Natural day, that it takes not up an Artificial one. 'Tis all included in the limits of three hours and a half, which is no more than is requir'd for the presentment on the Stage. A beauty perhaps not much observ'd; if it had, we should not have look'd on the Spanish Translation of five hours with so much wonder. The Scene of it is laid in *London;* the latitude of place is almost as little as you can imagine; for it lies all within the compass of two Houses, and after the first Act, in one. The continuity of Scenes is observ'd more than in any of our Playes, excepting his own Fox and Alchymist. They are not broken above twice or thrice at most in the whole Comedy; and in the two best of *Corneille's* Playes, the *Cid* and *Cinna,* they are interrupted once apiece. The action of the Play is intirely one; the end or aim of which is the setling *Morose's* estate on *Dauphine.* The Intrigue of it is the greatest and most noble of any pure unmix'd Comedy in any Language; you see in it many persons of various characters and humours, and all delightful: as first, *Morose,* or an old Man, to whom all noise but his own talking is offensive. Some who would be thought Criticks, say this humour of his is forc'd: but to remove that objection, we may consider him first to be naturally of a delicate hearing, as many are to whom all sharp sounds are unpleasant; and secondly, we may attribute much of it to the peevishness of his age, or the wayward authority of an old man in his own house, where he may make himself obeyed; and this the poet seems to allude to in his name *Morose.* Besides this, I am assur'd from divers persons, that *Ben. Johnson* was actually acquainted with such a man, one altogether as ridiculous as he is here represented. Others say it is not enough to find one man of such an humour; it must be common to more, and the more common the more natural. To prove this, they instance in the best of Comical Characters, *Falstaffe:* There are many men resembling him; Old, Fat, Merry, Cowardly, Drunken, Amorous, Vain, and Lying: But to convince these people, I need but tell them, that humour is the ridiculous extravagance of conversation, wherein one man differs from all others. If then it be common, or communicated to many, how differs it from other mens? or what indeed causes it to be ridiculous so much as the singularity of it? As for *Falstaffe*, he is not properly one humour, but a Miscellany of Humours or Images, drawn from so many several men; that wherein he is singular in his wit, or those things he sayes *præter expectatum,* unexpected by the Audience; his quick evasions, when you imagine him surpriz'd, which as they are extreamly diverting of themselves, so receive a great addition from his person; for the very sight of such an unwieldy old debauch'd fellow is a Comedy alone. And here having a place so proper for it, I cannot but enlarge somewhat upon this subject of humour into which I am fallen. The Ancients had little of it in their Comedies; for the τὸ γελοῖον [the ridiculous] of the old Comedy, of which *Aristophanes* was chief, was not so much to imitate a man, as to make the people laugh at some odd conceit, which had commonly somewhat of unnatural or obscene in it. Thus, when you see *Socrates* brought upon the Stage, you are not to imagine him made ridiculous by the imitation of his actions, but rather by making him perform something very unlike himself; something so childish and absurd, as by comparing it with the gravity of the true *Socrates*, makes a ridiculous object for the Spectators. In their new Comedy which succeeded, the Poets sought indeed to express the ἦθος, [character] as in their Tragedies the πάθος [suffering] of Mankind. But this ἦθος contain'd onely the general Characters of men and manners; as old men, Lovers, Servingmen, Courtizans, Parasites, and such other persons as we see in their Comedies; all which they made alike: that is, one old man or Father, one Lover, one Courtizan so like another, as if the first of them had begot the rest of every sort: *Ex homine hunc natum dicas.* [This man is born of man.] The same custome they observ'd likewise in their Tragedies. As for the *French*, though they have the word

humeur among them, yet they have small use of it in their Comedies, or Farces; they being but ill imitations of the *ridiculum,*
or that which stirr'd up laughter in the old Comedy. But among
the *English* 'tis otherwise: where by humour is meant some extravagant habit, passion, or affection; particular (as I said before) to some one person: by the oddness of which, he is immediately distinguish'd from the rest of men; which being lively
and naturally represented, most frequently begets that malicious
pleasure in the Audience which is testified by laughter; as all
things which are deviations from customes are ever the aptest to
produce it: though by the way this laughter is only accidental,
as the person represented is Fantastick or Bizarre, but pleasure
is essential to it, as the imitation of what is natural. The description of these humours, drawn from the knowledge and observation of particular persons, was the peculiar genius and talent of
Ben. Johnson; to whose Play I now return.

Besides *Morose,* there are at least 9 or 10 different Characters
and humours in the *Silent Woman;* all which persons have several concernments of their own, yet are all us'd by the Poet, to
the conducting of the main design to perfection. I shall not waste
time in commending the writing of this play; but I will give you
my opinion, that there is more wit and acuteness of Fancy in it
than in any of *Ben Johnson's.* Besides, that he has here describ'd
the conversation of Gentlemen in the persons of *True-Wit,* and
his Friends, with more gayety, ayre and freedom, than in the rest
of his Comedies. For the contrivance of the Plot, 'tis extream
elaborate, and yet withal easie; for the λυσις, or untying of it,
'tis so admirable, that when it is done, no one of the Audience
would think the Poet could have miss'd it; and yet it was conceal'd so much before the last Scene, that any other way would
sooner have enter'd into your thoughts. But I dare not take upon
me to commend the Fabrick of it, because it is altogether so
full of Art, that I must unravel every Scene in it to commend it
as I ought. And this excellent contrivance is still the more to be
admir'd, because 'tis Comedy, where the persons are onely of
common rank, and their business private, not elevated by Passions or high concernments as in serious Playes. Here every one
is a proper Judge of all he sees; nothing is represented but that
with which he daily converses: so that by consequence all faults

lie open to discovery, and few are pardonable. 'Tis this which
Horace has judiciously observed:

> *Creditur ex medio res arcessit, habere*
> *Sudoris minimum; sed habet Comedia tanto*
> *Plus oneris, quanto veniæ minus.*

[It is believed that comedy, because it draws its subject matter
from the middle class, involves the least amount of sweat; but
comedy is as much more burdensome as it receives less indulgence.]

But our Poet, who was not ignorant of these difficulties, had
prevail'd himself of all advantages; as he who designs a large
leap takes his rise from the highest ground. One of these advantages is that which *Corneille* has laid down as the greatest which
can arrive to any Poem, and which he himself could never compass above thrice in all his plays; *viz.* the making choice of some
signal and long-expected day, whereon the action of the Play is
to depend. This day was that design'd by *Dauphine* for the
settling of his Uncle's Estate upon him; which to compass he
contrives to marry him: that the marriage had been plotted by
him long beforehand is made evident by what he tells *Truwit* in
the second Act, that in one moment he had destroy'd what he
had been raising many months.

There is another artifice of the Poet, which I cannot here omit,
because by the frequent practice of it in his Comedies, he has
left it to us almost as a Rule; that is, when he has any Character
or humour wherein he would show a *coup de Maistre*, or his
highest skill, he recommends it to your observation by a pleasant
description of it before the person first appears. Thus, in *Bartholomew Fair* he gives you pictures of *Numps* and *Cokes*, and
in this those of *Daw, Lafoole, Morose*, and the *Collegiate Ladies;*
all which you hear describ'd before you see them. So that before
they come upon the stage, you have a longing expectation of
them, which prepares you to receive them favourably; and when
they are there, even from their first appearance you are so far
acquainted with them, that nothing of their humour is lost to
you.

I will observe yet one thing further of this admirable Plot; the
business of it rises in every Act. The second is greater then the
first; the third then the second; and so forward to the fifth. There

too you see, till the very last Scene, new difficulties arising to obstruct the action of the Play; and when the Audience is brought into despair that the business can naturally be effected, then, and not before, the discovery is made. But that the Poet might entertain you with more variety all this while, he reserves some new Characters to show you, which he opens not till the second and third Act. In the second *Morose, Daw,* the *Barber,* and *Otter;* in the third the *Collegiat Ladies:* All which he moves afterwards in by-walks, or under-Plots, as diversions to the main design, least it should grow tedious, though they are still naturally joyn'd with it, and somewhere or other subservient to it. Thus, like a skilful Chest-player, by little and little he draws out his men, and makes his pawns of use to his greater persons.

If this Comedy, and some others of his, were translated into French Prose (which would now be no wonder to them, since *Molière* has lately given them Playes out of Verse which have not displeas'd them), I believe the controversie would soon be decided betwixt the two Nations, even making them the Judges. But we need not call our Hero's to our ayde; Be it spoken to the honour of the English, our Nation can never want in any Age such who are able to dispute the Empire of Wit with any people in the Universe. And though the fury of a Civil War, and Power, for twenty years together, abandon'd to a barbarous race of men, Enemies of all good Learning, had buried the Muses under the ruines of Monarchy; yet with the restoration of our happiness, we see reviv'd Poesie lifting up its head, and already shaking off the rubbish which lay so heavy on it. We have seen since His Majeste's return, many Dramatick Poems which yield not to those of any forreign Nation, and which deserve all lawrels but the English. I will set aside Flattery and Envy: it cannot be deny'd but we have had some little blemish either in the Plot or writing of all those Playes which have been made within these seven years: (and perhaps there is no Nation in the world so quick to discern them, or so difficult to pardon them, as ours:) yet if we can perswade ourselves to use the candour of that Poet, who (though the most severe of criticks) has left us this caution by which to moderate our censures; *Ubi plura nitent in carmine non ego paucis offendar maculis;*—[Where many things shine in a poem, I shall not be offended by a few flaws.] If in consideration of their many and great beauties, we can wink at some slight, and little imperfections, if we, I say, can be thus equal to ourselves, I ask no favour from the French. And if I do not venture upon any particular judgment of our late Playes, 'tis out of the consideration which an Ancient Writer gives me: *Vivorum, ut magna admiratio ita censura difficilis:* betwixt the extreams of admiration and malice, 'tis hard to judge uprightly of the living. Onely I think it may be permitted me to say, that as it is no less'ning to us to yield to some Playes, and those not many, of our own Nation in the last Age, so can it be no addition to pronounce of our present Poets that they have far surpass'd all the Ancients, and the Modern Writers of other Countreys.

This, my Lord, was the substance of what was then spoke on that occasion; and *Lisideius,* I think was going to reply, when he was prevented thus by *Crites:* I am confident, said he, the most material things that can be said, have been already urg'd on either side; if they have not, I must beg of *Lisideius* that he will defer his answer till another time: for I confess I have a joynt quarrel to you both, because you have concluded, without any reason given for it, that Rhyme is proper for the Stage. I will not dispute how ancient it hath been among us to write this way; perhaps our ancestors knew no better till *Shakespeare's* time. I will grant it was not altogether left by him, and that *Fletcher* and *Ben Johnson* us'd it frequently in their Pastorals, and sometimes in other Playes. Farther, I will not argue whether we receiv'd it originally from our own Country-men, or from the French; for that is an inquiry of as little benefit, as theirs who, in the midst of the great Plague were not so solicitous to provide against it, as to know whether we had it from the malignity of our own air, or by transportation from *Holland.* I have therefore onely to affirm, that it is not allowable in serious Playes; for Comedies, I find you already concluding with me. To prove this, I might satisfie myself to tell you, how much in vain it is for you to strive against the stream of the peoples inclination; the greatest part of which are prepossess'd so much with those excellent Playes of *Shakespeare, Fletcher,* and *Ben Johnson,* (which have been written out of Rhyme) that except you could bring them such as were written better in it, and those too by persons of equal reputation with them, it will be impossible for you to

gain your cause with them, who will still be judges. This it is
to which in fine all your reasons must submit. The unanimous
consent of an Audience is so powerful, that even *Julius Cæsar*
(as *Macrobius* reports of him) when he was perpetual Dictator,
was not able to ballance it on the other side. But when *Laberius*,
a *Roman* Knight, at his request contended in the *Mime* with another poet, he was forc'd to cry out, *Etiam favente me victus es,
Laberi.* [Laberius, you are defeated even with my support.] But
I will not on this occasion, take the advantage of the greater number, but onely urge such reasons against Rhyme, as I find in the
Writings of those who have argu'd for the other way. First then,
I am of opinion, that Rhyme is unnatural in a play, because Dialogue there is presented as the effect of sudden thought. For a
play is the imitation of Nature; and since no man, without premeditation speaks in Rhyme, neither ought he to do it on the
Stage; this hinders not but the Fancy may be there elevated to
an higher pitch of thought then it is in ordinary discourse: for
there is a probability that men of excellent and quick parts may
speak noble things *ex tempore:* but those thoughts are never
fetter'd with the numbers or sound of Verse without study, and
therefore it cannot be but unnatural to present the most free way
of speaking, in that which is the most constrain'd. For this Reason, sayes *Aristotle*, 'Tis best to write Tragedy in that kind of
Verse which is the least such, or which is nearest Prose: and
this amongst the Ancients was the Iambique, and with us is blank
verse, or the measure of verse, kept exactly without rhyme.
These numbers therefore are fittest for a Play; the others for a
paper of Verses, or a Poem. Blank verse being as much below
them as rhyme is improper for the *Drama*. And if it be objected
that neither are blank verses made *ex tempore*, yet as nearest
Nature, they are still to be preferr'd. But there are two particular exceptions, which many besides myself have had to verse; by
which it will appear yet more plainly, how improper it is in
Playes. And the first of them is grounded upon that very reason
for which some have commended Rhyme: they say the quickness
of repartees in argumentative Scenes receives an ornament from
verse. Now what is more unreasonable then to imagine that a
man should not onely light upon the Wit, but the Rhyme too
upon the sudden? This nicking of him who spoke before both in

sound and measure, is so great an happiness, that you must at least suppose the persons of your Play to be born Poets, *Arcades omnes et cantare pares et respondere parati:* [We are all Arcadians, all equally capable of singing, and ready to reply.] they must have arriv'd to the degree of *quicquid conabar dicere:* to make Verses almost whether they will or no: if they are any thing below this, it will look rather like the design of two then the answer of one: it will appear that your Actors hold intelligence together, that they perform their tricks like Fortune-tellers, by confederacy. The hand of Art will be too visible in it, against that maxime of all Professions; *Ars est celare artem,* That it is the greatest perfection of Art to keep it self undiscover'd. Nor will it serve you to object, that however you manage it, 'tis still known to be a Play; and, consequently the Dialogue of two persons understood to be the labour of one Poet. For a play is still an imitation of Nature; we know we are to be deceiv'd, and we desire to be so; but no man ever was deceiv'd but with a probability of truth, for who will suffer a gross lie to be fasten'd on him? Thus we sufficiently understand that the scenes which represent Cities and Countries to us, are not really such, but only painted on boards and Canvas: But shall that excuse the ill Painture or designment of them; Nay rather ought they not be labour'd with so much the more diligence and exactness to help the imagination? since the mind of man does naturally tend to, and seek after Truth; and therefore the nearer any thing comes to the imitation of it, the more it pleases.

Thus, you see, your Rhyme is uncapable of expressing the greatest thoughts naturally, and the lowest it cannot with any grace: for what is more unbefitting the Majesty of Verse, then to call a Servant, or bid a door be shut in Rhime? And yet this miserable necessity you are forc'd upon. But Verse, you say, circumscribes a quick and luxuriant fancy, which would extend itself too far on every subject, did not the labour which is required to well-turn'd and polish'd Rhyme, set bounds to it. Yet this Argument, if granted, would onely prove that we may write better in Verse, but not more naturally. Neither is it able to evince that; for he who wants judgment to confine his fancy in blank verse, may want it as much in Rhyme; and he who has it will avoid errors in both kinds. Latine verse was as great a confinement to the imagination of those Poets, as Rhime to ours: and yet you find *Ovid* saying too much on every subject. *Nescivit* (sayes *Seneca*) *quod bene cessit relinquere:* [He did not know how to let well enough alone.] of which he gives you one famous instance in his Discription of the Deluge:

Omnia pontus erat, deerant quoque Litora ponto.

Now all was Sea, Nor had that Sea a shore.

Thus *Ovid's* fancy was not limited by verse, and *Virgil* needed not verse to have bounded his.

In our own language we see *Ben. Johnson* confining himself to what ought to be said, even in the liberty of blank Verse; and yet *Corneille,* the most judicious of the *French* Poets, is still varying the same sense an hundred wayes, and dwelling eternally on the same subject, though confin'd by Rhyme. Some other exceptions I have to Verse; but being these I have nam'd are for the most part already publick, I conceive it reasonable they should first be answer'd.

It concerns me less than any, said *Neander* (seeing he had ended) to reply to this Discourse; because when I should have prov'd that Verse may be natural in Playes, yet I should alwayes be ready to confess, that those which I have written in this kind come short of that perfection which is required. Yet since you are pleased I should undertake this Province, I will do it, though with all imaginable respect and deference, both to that person from whom you have borrow'd your strongest arguments, and to whose judgment, when I have said all, I finally submit. But before I proceed to answer your objections, I must first remember you, that I exclude all Comedy from my defence; and next that I deny not but blank verse may be also us'd, and content my self only to assert, that in serious Playes where the subject and characters are great, and the Plot unmix'd with mirth, which might allay or divert these concernments which are produc'd, Rhyme is there as natural, and more effectual than blank Verse.

And now having laid down this as a foundation, to begin with *Crites,* I must crave leave to tell him, that some of his Arguments against rhyme reach no farther then from the faults or defects of ill rhyme, to conclude against the use of it in general. May not I conclude against blank verse by the same reason? If the words of some Poets who write in it, are either ill chosen, or ill placed (which makes not onely rhime, but all kind of verse in any language unnatural;) Shall I, for their vitious affectation condemn those excellent lines of *Fletcher*, which are written in that kind? Is there any thing in rhyme more constrain'd than this line in blank verse? I Heav'n invoke, and strong resistance make? where you see both the clauses are plac'd unnaturally; that is, contrary to the common way of speaking, and that without the excuse of a rhyme to cause it: yet you would think me very ridiculous, if I should accuse the stubbornness of blank Verse for this, and not rather the stiffness of the Poet. Therefore, *Crites*, you must either prove that words, though well chosen, and duly plac'd, yet render not Rhyme natural in it self; or, that however natural and easy the rhyme may be, yet it is not proper for a Play. If you insist on the former part, I would ask you what other conditions are requir'd to make Rhyme natural in it self, besides an election of apt words, and a right disposing of them? For the due choice of your words expresses your sense naturally, and the due placing them adapts the rhyme to it. If you object that one verse may be made for the sake of another, though both the words and rhyme be apt, I answer it cannot possibly so fall out; for either there is a dependance of sense betwixt the first line and the second, or there is none: if there be that connection, then in the natural position of the words the latter line must of necessity flow from the former: if there be no dependance, yet still the due ordering of words makes the last line as natural in it self as the other: so that the necessity of a rhime never forces any but bad or lazy Writers to say what they would not otherwise. 'Tis true, there is both care and Art required to write in Verse; A good Poet never concludes upon the first line, till he has sought out such a rhime as may fit the sense, already prepar'd to heighten the second: many times the close of the sense falls into the middle of the next verse, or farther off, and he may often prevail himself of the same advantages in English which *Virgil* had in Latine; he may break off in the *Hemystich*, and begin another line: indeed, the not observing these two last things, makes Playes which are writ in verse so tedious: for though, most commonly, the sense is to be confin'd to the Couplet, yet nothing that does *perpetuo tenore fluere*, run in the same channel, can please alwayes. 'Tis like the murmuring of a stream, which not varying in the fall, causes at first attention, at last drowsiness.

Variety of cadences is the best rule, the greatest help to the Actors, and refreshment to the Audience.

If then Verse may be made natural in it self, how becomes it improper to a Play? You say the Stage is the representation of Nature, and no man in ordinary conversation speaks in rhime. But you foresaw when you said this, that it might be answer'd; neither does any man speak in blank verse, or in measure without rhime. Therefore you concluded, that which is nearest Nature is still to be preferr'd. But you took no notice that rhime might be made as natural as blank verse, by the well placing of the words, etc. All the difference between them, when they are both correct, is the sound in one, which the other wants; and if so, the sweetness of it, and all the advantage resulting from it, which are handled in the Preface to the *Rival Ladies,* will yet stand good. As for that place of *Aristotle,* where he sayes, Playes should be writ in that kind of Verse which is nearest Prose; it makes little for you; blank verse being properly but measur'd Prose. Now measure alone in any modern Language, does not constitute verse; those of the Ancients in Greek and Latine consisted in quantity of words, and a determinate number of feet. But when, by the inundation of the *Goths* and *Vandals* into *Italy,* new Languages were brought in, and barbarously mingled with the Latine (of which the *Italian, Spanish, French,* and ours (made out of them and the *Teutonick*) are dialects:) a new way of Poesie was practis'd; new, I say, in those Countries, for in all probability it was that of the Conquerors in their own Nations. This new way consisted in measure or number of feet and rhyme. The sweetness of Rhyme, and observation of Accent, supplying the place of quantity in words, which could neither exactly be observ'd by those *Barbarians,* who knew not the Rules of it, neither was it suitable to their tongues, as it has been to the Greek and Latine. No man is tied in modern Poesie to observe any farther rule in the feet of his verse, but that they be dissyllables; whether *Spondee, Trochee,* or *Iambique,* it matters not; onely he is obliged to rhyme: Neither do the *Spanish, French Italian,* or *Germans,* acknowledge at all, or very rarely, any such kind of Poesie as blank verse amongst them. Therefore at most 'tis but a Poetick Prose, a *Sermo pedestris;* and as such, most fit for Comedies, where I acknowledge Rhyme to be improper.

Farther; as to that quotation of *Aristotle,* our Couplet Verses may
be rendred as near Prose as blank verse it self, by using those
advantages I lately nam'd, as breaks in an Hemistick, or running
the sence into another line, thereby making Art and Order appear
as loose and free as Nature: or not tying ourselves to Couplets
strictly, we may use the benefit of the Pindarique way practised
in the Siege of *Rhodes;* where the numbers vary, and the rhyme
is dispose'd carelessly, and far from often chymeing. Neither is
that other advantage of the Ancients to be despis'd, of changing
the kind of verse when they please, with the change of the Scene,
or some new entrance; for they confine not themselves always to
Iambiques, but extend their liberty to all lyrique numbers, and
sometimes, even to Hexameter. But I need not go so far to prove
that Rhyme, as it succeeds to all other offices of Greek and Latin
Verse, so especially to this of Playes, since the custome of all
Nations at this day confirms it: all the *French, Italian,* and *Spanish* Tragedies are generally writ in it; and sure the Universal
consent of the most civiliz'd parts of the world ought in this, as
it doth in other customs, include the rest.

But perhaps you may tell me I have propos'd such a way to
make rhyme natural, and consequently proper to Playes, as is
unpracticable, and that I shall scarce find six or eight lines together in any play, where the words are so plac'd and chosen as
is requir'd to make it natural. I answer, no Poet need constrain
himself at all times to it. It is enough he makes it his general
Rule; for I deny not but sometimes there may be a greatness in
placing the words otherwise; and sometimes they may sound
better, sometimes also the variety it self is excuse enough. But
if, for the most part, the words be plac'd as they are in the negligence of Prose, it is sufficient to denominate the way practicable;
for we esteem that to be such, which in the Tryal oftener succeeds then misses. And thus far you may find the practice made
good in many Playes: where you do not, remember still, that if
you cannot find six natural Rhymes together, it will be as hard
for you to produce as many lines in blank Verse, even among the
greatest of our Poets, against which I cannot make some reasonable exception.

And this, Sir, calls to my remembrance the beginning of your
discourse, where you told us we should never find the Audience

favourable to this kind of writing, till we could produce as good Playes in Rhyme, as *Ben Johnson, Fletcher,* and *Shakespeare,* had writ out of it. But it is to raise envy to the living, to compare them with the dead. They are honour'd, and almost ador'd by us, as they deserve; neither do I know any so presumptuous of themselves as to contend with them. Yet give me leave to say thus much, without injury to their Ashes; that not onely we shall never equal them, but they could never equal themselves, were they to rise and write again. We acknowledge them our Fathers in Wit; but they have ruin'd their estates Themselves before they came to their childrens hands. There is scarce an Humour, a Character, or any kind of Plot, which they have not blown upon: all comes sullied or wasted to us: and were they to entertain this age, they could not make so plenteous treatments out of such decay'd Fortunes. This therefore will be a good Argument to us either not to write at all, or to attempt some other way. There is no bayes to be expected in their Walks: *Tentanda via est quà me quoque possum tollere humo.* [I must try to find the way by which I can raise myself from the earth.]

This way of writing in Verse, they have onely left free to us; our age is arriv'd to a perfection in it, which they never knew; and which (if we may guess by what of theirs we have seen in Verse, as the *Faithful Shepherdess,* and *Sad Shepherd*) 'tis probable they never could have reach'd. For the Genius of every Age is different, and though ours excel in this, I deny not but to imitate Nature in that perfection which they did in Prose, is a greater commendation then to write in verse exactly. As for what you have added, that the people are not generally inclin'd to like this way; if it were true, it would be no wonder, that betwixt the shaking off an old habit, and the introducing of a new, there should be difficulty. Do we not see them stick to *Hopkins* and *Sternholds* Psalmes, and forsake those of *David,* I mean *Sandys* his Translation of them? If by the people you understand the multitude, the οἱ πολλοί, 'tis no matter what they think; they are sometimes in the right, sometimes in the wrong: their judgment is a meer lottery. *Est ubi plebs rectè putat, est ubi peccat.* [Sometimes the mob is right in its opinion, sometimes wrong.] *Horace* sayes it of the vulgar, judging poesie. But if you mean the mix'd audience of the populace and the Noblesse, I dare confidently affirm that a great part of the latter sort are already favourable to verse; and that no serious Playes written since the Kings return have been more kindly receiv'd by them then the *Siege of Rhodes,* the *Mustapha, The Indian* Queen, and *Indian* Emperor.

But I come now to the inference of your first Argument. You said the Dialogue of Playes is presented as the effect of sudden thought, but no man speaks suddenly, or *ex tempore* in Rhyme; and you inferr'd from thence, that Rhyme, which you acknowledge to be proper to Epique Poesie, cannot equally be proper to Dramatick, unless we could suppose all men born so much more then Poets, that verses should be made in them, not by them.

It has been formerly urg'd by you, and confess'd by me, that since no man spoke any kind of verse *ex tempore,* that which was nearest Nature was to be preferr'd. I answer you therefore, by distinguishing betwixt what is nearest to the nature of Comedy, which is the imitation of common persons and ordinary speaking, and what is nearest the nature of a serious Play: this last is indeed the representation of Nature, but 'tis Nature wrought up to a higher pitch. The Plot, the Characters, the Wit, the Passions, the Descriptions, are all exalted above the level of common converse, as high as the imagination of the Poet can carry them, with proportion to verisimility. Tragedy we know is wont to image to us the minds and fortunes of noble persons, and to portray these exactly; Heroick Rhyme is nearest Nature, as being the noblest kind of modern verse.

> *Indignatur enim privatis et prope socco*
> *Dignis carminibus narria cæna Thyestæ*

[It is improper to tell the banquet of Thyestes in poems composed in colloquial language, and in comic style.]

(Sayes *Horace.*) And in another place,

> *Effutire leves indigna tragædia versus.*

[It is improper to babble out frivolous verses in tragedy.]

Blank Verse is acknowledg'd to be too low for a Poem, nay more, for a paper of verses; but if too low for an ordinary Sonnet, how much more for Tragedy, which is by *Aristotle* in the dispute betwixt the Epique Poesie and the Dramatick, for many reasons he there alledges, ranck'd above it.

But setting this defence aside, your Argument is almost as strong against the use of Rhyme in Poems as in Playes; for the

Epique way is every where interlac'd with Dialogue, or discour-
sive Scenes; and therefore you must either grant Rhyme to be
improper there, which is contrary to your assertion, or admit it
into Playes by the same title which you have given it to Poems.
For though Tragedy be justly preferr'd above the other, yet there
is a great affinity between them as may easily be discovered in
that definition of a Play which *Lisideius* gave us. The Genus of
them is the same, a just and lively Image of human nature, in its
Actions, Passions, and traverses of Fortune: so is the end, namely
for the delight and benefit of Mankind. The Characters and Persons are still the same, *viz.* the greatest of both sorts; onely the
manner of acquainting us with those Actions, Passions, and Fortunes is different. Tragedy performs it *viva voce,* or by action,
in Dialogue; wherein it excels the Epique Poem which does it
chiefly by narration, and therefore is not so lively an Image of
Human Nature. However, the agreement betwixt them is such,
that if Rhyme be proper for one, it must be for the other. Verse
'tis true is not the effect of sudden thought; but this hinders not
that sudden thought may be represented in verse, since those
thoughts are such as must be higher than Nature can raise them
without premeditation, especially to a continuance of them, even
out of verse, and consequently you cannot imagine them to have
been sudden either in the Poet, or in the Actors. A Play, as I
have said to be like Nature, is to be set above it; as Statues
which are placed on high are made greater then the life, that
they may descend to the sight in their just proportion.

Perhaps I have insisted too long upon this objection; but the
clearing of it will make my stay shorter on the rest. You tell us
Crites, that rhyme appears most unnatural in repartees, or short
replyes: when he who answers, (it being presumed he knew not
what the other would say, yet) makes up that part of the verse
which was left incompleat, and supplies both the sound and
measure of it. This, you say, looks rather like the confederacy
of two, than the answer of one.

This, I confess, is an objection which is in every ones mouth,
who loves not rhyme: but suppose, I beseech you, the repartee
were made onely in blank verse, might not part of the same
argument be turn'd against you? for the measure is as often sup-

ply'd there as it is in Rhyme. The latter half of the Hemystich as
commonly made up, or a second line subjoyn'd as a reply to
the former; which any one leaf in *Johnson's* Playes will sufficiently clear to you. You will often find in the Greek Tragedians,
and in *Seneca,* that when a Scene grows up into the warmth of
repartees (which is the close fighting of it) the latter part of
the Trimeter is supply'd by him who answers; and yet it was
never observ'd as a fault in them by any of the Ancient or Modern Criticks. The case is the same in our verse, as it was in theirs;
Rhyme to us being in lieu of quantity to them. But if no latitude
is to be allow'd a Poet, you take from him not only his licence
of *quidlibet audendi,* [trying anything] but you tie him up in a
straiter compass than you would a Philosopher. This is indeed
Musas colere severiores: [to worship severer Muses]. You would
have him follow Nature, but he must follow her on foot: you
have dismounted him from his *Pegasus.* But you tell us this supplying the last half of a verse, or adjoyning a whole second to
the former, looks more like the design of two, then the answer
of one. Suppose we acknowledge it: how comes this confederacy
to be more displeasing to you then in a Dance which is well contriv'd? You see there the united design of many persons to make
up one Figure: after they have seperated themselves in many
petty divisions, they rejoyn one by one into a gross: the confederacy is plain amongst them, for chance could never produce
anything so beautiful, and yet there is nothing in it that shocks
your sight. I acknowledge the hand of Art appears in repartee,
as of necessity it must in all kind of verse. But there is also the
quick and poynant brevity of it (which is an high imitation of
Nature in those sudden gusts of passion) to mingle with it; and
this joyn'd with the cadency and sweetness of the Rhyme, leaves
nothing in the soul of the hearer to desire. 'Tis an Art which appears; but it appears onely like the shadowings of Painture,
which being to cause the rounding of it, cannot be absent; but
while that is consider'd they are lost: so while we attend to the
other beauties of the matter, the care and labour of the Rhyme
is carry'd from us, or at least drown'd in its own sweetness, as
Bees are sometimes bury'd in their Honey. When a Poet has
found the repartee, the last perfection he can add to it, is to put

it into verse. However good the thought may be; however apt
the words in which 'tis couch'd, yet he finds himself at a little
unrest, while Rhyme is wanting: he cannot leave it till that comes
naturally, and then is at ease, and sits down contented.

From Replies, which are the most elevated thoughts of Verse,
you pass to the most mean ones: those which are common with
the lowest of household conversation. In these, you say, the
Majesty of Verse suffers. You instance in the calling of a servant,
or commanding a door to be shut in rhyme. This, *Crites,* is a
good observation of yours, but no argument: for it proves no
more but that such thoughts should be wav'd, as often as may be,
by the address of the Poet. But suppose they are necessary in
the places where he uses them, yet there is no need to put them
into rhyme. He may place them in the beginning of a Verse, and
break it off, as unfit, when so debas'd, for any other use: or granting the worst, that they require more room than the Hemystich
will allow, yet still there is a choice to be made of the best words,
and least vulgar (provided they be apt) to express such thoughts.
Many have blamed rhyme in general, for this fault, when the
Poet, with a little care, might have redress'd it. But they do it
with no more justice, then if English Poesie should be made
ridiculous for the sake of the Water Poet's Rhymes. Our language
is noble, full, and significant; and I know not why he who is
Master of it may not cloath ordinary things in it as decently as
the Latine, if he use the same diligence in his choice of words:
delectus verborum origo est eloquentiæ. [Choice of words is the
origin of eloquence.] It was the saying of *Julius Cæsar,* one so
curious in his, that none of them can be chang'd but for a worse.
One would think, unlock the door was a thing as vulgar as could
be spoken; and yet Seneca could make it sound high and lofty
in his Latin:

> *Reserate clusos Regii postes Laris.*

[Set wide the palace gates.]

But I turn from this exception, both because it happens not
above twice or thrice in any Play that those vulgar thoughts are
us'd; and then too (were there no other Apology to be made,
yet) the necessity of them (which is alike in all kind of writing)
may excuse them. Besides that the great eagerness and precipita-

tion with which they are spoken makes us rather mind the substance than the dress; that for which they are spoken, rather than
what is spoken. For they are alwayes the effect of some hasty
concernment, and something of consequence depends on them.

Thus, *Crites,* I have endeavour'd to answer your objections; it
remains onely that I should vindicate an Argument for Verse,
which you have gone about to overthrow. It had formerly been
said that the easiness of blank verse renders the Poet too luxuriant, but that the labour of Rhyme bounds and circumscribes an
over-fruitful fancy, the sense there being commonly confin'd to
the couplet, and the words so order'd that the Rhyme naturally
follows them, not they the Rhyme. To this you answer'd, that it
was no Argument to the question in hand, for the dispute was
not which way a man may write best; but which is most proper
for the subject on which he writes.

First, give me leave, Sir, to remember you that the Argument
against which you rais'd this objection, was onely secondary: it
was built upon this *Hypothesis,* that to write in verse was proper
for serious Playes. Which supposition being granted (as it was
briefly made out in that discourse, by showing how verse might
be made natural) it asserted, that this way of writing was an
help to the Poets judgment, by putting bounds to a wilde over-
flowing fancy. I think therefore it will not be hard for me to
make good what it was to prove: But you add, that were this let
pass, yet he who wants judgment in the liberty of his fancy, may
as well show the defect of it when he is confin'd to verse; for he
who has judgment will avoid errours, and he who has it not, will
commit them in all kinds of writing.

This Argument, as you have taken it from a most acute person,
so I confess it carries much weight in it: but by using the word
Judgment here indefinitely, you seem to have put a fallacy upon
us: I grant, he who has Judgment, that is, so profound, so strong,
so infallible a judgment, that he needs no helps to keep it always
pois'd and upright, will commit no faults either in rhyme or out
of it. And on the other extream, he who has a judgment so weak
and craz'd that no helps can correct or amend it, shall write
scurvily out of Rhyme, and worse in it. But the first of these
judgments is no where to be found, and the latter is not fit to

write at all. To speak therefore of judgment as it is in the best
Poets; they who have the greatest proportion of it, want other
helps than from it within. As for example, you would be loth to
say, that he who was endued with a sound judgment had no
need of History, Geography, or Moral Philosophy, to write correctly. Judgment is indeed the Master-workman in a Play; but
he requires many subordinate hands, many tools to his assistance.
And Verse I affirm to be one of these; 'tis a Rule and line by
which he keeps his building compact and even, which otherwise
lawless imagination would raise either irregularly or loosly. At
least if the Poet commits errours with this help, he would make
greater and more without it: 'tis (in short), a slow and painfull,
but the surest kind of working. *Ovid* whom you accuse for luxuri-
ancy in Verse, had perhaps been farther guilty of it, had he writ
in Prose. And for your instance of *Ben Johnson,* who, you say, writ
exactly without the help of Rhyme; you are to remember, 'tis
onely an aid to a luxuriant fancy, which his was not: As he did
not want imagination, so none ever said he had much to spare.
Neither was verse then refin'd so much to be an help to that Age
as it is to ours. Thus then the second thoughts being usually the
best, as receiving the maturest digestion from judgment, and the
last and most mature product of those thoughts being artful and
labour'd verse, it may well be inferr'd, that verse is a great help
to a luxuriant Fancy; and this is what the Argument which you
oppos'd was to evince.

   Neander was pursuing this Discourse so eagerly, that *Eugenius*
had call'd to him twice or thrice ere he took notice that the Barge
stood still, and that they were at the foot of *Somerset* Stairs,
where they had appointed it to land. The company were all sorry
to separate so soon, though a great part of the evening was already spent; and stood a-while looking back on the water, which
the Moon-beams played upon, and made it appear like floating
quick-silver: at last they went up through a crowd of French
people, who were merrily dancing in the open air, and nothing
concern'd for the noise of Guns which had allarm'd the Town
that afternoon. Walking thence together to the *Piazze,* they
parted there; *Eugenius* and *Lisideius* to some pleasant appointment they had made, and *Crites* and *Neander* to their several
Lodgings.

preface to

FABLES ANCIENT AND MODERN

[1700]

'TIS WITH A POET, as with a Man who designs to build, and is very exact, as he supposes, in casting up the Cost beforehand: But, generally speaking, he is mistaken in his Account, and reckons short of the Expence he first intended: He alters his Mind as the Work proceeds, and will have this or that Convenience more, of which he had not thought when he began. So has it hapned to me; I have built a House, where I intended but a Lodge: Yet with better Success than a certain Nobleman, who beginning with a Dog-kennil, never liv'd to finish the Palace he had contriv'd.

From translating the First of *Homer's Iliads,* (which I intended as an Essay to the whole Work) I proceeded to the Translation of the Twelfth Book of *Ovid's Metamorphoses,* because it contains, among other Things, the Causes, the Beginning, and Ending, of the *Trojan* War: Here I ought in reason to have stopp'd; but the Speeches of *Ajax* and *Ulysses* lying next in my way, I could not balk 'em. When I had compass'd them, I was so taken with the former Part of the Fifteenth Book, (which is the Master-piece of the whole *Metamorphoses*) that I enjoyn'd my self the pleasing Task of rendring it into *English.* And now I found, by the Number of my Verses, that they began to swell into a little Volume; which gave me an Occasion of looking backward on some Beauties of my Author, in his former Books: There occur'd to me the Hunting of the Boar, *Cinyras* and *Myrrha,* the good-natur'd Story of *Baucis* and *Philemon,* with the rest, which I hope I have translated closely enough, and given them the same Turn of Verse, which they had in the Original; and this, I may say without vanity, is not the Talent of every Poet: He who has arriv'd the nearest to it, is the Ingenious and Learned *Sandys,* the best Versifier of the former Age; if I may properly call it by that Name, which was the former Part of this concluding Century. For *Spencer* and *Fairfax* both flourish'd in the Reign of Queen *Elizabeth:* Great Masters in our Language; and who saw much farther into the Beauties of our Numbers, than those who immediately followed them. *Milton* was the Poetical Son of *Spencer,* and Mr. *Waller* of *Fairfax;* for we have our Lineal Descents and Clans, as well as other Families: *Spencer* more than once insinuates, that the Soul of *Chaucer* was transfus'd into his Body; and that he was begotten by him Two hundred years after his Decease. *Milton* has acknowledg'd to me, that *Spencer* was his Original; and many besides my self have heard our famous *Waller* own, that he deriv'd the Harmony of his Numbers from the *Godfrey of Bulloign,* which was turn'd into *English* by Mr. *Fairfax.* But to return: Having done with *Ovid* for this time, it came into my mind, that our old *English* Poet *Chaucer* in many Things resembled him, and that with no disadvantage on the Side of the Modern Author, as I shall endeavour to prove when I compare them: And as I am, and always have been studious to promote the Honour of my Native Country, so I soon resolv'd to put their Merits to the Trial, by turning some of the *Canterbury* Tales into our Language, as it is now refin'd: For by this Means both the Poets, being set in the same Light, and dress'd in the same *English* Habit, Story to be compar'd with Story, a certain Judgment may be made betwixt them, by the Reader, without obtruding my Opinion on him: Or if I seem partial to my Country-man, and Predecessor in the Laurel, the Friends of Antiquity are not few: And besides many of the Learn'd, *Ovid* has almost all the Beaux, and the whole Fair Sex his declar'd Patrons. Perhaps I have assum'd somewhat more to my self than they allow me; because I have adventur'd to sum up the Evidence: but the Readers are the Jury; and their Privilege remains entire to decide according to the Merits of the Cause; Or, if they please to bring it to another Hearing, before some other Court. In the mean time, to follow the Thrid of my Discourse, (as Thoughts, according to Mr. *Hobbs,* have always some Connexion) so from *Chaucer* I was led to think on *Boccace,* who was not only his Contemporary, but also pursu'd the same Studies; wrote Novels in Prose, and many Works in Verse; particularly is said to have invented the Octave Rhyme, or *Stanza* of Eight Lines, which ever since has been maintain'd by the Practice of all *Italian* Writers, who are, or at least assume the Title of *Heroick Poets:* He and *Chaucer,* among other Things, had this in common, that they refin'd their Mother-Tongues; but with this difference, that *Dante* had begun to file their Language, at least in Verse, before the time of Boccace, who likewise receiv'd no little Help from his Master *Petrarch:* But the Reformation of their Prose was wholly owing to *Boccace* himself; who is yet the Standard of Purity in the *Italian* Tongue; though many of his Phrases are become obsolete, as in process of Time it must needs happen. Chaucer (as you have formerly been told by our learn'd Mr. *Rhymer* [3]) first adorn'd and amplified our barren Tongue from the *Provencall,* which was then the most polish'd of all Modern Languages: But this Subject has been copiously treated by that great Critick, who deserves no little Commendation from us his Countrymen. For these Reasons of Time, and Resemblance of Genius, in *Chaucer* and *Boccace,* I resolv'd to join them in my present Work; to which I have added some Original Papers of my own; which whether they are equal or inferiour to my other Poems, an Author is the most improper Judge; and therefore I leave them wholly to the Mercy of the Reader: I will hope the best, that they will not be condemn'd; but if they should, I have the Excuse of an old Gentleman, who mounting on Horseback before some Ladies, when I was present, got up somewhat heavily, but desir'd of the Fair Spectators, that they would count Fourscore and eight before they judg'd him. By the Mercy of God, I am already come within Twenty Years of his Number, a Cripple in my Limbs, but what Decays are in my Mind, the Reader must determine. I think my self as vigorous as ever in the Faculties of my Soul, excepting only my Memory, which is not impaired to any great degree; and if I lose not more of it, I have no great reason to complain. What Judgment I had, increases rather than diminishes; and Thoughts, such as they are, come crowding in so fast upon me, that my only Difficulty is to chuse or to reject; to run them into Verse, or to give them the other Harmony of Prose, I have so long studied and

---

[3] Thomas Rymer (1641–1713), influential neo-classical critic, author of *The Tragedies of the Last Age Consider'd* (1678) and *A Short View of Tragedy* (1693).

practis'd both, that they are grown into a Habit, and become familiar to me. In short, though I may lawfully plead some part of the old Gentleman's Excuse; yet I will reserve it till I think I have greater need, and ask no Grains of Allowance for the Faults of this my present Work, but those which are given of course to Humane Frailty. I will not trouble my Reader with the shortness of Time in which I writ it; or the several Intervals of Sickness: They who think too well of their own Performances, are apt to boast in their Prefaces how little Time their Works have cost them; and what other Business of more importance interfer'd: But the Reader will be apt to ask the Question, Why they allow'd not a longer Time to make their Works more perfect? and why they had so despicable an Opinion of their Judges, as to thrust their indigested Stuff upon them, as if they deserv'd no better?

With this Account of my present Undertaking, I conclude the first Part of this Discourse: In the second Part, as at a second Sitting, though I alter not the Draught, I must touch the same Features over again, and change the Dead-colouring of the Whole. In general I will only say, that I have written nothing which savours of Immorality of Profaneness; at least, I am not conscious to my self of any such Intention. If there happen to be found an irreverent Expression, or a Thought too wanton, they are crept into my Verses through my Inadvertency: If the Searchers find any in the Cargo, let them be stav'd or forfeited, like Counterbanded Goods; at least, let their Authors be answerable for them, as being but imported Merchandise, and not of my own Manufacture. On the other Side, I have endeavour'd to chuse such Fables, both Ancient and Modern, as contain in each of them some instructive Moral, which I could prove by Induction, but the Way is tedious; and they leap foremost into fight, without the Reader's Trouble of looking after them. I wish I could affirm with a safe Conscience, that I had taken the same Care in all my former Writings; for it must be own'd, that supposing Verses are never so beautiful or pleasing, yet if they contain any thing which shocks Religion, or Good Manners, they are at best, what Horace says of good Numbers without good Sense, *versus inopes rerum, nugaeque canorae:* [verses without substance, trifles that can be sung]. Thus far, I hope, I am Right in Court, without renouncing to my other Right of Self-defence, where I have been wrongfully accus'd, and my Sense wire-drawn into Blasphemy or Bawdry, as it has often been by a Religious Lawyer, in a late Pleading against the Stage; in which he mixes Truth with Falshood, and has not forgotten the old Rule, of calumniating strongly, that something may remain.

I resume the Thrid of my Discourse with the first of my Translations, which was the First *Iliad* of *Homer*. If it shall please God to give me longer Life, and moderate Health, my Intentions are to translate the whole *Ilias;* provided still, that I meet with those Encouragements from the Publick, which may enable me to proceed in my Undertaking with some Chearfulness. And this I dare assure the World before-hand, that I have found by Trial, *Homer* a more pleasing Task than *Virgil,* (though I say not the Translation will be less laborious.) For the *Grecian* is more according to my Genius, than the *Latin* Poet. In the Works of the two Authors we may read their Manners, and natural Inclinations, which are wholly different. *Virgil* was of a quiet, sedate Temper; *Homer* was rapid in his Thoughts, and took all the Liberties both of Numbers, and of Expressions, which his Language, and the Age in which he liv'd allow'd him: *Homer's* Invention was more copious, *Virgil's* more confin'd: So that if *Homer* had not led the Way, it was not in *Virgil* to have begun Heroick Poetry: For, nothing can be more evident, than that the *Roman* Poem is but the Second Part of the *Ilias;* a Continuation of the same Story: And the Persons already form'd: The Manners of *Aeneas,* are those of *Hector* superadded to those which Homer gave him. The Adventures of *Ulysses* in the *Odysseis,* are imitated in the first Six Books of *Virgil's Aeneis:* And though the Accidents are not the same, (which would have argu'd him of a servile, copying, and total Barrenness of Invention) yet the Seas were the same, in which both the *Heroes* wander'd; and *Dido* cannot be deny'd to be the Poetical Daughter of *Calypso.* The Six latter Books of Virgil's Poem, are the Four and twenty *Iliads* contracted: A Quarrel occasion'd by a Lady, a Single Combate, Battels fought, and a Town besieg'd. I say not this in derogation to *Virgil,* neither do I contradict any thing which I have formerly said in his just Praise: For his *Episodes* are almost wholly of his own Invention; and the Form which he has given to the Telling, makes the Tale his own, even though the Original Story had been the same. But this proves, however, that *Homer* taught *Virgil* to design: And if Invention be the first Vertue of an Epick Poet, then the *Latin* Poem can only be allow'd the second Place. Mr. *Hobbs,*[4] in the Preface to his own bald Translation of the *Ilias,* (studying Poetry as he did Mathematicks, when it was too late) Mr. *Hobbs,* I say, begins the Praise of *Homer* where he should have ended it. He tells us, that the first Beauty of an Epick Poem consists in Diction, that is, in the Choice of Words, and Harmony of Numbers: Now, the Words are the Colouring of the Work, which in the Order of Nature is last to be consider'd. The Design, the Disposition, the Manners, and the Thoughts, are all before it: Where any of those are wanting or imperfect, so much wants or is imperfect in the Imitation of Humane Life; which is in the very Definition of a Poem. Words indeed, like glaring Colours, are the first Beauties that arise, and strike the Sight; but if the Draught be false or lame, the Figures ill dispos'd, the Manners obscure or inconsistent, or the Thoughts unnatural, then the finest Colours are but Dawbing, and the Piece is a beautiful Monster at the best. Neither Virgil nor Homer were deficient in any of the former Beauties; but in this last, which is Expression, the *Roman* Poet is at least equal to the *Grecian,* as I have said elsewhere; supplying the Poverty of his Language, by his Musical Ear, and by his Diligence. But to return: Our two Great Poets, being so different in their Tempers, one Cholerick and Sanguin, the other Phlegmatick and Melancholick; that which makes them excel in their several Ways, is, that each of them has follow'd his own natural Inclination, as well in Forming the Design, as in the Execution of it. The very Heroes shew their Authors: *Achilles* is hot, impatient, revengeful, *Impiger, iracundus, inexorabilis, acer,* etc. [energetic, irritable, fierce] *Aeneas* patient, considerate, careful of his People, and merciful to his Enemies; ever submissive to the Will of Heaven, *quo fata trahunt retrahuntque, sequamur.* [Let us follow wherever fate drags us to and fro]. I could please my self with enlarging on

---

[4] Thomas Hobbes (1588–1679), English philosopher, published his translations of the *Iliad* and the *Odyssey* when he was 87. To the translation he attached a prefatory essay, "Concerning Virtues of an Heroic Poem."

this Subject, but am forc'd to defer it to a fitter Time. From all I have said, I will only draw this Inference, That the Action of *Homer* being more full of Vigour than that of *Virgil*, according to the Temper of the Writer, is of consequence more pleasing to the Reader. One warms you by degrees; the other sets you on fire all at once, and never intermits his Heat. 'Tis the same Difference which *Longinus* makes betwixt the Effects of Eloquence in *Demosthenes*, and *Tully*. One persuades; the other commands. You never cool while you read *Homer*, even not in the Second Book, (a graceful Flattery to his Countrymen;) but he hastens from the Ships, and concludes not that Book till he has made you an Amends by the violent playing of a new Machine. From thence he hurries on his Action with Variety of Events, and ends it in less Compass than Two Months. This Vehemence of his, I confess, is more suitable to my Temper: and therefore I have translated his First Book with greater Pleasure than any Part of *Virgil*: But it was not a Pleasure without Pains: The continual Agitations of the Spirits, must needs be a Weakning of any Constitution, especially in Age: and many Pauses are required for Refreshment betwixt the Heats; the *Iliad* of its self being a third part longer than all *Virgil's* Works together.

This is what I thought needful in this Place to say of *Homer*. I proceed to *Ovid*, and *Chaucer*; considering the former only in relation to the latter. With *Ovid* ended the Golden Age of the *Roman* Tongue: From *Chaucer* the Purity of the *English* Tongue began. The Manners of the Poets were not unlike: Both of them were well-bred, well-natur'd, amorous, and Libertine, at least in their Writings, it may be also in their Lives. Their Studies were the same, Philosophy, and Philology. Both of them were knowing in Astronomy, of which *Ovid's* Books of the *Roman* Feasts, and *Chaucer's* Treatise of the *Astrolabe*, are sufficient Witnesses. But *Chaucer* was likewise an Astrologer, as were *Virgil, Horace, Persius*, and *Manilius*. Both writ with wonderful Facility and Clearness; neither were great Inventors: For *Ovid* only copied the *Grecian* Fables; and most of *Chaucer's* Stories were taken from his *Italian* Contemporaries, or their Predecessors: *Boccace* his *Decameron* was first publish'd; and from thence our *English-man* has borrow'd many of his *Canterbury* Tales: Yet that of

Palamon and *Arcite* was written in all probability by some *Italian* Wit, in a former Age; as I shall prove hereafter: The Tale of *Grizild* was the Invention of *Petrarch;* by him sent to Boccace; from whom it came to *Chaucer: Troilus* and *Cressida* was also written by a Lombard Author; but much amplified by our *English* Translatour, as well as beautified; the Genius of our Country-men in general being rather to improve an Invention, than to invent themselves; as is evident not only in our Poetry, but in many of our Manufactures. I find I have anticipated already, and taken up from *Boccace* before I come to him: But there is so much less behind; and I am of the Temper of most Kings, *who love to be in Debt,* are all for present Money, no matter how they pay it afterwards: Besides, the Nature of a Preface is rambling; never wholly out of the Way, nor in it. This I have learn'd from the Practice of honest *Montaign,* and return at my pleasure to *Ovid* and *Chaucer,* of whom I have little more to say. Both of them built on the Inventions of other Men; yet since Chaucer had something of his own, as *The Wife of Baths Tale, The Cock and the Fox,* which I have translated, and some others, I may justly give our Countryman the Precedence in that Part; since I can remember nothing of *Ovid* which was wholly his. Both of them understood the Manners; under which Name I comprehend the Passions, and, in a larger Sense, the Descriptions of Persons, and their very Habits: For an Example, I see *Baucis* and *Philemon* as perfectly before me, as if some ancient Painter had drawn them; and all the Pilgrims in the *Canterbury* Tales, their Humours, their Features, and the very Dress, as distinctly as if I had supp'd with them at the *Tabard* in *Southwark.* Yet even there too the Figures of *Chaucer* are much more lively, and set in a better Light: Which though I have not time to prove; yet I appeal to the Reader, and am sure he will clear me from Partiality. The Thoughts and Words remain to be consider'd, in the Comparison of the two Poets; and I have sav'd my self one half of that Labour, by owning that *Ovid* liv'd when the *Roman* Tongue was in its Meridian; *Chaucer,* in the Dawning of our Language: Therefore that Part of the Comparison stands not on an equal Foot, any more than the Diction of *Ennius* and *Ovid;* or of *Chaucer,* and our present *English.* The Words are given up as a Post not to be defended in our Poet, because he wanted the Modern Art of Fortifying. The Thoughts remain to be consider'd: And they are to be measur'd only by their Propriety; that is, as they flow more or less naturally from the Persons describ'd, on such and such Occasions. The Vulgar Judges, which are Nine Parts in Ten of all Nations, who call Conceits and Jingles Wit, who see *Ovid* full of them, and *Chaucer* altogether without them, will think me little less than mad, for preferring the *Englishman* to the Roman: Yet, with their leave, I must presume to say, that the Things they admire are only glittering Trifles, and so far from being Witty, that in a serious Poem they are nauseous, because they are unnatural. Wou'd any Man who is ready to die for Love, describe his Passion like *Narcissus*? Wou'd he think of *inopem me copia fecit*, and a Dozen more of such Expressions, pour'd on the Neck of one another, and signifying all the same Thing? If this were Wit, was this a Time to be witty, when the poor Wretch was in the Agony of Death? This is just *John Littlewit* in *Bartholomew Fair*, who had a Conceit (as he tells you) left him in his Misery; a miserable Conceit. On these Occasions the Poet shou'd endeavour to raise Pity: But instead of this, *Ovid* is tickling you to laugh. *Virgil* never made use of such Machines, when he was moving you to commiserate the Death of *Dido:* He would not destroy what he was building. *Chaucer* makes *Arcite* violent in his Love, and unjust in the Pursuit of it: Yet when he came to die, he made him think more reasonably: He repents not of his Love, for that had alter'd his Character; but acknowledges the Injustice of his Proceedings, and resigns *Emilia* to *Palamon*. What would *Ovid* have done on this Occasion? He would certainly have made *Arcite* witty on his Death-bed. He had complain'd he was farther off from Possession, by being so near, and a thousand such Boyisms, which *Chaucer* rejected as below the Dignity of the Subject. They who think otherwise, would by the same Reason prefer *Lucan* and *Ovid* to *Homer* and *Virgil*, and *Martial* to all Four of them. As for the Turn of Words, in which *Ovid* particularly excels all Poets; they are sometimes a Fault, and sometimes a Beauty, as they are us'd properly or improperly; but in strong Passions always to be shunn'd, because Passions are serious, and will admit no Playing. The *French* have a high Value for them; and

I confess, they are often what they call Delicate, when they are introduc'd with Judgment; but *Chaucer* writ with more Simplicity, and follow'd Nature more closely than to use them. I have thus far, to the best of my Knowledge, been an upright Judge betwixt the Parties in Competition, not medling with the Design nor the Disposition of it; because the Design was not their own; and in the disposing of it they were equal. It remains that I say somewhat of *Chaucer* in particular.

In the first place, As he is the Father of *English* Poetry, so I hold him in the same Degree of Veneration as the *Grecians* held *Homer*, or the *Romans Virgil*: He is a perpetual Fountain of good Sense; learn'd in all Sciences; and therefore speaks properly on all Subjects: As he knew what to say, so he knows also when to leave off; a Continence which is practis'd by few Writers, and scarcely by any of the Ancients, excepting *Virgil* and *Horace*. One of our late great Poets is sunk in his Reputation, because he cou'd never forgive any Conceit which came in his way; but swept like a Drag-net, great and small. There was plenty enough, but the Dishes were ill sorted; whole Pyramids of Sweetmeats, for Boys and Women; but little of solid Meat, for Men: All this proceeded not from any want of Knowledge, but of Judgment; neither did he want that in discerning the Beauties and Faults of other Poets; but only indulg'd himself in the Luxury of Writing; and perhaps knew it was a Fault, but hop'd the Reader would not find it. For this Reason, though he must always be thought a great Poet, he is no longer esteem'd a good Writer: And for Ten Impressions, which his Works have had in so many successive Years, yet at present a hundred Books are scarcely purchas'd once a Twelvemonth: For, as my last Lord *Rochester* said, though somewhat profanely, *Not being of God, he could not stand.*

Chaucer follow'd Nature every where; but was never so bold to go beyond her: And there is a great Difference of being *Poeta* and *nimus Poeta*, [A poet and too much of a poet], if we may believe *Catullus*, as much as betwixt a modest Behaviour and Affectation. The verse of *Chaucer*, I confess, is not Harmonious to us; but 'tis like the Eloquence of one whom Tacitus commends, it was *auribus istius temporis accommodata:* [accommodated to the ears of that time]: They who liv'd with him, and

some time after him, thought it Musical; and it continues so
even in our Judgment, if compar'd with the Numbers of *Lidgate*
and *Gower* his Contemporaries: There is the rude Sweetness of
a *Scotch* Tune in it, which is natural and pleasing, though not
perfect. 'Tis true, I cannot go so far as he who publish'd the
last Edition of him; for he would make us believe the Fault is
in our Ears, and that there were really Ten Syllables in a Verse
where we find but Nine: But this Opinion is not worth confut-
ing; 'tis so gross and obvious an Errour, that common Sense
(which is a Rule in every thing but Matters of Faith and
Revelation) must convince the Reader, that Equality of Numbers
in every Verse which we call Heroick, was either not known, or
not always practis'd in *Chaucer's* Age. It were an easie Matter
to produce some thousands of his Verses, which are lame for
want of half a Foot, and sometimes a whole one, and which no
Pronunciation can make otherwise. We can only say, that he
liv'd in the Infancy of our Poetry, and that nothing is brought
to Perfection at the first. We must be Children before we grow
Men. There was an *Ennius*, and in process of Time a *Lucilius*,
and a *Lucretius*, before *Virgil* and *Horace;* even after *Chaucer*
there was a *Spencer*, a *Harrington*, a *Fairfax*, before *Waller* and
Denham were in being: And our Numbers were in their Nonage
till these last appear'd. I need say little of his Parentage, Life,
and Fortunes: They are to be found at large in all the Editions
of his Works. He was employ'd abroad, and favour'd by *Edward*
the Third, *Richard* the Second, and *Henry* the Fourth, and was
Poet, as I suppose, to all Three of them. In *Richard's* Time, I
doubt, he was a little dipt in the Rebellion of the Commons;
and being Brother-in-Law to *John of Ghant*, it was no wonder
if he follow'd the Fortunes of that Family; and was well with
Henry the Fourth when he had depos'd his Predecessor. Neither
is it to be admir'd, that *Henry*, was a wise as well as a valiant
Prince, who claim'd by Succession, and was sensible that his
Title was not sound, but was rightfully in *Mortimer*, who had
married the Heir of *York*; it was not to be admir'd, I say, if
that great Politician should be pleas'd to have the greatest Wit
of those Times in his Interests, and to be the Trumpet of his
Praises. *Augustus* had given him the Example, by the Advice of
Mecaenas, who recommended *Virgil* and *Horace* to him; whose

Praises help'd to make him Popular while he was alive, and after his Death have made him Precious to Posterity. As for the Religion of our Poet, he seems to have some little Byas towards the Opinions of *Wickliff*, after *John of Ghant* his Patron; somewhat of which appears in the Tale of *Piers Plowman:* Yet I cannot blame him for inveighing so sharply against the Vices of the Clergy in his Age: Their Pride, their Ambition, their Pomp, their Avarice, their Worldly Interest, deserv'd the Lashes which he gave them, both in that, and in most of his *Canterbury Tales:* Neither has his Contemporary *Boccace,* spar'd them. Yet both those Poets liv'd in much esteem, with good and holy Men in Orders: For the Scandal which is given by particular Priests, reflects not on the Sacred Function. *Chaucer's Monk,* his *Chanon,* and his *Fryar,* took not from the Character of his *Good Parson.* A Satyrical Poet is the Check of the Laymen, on bad Priests. We are only to take care, that we involve not the Innocent with the Guilty in the same Condemnation. The Good cannot be too much honour'd, nor the Bad too coursly us'd: For the Corruption of the Best, becomes the Worst. When a Clergy-man is whipp'd, his Gown is first taken off, by which the Dignity of his Order is secur'd: If he be wrongfully accus'd, he has his Action of Slander; and 'tis at the Poet's Peril, if he transgress the Law. But they will tell us, that all kind of Satire, though never so well deserv'd by particular Priests, yet brings the whole Order into Contempt. Is then the Peerage of *England* any thing dishonour'd, when a Peer suffers for his Treason? If he be libell'd, or any way defam'd, he has his *Scandalum Magnatum* [5] to punish the Offendor. They who use this Kind of Argument, seem to be conscious to themselves of somewhat which has deserv'd the Poet's Lash; and are less concern'd for their Publick Capacity, then for their Private: At least, there is Pride at the bottom of their Reasoning. If the Faults of Men in Orders are only to be judg'd among themselves, they are all in some sort Parties: For, since they say the Honour of their Order is concern'd in every Member of it, how can we be sure, that they will be impartial Judges? How far I may be allow'd to speak my Opinions in this Case, I know not: But I am sure

---

[5] Literally "magnified scandal"; the penalties were greater for slandering a peer than for slandering a commoner.

a Dispute of this Nature caus'd Mischief in abundance betwixt a King of *England* and an Archbishop of *Canterbury;* one standing up for the Laws of his Land, and the other for the Honour (as he call'd it) of God's Church; which ended in the Murther of the Prelate, and in the whipping of his Majesty from Post to Pillar for his Penance. The learn'd and Ingenious Dr. *Drake* has sav'd me the Labour of inquiring into the Esteem and Reverence which the Priests have had of old; and I would rather extend than diminish any part of it: Yet I must needs say, that when a Priest provokes me without any Occasion given him, I have no Reason, unless it be the Charity of a *Christian,* to forgive him: *Prior laesit* is Justification sufficient in the Civil Law. If I answer him in his own Language, Self-defence, I am sure, must be allow'd me; and if I carry it farther, even to a sharp Recrimination, somewhat may be indulg'd to Humane Frailty. Yet my Resentment has not wrought so far, but that I have follow'd Chaucer in his Character of a Holy Man, and have enlarg'd on that Subject with some Pleasure, reserving to my self the Right, if I shall think fit hereafter, to describe another sort of Priests, such as are more easily to be found than the Good Parson; such as have given the last Blow to Christianity in this Age, by a Practice so contrary to their Doctrine. But this will keep cold till another time. In the mean while, I take up *Chaucer* where I left him. He must have been a Man of a most wonderful comprehensive Nature, because, as it has been truly observ'd of him, he has taken into the Compass of his *Canterbury Tales* the various Manners and Humours (as we now call them) of the whole *English* Nation, in his Age. Not a single Character has escap'd him. All his Pilgrims are severally distinguish'd from each other; and not only in their Inclinations, but in their very Phisiognomies and Persons. *Baptista Porta*[6] could not have describ'd their Natures better, than by the Marks which the Poet gives them. The Matter and Manner of their Tales, and of their Telling, are so suited to their different Educations, Humours, and Callings, that each of them would be improper in any other Mouth. Even the grave and serious Characters are distinguish'd by their several sorts of Gravity: Their

---

[6] Giambattista della Porta (*c.* 1538–1615), Italian natural philosopher.

Discourses are such as belong to their Age, their Calling, and their Breeding; such as are becoming of them, and of them only. Some of his Persons are Vicious, and some Vertuous; some are unlearn'd, or (as *Chaucer calls them*) Lewd, and some are Learn'd. Even the Ribaldry of the Low Characters is different: The *Reeve*, the *Miller*, and the Cook, are several Men, and distinguish'd from each other, as much as the mincing Lady Prioress, and the broad-speaking Wife of *Bathe*. But enough of this: There is such a Variety of Game springing up before me, that I am distracted in my Choice, and know not which to follow. 'Tis sufficient to say according to the Proverb, that here is God's Plenty. We have our Fore-fathers and Great Grand-dames all before us, as they were in *Chaucer's* Days; their general Characters are still remaining in Mankind, and even in England, though they are call'd by other Names than those of *Moncks*, and *Fryars*, and *Chanons*, and *Lady Abbesses*, and *Nuns:* For Mankind is ever the same, and nothing lost out of Nature, though every thing is alter'd. May I have leave to do my self the Justice, (since my Enemies will do me none, and are so far from granting me to be a good Poet, that they will not allow me so much as to be a Christian, or a Moral Man) may I have leave, I say, to inform my Reader, that I have confin'd my Choice to such Tales of *Chaucer*, as savour nothing of Immodesty. If I had desir'd more to please than to instruct, the *Reve*, the *Miller*, the *Shipman*, the *Merchant*, the *Sumner*, and above all, the *Wife of Bathe*, in the Prologue to her Tale, would have procur'd me as many Friends and Readers, as there are *Beaux* and Ladies of Pleasure in the Town. But I will no more offend against Good Manners: I am sensible as I ought to be of the Scandal I have given by my loose writings; and make what Reparation I am able, by this Publick Acknowledgment. If any thing of this Nature, or of Profaneness, be crept into these Poems, I am so far from defending it, that I disown it. *Totum hoc indictum volo.* [I wish it all unsaid.] *Chaucer* makes another manner of Apologie for his broad-speaking, and *Boccace* makes the like; but I will follow neither of them. Our Country-man, in the end of his Characters, before the *Canterbury Tales*, thus excuses the Ribaldry, which is very gross, in many of his Novels.

> *But first, I pray you, of your courtesy,*
> *That ye ne arrete it nought my villany,*
> *Though that I plainly speak in this mattere*
> *To tellen you her words, and eke her chere:*
> *Ne though I speak her words properly,*
> *For this ye knowen as well as I,*
> *Who shall tellen a tale after a man*
> *He mote rehearse as nye, as ever He can:*
> *Everich word of it been in his charge,*
> All speke he, never so rudely, ne large.
> *Or else he mote tellen his tale untrue,*
> *Or feine things, or find words new:*
> *He may not spare, altho he were his brother,*
> *He mote as well say o word as another.*
> Christ *spake himself full broad in holy Writ,*
> *And well I wote no Villany is it.*
> *Eke* Plato *saith, who so can him rede,*
> *The words mote been Cousin to the dede.*

Yet if a Man should have enquir'd of *Boccace* or of *Chaucer,* what need they had of introducing such Characters, where obscene Words were proper in their Mouths, but very undecent to be heard; I know not what Answer they could have made: For that Reason, such Tales shall be left untold by me. You have here a *Specimen* of *Chaucer's* Language, which is so obsolete, that his Sense is scarce to be understood; and you have likewise more than one Example of his unequal Numbers, which were mention'd before. Yet many of his Verses consist of Ten Syllables, and the words not much behind our present *English:* As for Example, these two Lines, in the Description of the Carpenter's Young Wife:

> *Wincing she was, as is a jolly Colt,*
> *Long as a Mast, and upright as a Bolt.*

I have almost done with Chaucer, when I have answer'd some Objections relating to my present Work. I find some People are offended that I have turn'd these Tales into modern *English;* because they think them unworthy of my Pains, and look on *Chaucer* as a dry, old-fashion'd Wit, not worth receiving. I have often heard the late Earl of *Leicester* say, that Mr. Cowley

himself was of that opinion; who having read him over at my
Lord's Request, declar'd he had no Taste of him. I dare not
advance my Opinion against the Judgment of so great an Author:
But I think it fair, however, to leave the Decision to the Publick:
Mr. *Cowley* was too modest to set up for a Dictatour; and being
shock'd perhaps with his old Style, never examin'd into the
depth of his good Sense. *Chaucer*, I confess, is a rough Diamond,
and must first be polish'd e'er he shines. I deny not likewise, that
living in our early Days of Poetry, he writes not always of a
piece; but sometimes mingles trivial Things, with those of greater
Moment. Sometimes also, though not often, he runs riot, like
Ovid, and knows not when he has said enough. But there are
more great Wits, beside *Chaucer*, whose Fault is their Excess of
Conceits, and those ill sorted. An Author is not to write all he
can, but only all he ought. Having observ'd this Redundancy
in *Chaucer*, (as it is an easie Matter for a Man of ordinary Parts
to find a Fault in one of greater) I have not ty'd my self to a
Literal Translation; but have often omitted what I judg'd unnecessary, or not of Dignity enough to appear in the Company
of better Thoughts. I have presum'd farther in some Places, and
added somewhat of my own where I thought my Author was
deficient, and had not given his Thoughts their true Lustre, for
want of Words in the Beginning of our Language. And to this
I was the more embolden'd, because (if I may be permitted
to say it of my self) I found I had a Soul congenial to his, and
that I had been conversant in the same Studies. Another Poet,
in another Age, may take the same Liberty with my Writings;
if at least they live long enough to deserve Correction. It was
also necessary sometimes to restore the Sense of *Chaucer*, which
was lost or mangled in the Errors of the Press: Let this Example
suffice at present in the Story of *Palamon* and *Arcite*, where the
Temple of Diana is describ'd, you find these Verses, in all the
Editions of our Author:

> *There saw I* Danè *turned unto a Tree,*
> *I mean not the Goddess* Diane,
> *But* Venus *Daughter, which that hight Danè.*

Which after a little Consideration I knew was to be reform'd
into this Sense, that *Daphne* the Daughter of *Peneus* was turn'd

into a Tree. I durst not make thus bold with *Ovid,* lest some future *Milbourn* [7] should arise, and say, I varied from my Author, because I understood him not.

But there are other Judges who think I ought not to have translated *Chaucer* into *English,* out of a quite contrary Notion: They suppose there is a certain Veneration due to his old Language; and that it is little less than Profanation and Sacrilege to alter it. They are farther of opinion, that somewhat of his good Sense will suffer in this Transfusion, and much of the Beauty of his Thoughts will infallibly be lost, which appear with more Grace in their old Habit. Of this Opinion was that excellent Person, whom I mention'd, the late Earl of *Leicester,* who valu'd *Chaucer* as much as Mr. *Cowley* despis'd him. My Lord dissuaded me from this Attempt, (for I was thinking of it some Years before his Death) and his Authority prevail'd so far with me, as to defer my Undertaking while he liv'd, in deference to him: Yet my Reason was not convinc'd with what he urg'd against it. If the first End of a Writer be to be understood, then as his Language grows obsolete, his Thoughts must grow obscure, *multa renascuntur quae nunc cecidere; cadentque quae nunc sunt in honore vocabula, si volet usus, quem penes arbitrum est et jus et norma loquendi.* [Many words which are now in disuse shall be revived, and words now held in honor will fall, if that is what usage wants. With usage rests the decision, the law, and the correct form of speech.] When an ancient Word for its Sound and Significancy deserves to be reviv'd, I have that reasonable Veneration for Antiquity, to restore it. All beyond this is Superstition. Words are not like Land-marks, so sacred as never to be remov'd: Customs are chang'd, and even Statutes are silently repeal'd, when the Reason ceases for which they were enacted. As for the other Part of the Argument, that his Thoughts will lose of their original Beauty, by the innovation of Words; in the first place, not only their Beauty, but their Being is lost, where they are no longer understood, which is the present Case. I grant, that something must be lost in all transfusion, that is, in all Translations; but the Sense will remain, which would

[7] Luke Milbourne (1649–1720), clergyman and poet, attacked Dryden's translation of Virgil.

otherwise be lost, or at least be maim'd, when it is scarce intelligible; and that but to a few. How few are there who can read Chaucer, so as to understand him perfectly? And if imperfectly, then with less Profit, and no Pleasure. 'Tis not for the Use of some old *Saxon* Friends, that I have taken these Pains with him: Let them neglect my Version, because they have no need of it. I made it for their sakes who understand Sense and Poetry, as well as they; when that Poetry and Sense is put into Words which they understand. I will go farther, and dare to add, that what Beauties I lose in some Places, I give to others which had them not originally: But in this I may be partial to my self; let the Reader judge, and I submit to his Decision. Yet I think I have just Occasion to complain of them, who because they understand *Chaucer,* would deprive the greater part of their Countrymen of the same Advantage, and hoord him up, as Misers do their Grandam Gold, only to look on it themselves, and hinder others from making use of it. In sum, I seriously protest, that no Man ever had, or can have, a greater Veneration for *Chaucer,* than my self. I have translated some part of his Works, only that I might perpetuate his Memory, or at least refresh it, amongst my Countrymen. If I have alter'd him any where for the better, I must at the same time acknowledge, that I could have done nothing without him: *Facile est inventis addere* [It is easy to add to what has already been invented], is no great Commendation; and I am not so vain to think I have deserv'd a greater. I will conclude what I have to say of him singly, with this one Remark: A Lady of my Acquaintance, who keeps a kind of Correspondence with some Authors of the Fair Sex in *France,* has been inform'd by them, that *Mademoiselle de Scudery,* who is as old as *Sibyl,* and inspir'd like her by the same God of Poetry, is at this time translating *Chaucer* into modern French. From which I gather, that he has been formerly translated to the old Provencall, (for, how she should come to understand Old *English,* I know not.) But the Matter of Fact being true, it makes me think, that there is something in it like Fatality; that after certain Periods of Time, the Fame and Memory of Great Wits should be renew'd, as *Chaucer* is both in *France* and *England.* If this be wholly Chance, 'tis extraordinary; and I dare not call it more, for fear of being tax'd with Superstition.

Boccace comes last to be consider'd, who living in the same Age with *Chaucer,* had the same Genius, and follow'd the same Studies: Both writ Novels, and each of them cultivated his Mother-Tongue: But the greatest Resemblance of our two Modern Authors being in their familiar Style, and pleasing way of relating Comical Adventures, I may pass it over, because I have translated nothing from *Boccace* of that Nature. In the serious Part of Poetry, the Advantage is wholly on *Chaucer's* Side; for though The *Englishman* has borrow'd many Tales from the *Italian,* yet it appears, that those of *Boccace* were not generally of his own making, but taken from Authors of former Ages, and by him only modell'd: So that what there was of Invention in either of them, may be judg'd equal. But *Chaucer* has refin'd on *Boccace,* and has mended the Stories which he has borrow'd, in his way of telling; though Prose allows more Liberty of Thought, and the Expression is more easie, when unconfin'd by Numbers. Our Countryman carries Weight, and yet wins the Race at disadvantage. I desire not the Reader should take my Word; and therefore I will set two of their Discourses on the same Subject, in the same Light, for every Man to judge betwixt them. I translated *Chaucer* first, and amongst the rest, pitch'd on the Wife of *Bath's* Tale; not daring, as I have said, to adventure on her Prologue; because 'tis too licentious: There *Chaucer* introduces an old Woman of mean Parentage, whom a youthful Knight of Noble Blood was forc'd to marry, and consequently loath'd her: The Crone being in bed with him on the wedding Night, and finding his Aversion, endeavours to win his Affection by Reason, and speaks a good Word for her self, (as who could blame her?) in hope to mollifie the sullen Bridegroom. She takes her Topiques from the Benefits of Poverty, the Advantages of old Age and Ugliness, the Vanity of Youth, and the silly Pride of Ancestry and Titles without inherent Vertue, which is the true Nobility. When I had clos'd *Chaucer,* I return'd to *Ovid,* and translated some more of his Fables; and by this time had so far forgotten the Wife of *Bath's* Tale, that when I took up *Boccace,* unawares I fell on the same Argument of preferring Virtue to Nobility of Blood, and Titles, in the Story of *Sigismonda;* which I had certainly avoided for the Resemblance of the two Discourses, if my Memory had not fail'd me. Let the Reader weigh them both; and if he thinks me partial to *Chaucer,* 'tis in him to right *Boccace.*

I prefer in our Countryman, far above all his other Stories, the Noble Poem of *Palamon* and *Arcite,* which is of the Epique kind, and perhaps not much inferiour to the *Ilias* or the *Aeneis:* the Story is more pleasing than either of them, the Manners as perfect, the Diction as poetical, the Learning as deep and various; and the Disposition full as artful: only it includes a greater length of time; as taking up seven years at least; but *Aristotle* has left undecided the Duration of the Action; which yet is easily reduc'd into the Compass of a year, by a Narration of what preceded the Return of *Palamon* to *Athens.* I had thought for the Honour of our Nation, and more particularly for his, whose Laurel, tho' unworthy, I have worn after him, that this Story was of *English* Growth, and *Chaucer's* own: But I was undeceiv'd by *Boccace;* for casually looking on the End of his seventh *Giornata,* I found *Dioneo* (under which name he shadows himself) and *Fiametta* (who represents his Mistress, the natural Daughter of *Robert* King of *Naples*) of whom these Words are spoken. *Dioneo e Fiametta gran pezza eantarono insieme d'Arcita, e di Palamone* [Dioneo and Fiametta would sing together much of the story of Arcite and Palamone]: by which it appears that this Story was written before the time of *Boccace;* but the Name of its Author being wholly lost, *Chaucer* is now become an Original; and I question not but the Poem has receiv'd many Beauties by passing through his Noble Hands. Besides this Tale, there is another of his own Invention, after the manner of the Provencalls, call'd *The Flower and the Leaf;* with which I was so particularly pleas'd, both for the Invention and the Moral; that I cannot hinder my self from recommending it to the Reader.

As a Corollary to this Preface, in which I have done Justice to others, I owe somewhat to my self: not that I think it worth my time to enter the Lists with one M——, or one B——, but barely to take notice, that such Men there are who have written scurrilously against me without any Provocation. M——, who is in Orders, pretends amongst the rest this Quarrel to me, that I have fallen foul on Priesthood; If I have, I am only to ask Pardon of good Priests, and am afraid his part of the Reparation will come to little. Let him be satisfied that he shall not be able to force himself upon me for an Adversary. I contemn him too much to enter into Competition with him. His own Translations of Virgil have answer'd his Criticisms on mine. If (as they say, he has declar'd in Print) he prefers the Version of Ogilby to mine, the World has made him the same Compliment: For 'tis agreed on all hands, that he writes even below Ogilby: That, you will say, is not easily to be done; but what cannot M—— bring about? I am satisfy'd however, that while he and I live together, I shall not be thought the worst Poet of the Age. It looks as if I had desir'd him underhand to write so ill against me: But upon my honest Word I have not brib'd him to do me this Service, and am wholly guiltless of his Pamphlet. 'Tis true I should be glad, if I could persuade him to continue his good Offices, and write such another Critique on any thing of mine: For I find by Experience he has a great Stroke with the Reader, when he condemns any of my Poems to make the World have a better Opinion of them. He has taken some Pains with my Poetry; but no body will be persuaded to take the same with his. If I had taken to the Church (as he affirms, but which was never in my Thoughts) I should have had more Sense, if not more Grace, than to have turn'd my self out of my Benefice by writing Libels on my Parishioners. But his Account of my Manners and my Principles, are of a Piece with his Cavils and his Poetry: And so I have done with him for ever.

As for the City Bard, or Knight Physician,[8] I hear his Quarrel to me is, that I was the Author of *Absalom* and *Architophel,* which he thinks is a little hard on his Fanatique Patrons in *London.*

But I will deal the more civilly with his two Poems, because nothing ill is to be spoken of the Dead: And therefore Peace be to the *Manes* of his *Arthurs.* I will only say that it was not for this Noble Knight that I drew the Plan of an Epick Poem on King *Arthur* in my Preface to the Translation of *Juvenal.* The

---

[8] Sir Richard Blackmore (d. 1729), physician and author, attacked Dryden's morals in the preface to his epic poem, *Prince Arthur.*

Guardian Angels of Kingdoms were Machines too ponderous for him to manage; and therefore he rejected them as *Dares* did the Whirl-bats of *Eryx* when they were thrown before him by *Entellus:* Yet from that Preface he plainly took his Hint: For he began immediately upon the Story; though he had the Baseness not to acknowledge his Benefactor; but in stead of it, to traduce me in a Libel.

I shall say the less of Mr. *Collier,*[9] because in many Things he has tax'd me justly; and I have pleaded Guilty to all Thoughts and Expressions of mine, which can be truly argu'd of Obscenity, Profaneness, or Immorality; and retract them. If he be my Enemy, let him triumph; if he be my Friend, as I have given him no Personal Occasion to be otherwise, he will be glad of my Repentance. It becomes me not to draw my Pen in the Defence of a bad Cause, when I have so often drawn it for a good one. Yet it were not difficult to prove, that in many Places he has perverted my Meaning by his Glosses; and interpreted my Words into blasphemy and Baudry, of which they were not guilty. Besides that, he is too much given to Horse-play in his Raillery; and comes to Battel, like a Dictatour from the Plough. I will not say, *The Zeal of Gods House has eaten him up;* but I am sure it has devour'd some Part of his Good Manners and Civility. It might also be doubted, whether it were altogether Zeal, which prompted him to this rough manner of Proceeding; perhaps it became not one of his Function to rake into the Rubbish of Ancient and Modern Plays; a Divine might have employ'd his Pains to better purpose, than in the Nastiness of *Plautus* and *Aristophanes;* whose Examples, as they excuse not me, so it might be possibly suppos'd, that he read them not without some Pleasure. They who have written Commentaries on those Poets, or on *Horace, Juvenal,* and *Martial,* have explain'd some Vices, which without their interpretation had been unknown to Modern Times. Neither has he judg'd impartially betwixt the former Age and us.

There is more Baudry in one Play of *Fletcher's,* call'd *The Custom of the Country,* than in all our together. Yet this has been often acted on the Stage in my remembrance. Are the

---

[9] Jeremy, Collier; see below, pp. 96–130.

Times so much more reform'd now, than they were Five and
Twenty Years ago? If they are, I congratulate the Amendment
of our Morals. But I am not to prejudice the Cause of my Fellow-
Poets, though I abandon my own Defence: They have some of
them answer'd for themselves, and neither they nor I can think
Mr. *Collier* so formidable an Enemy, that we should shun him.
He has lost Ground at the latter end of the Day, by pursuing his
Point too far, like the Prince of *Condé* at the Battel of *Senneph:*
From Immoral Plays, to No Plays; *ab abusu ad usum, non valet
consequentia.* [An inference drawn from misuse to use is in-
valid]. But being a Party, I am not to erect my self into a
Judge. As for the rest of those who have written against me,
they are such Scoundrels, that they deserve not the least Notice
to be taken of them. B—— and M—— are only distinguish'd from
the Crowd, by being remember'd to their Infamy.
    —*Demetri, Teque Tigelli*
    Discipularum inter jubeo plorare cathedras.
[I order you, Demetrius and Tegellius, to weep among the
benches of your students.]

William Congreve

[1670–1729]

৵৽৾৵

THOUGH CONGREVE IS ANYTHING BUT a major critic, he contributed lively essays to two of the important critical discussions of his time. "Concerning Humor in Comedy" continues the debate on the nature of wit and humor, and the relation of these terms to the English genius, which began with Ben Jonson and extends well into the nineteenth century (see Hazlitt's "Wit and Humor" in *English Literary Criticism: Romantic and Victorian* of this series). In this debate we can see the way in which humor is transformed from a psychological term, based on sixteenth-century medical theory, to a term meaning an amusing quality in speech or writing. In this process of transformation, Congreve stands midway; he speaks of "humor" characters in a way which reveals his debt to Jonson, but he also speaks of things which may, in a comedy, be "humorously" spoken, giving the term its modern meaning. Congreve's view that humor (in the Jonsonian sense of extreme eccentricity or ridiculousness) is "almost of English growth" was common in the seventeenth and eighteenth centuries, and influenced the way in which the theory of comedy as a genre developed (see Dryden's *Essay of Dramatic Poesy* above).

Congreve was one of the Restoration playwrights whose "immorality and profaneness" Jeremy Collier attacked (see below, pp. 96–130). Congreve replied to Collier in *Amendments of Mr. Collier's False and Imperfect Citations* (1698), an essay more notable for its good humor than for its logic.

BIBLIOGRAPHY. *Complete Works,* ed. Montague Summers, 4 vols. (London, 1923).

George Meredith, *On the Idea of Comedy and the Uses of the Comic Spirit* (London, 1877); D. C. Taylor, *Congreve* (London, 1931); J. W. Krutch, *Comedy and Conscience after the Restoration* (2nd ed., New York, 1949).

TEXT. *Letters Upon Several Occasions,* ed. John Dennis (London, 1696).

CONCERNING HUMOUR IN COMEDY

[1695]

Mr. Congreve *to Mr.* Dennis
Concerning Humour in Comedy

Dear Sir:

You write to me that you have Entertained your self two or three days with reading several Comedies, of several Authors; and your Observation is, that there is more of *Humour* in our English Writers, than in any of the other Comick Poets, Ancient or Modern. You desire to know my Opinion, and at the same time my Thought, of that which is generally call'd *Humour* in Comedy.

I agree with you, in an Impartial Preference of our English Writers, in that Particular. But if I tell you my Thoughts of *Humour*, I must at the same time confess, that what I take for true *Humour*, has not been so often written even by them, as is generally believed: And some who have valued themselves, and have been esteem'd by others, for that kind of Writing have seldom touch'd upon it. To make this appear to the World, would require a long and labour'd Discourse, and such as I neither am able nor willing to undertake. But such little Remarks, as may be contained within the Compass of a Letter, and such unpremeditated Thoughts, as may be Communicated between Friend and Friend, without incurring the Censure of the World, or setting up for a *Dictator,* you shall have from me, since you have enjoyn'd it.

To Define *Humour,* perhaps, were as difficult, as to Define *Wit;* for like that, it is of infinite variety. To Enumerate the several *Humours* of Men, were a Work as endless, as to sum up their several Opinions. And in my mind the *Quot homines tot Sententiæ* might have been more properly interpreted of *Humour;* since there are many Men, of the same Opinion in many things, who are yet quite different in Humours. But thô we cannot certainly tell what *Wit* is, or, what *Humour* is, yet we may

go near to shew something, which is not *Wit* or not *Humour;*
and yet often mistaken for both. And since I have mentioned
Wit and *Humour* together, let me make the first Distinction
between them, and observe to you that *Wit is often mistaken
for Humour.*

I have observed, that when a few things have been Wittily
and Pleasantly spoken by any Character in a Comedy; it has
been very usual for those, who make their Remarks on a Play,
while it is acting, to say, *Such a thing is very Humorously
spoken: There is a great Deal of Humour in that Part.* Thus the
Character of the Person speaking, may be, Surprizingly and
Pleasantly, is mistaken for a Character of *Humour;* which indeed
is a Character of *Wit.* But there is a great Difference between a
Comedy, wherein there are many things *Humorously,* as they
call it, which is *Pleasantly* spoken; and one, where there are
several Characters of *Humour,* distinguish'd by the Particular
and Different Humours, appropriated to the several Persons represented, and which naturally arise, from the different Con-
stitutions, Complexions, and Dispositions of Men. The saying of
Humorous Things, does not distinguish Characters; For every
Person in a Comedy may be allow'd to speak them. From a
Witty Man they are expected; and even a *Fool* may be permitted
to stumble on 'em by chance. Thô I make a Difference betwixt
Wit and *Humour;* yet I do not think that Humorous Characters
exclude Wit: No, but the Manner of *Wit* should be adapted to
the *Humour.* As, for Instance, a Character of a Splenetick and
Peevish *Humour,* should have a Satyrical Wit. A Jolly and Sanguine *Humour,* should have a Facetious Wit. The Former should
speak Positively; the Latter, Carelesly: For the former Observes,
and shews things as they are; the latter, rather overlooks Nature,
and speaks things as he would have them; and his *Wit* and
Humour have both of them a less Alloy of Judgment than the
others.

As *Wit,* so its opposite, *Folly, is sometimes mistaken for Humour.*

When a Poet brings a *Character* on the Stage, committing a
thousand Absurdities, and talking Impertinencies, roaring Aloud,
and Laughing immoderately on every, or rather upon no occasion; this is a Character of Humour.

Is any thing more common than to have a pretended Comedy, stuff'd with such Grotesques, Figures, and Farce Fools? Things, that either are not in Nature, or, if they are, are Monsters and Births of Mischance; and consequently, as such, should be stifled, and huddled out of the way, like *Sooterkins;* that Mankind may not be shock'd, with an appearing Possibility of the Degeneration of a God-like *Species.* For my part, I am as willing to Laugh, as any body, and as easily diverted with an Object truly ridiculous: but at the same time I can never care for seeing things, that force me to entertain low thoughts of my Nature. I dont know how it is with others, but I confess freely to you, I could never look long upon a Monkey, without very Mortifying Reflections; thô I never heard any thing to the Contrary, why that Creature is not Originally of a Distinct *Species.* As I dont think *Humour* exclusive of *Wit,* neither do I think it inconsistent with *Folly;* but I think the Follies should be only such as Mens Humours may incline 'em to; and not Follies intirely abstract from both Humour and Nature.

Sometimes *Personal Defects are misrepresented for Humours.*

I mean, sometimes Characters are barbarously exposed on the Stage, ridiculing Natural Deformities, Casual Defects in the Senses, and Infirmities of Age. Sure the Poet must both be very Ill-natur'd himself, and think his Audience so, when he proposes by shewing a Man Deform'd, or Deaf, or Blind, to give them an agreeable Entertainment; and hopes to raise their Mirth, by what is truly an object of Compassion. But much need not be said upon this Head to any body, especially to you, who, in one of your Letters to me concerning Mr. *Johnson's Fox,* have justly excepted against this Immoral part of *Ridicule* in *Corbaccio's* Character; and there I must agree with you to blame him, whom otherwise I cannot enough admire for his great Mastery of true Humour in Comedy.

External Habit of Body is often mistaken for Humour.

By *External Habit,* I do not mean the Ridiculous Dress or Cloathing of a Character, thô that goes a good way in some received Characters. (But undoubtedly a Man's Humour may incline him to dress differently from other People). But I mean a Singularity of Manners, Speech, and Behaviour, peculiar to all, or most of the same Country, Trade, Profession, or Education. I cannot think that a *Humour* which is only a Habit, or Disposition contracted by Use or Custom; for by a Disuse, or Complyance with other Customs, it may be worn off, or diversify'd.

Affectation is generally mistaken for Humour.

These are indeed so much alike, that at a Distance they may be mistaken one for the other. For what is *Humour* in one, may be *Affectation* in another; and nothing is more common, than for some to affect particular ways of saying, and doing things, peculiar to others whom they admire and would imitate. *Humour* is the Life, *Affectation* the Picture. He that draws a Character of *Affectation,* shews *Humour* at the Second Hand; he at best but publishes a Translation, and his Pictures are but Copies.

But as these two last distinctions are the Nicest, so it may be most proper to Explain them; by Particular Instances from some Author of Reputation. *Humour* I take, either to be born with us, and so of a Natural Growth; or else to be grafted into us, by some accidental change in the Constitution, or revolution of the Internal Habit of Body; by which it becomes, if I may so call it, Naturaliz'd.

Humour is from Nature, *Habit* from Custom; and *Affectation* from Industry.

Humour, shews us as we *are.*

Habit, shews us as we appear, under a forcible Impression.

Affectation, shews what we would be, under a Voluntary Disguise.

Thô here I would observe by the way, that a continued Affectation may in time become a Habit.

The Character of *Morose* in the *Silent Woman,* I take to be a Character of Humour. And I choose to Instance this Character to you, from many others of the same Author, because I know it has been Condemn'd by many as Unnatural and Farce: And you have your self hinted some dislike of it, for the same Reason, in a Letter to me, concerning some of *Johnson's* Plays.

Let us suppose *Morose* to be a Man Naturally Splenetick and Melancholly; is there any thing more offensive to one of such a Disposition, than Noise and Clamour? Let any Man that has the Spleen (and there are enough in *England*) be Judge. We see common Examples of this Humour in little every day. 'Tis ten to one, but three parts in four of the Company that you dine with, are Discompos'd and Startled at the Cutting of a Cork, or Scratching a Plate with a Knife: It is a Proportion of the same Humour, that makes such or any other Noise offensive to the Person that hears it; for there are others who will not be disturb'd at all by it. Well, But *Morose,* you will say, is so Extravagant, he cannot bear any Discourse or Conversation, above a Whisper. Why, It is his excess of this Humour, that makes him become Ridiculous, and qualifies his Character for Comedy. If the Poet had given him, but a Moderate proportion of that Humour, 'tis odds but half the Audience, would have sided with the Character, and have Condemn'd the Author, for Exposing a Humour which was neither Remarkable nor Ridiculous. Besides, the distance of the Stage requires the Figure represented, to be something larger than the Life; and sure a Picture may have Features larger in Proportion, and yet be very like the Original. If this Exactness of Quantity, were to be observed in Wit, as some would have it in Humour; what would become of those Characters that are design'd for Men of Wit? I believe if a Poet should steal a Dialogue of any Length from the *Extempore* Discourse of the two Wittiest Men upon Earth, he would find the Scene but coldly receiv'd by the Town. But to the purpose.

The Character of Sir *John Daw* in the same Play, is a Character of Affectation. He every where discovers an Affectation of Learning; when he is not only Conscious to himself, but the Audience also plainly perceives that he is Ignorant. Of this kind are the Characters of *Thraso* in the Eunuch of *Terence,* and *Pyrgopolinices* in the *Miles Gloriosus* of *Plautus.* They affect to be thought Valiant, when both themselves and the Audience know they are not. Now such a boasting of Valour in Men who were really Valiant, would undoubtedly be a *Humour;* for a Fiery Disposition might naturally throw a Man into the same Extravagance, which is only affected in the Characters I have mentioned.

The Character of *Cob* in *Every Man in his Humour* and most of the under Characters in *Bartholomew-Fair,* discover only a Singularity of Manners, appropriated to the several Educations and Professions of the Persons represented. They are not Hu-

mours but Habits contracted by Custom. Under this Head may
be ranged all Country-Clowns, Sailers, Tradesmen, Jockeys,
Gamesters, and such like, who make use of *Cants* or peculiar
Dialects in their several Arts and Vocations. One may almost
give a Receipt for the Composition of such a Character: For
the Poet has nothing to do, but to collect a few proper Phrases
and terms of Art, and to make the Person apply them by ridiculous Metaphors in his Conversation, with Characters of different
Natures. Some late Characters of this kind have been very successful; but in my mind they may be Painted without much Art
or Labour; since they require little more, than a good Memory
and Superficial Observation. But true *Humour* cannot be shewn,
without a Dissection of Nature, and a Narrow Search, to discover
the first Seeds, from whence it has its Root and growth.

If I were to write to the World, I should be obliged to dwell
longer, upon each of these Distinctions and Examples; for I
know that they would not be plain enough to all Readers. But
a bare hint is sufficient to inform you of the Notions which I
have on this Subject: And I hope by this time you are of my
Opinion, that Humour is neither Wit, nor Folly, nor Personal
defect; nor Affectation, nor Habit; and yet, that each and all of
these, have been both written and received for Humour.

I should be unwilling to venture even on a bare Description
of Humour, much more to make a Definition of it, but now my
hands is in, Ile tell you what serves me instead of either. I take
it to be, *A singular and unavoidable manner of doing or saying
any thing, Peculiar and Natural to one Man only; by which his
Speech and Actions are distinguish'd from those of other men.*

Our *Humour* has relation to us, and to what proceeds from us,
as the Accidents have to a Substance; it is a Colour, Taste, and
Smell, Diffused through all; thô our Actions are never so many,
and different in Form, they are all Splinters of the same Wood,
and have Naturally one Complexion, which thô it may be disguised by Art, yet cannot be wholly changed: We may Paint
it with other Colours, but we cannot change the Grain. So the
Natural sound of an Instrument will be distinguish'd, thô the
Notes expressed by it, are never so various, and the Divisions
never so many. Dissimulation, may by Degrees, become more
easy to our practice; but it can never absolutely transubstantiate

us into what we would seem: It will always be in some proportion a Violence upon Nature.

A Man may change his Opinion, but I believe he will find it a Difficulty, to part with his *Humour,* and there is nothing more provoking, than the being made sensible of that difficulty. Sometimes, one shall meet with those, who perhaps, Innocently enough, but at the same time impertinently, will ask the Question; *Why are you not Merry? Why are you not Gay, Pleasant, and Cheerful?* then, instead of answering, could I ask such a one; *Why are you not handsome? Why have you not Black Eyes* and a better Complexion? Nature abhors to be forced.

The two Famous Philosophers of *Ephesus* and *Abdera,* have their different Sects at this day. Some Weep, and others Laugh at one and the same thing.

I dont doubt, but you have observed several Men Laugh when they are Angry; others who are Silent; some that are Loud: Yet I cannot suppose that it is the passion of *Anger* which is in it self different, or more or less in one than t'other; but that it is the *Humour* of the Man that is Predominant, and urges him to express it in that manner. Demonstrations of pleasure are as Various; one Man has a Humour of retiring from all Company, when any thing has happen'd to please him beyond expectation; he hugs himself alone, and thinks it an Addition to the pleasure to keep it Secret. Another is upon Thorns till he has made Proclamation of it; and must make other people sensible of his happiness, before he can be so himself. So it is in Grief, and other Passions. Demonstrations of Love and the Effects of that Passion upon several Humours are infinitely different; but here the Ladies who abound in Servants are the best Judges. Talking of the Ladies, methinks something should be observed of the Humour of the Fair Sex, since they are sometimes so kind as to furnish out a Character for Comedy. But I must confess I have never made any observation of what I Apprehend to be true Humour in Women. Perhaps Passions are too powerful in that Sex, to let Humour have its Course; or may be by Reason of their Natural Coldness, Humour cannot Exert it self to that extravagant Degree, which it often does in the Male Sex. For if ever any thing does appear Comical or Ridiculous in a Woman, I think it is little more than an acquir'd Folly, or an Affectation. We may call them the weaker Sex, but I think the true Reason is, because our Follies are Stronger, and our Faults are more prevailing.

One might think that the Diversity of Humour, which must be allowed to be diffused throughout Mankind, might afford endless matter, for the support of Comedies. But when we come closely to consider that point, and nicely to distinguish the Difference of Humours, I believe we shall find the contrary. For thô we allow every Man something of his own, and a peculiar Humour; yet every Man has it not in quantity, to become Remarkable by it: Or, if many do become Remarkable by their Humours; yet all those Humours may not be Diverting. Nor is it only requisite to distinguish what Humour will be diverting, but also how much of it, what part of it to shew in Light, and what to cast in Shades; how to set it off by preparatory Scenes, and by opposing other humours to it in the same Scene. Thrô a wrong Judgment, sometimes, Mens Humours may be opposed when there is really no specific Difference between them; only a greater proportion of the same, in one than t'other, occasion'd by his having more Flegm, or Choller, or whatever the Constitution is, from whence their Humours derive their Source.

There is infinitely more to be said on this Subject; thô perhaps I have already said too much; but I have said it to a Friend, who I am sure will not expose it, if he does not approve of it. I believe the Subject is intirely new, and was never touch'd upon before; and if I would have any one to see this private Essay, it should be some one who might be provoked by my Errors in it to Publish a more Judicious Treatise on the Subject. Indeed I wish it were done, that the World being a little acquainted with the scarcity of true Humour, and the difficulty of finding and shewing it, might look a little more favourably on the Labours of them, who endeavour to search into Nature for it, and lay it open to the Publick View.

I dont say but that very entertaining and useful Characters, and proper for Comedy, may be drawn from Affectations, and those other Qualities, which I have endeavoured to distinguish from Humour; but I would not have such imposed on the World, for Humour, nor esteem'd of Equal value with it. It were perhaps, the Work of a long Life to make one Comedy true in all its Parts, and to give every Character in it a True and Distinct

Humour. Therefore every Poet must be beholding to other helps, to make out his Number of ridiculous Characters. But I think such a One deserves to be broke, who makes all false Musters; who does not shew one true Humour in a Comedy, but entertains his Audience to the end of the Play with every thing out of Nature.

I will make but one Observation to you more, and have done; and that is grounded upon an Observation of your own, and which I mention'd at the beginning of my Letter, *viz.* That there is more of Humour in our English Comick Writers than in any others. I do not at all wonder at it, for I look upon Humour to be almost of English Growth; at least, it does not seem to have found such Encrease on any other Soil. And what appears to me to be the reason of it, is the greater Freedom, Privilege, and Liberty which the Common People of *England* enjoy. Any Man that has a Humour, is under no restraint, or fear of giving it Vent; they have a Proverb among them, which, may be, will shew the Bent and Genius of the People, as well as a longer Discourse: *He that will have a May-pole, shall have a May-pole.* This is a Maxim with them, and their Practice is agreeable to it. I believe something Considerable too may be ascribed to their feeding so much on Flesh, and the Grossness of their Diet in general. But I have done, let the Physicians agree that. Thus you have my Thoughts of *Humour,* to my Power of Expressing them in so little Time and Compass. You will be kind to shew me wherein I have Err'd; and as you are very Capable of giving me Instruction, so I think I have a very Just title to demand it from you, being without Reserve,

July 10, 1695.

> *Your real Friend,*
> *and humble Servant,*
> W. Congreve.

Jeremy Collier

[1650–1726]

◆◆◆

COLLIER WAS A PRIEST of the Church of England whose principal occupation was religious controversy—he was twice imprisoned for his activities, and for the last 30 years of his life was technically an outlaw. He wrote more than 40 books and pamphlets, most of them on ecclesiastical and theological subjects, but only one—his *Short View of the Immorality and Profaneness of the English Stage*—is of literary interest.

Collier's book belongs to a tradition of critical controversy which goes back to Plato and Aristotle, and is still with us—the controversy over the relationship between art and morality. In post-Reformation England, the rising middle class, with its strong Puritan bias, gave a clamorous voice to the anti-art position. Stephen Gosson's *School of Abuse* (see *English Literary Criticism: The Renaissance*, in this series) is an Elizabethan example of this position; Collier's is the principal Restoration contribution, though there were others.

The fashionable bawdiness and license of the Restoration stage made it a particularly vulnerable target for moral censure, and even Dryden, who was not the worst offender, confessed that "in many things he [Collier] has taxed me justly." Collier shrewdly undermined his antagonists by basing his argument on the "rules" and common sense, and by supporting his case with citations from classical and neo-classical authorities. Against an argument that united neo-classical theory and moral scruples there was no adequate defense, and though distinguished opponents—including Dryden, Congreve, and Vanbrugh —wrote in their own cause, Collier had clearly won, and in winning altered the tone of English drama. The battle over the morality of comedy, particularly of Restoration comedy, continued; Lamb and Macaulay are still at it in the nineteenth century.

BIBLIOGRAPHY. There is no modern edition of the Collier pamphlets. A substantial selection of Collier's *Short View* is included in *Critical Essays of the Seventeenth Century*, ed. J. E. Spingarn, vol. III (Bloomington, Indiana, 1957).

J. W. Krutch, *Comedy and Conscience after the Restoration*, (2nd ed. New York, 1949); Sister Rose Anthony, *The Jeremy Collier Controversy* (Milwaukee, 1957).

TEXT. *A Short View of the Immorality and Profaneness of the English Stage* (3rd ed., London, 1698).

from

A SHORT VIEW OF THE IMMORALITY AND PROFANENESS OF THE ENGLISH STAGE

[1698]

The INTRODUCTION

THE BUSINESS OF *Plays* is to recommend Vertue, and discountenance Vice; to shew the Uncertainty of Humane Greatness, the suddain Turns of Fate, and the Unhappy Conclusions of Violence and Injustice: 'Tis to expose the Singularities of Pride and Fancy, to make Folly and Falsehood contemptible, and to bring every Thing that is Ill under Infamy, and Neglect. This Design has been oddly pursued by the *English Stage*. Our *Poets* write with a different view, and are gone into an other Interest. 'Tis true, were their Intentions fair, they might be *Serviceable* to this *Purpose*. They have in a great measure the Springs of Thought and Inclination in their Power. *Show, Musick, Action, and Rhetorick,* are moving Entertainments; and rightly employ'd, would be very significant. But Force and Motion are Things indifferent, and the Use lies chiefly in the Application. These Advantages are now, in the Enemies Hand, and under a very dangerous Management. Like Cannon seized, they are pointed the wrong way; and by the Strength of the Defence the Mischief is made the greater. That this Complaint is not unreasonable, I shall endeavor to prove by shewing the Misbehaviour of the *Stage*, with respect to *Morality*, and *Religion*. Their *Liberties* in the Following Particulars are intolerable, *viz.* Their *Smuttiness* of *Expression;* Their *Swearing, Prophaneness,* and *Lewd Application of*

Scripture; Their *Abuse* of the *Clergy,* Their *making* their *top Characters Libertines,* and giving them *Success* in their *Debauchery.* This Charge, with some other Irregularities, I shall make good against the *Stage,* and shew both the *Novelty* and *Scandal* of the *Practice.* And first, I shall begin with the *Rankness* and *Indecency* of their *Language.*

CHAP. IV.

The Stage-Poets make their Principal Persons Vitious, and reward them at the End of the Play.

THE LINES OF VIRTUE and Vice are Struck out by Nature in very Legible Distinctions; They tend to a different Point, and in the greater Instances the Space between them is easily perceiv'd. Nothing can be more unlike than the Original Forms of these Qualities: The First has all the sweetness, Charms, and Graces imaginable; The other has the Air of a *Post* ill Carved into a *Monster,* and looks both foolish and Frightful together. These are the Native Appearances of Good and Evil: And they that endeavour to blot the Distinctions, to rub out the Colours, or change the Marks, are extreamly to blame. 'Tis confessed as long as the Mind is awake, and Conscience goes true, there's no fear of being imposed on. But when Vice is varnish'd over with Pleasure, and comes in the Shape of Convenience, the case grows somewhat dangerous; for then the Fancy may be gain'd, and the Guards corrupted, and Reason suborn'd against it self. And thus a *Disguise* often passes when the Person would otherwise be stopt. To put *Lewdness* into a Thriving condition, to give it an Equipage of Quality, and to treat it with Ceremony and Respect, is the way to confound the Understanding, to fortifie the Charm, and to make the Mischief invincible. Innocence is often owing to Fear, and Appetite is kept under by Shame; But when these Restraints are once taken off, when Profit and Liberty lie on the same side, and a Man can Debauch himself into Credit, what can be expected in such a case, but that Pleasure should grow absolute and Madness carry all before it? The *Stage* seems eager to bring Matters to this Issue; They have made a considerable progress and are still pushing their Point with all the Vigour imaginable. If this be not their Aim, why is *Lewdness* so much consider'd in Character and Success? Why are their Favourites Atheistical, and their fine Gentlemen Debauched? To what purpose is *Vice* thus prefer'd, thus ornamented and caress'd, unless for Imitation? That matter of Fact stands thus, I shall make good by several Instances. To begin then with their Men of Breeding and Figure. *Wild-blood* sets up for *Debauchery*, Ridicules Marriage, and Swears by *Mahomet*. *Bellamy* makes sport with the Devil, and *Lorenzo* is vitious, and calls his Father *Bawdy Magistrate*. *Horner* is horridly Smutty, and *Harcourt* false to his Friend who used him kindly. In the *Plain Dealer*, *Freeman* talks coarsely, cheats the Widow, debauches her Son, and makes him undutiful. *Bellmour* is Lewd and Profane, And *Mellefont* puts *Careless* in the best way he can to debauch *Lady Plyant*.[1] These *Sparks* generally Marry the Top-Ladies, and those that do not, are brought to no penance, but go off with the Character of Fine Gentlemen. In *Don-Sebastian, Antonio*, an Atheistical Bully, is rewarded with the Lady *Moraima* and half the *Mufti's* Estate. *Valentine* in *Love for Love*, is (if I may so call him) the Hero of the *Play*. This Spark the *Poet* would pass for a Person of Virtue, but he speaks too late. 'Tis true, He was hearty in his Affection to *Angelica*. Now without question, to be in Love with a fine Lady of 30000 Pounds is a great Virtue! But then abating this single Commendation, *Valentine* is altogether compounded of Vice. He is a prodigal Debauchee, Unnatural and Profane, Obscene, Sawcy, and undutiful, And yet this Libertine is crown'd for the Man of Merit, has his Wishes thrown into his Lap, and makes the Happy *Exit*. I perceive we should have a rare Set of *Virtues* if these *Poets* had the making of them! How they hug a Vitious Character, and how profuse are they in their Liberalities to Lewdness! In the *Provok'd Wife, Constant* Swears at Length, solicits Lady *Brute*, Confesses himself Lewd, and prefers Debauchery to Marriage. He handles the last Subject very notably and worth the Hearing. *There is* (says he) *a poor sordid Slavery in Marriage, that turns the flowing Tide of Honour, and sinks it to the lowest ebb of Infamy. 'Tis a Corrupted Soil, Ill Nature, Avarice, Sloth, Cowardice, and Dirt are all its Product—*

---

[1] *The Mock Astrologer*, Dryden; *The Spanish Friar*, Dryden; *The Country Wife*, Wycherley; *The Double Dealer*, Congreve.

But then *Constancy (alias Whoring) is a Brave, Free, Haughty Generous Agent.* This is admirable stuff both for the Rhetorick and the Reason! The Character of *Young Fashion* in the *Relapse* is of the same Staunchness, but this the *Reader* may have in another Place.

To sum up the Evidence. A fine Gentleman, is a fine Whoring, Swearing, Smutty, Atheistical Man. These Qualifications it seems compleat, the *Idea* of Honour. They are the Top-Improvements of Fortune, and the distinguishing Glories of Birth and Breeding! This is the *Stage-Test* for *Quality,* and those that can't stand it ought to be *Disclaim'd.* The Restraints of Conscience and the Pedantry of Virtue are unbecoming a Cavalier: Future Securities, and Reaching beyond Life, are vulgar Provisions: If he falls a-Thinking at this rate, he forfeits his Honour; For his Head was only made to run against a Post! Here you have a Man of Breeding and Figure, that burlesques the *Bible,* Swears, and talks Smut to Ladies, speaks ill of his Friend behind his Back, and betrays his Interest: A fine Gentleman that has neither Honesty, nor Honour, Conscience, nor Manners, Good Nature, nor civil Hypocrisie: Fine, only in the Insignificancy of Life, the Abuse of Religion, and the Scandals of Conversation. These Worshipful Things are the *Poet's* Favourites: They appear at the Head of the *Fashion;* and shine in Character, and Equipage. If there is any Sense stirring, They must have it, tho' the rest of the *Stage* suffer never so much by the Partiality. And what can be the Meaning of this wretched Distribution of Honour? Is it not to give Credit and Countenance to Vice, and to shame young People out of all pretences to Conscience, and Regularity? They seem forc'd to turn Lewd in their own Defence: They can't otherwise justifie themselves to the Fashion, nor keep up the Character of Gentlemen: Thus People not well furnish'd with Thought and Experience, are debauch'd both in Practise and Principle. And thus Religion grows uncreditable, and passes for ill Education. The *Stage* seldom gives Quarter to any Thing that's serviceable or Significant, but persecutes Worth and Goodness under every Appearance. He that would be safe from their Satir must take care to disguise himself in Vice, and hang out the *Colours* of Debauchery. How often is Learning, Industry, and Frugality, ridiculed in Comedy? The rich Citizens are often

Misers, and Cuckolds, and the *Universities*, Schools of Pedantry upon this score. In short; Libertinism and Profaness, Dressing, Idleness, and Gallantry are the only valuable Qualities. As if People were not apt enough of themselves to be Lazy, Lewd, and Extravagant, unless they were prick'd forward, and provok'd by Glory, and Reputation. Thus the Marks of Honour, and Infamy are misapply'd, and the Idea's of Virtue and Vice confounded. Thus Monstrousness goes for Proportion, and the Blemishes of Human Nature make up the Beauties of it.

The fine Ladies are of the same Cut with the Gentlemen; *Moraima* is Scandalously rude to her Father, helps him to a beating, and runs away with *Antonio. Angelica* talks saucily to her Uncle, and *Belinda* confesses her Inclination for a Gallant.[2] And as I have observ'd already, the Toping Ladies in the *Mock Astrologer, Spanish Fryar, Country Wife, Old Batchelour, Orphan, Double Dealer,* and *Love Triumphant,* are smutty, and sometimes Profane.

And was Licentiousness and Irreligion always a mark of Honour? No I don't perceive but that the old *Poets* had an other Notion of Accomplishment, and bred their people of Condition a different way. *Philolaches* in *Plautus* laments his being debauch'd; and dilates upon the Advantages of Virtue, and Regularity. *Lusiteles* another Young Gentleman disputes handsomly by himself against Lewdness. And the discourse between him and *Philto* is Moral and well managed. And afterwards he lashes Luxury and Debauching with a great deal of Warmth and Satir. *Chremes* in *Terence* is a modest young Gentleman, he is afraid of being surpriz'd by *Thais,* and seems careful not to sully his Reputation. And *Pamphilus* in *Hecyra* resolves rather to be govern'd by Duty, than Inclination.

Plautus's Pinacium tells her Friend *Panegyris* that they ought to acquit themselves fairly to their Husbands, tho' These should fail in their Regards toward them. For all good People will do justice tho' they don't receive it. Lady *Brute* in the *Provok'd Wife* is govern'd by different maxims. She is debauch'd with ill Usage, says *Virtue is an Ass, and a Gallant's worth forty on't. Pinacium* goes on to another Head of Duty, and declares that a Daughter

2 *Don Sebastian,* Dryden; *Love for Love,* Congreve; *The Provok'd Wife,* Vanbrugh.

can never respect her Father too much, and that Disobedience has a great deal of scandal and Lewdness in't. The Lady *Jacinta* as I remember does not treat her Father at this rate of Decency. Let us hear a little of her Behaviour. The *Mock Astrologer* makes the Men draw, and frights the Ladies with the Apprehension of a Quarrel. Upon this, *Theodosia* crys *what will become of us! Jacinta* answers, *we'll die for Company: nothing vexes me but that I am not a Man, to have one thrust at that malicious old Father of mine before I go.* Afterwards the old Gentleman *Alonzo* threatens his Daughters with a Nunnery. *Jacinta* spars again, and says, *I would have thee to know thou graceless old Man, that I defy a Nunnery: name a Nunnery once more and I disown thee for my Father.* I could carry on the Comparison between the old and Modern Poets somwhat farther. But this may suffice.

Thus we see what a fine time Lewd People have on the *English Stage.* No Censure, no mark of Infamy, no Mortification must touch them. They keep their Honour untarnish'd, and carry off the Advantage of their Character. They are set up for the Standard of Behaviour, and the Masters of Ceremony and Sense. And at last that the Example may work the better, they generally make them rich and happy, and reward them with their own Desires.

Mr. *Dryden,* in the *Preface* to his *Mock-Astrologer,* confesses himself blamed for this Practise. *For making debauch'd Persons his* Protagonists, *or chief Persons of the Drama; And for making them happy in the Conclusion of the Play, against the Law of Comedy, which is to reward Virtue, and to punish Vice.* To this Objection He makes a lame Defence. And answers,

1st. *That he knows no such Law constantly observ'd in Comedy by the Ancient or Modern Poets.* What then? *Poets* are not always exactly in Rule. It may be a good Law tho' 'tis not constantly observ'd, some Laws are constantly broken, and yet ne'er the worse for all that. He goes on, and pleads the Authorities of *Plautus,* and *Terence.* I grant there are instances of Favour to vicious young People in those Authors, but to this I reply

1st, That those *Poets* had a greater compass of Liberty in their Religion. Debauchery did not lie under those Discouragements of Scandal and Penalty with them as it does with us. Unless therefore He can prove *Heathenism,* and *Christianity* the same, his *Precedents* will do him little service.

2ly, Horace who was as good a judge of the *Stage,* as either of those *Comedians,* seems to be of another Opinion. He condemns the obscenities of *Plautus,* and tells you Men of Fortune and Quality in his time, would not endure immodest Satir. He continues, that Poets were formerly admired for the great services they did. For teaching Matters relating to Religion, and Government; For refining the Manners, tempering the Passions, and improving the Understandings of Mankind: For making them more useful in Domestick Relations and the publick Capacities of Life. This is a demonstration that Vice was not the Inclination of the Muses in those days; and that *Horace* believ'd the chief business of a *Poem* was, to Instruct the Audience. He adds farther that the *Chorus* ought to turn upon the Argument of the *Drama,* and support the Design of the *Acts.* That They ought to speak in Defence of Virtue, and Frugality, and show a Regard to Religion. Now, from the Rule of the *Chorus,* we may conclude his Judgment for the *Play.* For, as he observes, there must be a Uniformity between the *Chorus* and the *Acts:* They must have the same View, and be all of a Piece. From hence 'tis plain that *Horace* would have no immoral *Character,* have either Countenance or good Fortune, upon the *Stage.* If 'tis said the very mention of the *Chorus* shews the Directions were intended for *Tragedy,* To this

I answer, that the Consequence is not good. For the use of a *Chorus* is not inconsistent with *Comedy.* The ancient *Comedians* had it. *Aristophanes* is an Instance. I know 'tis said the *Chorus* was left out in that they call the *New Comedy.* But I can't see the conclusiveness of this Assertion. For *Aristophanes* his *Plutus* is *New Comedy* with a *Chorus* in't. And *Aristotle* who lived after the Revolution of the *Stage,* mentions nothing of the Omission of the *Chorus.* He rather supposes its continuance by saying the *Chorus was added by the Government long after the Invention of Comedy.* 'Tis true *Plautus* and *Terence* have none, but those before them probably might. *Moliere* has now reviv'd them; And *Horace* might be of his Opinion for ought we know to the contrary.

Lastly. Horace having expresly mentioned the beginning and

progress of *Comedy,* discovers himself more fully: He advises a
Poet to form his Work upon the Precepts of *Socrates* and *Plato,*
and the Models of Moral Philosophy. This was the way to preserve Decency, and to assign a proper Fate and Behaviour to
every *Character.* Now if Horace would have his *Poet* govern'd
by the Maxims of Morality, he must oblige him to Sobriety of
Conduct, and a just distribution of Rewards and Punishments.

Mr. *Dryden* makes Homewards, and endeavours to fortifie
himself in Modern Authority. He lets us know that *Ben Johnson
after whom he may be proud to Err, gives him more than one
example of this Conduct;* [3] *That in the* Alchemist *is notorius,*
where neither *Face* nor his *Master* are corrected according to
their Demerits. But how Proud soever Mr. *Dryden* may be of
an Errour, he has not so much of *Ben Jonson's* company as he
pretends. His Instance of *Face &c.* in the *Alchemist* is rather
notorious against his purpose then for it.

For *Face* did not Council his Master *Lovewit* to debauch the
Widdow; neither is it clear that the Matter went thus far. He
might gain her consent upon Terms of Honour for ought appears to the contrary. 'Tis true *Face* who was one of the Principal
Cheats is Pardon'd and consider'd: But then his Master confesses
himself kind to a fault. He owns this Indulgence was a Breach
of Justice, and unbecoming the Gravity of old Man. And then
desires the Audience to excuse him upon the Score of the Temptation. But *Face continued in the Cousenage till the last without
Repentance.* Under favour I conceive this is a Mistake. For does
not *Face* make an Apology before he leaves the *Stage?* Does he
not set himself at the *Bar,* arraign his own Practise, and cast the
Cause upon the Clemency of the Company? And are not all
these Signs of the Dislike of what he had done? Thus careful
the *Poet* is to prevent the Ill Impressions of his *Play!* He brings
both Man and Master to Confession. He dismisses them like
Malefactours; And moves for their Pardon before he gives them
their Discharge. But the *Mock-Astrologer* has a gentler Hand:
Wild-Blood and *Jacinta* are more generously used: There is no
Acknowledgment exacted: no Hardship put upon them: They
are permitted to talk on in their Libertine way to the Last: And

[3] Preface to *The Mock Astrologer,* Dryden.

take Leave without the least appearance of Reformation. The *Mock-Astrologer* urges *Ben Johnson's Silent Woman* as an other Precedent to his purpose. For *there* Dauphine *confesses himself in Love with all the Collegiate Lady's. And yet this naughty* Dauphine *is Crowned in the end with the Posession of his Uncle's Estate, and with the hopes of all his Mistresses.* This Charge, as I take it, is somewhat too severe. I grant *Dauphine* Professes himself in Love with the Collegiate Ladies at first. But when they invited him to a private Visit, he makes them no Promise; but rather appears tired, and willing to disengage. *Dauphine* therefore is not altogether so naughty as this Author represents him.

Ben Johnson's Fox is clearly against Mr. *Dryden.* And here I have his own Confession for proof. He declares the *Poets end in this Play was the Punishment of Vice, and the Reward of Virtue.*[4] *Ben* was forced to strain for this piece of Justice, and break through the *Unity of Design.* This Mr. *Dryden* remarks upon him: However he is pleased to commend the Performance, and calls it an excellent *Fifth Act.*

Ben Johnson shall speak for himself afterwards in the Character of a Critick; In the mean time I shall take a Testimony or two from *Shakespear.* And here we may observe the admir'd *Falstaffe* goes off in Disappointment. He is thrown out of Favour as being a *Rake,* and dies like a Rat behind the Hangings. The Pleasure he had given, would not excuse him. The *Poet* was not so partial as to let his Humour compound for his Lewdness. If 'tis objected that this remark is wide of the Point, because *Falstaffe* is represented in Tragedy, where the Laws of Justice are more strickly observ'd. To this I answer, that you may call *Henry* the Fourth and Fifth, Tragedies if you please. But for all that, *Falstaffe* wears no *Buskins,* his Character is perfectly Comical from end to end.

The next Instance shall be in *Flowerdale* the *Prodigal.*[5] This Spark, notwithstanding his Extravagance, makes a lucky Hand on't at last, and marries up a rich Lady. But then the Poet qualifies him for his good Fortune, and mends his Manners with his

---

[4] *Essays of Dramatic Poesy* (see above, p. 37).
[5] *The London Prodigal* (1605), a play attributed to Shakespeare.

Circumstances. He makes him repent and leave off his Intemperance, Swearing, &c. And when his Father warn'd him against a Relapse, He answers very soberly,

Heaven helping me, I'le hate the Course of Hell.

I could give some Instances of this kind out of *Beaumount* and *Fletcher.* But there's no need of any farther Quotation; For Mr. *Dryden* is not satisfied with his Apology from Authority: He does as good as own that this may be construed no better than defending one ill practise by another. To prevent this very reasonable objection he endeavours to vindicate his *Precedents* from the Reason of the Thing. To this purpose he *makes a wide difference between the Rules of Tragedy and Comedy. That Vice must be impartially prosecuted in the first, because the Persons are great, &c.*

It seems, then *Executions* are only for *Greatness* and *Quality. Justice* is not to strike much *lower* than a *Prince. Private People* may do what they *please.* They are too *few* for *Mischief,* and too *Little* for *Punishment!* This would be admirable Doctrine for *Newgate,* and give us a general *Goal-Delivery* without more ado. But in *Tragedy* (says the *Mock Astrologer) the Crimes are likewise Horrid,* so that there is a necessity for Severity and Example. And how stands the matter in *Comedy?* Quite otherwise. There the *Faults are but the sallies of Youth, and the Frailties of Human Nature* For Instance. There is nothing but a little Whoring, Pimping, Gaming, Profaness, &c. And who could be so hard hearted to give a Man any Trouble for This? Such Rigours would be strangely Inhumane! A *Poet* is a better natur'd Thing I can assure you. These little Miscarriages *move Pity and Commiseration, and are not such as must of necessity be Punish'd.* This is comfortable Casuistry! But to be Serious. Is Dissolution of Manners such a Peccadillo? Does a Profligate Conscience deserve nothing but Commiseration? And are People damn'd only for *Humane Frailties?* I perceive the Laws of Religion and those of the *Stage* differ extreamly! The strength of his Defence lies in this choice Maxim, that the *Chief End of Comedy is Delight.* He questions *whether Instruction has any thing to do in Comedy.* If it has, he is sure *'tis no more then its secondary end: For the business of the Poet is to make you laugh.*

Granting the Truth of this Principle, I somewhat question the serviceableness of it. For is there no Diversion to be had unless Vice appears prosperous, and rides at the Head of Success? One would think such a preposterous distribution of Rewards, should rather shock the Reason, and raise the Indignation of the *Audience*. To laugh without reason is the Pleasure of Fools, and against it, of something worse. The exposing of Knavery, and making *Lewdness* ridiculous, is a much better occasion for Laughter. And this with submission I take to be the End of *Comedy*. And therefore it does not differ from *Tragedy* in the End, but in the *Means*. Instruction is the principal Design of both. The one works by Terror, the other by Infamy. 'Tis true, they don't move in the same Line, but they meet in the same point at last. For this Opinion I have good Authority, besides what has been cited already.

1st, Monsieur *Rapin* affirms 'That Delight is the End that Poetry aims at, but not the Principal one. For Poetry, being in Art, ought to be profitable by the quality of it's own nature, and by the Essential Subordination that all Arts should have to Polity, whose End in General is the publick Good. This is the Judgment of *Aristotle* and of *Horace* his chief Interpreter.' [6] *Ben Johnson*, in his Dedicatory Epistle of his *Fox* has somewhat considerable upon this Argument; And declaims with a great deal of zeal, spirit and good Sense against the Licentiousness of the *Stage*. He lays it down for a Principle, 'That 'tis impossible to be a good *Poet* without being a good *Man*. That he (a good Poet) is said to be able to inform Young Men to all good Discipline, and enflame grown Men to all great Virtues, &c.——That the general complaint was that the *Writers* of those days had nothing remaining in them of the Dignity of a *Poet* but the abused Name. That now, especially in Stage Poetry, nothing but Ribaldry, Profanation, *Blasphemy*, all Licence of Offence to God and Man, is practised. He confesses a great part of this Charge is over-true, and is sorry he dares not deny it. But then he hopes all are not embark'd in this bold Adventure for Hell. For my part (says he) I can, and from a most clear Conscience, affirm; That I have ever trembled to think towards the least Profaness, and loath'd the Use of such foul, and unwash'd Bawdry, as is now

6 René Rapin (1621–1687), *Réflexions sur la Poétique d'Aristote* (1674).

made the Food of the *Scene*.——The encrease of which Lust
in Liberty, what Learned or Liberal Soul does not abhor? In
whole *Enterludes* nothing but the Filth of the Time is utter'd
——with Brothelry able to violate the Ear of a *Pagan*, and Blasphemy, to turn the Blood of a Christian to Water.' He continues,
'that the Insolence of these Men had brought the *Muses* into
Disgrace, and made *Poetry* the lowest scorn of the Age.' He appeals to his Patrons the *Universities*, 'that his Labour has been
heretofore, and mostly in this his latest Work, to reduce not only
the ancient Forms, but Manners of the *Scene*, the Innocence and
the Doctrine, which is the PRINCIPAL END of Poesy, to inform
Men in the best Reason of Living.' Lastly, he adds, 'that he has
imitated the Conduct of the Ancients in this *Play*, The goings
out (or Conclusions) of whose *Comedies*, were not always joy-
ful but oft-times the Bawds, the Slaves, the Rivals, yea and the
Masters are Mulcted, and fitly, it being the Office of a *Comick
Poet* (mark that!) to imitate Justice and Instruct to Life,' &c.
Say you so! Why, then if *Ben Johnson* knew any thing of the
Matter, Divertisement and Laughing is not, as Mr. *Dryden* affirms, the *Chief End* of *Comedy*. This Testimony is so very full
and clear, that it needs no explaining, nor any enforcement from
Reasoning, and Consequence.

And because Laughing and Pleasure has such an unlimited
Prerogative upon the *Stage*, I shall add a Citation or two from
Aristotle concerning this Matter. Now, this great Man 'calls those
Buffoons, and Impertinents, who rally without any regard to
Persons and Things, to Decency, or good Manners. That there
is a great difference between Ribaldry and handsom Rallying.
He that would perform exactly must keep within the Character
of Virtue, and Breeding'. He goes on, and tells us that 'the old
Comedians entertain'd the Audience with Smut, but the Modern
ones avoided that Liberty, and grew more reserv'd. This latter
way he says was much more proper and Genteel then the other.
That in his Opinion Rallying, no less than Railing, ought to be
under the Discipline of Law; That he who is ridden by his *Jests*,
and minds nothing but the business of *Laughing*, is himself Ridiculous. And that a Man of Education and Sense, is so far from
going these Lengths that he wont so much as endure the hearing some sort of Buffoonry.'

And as to the point of Delight in general, the same Author affirms, 'that scandalous Satisfactions are not properly Pleasures. 'Tis only Distemper, and false Appetite which makes them Palatable. And a Man that is sick, seldom has his Tast true. Besides, supposing we throw Capacity out of the Question, and make Experiment and Sensation the Judge; Granting this, we ought not to chop at every Bait, nor Fly out at every Thing that strikes the Fancy. The meer Agreableness must not overbear us, without distinguishing upon the Quality, and the Means. Pleasure how charming soever, must not be fetched out of Vice. An Estate is a pretty thing, but if we purchase by Falshood, and Knavery, we pay too much for't. Some Pleasures are Childish, and others abominable; And upon the whole, pleasure, absolutely speaking, is no good Thing.' And so much for the Philosopher. And because *Ribaldry* is used for Sport, a passage or two from *Quintilian*, may not be unseasonable. This Orator does not only Condemn the grosser Instances, but cuts off all the *Double-Entendre's* at a Blow. He comes up to the Regularity of Thought, and tells us 'that the Meaning, as well as the Words of Discourse must be unsullied'. And in the same *Chapter* he adds that 'A Man of Probity has always a Reserve in his Freedoms, and Converses within the Rules of Modesty, and Character. And that Mirth at the expence of Virtue is an Over-purchase, *Nimium enim risus pretium est si probitatis impendio constat.*' [A laugh costs too much if it is achieved at the expense of integrity.]

Thus we see how these great *Masters* qualify Diversion, and tie it up to *Provisoes*, and Conditions. Indeed to make *Delight* the main business of *Comedy* is an unreasonable and dangerous Principle: It opens the way to all Licentiousness, and Confounds the distinction between Mirth, and Madness. For if Diversion is the *Chief End*, it must be had at any Price. No serviceable Expedient must be refused, tho' never so scandalous. And thus the worst Things are said, and the best abus'd; Religion is insulted, and the most serious Matters turn'd into Ridicule! As if the Blind side of an Audience ought to be caress'd, and their Folly and Atheism entertain'd in the first Place. Yes, if the Palate is pleas'd, no matter tho' the Body is Poyson'd! For can one die of an easier Disease than Diversion? But Raillery apart, certainly Mirth and Laughing without respect to the Cause, are not such supreme Satisfactions! A man has sometimes Pleasure in losing his Wits. Frensy and *Possession*, will shake the Lungs, and brighten the Face; and yet I suppose they are not much to be coveted. However, now we know the Reason of the Profaness, and Obscenity of the *Stage*, of their Hellish Cursing, and Swearing, and, in short, of their great Industry to make God and Goodness Contemptible: 'Tis all to Satisfie the Company, and make People Laugh! A most admirable justification! What can be more engaging to an *Audience*, then to see a *Poet* thus Atheistically brave? To see him charge up to the Canons Mouth, and defy the Vengeance of Heaven to serve them? Besides, there may be somewhat of Convenience in the Case. To fetch Diversion out of Innocence is no such easy matter. There's no succeeding it may be in this method, without Sweat, and Drudging. Clean Wit, inoffensive Humour, and handsom Contrivance, require Time, and Thought. And who would be at this Expence, when the Purchase is so cheap another way? 'Tis possible a *Poet* may not always have Sense enough by him for such an Occasion. And since we are upon supposals, it may be the *Audience* is not to be gain'd without straining a Point, and giving a Loose to Conscience: And when People are sick, are they not to be Humour'd? In fine, We must make them Laugh, right or wrong, for *Delight* is the *Chief End of Comedy. Delight!* He should have said *Debauchery:* That's the English of the Word, and the Consequence of the Practise. But the Original Design of *Comedy* was otherwise: And granting 'twas not so, what then? If the *Ends* of Things are naught, they must be mended. Mischief is the Chief end of Malice, would it be then a Blemish in Ill Nature to change Temper, and relent into Goodness? The Chief *End* of a Madman it may be is to Fire a House, must we not therefore bind him in his Bed? To conclude. If *Delight* without Restraint, or Distinction, without Conscience or Shame, is the Supream Law of *Comedy*, 'twere well if we had less on't. Arbitrary Pleasure, is more dangerous than Arbitrary Power. Nothing is more Brutal than to be abandon'd to Appetite; And nothing more wretched than to serve in such a Design. The *Mock-Astrologer* to clear himself of this Imputation, is glad to give up his Principle at Last. *Least any Man should think* (says he) *that I write this to make Libertinism amiable, or that I cared*

not to debase the end, and Institution of Comedy (It seems, then,
Delight is not the Chief end.) *I must farther declare that we
make not Vicious Persons Happy, but only as Heaven makes
Sinners so,* &c. If this will hold all's well. But *Heaven* does not
forgive without Repentance. Let us see then what Satisfaction
he requires from his *Wild-Blood,* and what Discipline he puts
him under. Why, He helps him to his Mistress, he Marries him
to a Lady of Birth and Fortune. And now do you think He
has not made him an Example, and punish'd him to some Purpose! These are frightful Severities! Who would be vicious when
such Terrors hang over his Head? And does *Heaven make Sinners happy* upon these Conditions? Sure, some People have a
good Opinion of Vice, or a very ill one of Marriage, otherwise
they would have Charged the Penance a little more. But I have
nothing farther with the *Mock-Astrologer.*

And now, for the Conclusion of a *Chapter,* I shall give some
Instances of the *Manners* of the *Stage,* and that with respect to
Poetry, and Ceremony. *Manners* in the Language of Poetry, is
a Propriety of actions, and Persons. To succeed in this business,
there must always be a regard had to Age, Sex, and Condition:
And nothing put into the Mouths of Persons which disagrees
with any of these Circumstances. 'Tis not enough to say a witty
Thing, unless it be spoken by a likely Person, and upon a proper
occasion. But my Design will lead me to this Subject afterwards,
and therefore I shall say no more of it at present, but proceed
to apply the Remark.

One instance of Impropriety in *Manners* both Poetical and
Moral, is their making Women, and Women of Quality talk
Smuttily. This I have proved upon them already, and could cite
many more places to the same purpose were it necessary.

But I shall go on, and give the *Reader* some other examples
of Decency, Judgment, and Probability. *Don Sebastian* will help
us in some measure. Here the *Mufty* makes a foolish Speech to
the Rabble, and jests upon his own Religion. He tells them,
*tho' your Tyrant is a Lawful Emperour, yet your Lawful Em-
perour is but a Tyrant,——That your Emperour is a Tyrant is
most Manifest, for you were born to be Turks, but he has play'd
the Turk with you.* And now is not this Man fit to Manage the
Alcoran, and to be set up for an Oracle of State? *Captain Tom*

should have had this Speech by right: But the *Poet* had a farther Design, and any thing is good enough for a *Mufti*.

Sebastian, after all the violence of his Repentance, his grasping at self Murther, and Resolutions for the *Cell*, is strangely pleased with the Remembrance of his *Incest*, and wishes the Repetition of it: And *Almeida* out of her Princely Modesty and singular Compunction, is of the same mind. This is somewhat surprising! *Oedipus* and *Jocasta* in *Sophocles* don't Repent at this Rate. No: The horror of the first Discovery continues upon their Spirits. They never relapse into any fits of Intemperance, nor entertain themselves with a lewd Memory. This sort of Behaviour is not only the more Instructive but more Natural too. It being very unlikely one should wish the Repeating a Crime, when He was almost Distracted at the thoughts on't, tho' 'twas committed under all the Circumstances of excuse. Now, when Ignorance and meer Mistakes are so very disquieting, 'tis very strange if a Man should plague his Mind with the aggravations of Knowledge. To carry Aversion, and Desire in their full strength upon the same Object; To fly and pursue with so much eagerness, is somewhat unusual.

If we step to the *Spanish Fryar* He will afford us a Flight worth the observing. 'Tis part of the Addresses of *Torrismond* to *Leonora:*

> *You are so Beautiful,*
> *So wondrous Fair, you justifie Rebellion;*
> *As if that faultless Face could make no Sin,*
> *But Heaven by looking on it must forgive.*

These are strange Compliments! *Torrismond* calls his Queen Rebel to her head, when he was both her General and her Lover. This is powerful Rhetorick to Court a Queen with; Enough, one would think, to have made the Affair desperate. But he has a Remedy at hand. The *Poet's Nostrum* of Profaneness cures all. He does as good as tell Her, she may Sin as much as she has a mind to. Her Face is a Protection to her Conscience. For Heaven is under a necessity to forgive a Handsom Woman. To say all this ought to be pass'd over in *Torrismond* on the score of his Passion, is to make the Excuse more scandalous than the Fault, if possible. Such Raptures are fit only for *Bedlam*, or a place which I shan't name. *Love Triumphant* will fur-

nish another Rant not altogether inconsiderable. Here *Celadea*
a Maiden Lady when she was afraid her Spark would be married
to another, calls out presently for a *Chaos*. She is for pulling
the World about her ears, tumbling all the Elements together,
and expostulates with Heaven for making Human Nature otherwise than it should have been:

> *Great Nature, break thy chain that links together*
> *The Fabrick of this Globe, and make a Chaos,*
> *Like that within my Soul.—*

Now to my fancy, if she had call'd for a *Chair* instead of a
Chaos, trip'd off, and kept her folly to her self, the Woman had
been much wiser. And since we have shown our Skill in vault-
ing on the High Ropes, a little *Tumbling* on the *Stage*, may
not do amiss for variety.

Now then for a jest or two. *Don Gomez* shall begin. And here
he'le give us a Gingle upon the double meaning of a word:

I think, says *Dominick* the Fryar, *it was my good Angel that
sent me hither so opportunely. Gomez* suspects him brib'd for
no creditable business, and answers.

Gom. *Ay, whose good Angels sent you hither, that you know
best Father.*

These *Spaniards* will entertain us with more of this fine Raillery. Colonel *Sancho* in *Love Triumphant* has a great stroak at
it. He says his Bride *Dalinda* is no more *Dalinda,* but *Dalilah*
the *Philistine.* This Colonel as great a Soldier as he is, is quite
puzzled at a *Herald.* He *thinks they call him* Herod, *or some
such Jewish Name.* Here you have a good Officer spoil'd for a
miserable jest. And yet after all, this *Sancho* tho' he can't pronounce *Herald,* knows what 'tis to be *Laconick,* which is somewhat more out of his way. *Thraso* in *Terence* was a man of the
same size in Sense, but for all that he does not quibble. *Albanact*
Captain of the Guards, is much about as witty as *Sancho.* It
seems *Emmeline* Heiress to the Duke of *Cornwal,* was Blind.
Albanact takes the rise of his Thought from hence; And observes *that as Blind as she is, Coswald would have no blind
Bargain of her. Carlos* tells *Sancho* he is sure of his Mistress and
has no more to do but to take out a License.

Sancho replies, *Indeed, I have her License for it. Carlos* is
somewhat angry at this Gingle, and cries, *what, quibbling too*

in your Prosperity? Adversity it seems is the only time for *punning.* Truly I think so too. For 'tis a sign a Man is much Distress'd when he flies to such an Expedient. However, *Carlos* needed not to have been so touchy: For He can stoop as low himself upon occasion. We must know then that *Sancho* had made Himself a Hunch'd-Back, to counterfeit the *Conde Alonzo.* The two Colonels being in the same Disguise, were just upon the edg of a Quarrel. After some Preliminaries in Railing, *Sancho* cries, *Don't provoke me; I am mischievously bent.*

Carlos replies, *Nay you are* BENT *enough, in Conscience, but I have a* BENT *Fist for Boxing.* Here you have a brace of Quibbles started in a Line and a half. And which is worst of all, they come from *Carlos,* from a *Character* of Sense; And therefore the Poet, not the *Soldier,* must answer for them.

I shall now give the *Reader* a few Instances of the Courtship of the *Stage,* and how decently they treat the Women, and *Quality* of both *Sexes.* The *Women,* who are secured from Affronts by Custom, and have a Privilege for Respect, are sometimes but roughly saluted by these Men of Address. And to bar the Defence, this Coarseness does not alwaies come from Clowns and Women-haters; but from *Persons* of Figure, neither singular nor ill Bred. And which is still worse, The Satir falls on blindly without Distinction, and strikes at the whole *Sex.*

Enter *Raymond,* a Noble-man, in the *Spanish Fryar.*

> *O Vertue! Vertue! What art thou become?*
> *That men should leave thee for that Toy a woman,*
> *Made from the dross and refuse of a Man;*
> *Heaven took him sleeping when he made her too,*
> *Had Man been waking he had ne'er consented.*

I did not know before that a Man's Dross lay in his *Ribs;* I believe sometimes it lies higher. But the Phylosophy, the Religion, and the Ceremony of these Lines, are too tender to be touched. *Creon* a Prince in *Oedipus,* Rails in General at the *Sex,* and at the same time is violently in Love with *Euridice.* This upon the matter, is just as natural, as 'tis Civil. If any one would understand what the *Curse of all tender hearted Women is, Belmour* will inform him.[7] What is it then? 'Tis the *Pox.* If this

---

[7] *The Old Bachelor,* Congreve.

be true, the Women had need lay in a stock of ill Nature betimes. It seems 'tis their only preservative. It guards their Virtue, and their Health, and is all they have to trust to. *Sharper* another Man of Sense in this *Play*, talks much at the same rate. *Belinda* would know of him *where he got that excellent Talent of Railing?*

Sharp. *Madam, the Talent was Born with me.——I confess I have taken care to improve it to qualifie me for the Society of Ladies.* Horner, a Topping *Character* in the *Country Wife*, is advised to *avoid Women, and hate them as they do him. He Answers:*

Because I do hate them, and would hate them yet more, I'll frequent e'm; you may see by Marriage, nothing makes a Man hate a Woman more than her Constant Conversation. There is still something more Coarse upon the *Sex* spoken by *Dorax*, but it is a privileged Expression; and as such I must leave it. The *Relapse* mends the Contrivance of the Satir, refines upon the manner, and to make the Discourse the more probable, obliges the Ladies to abuse themselves. And because I should be loath to tire the *Reader, Berinthia* shall close the Argument. This Lady, having undertook the Employment of a *Procuress,* makes this remark upon it to her self:

Berinth. *So here is fine work! But there was no avoiding it.—— Besides, I begin to Fancy there may be as much Pleasure in carrying on another Bodies Intrigue as ones own. This is at least certain, It exercises almost all the Entertaining Faculties of a Woman. For there is Employment for Hypocrisie, Invention, Deceit, Flattery, Mischief, and Lying.*

Let us now see what Quarter the *Stage* gives to *Quality*. And here we shall find them extreamly free, and familiar. They dress up the *Lords* in Nick-Names, and expose them in *Characters* of Contempt. *Lord Froth* is explained a *Solemn Coxcomb;* And *Lord Rake,* and *Lord Foplington* give you their Talent in their Title.[8] Lord *Plausible* in the *Plain Dealer* Acts a ridiculous Part, but is with all very civil. He tells *Manly, he never attempted to abuse any Person.* The other answers, *What! you were afraid? Manly* goes on, and declares *He would call a Rascal by no other*

---

[8] *The Double Dealer,* Congreve; *The Relapse,* Vanbrugh.

Title, tho' his Father had left him a Dukes. That is, he would
call a Duke a Rascal. This I confess is very much *Plain Dealing.*
Such Freedoms would appear but odly in Life, especially without provocation. I must own the *Poet* to be an Author of good
Sense; But under favour, these jests, if we may call them so,
are somewhat high season'd, the Humour seems overstrain'd, and
the *Character* push'd too far. To proceed. *Mustapha* was selling
Don Alvarez for a Slave. The Merchant asks *what Virtues he
has. Mustapha* replies, *Virtues, quoth ah! He is of a great Family
and Rich, what other Virtues would'st thou have in a Nobleman?* [9] Don *Carlos,* in *Love Triumphant,* stands for a Gentleman and a Man of Sense, and out-throws *Mustapha* a Bar's
Length. He tells us *Nature has given* Sancho *an empty Noddle,
but Fortune in revenge has fill'd his Pockets: just a Lords Estate
in Land and Wit.* This is a handsom Complement to the Nobility! And my Lord *Salisbury* had no doubt of it a good Bargain
of the *Dedication. Teresa's* general Description of a Countess
is considerable in its Kind: But only 'tis in no Condition to appear. In the *Relapse,* Sir *Tunbelly* who had Mistaken Young
Fashion for Lord *Foplington,* was afterwards undeceiv'd; and
before the surprize was quite over, puts the Question, *is it then
possible that this should be the true Lord* Foplington *at last?*
The Nobleman removes the scruple with great Civility and Discretion! *Lord* Fopl. *Why, what do you see in his Face to make
you doubt of it? Sir, without presuming to have an extraordinary
Opinion of my Figure, give me leave to tell you, if you had
seen as many Lords as I have done, you would not think it Impossible a Person of a worse Taille then mine might be a Modern
Man of Quality.*

I'm sorry to hear *Modern Quality* degenerates so much. But,
by the way, these Liberties are altogether new. They are un-
practised by the Latin *Comedians,* and by the *English* too till
very lately, as the *Plain Dealer* observes. And as for *Moliere* in
France, he pretends to fly his Satir no higher than a Marquis.

And has our *Stage* a particular Privilege? Is their *Charter* in-
larg'd, and are they on the same Foot of Freedom with the
Slaves in the *Saturnalia?* Must all Men be handled alike? Must

[9] *Don Sebastian,* Dryden.

their Roughness be needs play'd upon Title? And can't they lash the Vice without pointing upon the *Quality*? If, as Mr. *Dryden* rightly defines it, a *Play ought to be a just Image of Humane Nature*,[10] Why are not the Decencies of Life, and the Respects of Conversation observ'd? Why must the Customes of Countries be Cross'd upon, and the Regards of Honour overlook'd? What necessity is there to kick the *Coronets* about the *Stage*, and to make a Man a Lord, only in order to make him a Coxcomb? I hope the *Poets* don't intend to revive the old Project of Levelling, and *Vote* down the House of *Peers*. In earnest, the *Play-house* is an admirable School of Behaviour! This is their way of managing Ceremony, distinguishing Degree, and Entertaining the *Boxes*! But I shall leave them at present to the Enjoyment of their Talent, and proceed to another Argument.

CHAP. V.

SECTION III.

Remarks upon the Relapse.

THE *Relapse* SHALL FOLLOW *Don Quixot*, upon the account of some Alliance between them. And because this *Author* swaggers so much in his *Preface*, and seems to look big upon his Performance, I shall spend a few more thoughts than ordinary upon his *Play*, and examine it briefly in the *Fable*, the *Moral*, the *Characters*, &c. The Fable I take to be as follows.

Fashion, *a Lewd, Prodigal, younger Brother, is reduced to extremity: Upon his arrival from his Travels, he meets with* Coupler, *an old sharping Match-maker; This Man puts him upon a project of cheating his Elder Brother, Lord* Foplington, *of a rich Fortune. Young* Fashion, *being refused a Summ of Money by his Brother, goes into* Couplers *Plot, bubbles Sir* Tunbelly *of his Daughter, and makes himself Master of a fair Estate.*

From the Form and Constitution of the *Fable*, I observe

1st. That there is a *Misnommer* in the Title. The *Play* should not have been call'd the *Relapse*, or *Virtue* in *Danger*. *Lovelace*, and *Amanda*, from whose *Characters* these Names are drawn, are

---

[10] *Essay of Dramatic Poesy* (see above, p. 8).

Persons of Inferiour Consideration. *Lovelace* sinks in the middle of the *Fourth* Act, and we hear no more of him till towards the End of the *Fifth,* where he enters once more, but then 'tis as *Cato* did the Senate house, only to go out again. And as for *Amanda* she has nothing to do but to stand a shock of Courtship, and carry off her Virtue. This I confess is a great task in the *Play-house,* but no main matter in the *Play.*

The *Intrigue,* and the *Discovery,* the great Revolution and success, turns upon *Young Fashion.* He without Competition, is the Principal Person in the *Comedy.* And therefore the *Younger Brother,* or the *Fortunate Cheat,* had been much a more proper Name. Now when a *Poet* can't rig out a *Title Page,* 'tis but a bad sign of his holding out to the *Epilogue.*

2ly. I observe the Moral is vitious: It points the wrong way, and puts the *Prize* into the wrong Hand. It seems to make *Lewdness* the reason of *Desert,* and gives *Young Fashion* a Second Fortune, only for Debauching away his First. A short view of his *Character,* will make good this Reflection. To begin with him: He confesses himself a *Rake,* Swears, and Blasphemes, Curses, and Challenges his Elder Brother, cheats him of his Mistress, and gets him laid by the Heels in a Dog-Kennel. And what was the ground of all this unnatural quarrelling and outrage? Why, the main of it was only because Lord *Foplington* refused to supply his Luxury and make good his Extravagance. This *Young Fashion,* after all, is the *Poet's* Man of Merit, He provides a *Plot* and a Fortune, on purpose for him. To speak freely, A Lewd Character seldom wants good Luck in *Comedy.* So that when ever you see a thorough Libertine, you may always swear he is in a rising way, and that the *Poet* intends to make him a great Man. In short; This *Play* perverts the End of *Comedy*: Which as Monsieur *Rapin* observes ought to regard Reformation and publick Improvement. But the *Relapser* had a more fashionable Fancy in his Head. His *Moral* holds forth this notable Instruction.

1st. That all *Younger Brothers* should be careful to run out their Circumstances as Fast, and as Ill as they can. And when they have put their Affairs in this posture of Advantage, they may conclude themselves in the high Road to Wealth, and Success. For, as *Fashion* Blasphemously applies it, *Providence takes care of Men of Merit.*

2ly. That when a Man is press'd, his business is not to be govern'd by Scruples, or formalize upon Conscience and Honesty. The quickest Expedients are the best; For in such cases the Occasion justifies the Means, and a Knight of the *Post*, is as good as one of the *Garter*. In the

3d Place it may not be improper to look a little into the *Plot*. Here the *Poet* ought to play the Politician if ever. This part should have some stroaks, of Conduct and strains of Invention more then ordinary. There should be something that is admirable, and unexpected to surprize the Audience. And all this Fineness must work by gentle degrees, by a due preparation of *Incidents*, and by Instruments which are probable. 'Tis Mr. *Rapins* remark that, without probability *every Thing is lame and Faulty*. Where there is no pretence to *Miracle* and *Machine*, matters must not exceed the force of Belief. To produce effects without proportion and likelyhood in the Cause, is Farce and Magick, and looks more like Conjuring than Conduct. Let us examine the *Relapser* by these Rules. To discover his *Plot*, we must lay open somewhat more of the *Fable*.

'Lord *Foplington* a Town Beau, had agreed to Marry the Daughter of Sir *Tun-belly Clumsey* a Country Gentleman, who lived Fifty miles from *London*. Notwithstanding this small distance, the Lord had never seen his Mistress, nor the Knight his Son in Law. Both parties out of their great Wisdom, leave the treating the Match to *Coupler*. When all the preliminaries of Settlement were adjusted, and Lord *Foplington* expected by Sir *Tun-belly* in a few days, *Coupler* betrays his Trust to *Young Fashion*. He advises him to go down before his Brother: To Counterfeit his Person, and pretend that the strength of his Inclinations brought him thither before his time and without his Retinue. And to make him pass upon Sir *Tun-belly*, *Coupler* gives him his *Letter*, which was to be Lord *Foplington's* Credential. *Young Fashion* thus provided, posts down to Sir *Tunbelly*, is recieved for Lord *Foplington,* and by the help of a little Folly and Knavery in the Family, Marries the young Lady without her Father's Knowledge, and a week before the Appointment.'

This is the Main of the Contrivance. The Counterturn in Lord *Foplington's* appearing afterwards, and the Support of the main *Plot*, by *Bull's,* and *Nurse's* attesting the Marriage, contain's little of Moment. And here we may observe that Lord *Foplington* has an unlucky Disagreement in his *Character;* This Misfortune sits hard upon the credibility of the Design. 'Tis true he was Formal and Fantastick, Smitten with Dress, and Equipage, and it may be vapour'd by his Perfumes; But his Behaviour is far from that of an Ideot. This being granted, 'tis very unlikely this Lord with his five Thousand pounds *per annum,* should leave the choise of his Mistress to *Coupler,* and take her Person and Fortune upon *Content.* To court thus blindfold, and by *Proxy,* does not agree with the Method of an Estate, nor the Niceness of a *Beau.* However the *Poet* makes him engage Hand over Head, without so much as the sight of her Picture. His going down to Sir *Tun-belly* was as extraordinary as his Courtship. He had never seen this Gentleman. He must know him to be beyond Measure suspicious, and there was no Admittance without *Couplers* Letter. This *Letter,* which was the Key to the Castle, he forgot to take with him, and tells you *'twas stolen by his Brother Tam.* And for his part he neither had the Discretion to get another, nor yet to produce that written by him to Sir *Tun-belly.* Had common Sense been consulted upon this Occasion, the *Plot* had been at an End, and the *Play* had sunk in the Fourth *Act.* The Remainder subsists purely upon the strength of Folly, and of Folly altogether improbable, and out of *Character.* The *Salvo* of Sir *John Friendly's* appearing at last and vouching for Lord *Foplington* won't mend the matter. For, as the *Story* informs us, Lord *Foplington* never depended on this Reserve: He knew nothing of this Gentleman being in the Country, nor where he Lived. The truth is, Sir *John* was left in *Town,* and the Lord had neither concerted his journey with him nor engaged his Assistance.

Let us now see how Sir *Tun-belly* hangs together. This Gentleman the *Poet* makes a *Justice* of *Peace* and a *Deputy Lieutenant,* and seats him fifty Miles from London: But by his Character you would take him for one of *Hercules's* Monsters, or some Gyant in *Guy* of *Warwick.* His Behaviour is altogether *Romance,* and has nothing agreeable to Time, or Country. When *Fashion,* and *Lory,* went down, they find the Bridge drawn up, the Gates barr'd, and the Blunderbuss cock'd at the first civil Question. And when Sir *Tun-belly* had notice of this formidable Appearance, he Sallies out with the *Posse* of the Family, and marches against a Couple of Strangers with a *Life Guard* of Halberds, Sythes, and Pitchforks. And to make sure work, Young *Hoyden* is lock'd up at the first approach of the Enemy. Here you have prudence and wariness to the excess of Fable, and Frensy. And yet this mighty man of suspition, trusts *Coupler* with the Disposal of his only Daughter, and his Estate into the Bargain. And what was this *Coupler?* Why, a sharper by *Character,* and little better by Profession. Farther. Lord *Foplington* and the Knight, are but a days Journey asunder, and yet by their treating by Proxy and Commission one would Fancy a dozen Degrees of *Latitude* betwixt them. And as for Young *Fashion,* excepting *Couplers* Letter, he has all imaginable Marks of Imposture upon him. He comes before his Time, and without the Retinue expected, and has nothing of the Air of Lord *Foplington's* Conversation. When Sir *Tun-belly* ask'd him, *pray where are your Coaches and Servants, my Lord?* He makes a trifling excuse. *Sir, that I might give you and your Fair Daughter a proof how impatient I am to be nearer akin to you, I left my Equipage to follow me, and came away Post, with only one Servant.* To be in such a Hurry of Inclination for a Person he never saw is somewhat strange! Besides, 'tis very unlikely Lord *Foplington* should hazard his Complexion on Horseback, out-ride his Figure, and appear a Bridegroom in *Deshabille.* You may as soon perswade a Peacock out of his Train, as a *Beau* out of his Equipage; especially upon such an Occasion. Lord *Foplington* would scarsely speak to his Brother just come a *Shore,* till the Grand Commitee of *Taylors, Seamtresses, &c.,* was dispatch'd. Pomp and Curiosity were this Lords Inclination; why then should he mortifie without necessity, make his first Approaches thus out of Form, and present himself to his Mistress at such Disadvantage? And as this is the Character of Lord *Foplington,* so 'tis reasonable to suppose Sir *Tunbelly* acquainted with it. An enquiry into the Humour and management of a Son in Law, is very natural and Customary. So that we can't without Violence to Sense, suppose Sir *Tunbelly* a Stranger to Lord *Foplington's* Singularities. These Reasons were enough in all Conscience to make Sir *Tunbelly* suspect a Juggle, and that *Fashion* was no better than a Counterfeit. Why then was the *Credential*

swallow'd without chewing, why was not *Hoyden* lock'd up, and
a pause made for farther Enquiry? Did this *Justice* never hear
of such a Thing as Knavery, or had he ever greater reason to
guard against it? More wary steps might well have been expected from Sir *Tunbelly.* To run from one extream of Caution
to, another of Credulity, is highly improbable. In short, either
Lord *Foplington* and Sir *Tunbelly* are Fools, or they are not.
If they are, where lies the Cunning in over-reaching them? What
Conquest can there be without Opposition? If they are not Fools,
why does the *Poet* make them so? Why is their Conduct so
gross, so particolour'd, and inconsistent? Take them either way,
and the *Plot* miscarries. The first supposition makes it dull, and
the later, incredible. So much for the *Plot.* I shall now in the
4*th* Place touch briefly upon the *Manners.*

The *Manners* in the Language of the *Stage* have a significa-
tion somewhat particular. *Aristotle* and *Rapin* call them the
Causes and Principles of Action. They are formed upon the
Diversities of Age and Sex, of Fortune, Capacity, and Education.
The propriety of *Manners* consists in a Conformity of Practise,
and Principle, of Nature, and Behaviour. For the purpose. An
old Man must not appear with the Profuseness and Levity of
Youth; A Gentleman must not talk like a Clown, nor a Country
Girl like a Town Jilt. And when the *Characters* are feign'd, 'tis
Horace's Rule to keep them Uniform, and consistent, and agreeable to their first setting out. The *Poet* must be careful to hold
his *Persons* tight to their *Calling* and pretentions. He must not
shift and shuffle their Understandings; Let them skip from Wits
to Blockheads, nor from Courtiers to Pedants. On the other
hand. If their business is playing the Fool, keep them strictly
to their Duty, and never indulge them in fine Sentences. To
manage otherwise is to desert *Nature,* and makes the *Play* appear monstrous, and Chimerical. So that instead of an *Image
of Life,* 'tis rather an Image of Impossibility. To apply some of
these remarks to the *Relapser.*

The fine *Berinthia,* one of the Top-Characters, is impudent
and Profane. *Lovelace* would engage her Secrecy, and bids her
Swear. She answers, *I do.*

> Lov. *By what?*
> Berinth. *By Woman.*

Lov. *That's Swearing by my Deity, do it by your own, or I shan't believe you.*

Berinth. *By Man then.*

This Lady promises *Worthy* her Endeavours to corrupt *Amanda;* and then They make a Profane jest upon the Office. In the progress of the *Play* after a great deal of Lewd Discourse with *Lovelace, Berinthia* is carried off into a Closet, and Lodged in a *Scene* of Debauch. Here is Decency, and Reservedness, to a great exactness! Monsieur *Rapin* blames *Ariosto,* and *Tasso,* for representing two of their Women over free, and airy. These *Poets* says he, *rob Women of their Character, which is Modesty.* Mr. *Rymer* is of the same Opinion. His words are these. *Nature knows nothing in the Manners which so properly, and particularly distinguished a Woman as her Modesty.—An impudent Woman is fit only to be kicked, and expos'd in Comedy.*[11]

Now, *Berinthia* appears in *Comedy* 'tis true; but neither to be *kick'd* nor *expos'd.* She makes a Considerable Figure, has good Usage, keeps the best Company, and goes off without Censure, or Disadvantage. Let us now take a Turn or two with Sir *Tunbelly's* Heiress of 1500 pounds a year. This Young Lady Swears, talks Smut, and is upon the matter just as rag-manner'd as *Mary the Buxsome.* 'Tis plain the *Relapser* copied Mr. *Durfey's* Original, which is a sign he was somewhat Pinch'd. Now, this *Character* was no great Beauty in *Buxsome;* But it becomes the Knights Daughter much worse. *Buxsome* was a poor Peasant, which made her Rudeness more natural and expected. But *Deputy Lieutenants* Children don't use to appear with the Behaviour of Beggars. To breed all People alike, and make no distinction between a *Seat,* and a *Cottage,* is not over artful, nor very ceremonious to the Country Gentlemen. The *Relapser* gives *Miss* a pretty *Soliloquy,* I'll transcribe it for the *Reader.*

She swears by her Maker, *'tis well I have a Husband a coming, or I'de Marry the Baker, I would so. No body can knock at the Gate, but presently I must be lock'd up; and here's the Young Gray-hound —— can run loose about the House all day long, she can, 'tis very well!* Afterwards her Language is too Lewd to be Quoted. Here is a Compound of Ill Manners and Contra-

[11] Thomas Rymer (1641–1713), *Tragedies of the Last Age Considered* (1678).

diction! Is this a good Resemblance of Quality; a Description of
a great Heiress, and the effect of a Cautious Education? By her
Coarsness you would think her Bred upon a Common, and by
her Confidence, in the Nursery of the *Play-house.* I suppose the
Relapser Fancies the calling her *Miss Hoyden* is enough to justifie her Ill Manners. By his favour, this is a Mistake. To represent
her thus unhewn, he should have suited her Condition to her
Name a little better. For there is no charm in *Words* as to matters of Breeding, An unfashionable Name won't make a Man a
Clown. Education is not form'd upon Sounds and Syllables, but
upon Circumstances, and Quality. So that if he was resolv'd
to have shown her thus unpolish'd, he should have made her
keep *Sheep,* or brought her up at the *Wash-Boul.*

Sir *Tun-Belly* accosts Young *Fashion* much at the same rate of
Accomplishment. My Lord, —— *I humbly crave leave to bid you
Welcome in a Cup of Sack-wine.* One would imagine the *Poet*
was overdozed before he gave the *Justice* a Glass. For *Sack-wine*
is too low for a *Petty Constable.* This Peasantly expression agrees
neither with the Gentlemans Figure, nor with the rest of his Behaviour. I find we should have a Creditable *Magistracy,* if the
Relapser had the Making them. Here the *Characters* are pinch'd
in Sense, and stinted to short Allowance. At an other time they
are over-indulged, and treated above Expectation.

For the purpose: Vanity and Formalizing is Lord *Foplington's*
part. To let him speak without Aukwardness, and Affectation,
is to put him out of his Element. There must be Gumm and
stiffening in his Discourse to make it natural. However, the *Relapser* has taken a fancy to his Person, and given him some of
the most Gentile raillery in the whole *Play.* To give an Instance
or two. This Lord in Discourse with *Fashion* forgets his Name,
flies out into Sense, and smooth expression, out-talks his Brother,
and abating the starch'd Similitude of a *Watch,* discovers nothing
of Affectation for almost a *Page* together. He relapses into the
same Intemperance of good Sense, in an other Dialogue between him and his Brother. I shall cite a little of it.

Y. Fash. *Unless you are so kind to assist me in redeeming my
Annuity, I know no Remedy, but to go take a Purse.*

L. Fopl. *Why, Faith, Tam——to give you my Sense of the
Thing, I do think taking a Purse the best Remedy in the World,*

*for if you succeed, you are reliev'd that way; if you are taken
——you are reliev'd t'other.*

Fashion being disappointed of a supply quarrels his Elder
Brother, and calls him *the Prince of Coxcombs.*

L. Fopl. *Sir, I am proud of being at the Head of so prevailing
a party.*

Y. Fash. *Will nothing then provoke thee? draw, Coward.*

L. Fopl. *Look you* Tam, *your poverty makes your Life so
burdensome to you, you would provoke me to a Quarrel, in
hopes to slip through my Lungs into my Estate, or else to get
your self run through the Guts, to put an end to your Pain. But
I shall disappoint you in both,* &c.

This Drolling has too much Spirit, the Air of it is too free,
and too handsomly turn'd for Lord *Foplington's* Character. I
grant the *Relapser* could not afford to lose these Sentences. The
Scene would have suffer'd by the Omission. But then he should
have contriv'd the matter so, as that they might have been
spoken by Young *Fashion* in *Asides,* or by some other more
proper Person. To go on. Miss *Hoyden* sparkles too much in
Conversation. The *Poet* must needs give her a shining Line or
two, which serves only to make the rest of her dullness the
more remarkable. Sir *Tun-belly* falls into the same Misfortune
of a Wit, and rallies above the force of his Capacity: But the
place having a mixture of Profaness, I shall forbear to cite it.
Now, to what purpose should a Fools Coat be embroider'd?
Finery in the wrong place is but expensive Ridiculousness. Besides, I don't perceive the *Relapser* was in any Condition to be
thus liberal. And when a *Poet* is not overstock'd, to squander
away his Wit among his *Block-heads* is meer Distraction. His
men of Sense will smart for this prodigality. *Lovelace* in his
discourse of *Friendship,* shall be the first Instance. *Friendship*
(says he) *is said to be a plant of tedious growth, its Root composed of tender* Fibers, nice in their Tast, *&c.* By this Description the Palate of a *Fiber,* should be somewhat more *nice* and
distinguishing then the *Poets* Judgment. Let us examin some
more of his Witty People. Young *Fashion* fancies by *Misses* for
ward Behaviour, she would have a whole *Kennel* of *Beaux* after
her at *London.* And then, *Hey to the Park, and the Play, and
the Church, and the Devil.* Here I conceive the ranging of the

Period is amiss. For if he had put the *Play* and the *Devil* together, the Order of Nature and the Air of Probability had been much better observ'd.

Afterwards *Coupler* being out of Breath in coming up stairs to *Fashion*, asks him, *why the ——— can'st thou not lodge upon the Ground-floor?*

Y. Fash. *Because I love to lye as near Heaven as I can.* One would think a Spark just come off his Travels, and had made the *Tour* of *Italy* and *France*, might have rallied with a better Grace! However if he lodg'd in a *Garret*, 'tis a good *Local* jest. I had almost forgot one pretty remarkable Sentence of *Fashion* to *Lory. I shall shew thee* (says he) *the excess of my Passion by being very calm.* Now, since this *Gentleman* was in a vein of talking Philosophy to his Man, I'm sorry he broke of so quickly. Had he gone on and shown him the *Excess* of a Storm and no Wind stirring, the Topick had been spent and the Thought improv'd to the utmost.

Let us now pass on to *Worthy*, the *Relapser's* fine Gentleman. This Spark sets up for Sense and Address, and is to have nothing of Affectation or Conscience to spoil his Character. However, to say no more of him, he grows Foppish in the last *Scene*, and courts *Amanda* in Fustian, and Pedantry. First, He gives his Periods a turn of Versification, and talks *Prose* to her in *Meeter*. Now this is just as agreeable as it would be to *Ride* with one Leg and *Walk* with the other. But let him speak for himself. His first business is to bring *Amanda* to an Aversion for her Husband; And therefore he perswades her to *Rouse up that Spirit Women ought to bear; and slight your God if he neglects his Angel.* He goes on with his Orisons. *With Arms of Ice receive his Cold Embraces, and keep your Fire for those that come in Flames.* Fire and Flames is Mettal upon Mettal; 'Tis false Heraldry. *Extend the Arms of Mercy to his Aid. His zeal may give him Title to your Pity, altho' his Merit cannot claim your Love.* Here you have *Arms* brought in again by Head and shoulders. I suppose the design was to keep up the Situation of the *Allegory*. But the latter part of the Speech is very Pithy. He would have her resign her Virtue out of Civility, and abuse her Husband on Principles of good Nature. *Worthy* pursues his point, and Rises in his Address. He falls into a Fit of Dissection, and hopes to gain his Mistress by Cutting his Throat. He is for *Ripping up his Faithful Breast*, to prove the Reality of his Passion. Now, when a Man Courts with his Heart in his Hand, it must be great Cruelty to refuse him! No Butcher could have Thought of a more moving Expedient! However, *Amanda* continues obstinate, and is not in the usual Humour of the *Stage*. Upon this, like a well bred Lover he seizes her by Force and threatens to Kill her. *Nay struggle not for all's in vain, or Death, or Victory, I am determin'd.* In this rencounter the Lady proves too nimble, and slips through his Fingers. Upon this disappointment, he cries, *there's Divinity about her, and she has dispenc'd some Portion on't to me.* His Passion is Metamorphos'd in the Turn of a hand: He is refin'd into a *Platonick* Admirer, and goes off as like a *Town Spark* as you would wish. And so much for the *Poet's* fine Gentleman.

I should now examine the *Relapser's Thoughts and Expressions*, which are two other Things of Consideration in a *Play*. The *Thoughts* or *Sentiments are the Expressions of the Manners as Words are of the Thoughts.* But the view of the *Characters* has in some measure prevented this Enquiry. Leaving this Argument, therefore, I shall consider his *Play* with respect to the *Three Unities* of Time, Place, and Action.

And here the *Reader* may please to take notice, that the Design of these Rules, is to conceal the Fiction of the *Stage*, to make the *Play* appear Natural, and to give it an Air of Reality, and *Conversation*.

The largest compass for the first *Unity* is Twenty Four Hours: But a lesser proportion is more regular. To be exact, the Time of the History, or *Fable*, should not exceed that of the *Representation*: Or in other words, the whole Business of the *Play* should not be much longer than the Time it takes up in *Playing*.

The Second *Unity* is that of *Place*. To observe it, the *Scene* must not wander from one Town or Country to another. It must continue in the same House, Street, or at farthest in the same City, where it was first laid. The Reason of this Rule depends upon the *First*. Now, the Compass of *Time* being strait, that of *Space* must bear a Correspondent Proportion. Long journeys in

Plays are impracticable. The Distances of *Place* must be suited to Leisure and Possibility; otherwise the supposition will appear unnatural and absurd. The

Third *Unity* is that of *Action;* It consists in contriving the chief Business of the *Play* single, and making the concerns of one Person distinguishably great above the rest. All the Forces of the *Stage* must as it were serve Under one *General:* And the lesser Intrigues or Under-plots, have some Relation to the Main. The very Oppositions must be useful, and appear only to be Conquer'd and Countermin'd. To represent Two considerable Actions independent of each other, Destroys the beauty of Subordination, weakens the Contrivance, and dilutes the pleasure. It splits the *Play,* and makes the *Poem* double. He that would see more upon this subject may consult *Corneille.*[12] To bring these Remarks to the Case in hand: And here we may observe how the *Relapser* fails in all the *Rules* above mention'd.

1st. His *Play* by modest Computation, takes up a weeks Work, but five days you must allow it at the lowest. One day must be spent in the First, Second, and part of the Third *Act,* before Lord *Foplington* sets forward to Sir *Tun-belly.* Now, the Length of the Distance, the Pomp of the Retinue, and the Niceness of the Person being consider'd; the journey down, and up again, cannot be laid under four days. To put this out of doubt, Lord *Foplington* is particularly careful to tell *Coupler,* how concern'd he was not to overdrive, *for fear of disordering his Coach-Horses.* The Laws of *Place,* are no better observ'd than those of *Time.* In the Third *Act* the *Play* is in *Town,* in the Fourth *Act* 'tis stroll'd Fifty Miles off, and in the Fifth *Act* in *London* again. Here *Pegasus* stretches it to purpose! This *Poet* is fit to ride a Match with Witches. *Juliana Cox* never Switched a Broom stock with more Expedition! This is exactly

> *Titus* at *Walton Town,* and *Titus* at *Islington.*

One would think, by the probability of matters, the *Plot* had been stolen from Dr. *O—s.*[13]

---

[12] *Discours des Trois Unités* (1660).
[13] Titus Oates (1649–1705), inventor of sensational charges of "Popish Plots" against the king and the realm.

The *Poet's* Success in the last *Unity* of *Action* is much the same with the former. *Lovelace, Amanda,* and *Berinthia* have no share in the main Business. These Second rate *Characters* are a detatched Body: Their Interest is perfectly Foreign, and they are neither Friends nor Enemies to the *Plot. Young Fashion* does not so much as see them till the Close of the Fifth *Act,* and then they meet only to fill the *Stage.* And yet these *Persons* are in the *Poet's* account very considerable; Insomuch that he has misnamed his *Play* from the Figure of two of them. The strangness of *Persons,* distinct Company, and inconnexion of Affairs, destroys the Unity of the *Poem.* The contrivance is just as wise as it would be to cut a Diamond in two. There is a loss of Lustre in the Division. Increasing the Number, abates the Value; and by making it more, you make it less.

Thus far I have examin'd the *Dramatick* Merits of the *Play.* And upon enquiry, it appears a Heap of Irregularities. There is neither Propriety in the *Name,* nor Contrivance in the *Plot,* nor Decorum in the *Characters.* 'Tis a thorough Contradiction to Nature, and impossible in *Time,* and *Place.* Its *Shining Graces* as the Author calls them, are *Blasphemy* and *Baudy,* together with a mixture of *Oaths,* and *Cursing.* Upon the whole; The *Relapser's* Judgment, and his Morals, are pretty well adjusted. The *Poet,* is not much better than the *Man.* As for the *Profane* part, 'tis hideous and superlative. But this I have consider'd elsewhere. All that I shall observe here is, that the Author was sensible of this Objection. His Defence in his *Preface* is most wretched: He pretends to know nothing of the Matter, and that *'tis all Printed;* Which only proves his Confidence equal to the rest of his Virtues. To out-face Evidence in this manner is next to the affirming there's no such sin, as *Blasphemy,* which is the greatest Blasphemy of all. His Apology consists in railing at the *Clergy;* a certain sign of ill Principles, and ill Manners. This He does at an unusual rate of Rudeness and Spite. He calls them the Saints with Screw'd *Faces and wry Mouths.* And after a great deal of scurrilous Abuse, too gross to be mention'd, he adds; *If any Man happens to be offended at a story of a Cock and a Bull, and a Priest and a Bull-dog, I beg his Pardon, &c.* This is brave *Bear-Garden* Language! The *Relapser* would do well to transport his Muse to *Samourgan*.[14] There 'tis likely he might find Leisure to lick his *Abortive Brat* into shape; And meet with proper Business for his Temper, and encouragement for his Talent.

[14] An Academy in Lithuania, for the Education of Bears. Pere Aurill, *Voyage en Divers Etats, etc.,* p. 240. [Collier's note.]

Sir John Vanbrugh

[1664–1726]

᪐᪐᪐

VANBRUGH DIVIDED HIS MATURE YEARS between two careers—playwriting and architecture. His best-known building is the Duke of Marlborough's Blenheim Palace; his best-known plays (and the only ones which are not adaptations of French, Spanish, or English sources) are *The Relapse* (1696) and *The Provok'd Wife* (1697). These two were among the plays attacked by Jeremy Collier in his *Short View of the Immorality and Profaneness of the English Stage* (see above, pages 97 to 130). Collier devoted an entire chapter of his book to *The Relapse*, criticizing it for breaches of probability, morality, and decorum, for violations of all the classical unities, and for abuse of the clergy. Faced with this two-fold attack on his morals and his art, Vanbrugh was forced to defend his witty, mannered exaggerations by drawing upon the two traditional defenses of comic impropriety: that comedy represents "people as they are," and that its function is corrective—"a Discouragement to Vice and Folly." Neither argument is appropriate to Vanbrugh's plays, and one must conclude that Collier won this round. (See headnote to Collier, p. 96).

BIBLIOGRAPHY. *Complete Works,* ed. B. Dobree and G. Webb, 4 vols. (London, 1927).

J. W. Krutch, *Comedy and Conscience after the Restoration* (2nd ed., New York, 1949).

TEXT. *A Short Vindication of the "Relapse" and the "Provok'd Wife"* from *Immorality and Profaneness* (London, 1698).

from

A SHORT VINDICATION OF THE "RELAPSE" AND THE "PROVOK'D WIFE" FROM IMMORALITY AND PROFANENESS

[1698]

WHEN FIRST I SAW Mr. *Collier's* Performance upon the Irregularities of the Stage (in which amongst the rest of the Gentlemen, he's pleas'd to afford me some particular Favours), I was far from designing to trouble either my self or the Town with a Vindication; I thought his Charges against me for Immorality and Profaneness were grounded upon so much Mistake, that every one (who had had the curiosity to see the Plays, or on this Occasion should take the trouble to read 'em) would easily discover the Root of the Invective, and that 'twas the Quarrel of his Gown, and not of his God, that made him take Arms against me.

I found the Opinion of my Friends and Acquaintance the same, (at least they told me so) and the Righteous as well as the Unrighteous persuaded me, The Attack was so weak, the Town wou'd defend it self; that the General's Head was too hot for his Conduct to be wise; his Shot too much at Random ever to make a Breach; and that the Siege wou'd be raised, without my taking the Field.

I easily believ'd, what my Laziness made me wish; but I have since found, That by the Industry of some People, whose Temporal Interest engages 'em in the Squabble; and the Natural Propensity of others, to be fond of anything that's Abusive; this Lampoon has got Credit enough in some Places to brand the Persons it mentions with almost as bad a Character, as the Author of it has fixt upon himself, by his Life and Conversation in the World.

I think 'tis therefore now a thing no farther to be laught at. Should I wholly sit still, those People who are so much mistaken to think I have been busy to encourage Immorality, may double their Mistake, and fancy I profess it: I will therefore endeavor, in a very few Pages to convince the World, I have brought nothing upon the Stage, that proves me more an Atheist than a Bigot.

I may be blind in what relates to myself; 'tis more than possible, for most People are so: But if I judge right, what I have done is in general a Discouragement to Vice and Folly; I am sure I intended it, and I hope I have performed it. Perhaps I have not gone the common Road, nor observed the strictest Prescriptions: But I believe those who know this Town, will agree, That the Rules of a College of Divines will in an Infinity of Cases, fall as short of the Disorders of the Mind, as those of the Physicians do in the Diseases of the Body; and I think a man may vary from 'em both, without being a Quack in either.

The real Query is, Whether the Way I have varied, be likely to have a good Effect, or a bad one? That's the true State of the Case; which if I am cast in, I don't question however to gain at least thus much of my Cause, That it shall be allow'd I aim'd at the Mark, whether I hit it or not. This, if it won't vindicate my Sense, will justify my Morals; and shew the World, That this Honest Gentleman, in stretching his Malice, and curtailing his Charity, has play'd a Part which wou'd have much better become a Licentious Poet than a Reverend Divine. . . .

The next Chapter is upon the Encouragement of Immorality by the Stage: and here *Constant* is fallen upon, for pretending to be a Fine Gentleman, without living up to the Exact Rules of Religion. If Mr. *Collier* excludes everyone from that Character, that does not, I doubt he'll have a more general Quarrel to make up with the Gentlemen of *England*, than I have with the Lords, tho' he tells 'em I have highly affronted 'em.

But I wou'd fain know after all, upon what Foundation he lays so positive a Position, that *Constant* is my Model for a Fine Gentleman; and that he is brought upon the Stage for Imitation.

He might as well say, if I brought His Character upon the Stage, I design'd it a Model to the Clergy: And yet I believe most People wou'd take it t'other way. O, but these kind of

Fine Gentlemen, he says, are always prosperous in their Undertakings, and their Vice under no kind of Detection; for in the Fifth Act of the Play, they are usually rewarded with a Wife or a Mistress. And suppose I shou'd reward him with a Bishoprick in the Fifth Act, wou'd that mend his Character? I have too great a Veneration for the Clergy, to believe that wou'd make 'em follow his steps. And yet (with all due Respect to the Ladies) take one Amour with another, the Bishoprick may prove as weighty a Reward as a Wife or a Mistress either. He says, Mr. *Bull* was abused upon the stage, yet he got a Wife and a Benefice too. Poor *Constant* has neither, nay, he has not got even his Mistress yet, he had not, at least, when the Play was last Acted. But this honest Doctor, I find, does not yet understand the Nature of Comedy, though he has made it his Study so long. For the Business of Comedy is to shew People what they shou'd do, by representing them upon the Stage, doing what they shou'd not. Nor is there any necessity a Philosopher shou'd stand by, like an Interpreter at a Puppet-show, to explain the Moral to the Audience: The Mystery is seldom so deep, but the Pit and Boxes can dive into it; and 'tis their Example out of the Playhouse, that chiefly influences the Galleries. The stage is a Glass for the World to view it self in; People ought therefore to see themselves as they are; if it makes their Faces too Fair, they won't know they are Dirty, and by consequence will neglect to wash 'em. If therefore I have shewed *Constant* upon the Stage, what generally the Thing call'd a Fine Gentleman is off on't, I think I have done what I shou'd do. I have laid open his Vices as well as his Virtues: 'Tis the Business of the Audience to observe where his Flaws lessen his Value; and by considering the Deformity of his Blemishes, become sensible how much a Finer Thing he would be without 'em. But after all, *Constant* says nothing to justify the Life he leads, except where he's pleading with Lady *Brute* to debauch her; and sure nobody will suppose him there to be speaking much of his Mind. Besides, his Mistress in all her Answers makes the Audience observe the Fallacy of his Arguments. And I think Young Ladies may without much Penetration make this use of the Dialogue, That they are not to take all for Gospel, Men tell 'em upon such occasions.

The *Provok'd Wife* is charg'd with nothing more, except *Bellinda* for declaring she'd be glad of a Gallant, and Lady *Brute* for saying, *Virtue's an Ass, and a Gallant's worth forty on't.*

I need make no other Defence for the Ladies, than I have already done for the Gentlemen, the Case being much the same. However, to shew how unfair an Adversary I have to deal with, I must acquaint the Reader, that *Bellinda* only says, *If her Pride shou'd make her marry a Man she hated, her Virtue wou'd be in danger from the Man she lov'd.* Now her Reflection upon this, I take to be a useful Caution both to Mothers and Daughters (who think Chastity a Virtue) to consider something in their Matches, besides a Page and a Coronet.

Lady *Brute's* Words are fairly recited, but wrongly apply'd. Mr. *Collier's* mistaken; 'tis not Virtue she exposes, but her self, when she says 'em: Nor is it me he exposes, but himself, when he quotes 'em.

He gives me no farther occasion to mention the *Provok'd Wife,* I'll therefore take this to make an Observation or two upon the Moral of it, it being upon that account he has called it in question, and endeavour'd to make it pass for a Play that has none.

This Play was writ many years ago, and when I was very young; if therefore there had been some small Flaws in the Moral, I might have been excus'd for the Writing, tho' liable to some Blame for the Publishing it. But I hope it is not so loose, but I may be pardon'd for Both, whether Mr. *Collier* sets his Seal to't or not.

As for Sir *John Brute,* I think there are an Infinity of Husbands who have a very great share of his Vices: And I think his Business throughout the Play is a visible Burlesque upon his Character. 'Tis this Gentleman that gives the Spring to the rest of the Adventures: And tho' I own there is no mighty Plot in the whole matter, yet what there is, tends to the Reformation of Manners. For besides the hateful Idea his Figure needs must give of his Character, the ill Consequence of his Brutality appears in the Miscarriage of his Wife: For though his ill usage of her does not justify her Intrigue, her intriguing upon his ill usage, may be a Caution for some. I don't find our Women in *England* have much of the *Muscovite* Temper in 'em: if you'll make 'em think you are their Friend, you must give 'em softer strokes of your Kindness; if you don't, the Gallant has a dangerous Plea, and such a one as, I doubt, has carri'd many a Cause. Religion, I own, (when a woman has it) is a very great Bulwark for her Husband's Security: And so is Modesty, and so is Fear, and so is Pride; and yet all are little enough, if the Gallant has a Friend in the Garison. I therefore think That Play has a very good End, which puts the Governor in mind, let his Soldiers be ever so good, 'tis possible he may provoke 'em to a Mutiny.

The rest of the Characters, as they have no very great good, so they have very little mischief in 'em. Lady *Fanciful* is ridicul'd for her Vanity and her Affectation. *Mademoiselle* brings to mind what may often be expected from a *Suivante* of her Countrey. *Heartfree* is catch'd for his extravagant Railing at Womankind: and *Constant* gives himself a great deal of trouble, for a thing that is not worth his Pains. In short, they are most of 'em busy about what they shou'd not be; and those who observe they are so, may take warning to employ their time better.

I have nothing more to answer for in this Chapter, but making the Women speak against their own Sex: And having the Presumption to bring a Fop upon the Stage with the Title of a Lord.

This is a bungling Piece of Policy, to make the Women and the Nobility take up Arms in his Quarrel. I'm asham'd a Churchman should spin his Mischief no finer: The Sollicitors to the Holy War had almost as good a Plea. But he had one Consideration farther in this: He remember'd he had positively declar'd, Let a Clergyman be guilty of what Crimes he wou'd, he was God's Ambassador, and therefore a Privileg'd Person, whom the Poets ought never to take into Custody. This, upon second thoughts, he found wou'd hardly go down, if he monopoliz'd the Privilege to them alone; and so lest the Company shou'd bring their Charter to a Dispute, he has open'd the Books for New Subscriptions; the Lords and the Ladies are invited to come in; the Gentlemen, I suppose, may do so too, if they please; and, in short, rather than the Committee of Religion shall be expos'd for their Faults, all Mankind shall be admitted to Trade in Sin as they please.

But I dare answer for the Laity, of what Quality soever they may be, they are willing their Vices shou'd be scourg'd upon the Stage; at least, I never yet heard one of 'em declare the contrary. If the Clergy insist upon being exempted by themselves, I believe they may obtain it: But I'm apt to fancy, if they protect their Loose Livers from being expos'd in the Play-house, they'll find 'em grow the bolder to expose themselves in the Streets. A Clergyman is not in any Countrey exempted from the Gallows: And Mr. *Collier* has seen one of his Brethren peep through a worse Place than a Garret-Window: Nay (in a Reign he reckons a Just One) amble through the Town at the Tayl of a Cart, with his Sins in Red Letters upon his Shoulders. A Hangman then may jerk him; Why not a Poet? Perhaps 'tis feared he might give him more Sensible Strokes.

I am now come to thank the Gentleman for the last of his Favours; in which he is so generous to bestow a Chapter entire upon me.

I'm extremely oblig'd to him for it, since 'tis more than ever he promis'd me; For in the Title of his Book, he designs to Correct the Stage only for the Immorality and Profaneness of it. And indeed I think that was all his business with't. But he has since consider'd better of the matter, and rather than *quit his hold*, falls a Criticizing upon Plots, Characters, Words, Dialogue, &c., even to telling us when our fine Gentlemen make Love in the prevailing Strein, and when not. This gives us a farther view of his Studies; but, I think, if he kept to his Text, he had given us a better View of a Clergyman.

It may, perhaps, be expected I shou'd say more in answer to this Chapter, than to all that has gone before it; the Sense of the Play being attack'd here, much more than the Moral, which those who will take Mr. *Collier's* word for my Principles, must believe I am least concern'd for. But I shall satisfy 'em of the contrary, by leaving the Sense to answer for it self if it can. I'll only say this for't in general; That it looks as if a Play were not overloaded with Blunders, when so Pains-taking a Corrector is reduc'd to the wretched necessity of spending his Satyr upon *Fire* and *Flames*, being in the same Line; and *Arms* twice in the same Speech, though at six lines distance one from t'other. This looks as if the Critick were rather duller than the Poet: But when men fight in a Passion, 'tis usual to make insignificant Thrusts; most of his are so wide, they need no parrying; and those that hit, are so weak, they make no Wound.

I don't pretend however to have observ'd the nicety of Rule in this Play; I writ it in as much haste (though not in so much fury) as he has done his Remarks upon it; 'Tis therefore possible I may have made as many foolish Mistakes.

I could however say a great deal against the too exact observance of what's call'd the Rules of the Stage, and the crowding a Comedy with a great deal of Intricate Plot. I believe I could shew, that the chief entertainment, as well as the Moral, lies much more in the Characters and the Dialogue, than in the Business and the Event. And I can assure Mr. *Collier*, if I wou'd have weak'ned the Diversion, I cou'd have avoided all his Objections, and have been at the expence of much less pains than I have: And this is all the Answer I shall make to 'em, except what tumbles in my way, as I'm observing the foul play he shews me, in setting the *Relapse* in so wrong a Light as he does, at his opening of the Fable on't. . . .

Jonathan Swift

[1667–1745]

꠸꠸꠸

SWIFT'S CRITICAL WRITINGS are the occasional products of a life principally devoted to political and ecclesiastical controversy. Swift was
a priest of the Church of England and later Dean of Saint Patrick's,
Dublin, and he was for many years the leading political writer of the
Tory ministry. Perhaps it was his taste for controversy that led him
to enter two of the liveliest critical battles of his time.

The battle between the Ancients and the Moderns was fought
throughout the seventeenth century, both in England and in France:
Jonson argued it in *Timber* (1641), using the same bee metaphor that
Swift later used; Dryden made it the core of his four-cornered debate
in his *Essay of Dramatic Poesy* (see above, pp. 2 to 62); and
Swift's patron, Sir William Temple, re-fought it in his *Essay Upon
the Ancient and Modern Learning* (1690). The critical question over
which the battle was fought is essentially this: is the development of
literature from ancient to modern times progressive, regressive, or
cyclical? Temple had argued the superiority of the Ancients, and it
was in reply to "Modernist" attacks on Temple that Swift wrote his
satire. However, though Swift clearly favors his Ancients, the party
of "sweetness and light," over the Moderns, the party of "excrement
and venom," *The Battle of the Books* is more a satire on the entire
controversy than a contribution to it. The battle is left unfinished, and
the very fact that Swift chose to write of it as a mock epic suggests a
less than reverent attitude toward both sides.

Swift's *Tatler* essay is one of many in which he attacked contemporary corruptions of style, and urged the establishment of an English
Academy to standardize English usage. (See also Swift's *A Proposal
for Correcting, Improving, and Ascertaining the English Tongue,*
1712). Swift's was one of many neo-classical arguments for a fixed
language; Dryden took the same position, though more moderately,
in the Dedication to his *Troilus and Cressida* (1679), and Addison
supported Swift in *Spectator* no. 135. But by the middle of the century, the movement for an academy had died, partly because of the

opposition of Dr. Johnson, who ridiculed the idea in the Preface to his *Dictionary* (1755) and later in his life of Swift (*Lives of the Poets*, 1778), and partly because the *Dictionary* itself was a sufficient standardizing force.

BIBLIOGRAPHY. *Prose Works,* ed. Herbert Davis, 14 vols. (Oxford and Princeton, 1939—[in progress]).

Herbert Davis, *The Satire of Jonathan Swift* (New York, 1947); R. F. Jones, *Ancients and Moderns: a Study of the Background of the "Battle of the Books"* (St. Louis, 1936); R. Quintana, *Mind and Art of Jonathan Swift* (New York, 1936; rev. ed. 1953); M. K. Starkman, *Swift's Satire on Learning in A Tale of a Tub* (Princeton, 1950).

TEXT. *Works,* 11 vols. (Dublin, 1762), vols. I and XI.

SWEETNESS AND LIGHT *

[1696–1697]

THINGS WERE AT THIS CRISIS, when a material Accident fell out. For, upon the highest Corner of a large Window there dwelt a certain *Spider,* swollen up to the first Magnitude, by the Destruction of infinite Numbers of *Flies,* whose Spoils lay scattered before the Gates of his Palace, like Human Bones before the Cave of some Giant. The Avenues to his Castle were guarded with Turnpikes and Palisadoes, all after the *Modern* way of Fortification. After you had passed several Courts, you came to the Center, wherein you might behold the *Constable* himself in his own Lodgings, which had Windows fronting to each Avenue, and Ports to sally out upon all Occasions of Prey or Defence. In this Mansion he had for some Time dwelt in Peace and Plenty, without Danger to his *Person* by *Swallows* from above, or to his *Palace* by *Brooms* from below: when it was the Pleasure of Fortune to conduct thither a wandering *Bee,* to whose Curiosity a broken Pane in the Glass had discovered itself; and in he went,

---

* FROM *A Full and True Account of the Battle Fought last Friday Between the Ancient and Modern Books in St. James's Library,* better known as *The Battle of the Books,* written in 1696–7 and first published in 1704.

where expatiating a while, he at last happened to alight upon one of the outward Walls of the *Spider's* Citadel; which, yielding to the unequal Weight, sunk down to the very Foundation. Thrice he endeavored to force his Passage, and Thrice the Center shook. The *Spider* within, feeling the terrible Convulsion, supposed at first, that *Nature* was approaching to her final Dissolution; or else, that *Beelzebub*, with all his Legions, was come to revenge the Death of many thousands of his Subjects, whom his Enemy had slain and devoured. However, he at length valiantly resolved to issue forth, and meet his Fate. Meanwhile, the *Bee* had acquitted himself of his Toils, and, posted securely at some Distance, was employed in cleansing his Wings, and disengaging them from the ragged Remnants of the Cobweb. By this Time the *Spider* was adventured out, when beholding the Chasms, and Ruins, and Dilapidations of his Fortress, he was very near at his Wit's end, he stormed and swore like a Madman, and swelled until he was ready to burst. At length, casting his Eye upon the *Bee*, and wisely gathering Causes from Events, (for they knew each other by Sight) *A Plague split you*, said he, *for a giddy Son of a Whore; Is it you, with a Vengeance, that have made this Litter here? Could you not look before you, and be d—n'd? Do you think I have nothing else to do (in the Devil's Name) but to Mend and Repair after your Arse? Good Words, Friend*, said the *Bee* (having pruned himself, and being disposed to drole), *I'll give you my Hand and Word to come near your Kennel no more; I was never in such a confounded Pickle since I was born. Sirrah*, replied the *Spider*, *if it were not for breaking an old Custom in our Family, never to stir abroad against an Enemy, I should come and teach you better Manners. I pray, have Patience*, said the *Bee*, *or you will spend your Substance, and for ought I see, you may stand in need of it all, towards the Repair of your House. Rogue, Rogue*, replied the *Spider, yet, methinks, you should have more Respect to a Person, whom all the World allows to be so much your Betters. By my Troth*, said the *Bee, the Comparison will amount to a very good Jest, and you will do me a Favour, to let me know the Reason, that all the World is pleased to use in so hopeful a Dispute.* At this, the *Spider* having swelled himself into the Size and Posture of a Disputant, began his Argument in the true Spirit of Controversy, with a

Resolution to be heartily scurrilous and angry, to urge *on* his own Reasons, without the least Regard to the Answers or Objections of his Opposite; and fully predetermined in his Mind against all Conviction.

Not to disparage myself, said he, *by the Comparison with such a Rascal; What art thou but a Vagabond, without House or Home, without Stock or Inheritance? Born to no Possession of your own, but a Pair of Wings, and a Drone-Pipe. Your Livelihood is an universal Plunder upon Nature; a Freebooter over Fields and Gardens; and for the sake of Stealing, will rob a Nettle as readily as a Violet. Whereas I am a domestick Animal, furnished with a Native Stock within my self. This large Castle (to show my Improvements in the Mathematicks) is all built with my own Hand, and the Materials extracted altogether out of my own Person.*

I am glad, answered the Bee, *to hear you grant, at least, that I am come honestly by my Wings and my Voice; for then, it seems, I am obliged to Heaven alone for my Flights and my Musick; and Providence would never have bestowed on me two such Gifts, without designing them for the noblest Ends. I visit, indeed, all the Flowers and Blossoms of the Field and the Garden; but whatever I collect from thence, enriches my self, without the least Injury to their Beauty, their Smell, or their Taste. Now, for you and your skill in Architecture, and other Mathematicks, I have little to say: In that Building of yours, there might, for ought I know, have been Labor and Method enough, but by woful Experience for us both, 'tis too plain, the Materials are nought, and I hope, you will henceforth take Warning, and consider Duration and Matter, as well as Method and Art. You boast, indeed, of being obliged to no other Creature, but of drawing and spinning out all from your self; that is to say, if we may judge of the Liquor in the Vessel by what issues out, You possess a good plentiful Store of Dirt and Poison in your Breast; And, although I would by no means lessen or disparage your genuine Stock of either, yet I doubt you are somewhat obliged for an Increase of both to a little foreign Assistance. Your inherent Portion of Dirt does not fail of Acquisitions, by Sweepings exhaled from below: and one Insect furnishes you with a share of Poison to destroy another. So that, in short, the*

Question comes all to this, Whether is the nobler Being of the two, That, which by a lazy Contemplation of four Inches round, by an overweening Pride, which feeding and engendering on itself, turns all into Excrement and Venom, producing nothing at all, but Flybane and a Cobweb: or That, by an universal Range, with long Search, much Study, true Judgment, and Distinction of Things, brings home Honey and Wax.

This Dispute was managed with such Eagerness, Clamour, and Warmth, that the two Parties of *Books* in Arms below stood Silent a while, waiting in Suspense what would be the Issue; which was not long undetermined: For the *Bee*, grown impatient at so much loss of Time, fled strait away to a Bed of Roses, without looking for a Reply; and left the *Spider*, like an Orator, *collected* in himself, and just prepared to burst out.

It happened upon this Emergency, that *Æsop* broke Silence first. He had been of late most barbarously treated by a strange Effect of the *Regent's Humanity*, who had tore off his Title-page, sorely defaced one half of his Leaves, and chained him fast among a Shelf of *Moderns;* where soon discovering how high the Quarrel was like to proceed, He tried all his Arts, and turned himself to a thousand Forms: At length in the borrowed Shape of an *Ass,* the *Regent* mistook him for a *Modern;* by which means, he had Time and Opportunity to escape to the Antients, just when the *Spider* and the *Bee* were entering into their Contest; to which he gave His Attention with a World of Pleasure; and when it was ended, swore in the loudest Key, that in all his Life he had never known two Cases so parallel and adapt to each other, as That in the Window, and this upon the Shelves. The *Disputants,* said he, *have admirably managed the Dispute between them, have taken in the full Strength of all that is to be said on both sides, and exhausted the Substance of every Argument pro and con. It is but to adjust the Reasonings of both to the present Quarrel, then to compare and apply the Labors and Fruits of each, as the* Bee *has learnedly deduced them, and we shall find the Conclusion fall plain and close upon the* Moderns *and Us. For, pray, Gentlemen, was ever any Thing so* Modern *as the* Spider *in his Air, his Turns, and his Paradoxes? He argues in the Behalf of* You *his Brethren, and Himself, with many Boastings of his native Stock, and great Genius; that he spins and spits wholly from himself, and scorns to own any Obligation or Assistance from without. Then he displays to you his great Skill in Architecture, and Improvement in the Mathematicks. To all this, the* Bee, *as an Advocate, retained by us the* Antients, *thinks fit to Answer, That if one may judge of the great* Genius *or Inventions of the* Moderns, *by what they have produced, you will hardly have Countenance to bear you out in boasting of either. Erect your Schemes with as much Method and Skill as you please; yet, if the materials be nothing but Dirt, spun out of your own Entrails (the* Guts *of Modern* Brains) *the Edifice will conclude at last in a* Cobweb: *the Duration of which, like that of other* Spiders Webs, *may be imputed to their being forgotten, or neglected, or hid in a Corner. For any Thing else of Genuine, that the* Moderns *may pretend to, I cannot recollect; unless it be a large* Vein *of Wrangling and Satyr, much of a Nature and Substance with the* Spider's *Poison; which, however, they pretend to spit wholly out of themselves, is improved by the same Arts, by feeding upon the* Insects *and* Vermin *of the Age. As for Us, the* Antients, *We are content with the* Bee, *to pretend to Nothing of our own, beyond our* Wings *and our* Voice: *that is to say, our* Flights *and our* Language; *For the rest, whatever we have got has been by infinite Labour, and Search, and ranging through every Corner of Nature: The Difference is, that instead of* Dirt *and* Poison, *we have rather chose to fill our Hives with* Honey *and* Wax, *thus furnishing Mankind with the two Noblest of Things, which are* Sweetness *and* Light. . . .

ON THE CORRUPTION OF
THE ENGLISH TONGUE

(Tatler *CCXXX, Sept. 28, 1710*)

THE FOLLOWING LETTER hath laid before me many great and manifest Evils, in the World of Letters, which I had overlooked; but they open to me a very busy Scene, and it will require no small Care and Application to amend Errors which are become so universal. The Affectation of Politeness is exposed in this Epistle with a great deal of Wit and Discernment; so that, what-

ever Discourses I may fall into hereafter upon the Subjects the
Writer treateth of, I shall at present lay the Matter before the
World, without the least Alteration from the Words of my Cor-
respondent.

To ISAAC BICKERSTAFF, *Esq.;* [1]

'SIR,

There are some Abuses among us of great Consequence, the
Reformation of which is properly your Province; although, as
far as I have been conversant in your Papers you have not yet
considered them. These are the deplorable Ignorance that for
some Years hath reigned among our *English* Writers; the great
Depravity of our Taste; and the continual Corruption of our
Style. I say nothing here of those who handle particular Sciences,
Divinity, Law, Physick, and the like; I mean the Traders in
History and Politicks, and the *Belles Lettres;* together with those
by whom Books are not translated, but (as the common Expressions are) *Done out of French, Latin,* or other Language, and
made English. I cannot but observe to you, that until of later
Years, a *Grub-street* Book was always bound in Sheep-skin, with
suitable Print and Paper; the Price never above a Shilling; and
taken off wholly by common Tradesmen, or Country Pedlars. But
now they appear in all Sizes and Shapes, and in all Places: They
are handed about from Lapfulls in every Coffee-house to Persons of Quality; are shewn in *Westminster-Hall,* and the *Court
of Requests.* You may see them gilt, and in Royal Paper of five
or six Hundred Pages, and rated accordingly. I would engage
to furnish you with a Catalogue of *English* Books published
within the Compass of seven Years past, which at the first Hand
would cost you an Hundred Pounds; wherein you shall not be
able to find ten Lines together of common Grammar or common
Sense.

These two Evils, Ignorance and want of Taste, have produced
a Third; I mean a continual Corruption of our *English* Tongue;
which, without some timely Remedy, will suffer more by the false
Refinements of Twenty Years past, than it hath been improved in

---

[1] A pseudonym used by Swift in his attack on John Partridge, an almanac-
maker, in 1708. The name was later adopted by Steele for other *Tatler*
papers.

the foregoing Hundred. And this is what I design chiefly to enlarge upon; leaving the former Evils to your Animadversion.

But, instead of giving you a List of the late Refinements crept
into our Language; I here send you the Copy of a Letter I re-
ceived some Time ago from a most accomplished Person in this
Way of Writing; upon which I shall make some Remarks.
It is in these Terms:
"Sir,

I Cou'dn't *get the Things you sent for all* about Town—*I* tho't
to ha' *come down myself, and then* I'd ha' bro't 'um: *but* I ha'n't
don't, *and I believe* I can't do't, that's pozz—Tom *begins to*
gi'mself *Airs, because* he's *going with the* Plenipo's.—'Tis *said
the* French *King will* bambozzel *us* agen, *which* causes many
Speculations. *The* Jacks, *and others of that* Kidney, *are very*
uppish, *and* alert upon't, *as you may see by their* Phizz's.—Will
Hazard *has got the* Hipps, *having lost* to the Tune *of five* Hundr'd
Pound, tho' *he understands Play very well,* no Body better. *He
has* promis't *me upon* Rep, *to leave off Play; but you know* 'tis
a Weakness he's *apt to* give into, tho' *he has as·much Wit as
any Man, no body more. He has lain* incog *ever since*—*The* Mob's
very quiet with us now—*I believe you* tho't *I* banter'd *you in
my last like a* Country Put.—*I* shan't *leave Town this Month,*
etc."

This Letter is in every Point an admirable Pattern of the
present polite Way of Writing; nor is it of less Authority for being an Epistle: You may gather every Flower of it, with a Thousand more of equal Sweetness, from the Books, Pamphlets, and
single Papers, offered us every Day in the Coffee-houses: And
these are the Beauties introduced to supply the Want of Wit,
Sense, Humour, and Learning; which formerly were looked upon
as Qualifications for a Writer. If a Man of Wit, who died Forty
Years ago, were to rise from the Grave on Purpose; how would
he be able to read this Letter? and after he had got through that
Difficulty, how would he be able to understand it? The first
Thing that strikes your Eye, is the *Breaks* at the End of almost
every Sentence; of which I know not the Use, only that it is a
Refinement, and very frequently practised. Then you will observe the Abbreviations and Elisions, by which Consonants of
most obdurate Sound are joined together, without one softening

Vowel to intervene: And all this only to make one Syllable of two, directly contrary to the Example of the *Greeks* and *Romans;* altogether of the *Gothick* Strain, and a natural Tendency towards relapsing into Barbarity, which delighteth in Monosyllables, and uniting of mute Consonants; as it is observable in all the *Northern* Languages. And this is still more visible in the next Refinement, which consisteth in pronouncing the first Syllable in a Word that hath many, and dismissing the rest; such as *Phizz, Hipps, Mobb, Pozz, Rep,* and many more; when we are already over-loaded with Monosyllables, which are the Disgrace of our Language. Thus we cram one Syllable, and cut off the rest; as the Owl fattened her Mice after she had bit off their Legs, to prevent them from running away; and if ours be the same Reason for maiming of Words, it will certainly answer the End, for I am sure no other Nation will desire to borrow them. Some Words are hitherto but fairly split; and therefore only in their Way to Perfection; as *Incog.* and *Plenipo's:* But in a short Time, it is to be hoped, they will be further docked to *Inc* and *Plen.* This Reflection had made me, of late Years, very impatient for a Peace; which, I believe, would save the Lives of many brave Words, as well as Men. The War hath introduced abundance of Polysyllables, which will never be able to live many more Campaigns. *Speculations, Operations, Preliminaries, Ambassadors, Pallisadoes, Communication, Circumvallation, Battallions,* as numerous as they are, if they attack us too frequently in our Coffee-houses, we shall certainly put them to Flight, and cut off the Rear.

The third Refinement observable in the Letter I send you, consisteth in the Choice of certain Words, invented by some *pretty Fellows,* such as *Banter, Bamboozle, Country Put,* and *Kidney,* as it is there applied; some of which are now struggling for the Vogue, and others are in Possession of it. I have done my utmost for some Years past, to stop the Progress of *Mob* and *Banter;* but have been plainly born down by Numbers, and betrayed by those who promised to assist me.

In the last Place, you are to take Notice of certain choice Phrases scattered through the Letter; some of them tolerable enough, till they were worn to Rags by servile Imitators. You might easily find them, although they were not in a different Print; and therefore I need not disturb them.

These are the false Refinements in our Style, which you ought
to correct: First, by Arguments and fair Means; but if those fail,
I think you are to make Use of your Authority as Censor, and by
an annual *Index Expurgatorius,* expunge all Words and Phrases
that are offensive to good Sense, and condemn those barbarous
Mutilations of Vowels and Syllables. In this last Point, the usual
Pretence is, that they spell as they speak: A noble Standard for
Language! To depend upon the Caprice of every Coxcomb; who,
because Words are the Cloathing of our Thoughts, cuts them
out, and shapes them as he pleases, and changes them oftner
than his Dress. I believe, all reasonable People would be content, that such Refiners were more sparing of their Words, and
liberal in their Syllables. On this Head, I should be glad you
would bestow some Advice upon several young Readers in our
Churches; who coming up from the University, full fraught with
Admiration of our Town Politeness, will needs correct the Style
of their Prayer-Books. In reading the Absolution they are very
careful to say *Pardons* and *Absolves;* and in the Prayer for the
Royal Family, it must be *endu'm, enrich'um, prosper'um,* and
bring'um. Then, in their Sermons they use all the modern Terms
of Art; *Sham, Banter, Mob, Bubble, Bully, Cutting, Shuffling,*
and *Palming:* All which, and many more of the like Stamp, as I
have heard them often in the Pulpit from some young Sophisters;
so I have read them in some of *those Sermons that have made a
great Noise of late.* The Design, it seemeth, is to avoid the dreadful Imputation of Pedantry; to shew us, that they *know the
Town, understand Men and Manners,* and have not been poring
upon old unfashionable Books in the University.

I should be glad to see you the Instrument of introducing into
our Style that Simplicity which is the best and truest Ornament
of most Things in human Life, which the politer Ages always
aimed at in their Building and Dress, *(Simplex munditiis)* as well
as their Productions of Wit. It is manifest, that all new affected
Modes of Speech, whether borrowed from the Court, the Town,
or the Theatre, are the first perishing Parts in any Language;
and, as I could prove by many Hundred Instances, have been
so in ours. The Writings of *Hooker,* who was a Country Clergyman, and of *Parsons* the Jesuit, both in the Reign of Queen *Elizabeth;* are in a Style that, with very few Allowances, would not

offend any present Reader; much more clear and intelligible than those of Sir *H. Wooton,* Sir *Robert Naunton, Osburn, Daniel* the Historian, and several others who writ later; but being Men of the Court, and affecting the Phrases then in Fashion; they are often either not to be understood, or appear perfectly ridiculous.

What Remedies are to be applied to these Evils I have not Room to consider; having, I fear, already taken up most of your Paper. Besides, I think it is our Office only to represent Abuses, and yours to redress them.

> *I am, with great Respect,*
> SIR,
> *Yours, etc.'*

Alexander Pope

[1688–1744]

UNLIKE HIS CONTEMPORARIES, Swift and Addison, Pope had no career outside literature. His Roman Catholicism excluded him from public office, and ill-health from the ordinary activities of life. Poetry, which was his only serious interest, was also his livelihood. His poetic career began with the *Pastorals,* written, according to Pope, when he was 16. The *Essay on Criticism,* published in 1711, won him the admiration of Addison; he later became the friend of Swift and Gay, and moved in fashionable literary and social circles. The success of Pope's translations of Homer (*Iliad,* 1715–20; *Odyssey,* 1725–6) made him famous and financially independent.

Pope's "Discourse on Pastoral Poetry," the preface to his *Pastorals* (1709), is another phase of the Ancients-Moderns quarrel. Pope, a thorough-going Ancient, takes Virgil as his model, and sees the pastoral as "an image of . . . the golden age"; the Moderns argued for an adaptation of the form to differences of habits, customs, and climate—in other words, for an element of realism. At issue are both the authority of the Ancients, and the meaning of "imitation."

Another instance of "imitation" is Pope's *Essay on Criticism,* an example of a traditional genre, the critical essay in verse. Horace's *Ars Poetica* provided the classical model, and there were many seventeenth-century imitations of it. In substance Pope's *Essay* is composed largely of the critical commonplaces of neo-classical theory—the authority of the Ancients, the rightness of the Rules, the importance of judgment, common sense, and wit—drawn from a wide variety of sources. In his reverent eclecticism Pope is, of course, simply advocating one of the basic neo-classical principles which is that the rules of art, being founded on the universal truths of natural order and human nature, will be true from age to age, and can therefore be discovered either in Nature directly, or in Art ("Nature methodized"). Pope is not, however, arguing for slavish imitation; rules without talent are worthless: "Some beauties yet no precepts can declare,/ For there's a happiness as well as care."

Though it contains a comprehensive summary of neo-classical premises, the *Essay* also offers shrewd technical advice to both critics and poets, and one of its original aspects is the attention it gives to the art of criticism. It is also, of course, an example of what it teaches— a brilliant neo-classical poem.

BIBLIOGRAPHY. *Poems,* the Twickenham Edition, ed. John Butt and others, 6 vols. (London and New Haven, 1940–61); *Prose Works,* ed. Norman Ault (Oxford, 1936).
  J. E. Congleton, *Theories of Pastoral Poetry in England, 1684–1798* (Gainesville, Fla., 1952); Geoffrey Tillotson, *On the Poetry of Pope* (London, 1938) and *Pope and Human Nature* (Oxford, 1958); Austin Warren, *Alexander Pope as Critic and Humanist* (Princeton, 1929).

TEXT. *Works,* ed. Warburton (9 vols., London, 1751), vol. I. (I have omitted those notes by Pope which merely cite classical parallels to his remarks, and also a number of Warburton's.)

A DISCOURSE ON PASTORAL POETRY [1]

[1709]

THERE are not, I believe, a greater number of any sort of verses than of those which are called Pastorals; nor a smaller, than of those which are truly so. It therefore seems necessary to give some account of this kind of Poem, and it is my design to comprize in this short paper the substance of those numerous dissertations the Critics have made on the subject, without omitting any of their rules in my own favour. You will also find some points reconciled, about which they seem to differ, and a few remarks, which, I think, have escaped their observation.
  The original of Poetry is ascribed to that Age which succeeded the creation of the world: and as the keeping of flocks seems to have been the first employment of mankind, the most ancient sort of poetry was probably *pastoral*. It is natural to imagine, that the leisure of those ancient shepherds admitting and inviting

---

[1] Written at sixteen years of age. [Pope's note].

some diversion, none was so proper to that solitary and sedentary life as singing; and that in their songs they took occasion to celebrate their own felicity. From hence a Poem was invented, and afterwards improved to a perfect image of that happy time; which by giving us an esteem for the virtues of a former age, might recommend them to the present. And since the life of shepherds was attended with more tranquillity than any other rural employment, the Poets chose to introduce their Persons, from whom it received the name of Pastoral.

A Pastoral is an imitation of the action of a shepherd, or one considered under that character. The form of this imitation is dramatic, or narrative, or mixed of both; the fable simple, the manners not too polite nor too rustic: the thoughts are plain, yet admit a little quickness and passion, but that short and flowing: the expression humble, yet as pure as the language will afford; neat, but not florid; easy, and yet lively. In short, the fable, manners, thoughts, and expressions are full of the greatest simplicity in nature.

The complete character of this poem consists in simplicity, brevity, and delicacy; the two first of which render an eclogue natural, and the last delightful.

If we would copy Nature, it may be useful to take this Idea along with us, that Pastoral is an image of what they call the golden age. So that we are not to describe our shepherds as shepherds at this day really are, but as they may be conceived then to have been; when the best of men followed the employment. To carry this resemblance yet farther, it would not be amiss to give these shepherds some skill in astronomy, as far as it may be useful to that sort of life. And an air of piety to the Gods should shine through the Poem, which so visibly appears in all the works of antiquity: and it ought to preserve some relish of the old way of writing; the connection should be loose, the narrations and descriptions short, and the periods concise. Yet it is not sufficient, that the sentences only be brief, the whole Eclogue should be so too. For we cannot suppose Poetry in those days to have been the business of men, but their recreation at vacant hours.

But with a respect to the present age, nothing more conduces to make these composures natural, than when some Knowledge in rural affairs is discovered. This may be made to appear rather done by chance than on design, and sometimes is best shewn by inference; lest by too much study to seem natural, we destroy that easy simplicity from whence arises the delight. For what is inviting in this sort of poetry proceeds not so much from the Idea of that business, as of the tranquility of a country life.

We must therefore use some illusion to render a Pastoral delightful; and this consists in exposing the best side only of a shepherd's life, and in concealing its miseries. Nor is it enough to introduce shepherds discoursing together in a natural way; but a regard must be had to the subject; that it contain some particular beauty in itself, and that it be different in every Eclogue. Besides, in each of them a designed scene or prospect is to be presented to our view, which should likewise have its variety. This variety is obtain'd in a great degree by frequent comparisons, drawn from the most agreeable objects of the country; by interrogations to things inanimate; by beautiful digressions, but those short; sometimes by insisting a little on circumstances; and lastly, by elegant turns on the words, which render the numbers extremely sweet and pleasing. As for the numbers themselves, though they are properly of the heroic measure, they should be the smoothest, the most easy and flowing imaginable.

It is by rules like these that we ought to judge of Pastoral. And since the instructions given for any art are to be delivered as that art is in perfection, they must of necessity be derived from those in whom it is acknowledged so to be. It is therefore from the practice of Theocritus and Virgil (the only undisputed authors of Pastoral) that the Critics have drawn the foregoing notions concerning it.

Theocritus excels all others in nature and simplicity. The subjects of his Idyllia are purely pastoral; but he is not so exact in his persons, having introduced reapers and fishermen as well as shepherds. He is apt to be too long in his descriptions, of which that of the Cup in the first pastoral is a remarkable instance. In the manners he seems a little defective, for his swains are sometimes abusive and immodest, and perhaps too much inclining to rusticity; for instance, in his fourth and fifth Idyllia. But 'tis enough that all others learnt their excellencies from him, and that his Dialect alone has a secret charm in it, which no other could ever attain.

Virgil, who copies Theocritus, refines upon his original: and in all points where judgment is principally concerned, he is much superior to his master. Though some of his subjects are not pastoral in themselves, but only seem to be such; they have a wonderful variety in them, which the Greek was a stranger to. He exceeds him in regularity and brevity, and falls short of him in nothing but simplicity and propriety of style; the first of which perhaps was the fault of his age, and the last of his language.

Among the moderns, their success has been greatest who have most endeavoured to make these ancients their pattern. The most considerable Genius appears in the famous Tasso, and our Spenser. Tasso in his Aminta has as far excelled all the Pastoral writers, as in his Gierusalemme he has outdone the Epic poets of his country. But as this piece seems to have been the original of a new sort of poem, the Pastoral Comedy, in Italy, it cannot so well be considered as a copy of the ancients. Spenser's Calendar, in Mr. Dryden's opinion, is the most complete work of this kind which any nation has produced ever since the time of Virgil. Not but that he may be thought imperfect in some few points. His Eclogues are somewhat too long, if we compare them with the ancients. He is sometimes too allegorical, and treats of matters of religion in a pastoral style, as Mantuan had done before him. He has employed the Lyric measure, which is contrary to the practice of the old Poets. His Stanza is not still the same, nor always well chosen. This last may be the reason his expression is sometimes not concise enough: for the Tetrastic has obliged him to extend his sense to the length of four lines, which would have been more closely confined in the Couplet.

In the manners, thoughts, and characters, he comes near to Theocritus himself; tho', nothwithstanding all the care he has taken, he is certainly inferior in his Dialect: For the Doric had its beauty and propriety in the time of Theocritus; it was used in part of Greece, and frequent in the mouths of many of the greatest persons: whereas the old English and country phrases of Spenser were either entirely obsolete, or spoken only by people of the lowest condition. As there is a difference betwixt simplicity and rusticity, so the expression of simple thoughts should be plain, but not clownish. The addition he has made of a Calendar to his Eclogues, is very beautiful; since by this, besides the general moral of innocence and simplicity, which is common to other authors of Pastoral, he has one peculiar to himself; he compares human Life to the several Seasons, and at once exposes to his readers a view of the great and little worlds, in their various changes and aspects. Yet the scrupulous division of his Pastorals into Months, has obliged him either to repeat the same description, in other words, for three months together; or, when it was exhausted before, entirely to omit it: whence it comes to pass that some of his Eclogues (as the sixth, eighth, and tenth for example) have nothing but their Titles to distinguish them. The reason is evident, because the year has not that variety in it to furnish every month with a particular description, as it may every season.

Of the following Eclogues I shall only say, that these four comprehend all the subjects which the Critics upon Theocritus and Virgil will allow to be fit for pastoral: That they have as much variety of description, in respect of the several seasons, as Spenser's: that in order to add to this variety, the several times of the day are observed, the rural employments in each season or time of day, and the rural scenes or places proper to such employments; not without some regard to the several ages of man, and the different passions proper to each age.

But after all, if they have any merit, it is to be attributed to some good old Authors, whose works as I had leisure to study, so I hope I have not wanted care to imitate.

AN ESSAY ON CRITICISM

[1711]

PART I

Introduction. That 'tis as great a fault to judge ill, as to write ill, and a more dangerous one to the public, v. 1.

That a *true Taste* is as rare to be found, as a *true Genius,* v. 9–18.

That most men are born with some Taste, but spoil'd by false *Education,* v. 19–25.

The multitude of *Critics,* and causes of them, v. 26–45.

'TIS HARD TO SAY, if greater want of skill
Appear in writing or in judging ill;
But, of the two, less dang'rous is th' offence
To tire our patience, than mislead our sense.
Some few in that, but numbers err in this,   5
Ten censure wrong, for one who writes amiss;
A fool might once himself alone expose,
Now one in verse makes many more in prose.
   'Tis with our judgments as our watches, none
Go just alike, yet each believes his own.   10
In Poets as true genius is but rare,
True Taste as seldom is the Critic's share;
Both must alike from Heaven derive their light,
These born to judge, as well as those to write.
Let such teach others who themselves excel,   15
And censure freely who have written well.
Authors are partial to their wit, 'tis true,
But are not Critics to their judgment too?
   Yet if we look more closely, we shall find
Most have the seeds of judgment in their mind: 20
Nature affords at least a glimm'ring light;
The lines, tho' touched but faintly, are drawn right.
But as the slightest sketch, if justly trac'd,
Is by ill colouring but the more disgrac'd,
So by false learning is good sense defac'd: 25
Some are bewilder'd in the maze of schools,
And some made coxcombs Nature meant but fools.
In search of wit these lose their common sense,
And then turn Critics in their own defence:

Each burns alike, who can, or cannot write,   30
Or with a Rival's, or an Eunuch's spite.
All fools have still an itching to deride,
And fain would be upon the laughing side.
If Mævius scribble in Apollo's spite,
There are, who judge still worse than he can write.   35
   Some have at first for Wits, then Poets past,
Turn'd Critics next, and prov'd plain fools at last
Some neither can for Wits nor Critics pass,
As heavy mules are neither horse nor ass.
Those half-learn'd witlings, num'rous in our isle,   40
As half-form'd insects on the banks of Nile;
Unfinish'd things, one knows not what to call,
Their generation's so equivocal:
To tell 'em, would a hundred tongues require,
Or one vain wit's, that might a hundred tire.   45
   But you who seek to give and merit fame,
And justly bear a Critic's noble name,
Be sure yourself and your own reach to know,
How far your genius, taste, and learning go;
Launch not beyond your depth, but be discreet,   50
And mark that point where sense and dulness meet.
   Nature to all things fix'd the limits fit,
And wisely curbed proud man's pretending wit.
As on the land while here the ocean gains,
In other parts it leaves wide sandy plains;   55
Thus in the soul while memory prevails,
The solid pow'r of understanding fails;
Where beams of warm imagination play,
The memory's soft figures melt away.
One science only will one genius fit;   60
So vast is art, so narrow human wit:
Not only bounded to peculiar arts,
But oft' in those confin'd to single parts.
Like Kings we lose the conquests gain'd before,
By vain ambition still to make them more;   65
Each might his sev'ral province well command,
Would all but stoop to what they understand.
   First follow Nature, and your judgment frame

By her just standard, which is still the same:
Unerring NATURE, still divinely bright,   70
One clear, unchang'd, and universal light,
Life, force, and beauty, must to all impart,
At once the source, and end, and test of Art.
Art from that fund each just supply provides,
Works without show, and without pomp presides: 75
In some fair body thus th' informing soul
With spirits feeds, with vigour fills the whole,
Each motion guides, and ev'ry nerve sustains;
Itself unseen, but in th' effects, remains.
Some, to whom Heav'n in wit has been profuse,   80
Want as much more to turn it to its use;
For wit and judgment often are at strife,
Tho' meant each other's aid, like man and wife.
'Tis more to guide, than spur the Muse's steed;
Restrain his fury, than provoke his speed;   85
The wingèd courser, like a gen'rous horse,
Shows most true mettle when you check his course.
    Those RULES of old discovered, not devis'd,
Are Nature still, but Nature methodiz'd;
Nature, like Liberty, is but restrain'd   90
By the same Laws which first herself ordain'd.
    Hear how learn'd Greece her useful rules indites,
When to repress, and when indulge our flights:
High on Parnassus' top her sons she show'd,
And pointed out those arduous paths they trod;   95
Held from afar, aloft, th' immortal prize,
And urg'd the rest by equal steps to rise.
Just precepts thus from great examples giv'n,
She drew from them what they deriv'd from Heaven.
The generous Critic fann'd the Poet's fire,   100
And taught the world with reason to admire.
Then Criticism the Muses' handmaid prov'd,
To dress her charms, and make her more belov'd:
But following wits from that intention stray'd,
Who cou'd not win the mistress, wooed the maid;   105
Against the Poets their own arms they turn'd,
Sure to hate most the men from whom they learn'd.

So modern 'Pothecaries, taught the art
By Doctor's bills to play the Doctor's part,
Bold in the practice of mistaken rules,   110
Prescribe, apply, and call their masters fools.
Some on the leaves of ancient authors prey,
Nor time nor moths e'er spoil'd so much as they.
Some drily plain, without invention's aid,
Write dull receipts how poems may be made.   115
These leave the sense, their learning to display,
And those explain the meaning quite away.
   You then whose judgment the right course would steer,
Know well each ANCIENT's proper character;
His Fable, Subject, scope in ev'y page;   120
Religion, Country, genius of his Age:
Without all these at once before your eyes,
Cavil you may, but never criticize.
Be Homer's works your study and delight,
Read them by day, and meditate by night;   125
Thence form your judgment, thence your maxims bring,
And trace the Muses upward to their spring.
Still with itself compar'd, his text peruse;
And let your comment be the Mantuan Muse.
   When first young Maro in his boundless mind   130
A work t' outlast immortal Rome design'd,
Perhaps he seem'd above the Critic's law,
And but from Nature's fountains scorn'd to draw:
But when t' examine ev'ry part he came,
Nature and Homer were, he found, the same.   135
Convinc'd, amaz'd, he checks the bold design;
And rules as strict his labour'd work confine,
As if the Stagirite o'erlook'd each line.
Learn hence for ancient rules a just esteem;
To copy nature is to copy them.   140
   Some beauties yet no Precepts can declare,
For there's a happiness as well as care.
Music resembles Poetry, in each
Are nameless graces which no methods teach,
And which a master-hand alone can reach.   145
If, where the rules not far enough extend,

(Since rules were made but to promote their end)
Some lucky Licence answer to the full
Th' intent propos'd, that Licence is a rule.
Thus Pegasus, a nearer way to take,   150
May boldly deviate from the common track;
From vulgar bounds with brave disorder part,
And snatch a grace beyond the reach of art,
Which without passing thro' the judgment, gains
The heart, and all its end at once attains.   155
In prospects thus, some objects please our eyes,
Which out of nature's common order rise,
The shapeless rock, or hanging precipice.
Great Wits sometimes may gloriously offend,
And rise to faults true Critics dare not mend.   160
But tho' the Ancients thus their rules invade,
(As Kings dispense with laws themselves have made)
Moderns, beware! or if you must offend
Against the precept, ne'er transgress its End;
Let it be seldom, and compell'd by need;   165
And have, at least, their precedent to plead.
The Critic else proceeds without remorse,
Seizes your fame, and puts his laws in force.
    I know there are, to whose presumptuous thoughts
Those freer beauties, ev'n in them, seem faults.   170
Some figures monstrous and mis-shap'd appear,
Consider'd singly, or beheld too near,
Which, but proportion'd to their light, or place,
Due distance reconciles to form and grace.
A prudent chief not always must display   175
His pow'rs in equal ranks, and fair array,
But with th' occasion and the place comply,
Conceal his force, nay seem sometimes to fly.
Those oft are stratagems which error seem,
Nor is it Homer nods, but we that dream.   180
    Still green with bays each ancient Altar stands,
Above the reach of sacrilegious hands;
Secure from Flames, from Envy's fiercer rage,
Destructive War, and all-involving Age.
See, from each clime the learn'd their incense bring!   185

Hear, in all tongues consenting Pæans ring!
In praise so just let ev'ry voice be joined,
And fill the gen'ral chorus of mankind.
Hail, Bards triumphant! born in happier days;   190
Immortal heirs of universal praise!
Whose honours with increase of ages grow,
As streams roll down, enlarging as they flow;
Nations unborn your mighty names shall sound,
And worlds applaud that must not yet be found!   195
Oh may some spark of your celestial fire,
The last, the meanest of your sons inspire,
(That on weak wings, from far, pursues your flights;
Glows while he reads, but trembles as he writes)
To teach vain Wits a science little known,
T' admire superior sense, and doubt their own!   200

PART II

Causes hindering a *true Judgment.* 1. *Pride,* v. 201. 2. *Imperfect
Learning,* v. 215. 3. Judging by *parts,* and not by the whole, v. 233–
288. Critics in *Wit, Language, Versification,* only, v. 288, 305, 339 ff.
4. Being too hard to please, or too apt to admire, v. 384. 5. *Partiality—*
too much Love to a *Sect,*—to the *Ancients* or *Moderns,* v. 394. 6.
Prejudice or *Prevention,* v. 408. 7. *Singularity,* v. 424. 8. *Inconstancy,*
v. 430. 9. *Party Spirit,* v. 452 ff. 10. *Envy,* v. 466. Against Envy, and
in praise of Good Nature, v. 508 ff. When Severity is chiefly to be used
by Critics, v. 526 ff.

Of all the Causes which conspire to blind
Man's erring judgment, and misguide the mind,
What the weak head with strongest bias rules,
Is *Pride,* the never-failing vice of fools.
Whatever Nature has in worth deny'd,   205
She gives in large recruits of needful Pride;
For as in bodies, thus in souls, we find
What wants in blood and spirits, swell'd with wind:
Pride, where Wit fails, steps in to our defence,
And fills up all the mighty Void of sense.   210
If once right reason drives that cloud away,
Truth breaks upon us with resistless day.
Trust not yourself; but your defects to know,

Make use of ev'ry friend—and every foe.

A *little learning* is a dang'rous thing;   215
Drink deep, or taste not the Pierian spring:
There shallow draughts intoxicate the brain,
And drinking largely sobers us again.
Fir'd at first sight with what the Muse imparts,
In fearless youth we tempt the heights of Arts,   220
While from the bounded level of our mind,
Short views we take, nor see the lengths behind;
But more advanc'd, behold with strange surprise
New distant scenes of endless science rise!
So pleased at first the tow'ring Alps we try,   225
Mount o'er the vales, and seem to tread the sky,
Th' eternal snows appear already past,
And the first clouds and mountains seem the last;
But, those attain'd, we tremble to survey
The growing labours of the lengthen'd way,   230
Th' increasing prospect tires our wand'ring eyes,
Hills peep o'er hills, and Alps on Alps arise!

A perfect Judge will read each work of Wit
With the same spirit that its author writ:
Survey the Whole, nor seek slight faults to find   235
Where nature moves, and rapture warms the mind;
Nor lose, for that malignant dull delight,
The gen'rous pleasure to be charmed with wit.
But in such lays as neither ebb, nor flow,
Correctly cold, and regularly low,   240
That shunning faults, one quiet tenour keep;
We cannot blame indeed——but we may sleep.
In Wit, as Nature, what affects our hearts
Is not th' exactness of peculiar parts;
'Tis not a lip, or eye, we beauty call,   245
But the joint force and full result of all.
Thus when we view some well-proportion'd dome,
(The world's just wonder, and ev'n thine, O Rome!)
No single parts unequally surprize,
All comes united to th' admiring eyes;   250
No monstrous height, or breadth, or length appear;

The Whole at once is bold, and regular.
  Whoever thinks a faultless piece to see,
Thinks what ne'er was, nor is, nor e'er shall be.
In every work regard the writer's End, 255
Since none can compass more than they intend;
And if the means be just, the conduct true,
Applause, in spite of trivial faults, is due.
As men of breeding, sometimes men of wit,
T' avoid great errors, must the less commit: 260
Neglect the rules each verbal Critic lays,
For not to know some trifles, is a praise.
Most Critics, fond of some subservient art,
Still make the Whole depend upon a Part:
They talk of principles, but notions prize, 265
And all to one lov'd Folly sacrifice.
  Once on a time, La Mancha's Knight, they say,[1]
A certain Bard encountering on the way,
Discours'd in terms as just, with looks as sage,
As e'er could Dennis, of the Grecian stage; 270
Concluding all were desp'rate sots and fools,
Who durst depart from Aristotle's rules.
Our Author, happy in a judge so nice,
Produc'd his Play, and begg'd the Knight's advice;
Made him observe the subject, and the plot, 275
The manners, passions, unities; what not?
All which, exact to rule, were brought about,
Were but a Combat in the lists left out.
"What! leave the Combat out?" exclaims the Knight;
Yes, or we must renounce the Stagirite. 280
"Not so by Heaven" (he answers in a rage)
"Knights, squires, and steeds, must enter on the stage."
So vast a throng the stage can ne'er contain.
"Then build a new, or act it in a plain."
  Thus Critics, of less judgment than caprice, 285
Curious not knowing, not exact but nice,
Form short Ideas; and offend in arts

[1] A story taken by our Author from the *Spurious Don Quixote*. [Warburton's note.]

(As most in manners) by a love to parts.
　　Some to *Conceit* alone their taste confine,
And glitt'ring thoughts struck out at every line;   290
Pleas'd with a work where nothing's just or fit;
One glaring Chaos and wild heap of wit.
Poets like painters, thus, unskill'd to trace
The naked nature and the living grace,
With gold and jewels cover ev'ry part,   295
And hide with ornaments their want of art.
True Wit is Nature to advantage dress'd,
What oft was thought, but ne'er so well express'd;
Something, whose truth convinc'd at sight we find,
That gives us back the image of our mind.   300
As shades more sweetly recommend the light,
So modest plainness sets off sprightly wit.
For works may have more wit than does 'em good,
As bodies perish thro' excess of blood.
　　Others for *Language* all their care express,   305
And value books, as women men, for Dress:
Their praise is still,—the Style is excellent:
The Sense, they humbly take upon content.
Words are like leaves; and where they most abound,
Much fruit of sense beneath is rarely found.   310
False Eloquence, like the prismatic glass,
Its gaudy colours spreads on ev'ry place;
The face of Nature we no more survey,
All glares alike, without distinction gay:
But true Expression, like th' unchanging Sun,   315
Clears, and improves whate'er it shines upon,
It gilds all objects, but it alters none.
Expression is the dress of thought, and still
Appears more decent, as more suitable;
A vile conceit in pompous words express'd,   320
Is like a clown in regal purple dress'd:
For diff'rent styles with different subjects sort,
As several garbs with country, town, and court.
Some by old words to fame have made pretence,
Ancients in phrase, meer moderns in their sense;   325
Such labour'd nothings, in so strange a style,

Amaze th' unlearn'd, and make the learnèd smile.
Unlucky, as Fungoso in the Play,[2]
These sparks with aukward vanity display
What the fine gentleman wore yesterday;   330
And but so mimic ancient wits at best,
As apes our grandsires, in their doublets drest.
In words, as fashions, the same rule will hold;
Alike fantastick, if too new, or old:
Be not the first by whom the new are try'd,   335
Nor yet the last to lay the old aside.
   But most by Numbers judge a Poet's song;
And smooth or rough, with them is right or wrong:
In the bright Muse tho' thousand charms conspire,
Her Voice is all these tuneful fools admire;   340
Who haunt Parnassus but to please their ear,
Not mend their minds; as some to Church repair,
Not for the doctrine, but the music there.
These equal syllables alone require,
Tho' oft the ear the open vowels tire;   345
While expletives their feeble aid do join;
And ten low words oft creep in one dull line:
While they ring round the same unvary'd chimes,
With sure returns of still expected rhymes;
Where-e'er you find "the cooling western breeze,"   350
In the next line, it "whispers thro' the trees:"
If crystal streams "with pleasing murmurs creep,"
The reader's threaten'd (not in vain) with "sleep:"
Then, at the last and only couplet fraught
With some unmeaning thing they call a thought,   355
A needless Alexandrine ends the song,
That, like a wounded snake, drags its slow length along.
Leave such to tune their own dull rhymes, and know
What's roundly smooth, or languishingly slow;
And praise the easy vigour of a line,   360
Where Denham's strength, and Waller's sweetness join.
True ease in writing comes from art, not chance,
As those move easiest who have learn'd to dance.

---

[2] See Ben Johnson's *Every Man in his Humour.* [Pope's note. Pope has confused this play with *Every Man out of his Humour.*]

'Tis not enough no harshness gives offence,
The sound must seem an Echo to the sense: 365
Soft is the strain when Zephyr gently blows,
And the smooth stream in smoother numbers flows;
But when loud surges lash the sounding shoar,
The hoarse, rough verse should like the torrent roar:
When Ajax strives some rock's vast weight to throw,   370
The line too labours, and the words move slow;
Not so, when swift Camilla scours the plain,
Flies o'er th' unbending corn, and skims along the main.
Hear how Timotheus' varied lays surprize,[3]
And bid alternate passions fall and rise!   375
While, at each change, the son of Libyan Jove
Now burns with glory, and then melts with love;
Now his fierce eyes with sparkling fury glow,
Now sighs steal out, and tears begin to flow:
Persians and Greeks like turns of nature found,   380
And the World's victor stood subdued by Sound!
The pow'r of Music all our hearts allow,
And what Timotheus was, is DRYDEN now.
    Avoid Extremes; and shun the fault of such,
Who still are pleas'd too little or too much.   385
At ev'ry trifle scorn to take offence,
That always shows great pride, or little sense;
Those heads, as stomachs, are not sure the best,
Which nauseate all, and nothing can digest.
Yet let not each gay Turn thy rapture move;   390
For fools admire, but men of sense approve:
As things seem large which we tho' mists descry,
Dulness is ever apt to magnify.
    Some foreign writers, some our own despise;
The Ancients only, or the Moderns prize.   395
Thus Wit, like Faith, by each man is apply'd
To one small sect, and all are damn'd beside.
Meanly they seek the blessing to confine,
And force that sun but on a part to shine,
Which not alone the southern wit sublimes,   400

---

[3] See *Alexander's Feast,* or *the Power of Music:* an Ode by Mr. Dryden.
[Pope.]

But ripens spirits in cold northern climes;
Which from the first has shone on ages past,
Enlights the present, and shall warm the last;
Though each may feel encreases and decays,
And see now clearer and now darker days.   405
Regard not then if Wit be old or new,
But blame the false, and value still the true.
   Some ne'er advance a Judgment of their own,
But catch the spreading notion of the Town;
They reason and conclude by precedent,   410
And own stale nonsense which they ne'er invent.
Some judge of authors names, not works, and then
Nor praise nor blame the writings, but the men.
Of all this servile herd, the worst is he
That in proud dulness joins with Quality.   415
A constant Critic at the great man's board,
To fetch and carry nonsense for my Lord.
What woful stuff this madrigal would be,
In some starv'd hackney sonnetteer, or me?
But let a Lord once own the happy lines,   420
How the wit brightens! how the style refines!
Before his sacred name flies ev'ry fault,
And each exalted stanza teems with thought!
   The Vulgar thus thro' Imitation err;
As oft the Learn'd by being singular;   425
So much they scorn the crowd, that if the throng
By chance go right, they purposely go wrong:
So Schismatics the plain believers quit,
And are but damn'd for having too much wit.
Some praise at morning what they blame at night; 430
But always think the last opinion right.
A Muse by these is like a mistress us'd,
This hour she's idoliz'd, the next abus'd;
While their weak heads like towns unfortify'd,
Twixt sense and nonsense daily change their side. 435
Ask them the cause; they're wiser still, they say;
And still tomorrow's wiser than to-day.
We think our fathers fools, so wise we grow;
Our wiser sons, no doubt, will think us so.

Once School-divines this zealous isle o'er-spread;   440
Who knew most Sentences, was deepest read;
Faith, Gospel, all, seem'd made to be disputed,
And none had sense enough to be confuted:
Scotists and Thomists, now, in peace remain,
Amidst their kindred cobwebs in Duck Lane.[4]   445
If Faith itself has diff'rent dresses worn,
What wonder modes in Wit should take their turn?
Oft', leaving what is natural and fit,
The current folly proves the ready wit;
And authors think their reputation safe,   450
Which lives as long as fools are pleas'd to laugh.
  Some valuing those of their own side or mind,
Still make themselves the measure of mankind:
Fondly we think we honour merit then,
When we but praise ourselves in other men.   455
Parties in Wit attend on those of State,
And public faction doubles private hate.
Pride, Malice, Folly, against Dryden rose,
In various shapes of Parsons, Critics, Beaus;
But sense surviv'd, when merry jests were past;   460
For rising merit will buoy up at last.
Might he return, and bless once more our eyes,
New Blackmores and new Milbourns must arise:
Nay should great Homer lift his awful head,
Zoilus again would start up from the dead.   465
Envy will merit, as its shade, pursue;
But like a shadow, proves the substance true;
For envy'd Wit, like Sol eclips'd, makes known
Th' opposing body's grossness, not its own.
When first that sun too pow'rful beams displays,   470
It draws up vapours which obscure its rays;
But ev'n those clouds at last adorn its way,
Reflect new glories, and augment the day.
  Be thou the first true merit to befriend;
His praise is lost, who stays 'till all commend.   475
Short is the date, alas, of modern rhymes,

---

[4] A place where old and secondhand books were sold formerly, near Smithfield. [Pope.]

And 'tis but just to let them live betimes.
No longer now that golden age appears,
When Patriarch-wits survived a thousand years:
Now length of Fame (our second life) is lost,   480
And bare threescore is all ev'n that can boast;
Our sons their fathers' failing language see,
And such as Chaucer is, shall Dryden be.
So when the faithful pencil has design'd
Some bright Idea of the master's mind,   485
Where a new world leaps out at his command,
And ready Nature waits upon his hand;
When the ripe colours soften and unite,
And sweetly melt into just shade and light;
When mellowing years their full perfection give,   490
And each bold figure just begins to live,
The treach'rous colours the fair art betray,
And all the bright creation fades away!
    Unhappy Wit, like most mistaken things,
Atones not for that envy which it brings.   495
In youth alone its empty praise we boast,
But soon the short-liv'd vanity is lost:
Like some fair flow'r the early spring supplies,
That gaily blooms, but ev'n in blooming dies.
What is this Wit, which must our cares employ?   500
The owner's wife, that other men enjoy;
Then most our trouble still when most admir'd,
And still the more we give, the more requir'd;
Whose fame with pains we guard, but lose with ease,
Sure some to vex, but never all to please;   505
'Tis what the vicious fear, the virtuous shun,
By fools 'tis hated, and by knaves undone!
    If Wit so much from Ign'rance undergo,
Ah let not Learning too commence its foe!
Of old, those met rewards who could excell,   510
And such were prais'd who but endeavour'd well:
Tho' triumphs were to gen'rals only due,
Crowns were reserv'd to grace the soldiers too.
Now, they who reach Parnassus' lofty crown,
Employ their pains to spurn some others down;   515

And while self-love each jealous writer rules,
Contending wits become the sport of fools:
But still the worst with most regret commend,
For each ill Author is as bad a Friend.
To what base ends, and by what abject ways,   520
Are mortals urg'd thro' sacred lust of praise!
Ah ne'er so dire a thirst of glory boast,
Nor in the Critic let the Man be lost.
Good-nature and good-sense must ever join;
To err is human, to forgive, divine.   525
  But if in noble minds some dregs remain
Not yet purg'd off, of spleen and sour disdain;
Discharge that rage on more provoking crimes,
Nor fear a dearth in these flagitious times.
No pardon vile Obscenity should find,   530
Tho' wit and art conspire to move your mind;
But Dulness with Obscenity must prove
As shameful sure as Impotence in love.
In the fat age of pleasure, wealth and ease,
Sprung the rank weed, and thrived with large increase: 535
When love was all an easy Monarch's care;
Seldom at council, never in a war:
Jilts rul'd the state, and statesmen farces writ;
Nay wits had pensions, and young Lords had wit:
The Fair sate panting at a Courtier's play,   540
And not a Mask went unimprov'd away:
The modest fan was lifted up no more,
And Virgins smil'd at what they blush'd before.
The following licence of a Foreign reign
Did all the dregs of bold Socinus drain;   545
Then unbelieving Priests reform'd the nation,
And taught more pleasant methods of salvation;
Where Heav'n's free subjects might their rights dispute,
Lest God himself should seem too absolute:
Pulpits their sacred satire learn'd to spare,   550
And Vice admir'd to find a flatt'rer there!
Encourag'd thus, Wit's Titans brav'd the skies,
And the press groan'd with licens'd blasphemies.
These monsters, Critics! with your darts engage,

Here point your thunder, and exhaust your rage! 555
Yet shun their fault, who, scandalously nice,
Will needs mistake an author into vice;
All seems infected that th' infected spy,
As all looks yellow to the jaundic'd eye.

PART III

Rules for the *Conduct* of *Manners* in a Critic. 1. *Candour*, v. 563.
Modesty, v. 566. *Good Breeding*, v. 572. *Sincerity*, and *Freedom* of
advice, v. 578. 2. When one's Counsel is to be restrained, v. 584. Character of an *incorrigible Poet*, v. 600. And of an *impertinent Critic*,
v. 610 ff. Character of a *good Critic*, v. 629. The *History* of *Criticism*,
and Characters of the best Critics: Aristotle, v. 645. *Horace*, v. 653.
Dionysius, v. 665. *Petronius*, v. 667, *Quintilian*, v. 670. *Longinus*, v.
675. Of the Decay of Criticism, and its Revival. *Erasmus*, v. 693. *Vida*,
v. 705. *Boileau*, v. 714. *Lord Roscommon*, etc., v. 725. Conclusion.

LEARN then what MORALS Critics ought to show, 560
For 'tis but half a Judge's task, to know.
'Tis not enough, taste, judgment, learning, join;
In all you speak, let truth and candour shine:
That not alone what to your sense is due
All may allow; but seek your friendship too. 565
Be silent always when you doubt your sense;
And speak, though sure, with seeming diffidence:
Some positive, persisting fops we know,
Who, if once wrong, will needs be always so;
But you, with pleasure own your errors past, 570
And make each day a Critic on the last.
'Tis not enough, your counsel still be true;
Blunt truths more mischief than nice falshoods do;
Men must be taught as if you taught them not,
And things unknown propos'd as things forgot. 575
Without Good Breeding, truth is disapprov'd;
That only makes superior sense belov'd.
Be niggards of advice on no pretence;
For the worst avarice is that of sense.
With mean complacence ne'er betray your trust, 580
Nor be so civil as to prove unjust.
Fear not the anger of the wise to raise;

Those best can bear reproof, who merit praise.
   'Twere well might Critics still this freedom take,
But Appius reddens at each word you speak,   585
And stares, tremendous, with a threat'ning eye,[5]
Like some fierce Tyrant in old tapestry.
Fear most to tax an Honourable fool,
Whose right it is, uncensur'd, to be dull;
Such, without wit, are Poets when they please,   590
As without learning they can take Degrees.
Leave dang'rous truths to unsuccessful Satires,
And flattery to fulsome Dedicators,
Whom, when they praise, the world believes no more,
Than when they promise to give scribbling o'er.   595
'Tis best sometimes your censure to restrain,
And charitably let the dull be vain:
Your silence there is better than your spite,
For who can rail so long as they can write?
Still humming on, their drouzy course they keep, 600
And lash'd so long, like tops, are lash'd asleep.
False steps but help them to renew the race,
As, after stumbling, Jades will mend their pace.
What crouds of these, impenitently bold,
In sounds and jingling syllables grown old,   605
Still run on Poets, in a raging vein,
Ev'n to the dregs and squeezings of the brain,
Strain out the last dull droppings of their sense,
And rhyme with all the rage of Impotence.
   Such shameless Bards we have; and yet 'tis true, 610
There are as mad abandon'd Critics too.
The bookful blockhead, ignorantly read,
With loads of learnèd lumber in his head,
With his own tongue still edifies his ears,
And always list'ning to himself appears.   615
All books he reads, and all he reads assails,
From Dryden's Fables down to Durfey's Tales.

[5] This picture was taken to himself by *John Dennis,* a furious old Critic by profession, who, upon no other provocation, wrote against this Essay and its author, in a manner perfectly lunatic: For, as to the mention made of him in l. 270, he took it as a Compliment, and said it was treacherously meant to cause him to overlook this *Abuse* of his *Person.* [Pope.]

With him, most authors steal their works, or buy;
Garth did not write his own Dispensary.[6]
Name a new Play, and he's the Poet's friend,   620
Nay show'd his faults—but when would Poets mend?
No place so sacred from such fops is barr'd,
Nor is Paul's church more safe than Paul's church yard:
Nay, fly to Altars; there they'll talk you dead:
For Fools rush in where Angels fear to tread.   625
Distrustful sense with modest caution speaks,
It still looks home, and short excursions makes;
But rattling nonsense in full volleys breaks,
And never shock'd, and never turn'd aside,
Bursts out, resistless, with a thund'ring tide.   630
    But where's the man, who counsel can bestow,
Still pleas'd to teach, and yet not proud to know?
Unbias'd, or by favour, or by spite;
Not dully prepossess'd, nor blindly right;
Tho' learn'd, well-bred; and tho' well-bred, sincere;
Modestly bold, and humanly severe: 636
Who to a friend his faults can freely show,
And gladly praise the merit of a foe?
Blest with a taste exact, yet unconfin'd;
A knowledge both of books and human kind;   640
Gen'rous converse; a soul exempt from pride;
And love to praise, with reason on his side?
    Such once were Critics; such the happy few,
Athens and Rome in better ages knew.
The mighty Stagirite first left the shore,   645
Spread all his sails, and durst the deeps explore;
He steer'd securely, and discover'd far,
Led by the light of the Mæonian Star.
Poets, a race long unconfin'd, and free,
Still fond and proud of savage liberty,   650
Receiv'd his laws; and stood convinc'd 'twas fit,
Who conquer'd Nature, should preside o'er Wit.
    Horace still charms with graceful negligence,

[6] A common slander at that time in prejudice of that deserving Author.
Our Poet did him this justice, when that slander most prevailed; and it is
now (perhaps the sooner for this very verse) dead and forgotten. [Pope.]

And without method talks us into sense,
Will, like a friend, familiarly convey   655
The truest notions in the easiest way.
He, who supreme in judgment, as in wit,
Might boldly censure, as he boldly writ,
Yet judg'd with coolness, though he sung with fire;
His Precepts teach but what his works inspire.   660
Our Critics take a contrary extreme,
They judge with fury, but they write with fle'me: [7]
Nor suffers Horace more in wrong Translations
By Wits, than Critics in as wrong Quotations.
   See Dionysius Homer's thoughts refine,   665
And call new beauties forth from ev'ry line!
   Fancy and art in gay Petronius please,
The scholar's learning, with the courtier's ease.
   In grave Quintilian's copious work, we find
The justest rules, and clearest method join'd: 670
Thus useful arms in magazines we place,
All rang'd in order, and dispos'd with grace,
But less to please the eye, than arm the hand,
Still fit for use, and ready at command.
   Thee, bold Longinus! all the Nine inspire,   675
And bless their Critic with a Poet's fire.
An ardent Judge, who zealous in his trust,
With warmth gives sentence, yet is always just;
Whose own example strengthens all his laws;
And is himself that great Sublime he draws.   680
  Thus long succeeding Critics justly reign'd,
License repress'd, and useful laws ordain'd.
Learning and Rome alike in empire grew;
And Arts still follow'd where her Eagles flew;
From the same foes, at last, both felt their doom,   685
And the same age saw Learning fall, and Rome.
With Tyranny, then Superstition join'd,
As that the body, this enslav'd the mind;
Much was believ'd, but little understood,
And to be dull was constru'd to be good;   690
A second deluge Learning thus o'er-run,

   [7] Phlegm.

And the Monks finish'd what the Goths begun.
　At length Erasmus, that great injur'd name,
(The glory of the Priesthood, and the shame!)
Stemmed the wild torrent of a barb'rous age,　　　695
And drove those holy Vandals off the stage.
　But see! each Muse, in LEO's golden days,
Starts from her trance, and trims her wither'd bays,
Rome's ancient Genius, o'er its ruins spread,
Shakes off the dust, and rears his rev'rend head.　　700
Then Sculpture and her sister-arts revive;
Stones leap'd to form, and rocks began to live;
With sweeter notes each rising Temple rung;
A Raphael painted, and a Vida sung.
Immortal Vida: on whose honour'd brow　　　705
The Poet's bays and Critic's ivy grow:
Cremona now shall ever boast thy name,
As next in place to Mantua, next in fame!
　But soon by impious arms from Latium chas'd,
Their ancient bounds the banish'd Muses pass'd;　　710
Thence Arts o'er all the northern world advance,
But Critic-learning flourish'd most in France:
The rules a nation, born to serve, obeys;
And Boileau still in right of Horace sways.
But we, brave Britons, foreign laws despis'd,　　715
And kept unconquer'd, and unciviliz'd;
Fierce for the liberties of wit, and bold,
We still defied the Romans, as of old.
Yet some there were, among the sounder few
Of those who less presum'd, and better knew,　　720
Who durst assert the juster ancient cause,
And here restor'd Wit's fundamental laws.
Such was the Muse, whose rules and practice tell,[8]
"Nature's chief Masterpiece is writing well."
Such was Roscommon, not more learn'd than good,　　725
With manners generous as his noble blood;
To him the wit of Greece and Rome was known,

---

[8] *Essay on Poetry* by the Duke of Buckingham . . . Our Author . . .
was honour'd very young with his friendship, and it continued till his death
in all the circumstances of a familiar esteem. [Warburton.]

And every author's merit, but his own.
Such late was Walsh—the Muse's judge and friend,
Who justly knew to blame or to commend;   730
To failings mild, but zealous for desert;
The clearest head, and the sincerest heart.
This humble praise, lamented shade! receive,
This praise at least a grateful Muse may give:
The Muse, whose early voice you taught to sing,   735
Prescrib'd her heights, and pruned her tender wing,
(Her guide now lost) no more attempts to rise,
But in low numbers short excursions tries:
Content, if hence th' unlearn'd their wants may view,
The learn'd reflect on what before they knew: 740
Careless of censure, nor too fond of fame;
Still pleas'd to praise, yet not afraid to blame;
Averse alike to flatter, or offend;
Not free from faults, nor yet too vain to mend.

Joseph Addison

[1672–1719]

᪥

LIKE MANY LITERARY MEN of his time, Addison was also a man of affairs; during his successful political career he held public offices in England and Ireland, was a Member of Parliament, and Secretary of State. His *Works* include attempts at many literary forms—occasional poems, a tragedy, a comedy, the libretto of an opera—but his reputation rests almost entirely on the essays which he wrote for the *Tatler* and the *Spectator*.

Addison is not the best eighteenth-century critic, but he is the most representative. In his essays, the principal influences on Augustan criticism—Aristotle, Horace and Longinus, Boileau and Rapin, Dryden and Locke—are all evident; and so are the stock critical terms of his day—wit and judgment, imagination and fancy, correctness, sublimity, taste, common sense, the rules. His essays are, in fact, an index to the critical thought of the century.

Addison's critical essays can be divided into three categories: essays on single literary works, essays on genres and critical terms, and essays on aesthetics. To the first group belong the two essays on *Chevy Chase,* and the ambitious series of eighteen on *Paradise Lost;* in these Addison shows an orthodox dependence on classical authority, as well as an Augustan distaste for what he calls "the Gothic manner of writing." The second group includes essays on tragedy, the remarks on epic in the *Paradise Lost* series, and the essays on true and false wit. The third, and critically the most important group, contains the eleven essays "On the Pleasures of the Imagination," which have been called "the first attempt at a general theory of aesthetics in English."

As a theory of aesthetics, the "Imagination" essays are more interesting historically than critically. Certainly they did much to establish the direction which aesthetic thought took for the next hundred years. The questions which Addison raises—Why are the ideas of objects often more vivid than the objects themselves? Why are we pleasurably moved by the disagreeable and catastrophic in art? What

177

is the peculiar imaginative force of the vast and the strange?—were repeated through the century as speculation on the psychology of aesthetic experience continued, and as the influence of Longinus, with his emphasis on the emotional in art, increased. The answers that Addison offers are often extremely literal-minded and naïve—the too-easy application of Locke and Longinus to aesthetics—but one must allow that in some cases they were the *first* answers, and that they were written for the readers of a popular journal. "His purpose," Dr. Johnson wrote, "was to infuse literary curiosity by gentle and unsuspected conveyance into the gay, the idle, and the wealthy: he therefore presented knowledge in the most alluring form, not lofty and austere, but accessible and familiar." In this purpose, he was entirely successful.

BIBLIOGRAPHY. *The Spectator,* ed. G. A. Aitken, 8 vols. (London, 1898); *The Tatler,* ed. Aitken, 4 vols. (London, 1898–9).

Walter Graham, *English Literary Periodicals* (New York, 1930); C. S. Lewis, "Addison," in *Essays on the Eighteenth Century Presented to David Nichol Smith* (Oxford, 1945); Peter Smithers, *The Life of Joseph Addison* (Oxford, 1954).

TEXT. *The Spectator,* 9 vols. (London, 1712–15), vols. I and VI.

ON THE BALLAD OF CHEVY CHASE

(The Spectator *LXX, May 21, 1711*)

Interdum vulgus rectum videt.
[Sometimes the people see correctly. Horace, *Epist.* II. i. 63.]

WHEN I TRAVELLED, I took a particular Delight in hearing the Songs and Fables that are come from Father to Son, and are most in Vogue among the Common People of the Countries through which I passed; for it is impossible that any thing should be universally tasted and approved by a Multitude, tho' they are only the Rabble of a Nation, which hath not in it some peculiar Aptness to please and gratify the Mind of Man. Human Nature is the same in all reasonable Creatures; and whatever falls in with it, will meet with Admirers amongst Readers of all Qualities and Conditions. *Moliere,* as we are told by Monsieur *Boileau,* used to read all his Comedies to an old Woman who was his House-keeper, as she sat with him at her Work by the Chimney-Corner; and could foretel the Success of his Play in the Theatre, from the Reception it met at his Fire-Side: For he tells us the Audience always followed the old Woman, and never failed to laugh in the same Place.

I know nothing which more shews the essential and inherent Perfection of Simplicity of Thought, above that which I call the Gothick Manner in Writing, than this, that the first pleases all Kinds of Palates, and the latter only such as have formed to themselves a wrong artificial Taste upon little fanciful Authors and Writers of Epigram. *Homer, Virgil,* or *Milton,* so far as the Language of their Poems is understood, will please a Reader of plain common Sense, who would neither relish nor comprehend an Epigram of *Martial,* or a Poem of *Cowley:* So, on the contrary, an ordinary Song or Ballad that is the Delight of the common People, cannot fail to please all such Readers as are not un-qualified for the Entertainment by their Affectation or Ignorance; and the Reason is plain, because the same Paintings of Nature which recommend it to the most ordinary Reader, will appear Beautiful to the most refined.

The old Song of *Chevy-Chase* is the favourite Ballad of the common People of *England;* and *Ben. Johnson* used to say he had rather have been the Author of it than of all his Works. Sir *Philip Sidney* in his Discourse of Poetry [1] speaks of it in the fol-lowing Words; *I never heard the old Song of* Piercy *and* Douglas, *that I found not my Heart more moved than with a Trumpet; and yet it is sung by some blind Crowder with no rougher Voice than rude Stile; which being so evil apparelled in the Dust and Cobweb of that uncivil Age, what would it work trimmed in the gorgeous Eloquence of* Pindar? For my own Part, I am so pro-fessed an Admirer of this antiquated Song, that I shall give my Reader a Critick upon it, without any further Apology for so doing.

The greatest Modern Criticks have laid it down as a Rule, That an Heroick Poem should be founded upon some important Precept of Morality, adapted to the Constitution of the Country in which the Poet writes. *Homer* and *Virgil* have formed their

[1] *Defense of Poesy* (see vol. I of this series).

Plans in this View. As *Greece* was a Collection of many Governments, who suffered very much among themselves, and gave the *Persian* Emperor, who was their common Enemy, many Advantages over them by their mutual Jealousies and Animosities, *Homer,* in order to establish among them an Union, which was so necessary for their Safety, grounds his Poem upon the Discords of the several *Grecian* Princes who were engaged in a Confederacy against an *Asiatick* Prince, and the several Advantages which the Enemy gained by such their Discords. At the Time the Poem we are now treating of was written, the Dissentions of the Barons, who were then so many petty Princes, ran very high, whether they quarrelled among themselves, or with their Neighbours, and produced unspeakable Calamities to the Country: The Poet, to deter Men from such unnatural Contentions, describes a bloody Battel and dreadful Scene of Death, occasioned by the mutual Feuds which reigned in the Families of an *English* and *Scotch* Nobleman. That he designed this for the Instruction of his Poem, we may learn from his four last Lines, in which, after the Example of the modern Tragedians, he draws from it a Precept for the Benefit of his Readers.

> *God save the King, and bless the Land*
> *In Plenty, Joy, and Peace;*
> *And grant henceforth that foul Debate*
> *'Twixt Noblemen may cease.*

The next Point observed by the greatest Heroic Poets, hath been to celebrate Persons and Actions which do Honour to their Country: Thus *Virgil's* Hero was the Founder of *Rome, Homer's* a Prince of *Greece;* and for this Reason *Valerius Flaccus* and *Statius,* who were both *Romans,* might be justly derided for having chosen the Expedition of the *Golden Fleece* and the *Wars of Thebes,* for the Subjects of their Epic Writings.

The Poet before us, has not only found out an Hero in his own Country, but raises the Reputation of it by several beautiful Incidents. The *English* are the first who take the Field, and the last who quit it. The *English* bring only Fifteen hundred to the Battel, the *Scotch* Two thousand. The *English* keep the Field with Fifty three: The *Scotch* retire with Fifty five: All the rest on each Side being slain in Battel. But the most remarkable Circumstance of this Kind is the different Manner in which the *Scotch* and *English* Kings receive the News of this Fight, and of the great Mens Deaths who commanded in it.

> *This News was brought to* Edinburgh,
>   *Where* Scotland's *King did reign,*
> *That brave Earl* Douglas *suddenly*
>   *Was with an Arrow slain.*
>
> *O heavy News, King* James *did say,*
>   Scotland *can Witness be,*
> *I have not any Captain more*
>   *Of such Account as he.*
>
> *Like Tydings to King* Henry *came*
>   *Within as short a Space,*
> *That Piercy of* Northumberland
>   *Was slain in* Chevy-Chace.
>
> *Now God be with him said our King,*
>   *Sith 'twill no better be,*
> *I trust I have within my Realm*
>   *Five hundred as good as he.*
>
> *Yet shall not* Scot *nor* Scotland *say*
>   *But I will Vengeance take,*
> *And be revenged on them all*
>   *For brave Lord* Piercy's *sake.*
>
> *This Vow full well the King perform'd*
>   *After on* Humble-down,
> *In one Day Fifty Knights were slain*
>   *With Lords of great Renown.*
>
> *And of the rest of small Account*
>   *Did many Thousands dye,* &c.

At the same Time that our Poet shews a laudable Partiality to his Country-men, he represents the *Scots* after a Manner not unbecoming so bold and brave a People.

> *Earl* Douglas *on a milk-white Steed,*
>   *Most like a Baron bold,*
> *Rode foremost of the Company*
>   *Whose Armour shone like Gold.*

His Sentiments and Actions are every Way suitable to an Hero. One of us two, says he, must dye: I am an Earl as well as your self, so that you can have no Pretence for refusing the Combat: However, says he, 'tis Pity, and indeed would be a Sin, that so many innocent Men should perish for our Sakes, rather let you and I end our Quarrel in single Fight.

> *E'er thus I will out-braved be,*
>   *One of us two shall dye:*
> *I know thee well, an Earl thou art,*
>   *Lord* Piercy, *so am I.*
>
> *But trust me,* Piercy, *Pity it were,*
>   *And great Offence, to kill*
> *Any of these our harmless Men,*
>   *For they have done no Ill.*
>
> *Let thou and I the Battel try,*
>   *And set our Men aside;*
> *Accurst be he, Lord* Piercy *said,*
>   *By whom this is deny'd.*

When these brave Men had distinguished themselves in the Battel and in single Combat with each other, in the Midst of a generous Parly, full of heroic Sentiments, the *Scotch* Earl falls; and with his Dying Words encourages his Men to revenge his Death, representing to them, as the most bitter Circumstance of it, that his Rival saw him fall.

> *With that there came an Arrow keen*
>   *Out of an* English *bow,*
> *Which struck Earl* Douglas *to the Heart*
>   *A deep and deadly Blow.*
>
> *Who never spoke more Words than these,*
>   *Fight on my merry Men all;*
> *For why, my Life is at an End,*
>   *Lord* Piercy *sees my fall.*

Merry Men, in the Language of those Times, is no more than a chearful Word for Companions and Fellow-Soldiers. A passage in the Eleventh Book of *Virgil's Aeneids* is very much to be admired, where *Camilla* in her last agonies, instead of weeping over the Wound she had received, as one might have expected from a Warrior of her Sex, considers only (like the Hero of whom we are now speaking) how the Battel should be continued after her Death.

Tum sic expirans, &c.

A gathering Mist o'erclouds her chearful Eyes;
And from her Cheeks the rosy colour flies.
Then, turns to her, whom, of her Female Train,
She trusted most, and thus she speaks with Pain.
Acca, 'tis past! He swims before my Sight,
Inexorable Death; and claims his Right.
Bear my last Words to Turnus, *fly with speed,*
And bid him timely to my Charge succeed:
Repel the Trojans, *and the Town relieve:*
Farewell. . . .

Turnus did not die in so Heroic a Manner; tho' our Poet seems to have had his eye upon *Turnus*'s Speech in the last Verse.

Lord Piercy *sees my Fall.*

. . . Vicisti, & victum tendere palmas
Ausonii videre . . .

[You have conquered, and the Ausoniaus have seen me, vanquished, stretch out my hands . . . *Aeneid,* xii. 936.]

Earl *Piercy*'s Lamentation over his Enemy is generous, beautiful, and passionate; I must only caution the Reader not to let the Simplicity of the Stile, which one may well pardon in so old a Poet, prejudice him against the Greatness of the Thought.

Then leaving Life Earl Piercy *took*
The dead Man by the Hand,
And said, Earl Douglas *for thy Life*
Would I had lost my Land.

O Christ! My very Heart doth bleed
With Sorrow for thy Sake;
For sure a more renowned Knight
Mischance did never take.

That beautiful Line *Taking the dead Man by the Hand*, will put the Reader in Mind of *Aenea's* Behaviour towards *Lausus*, whom he himself had Slain as he came to the Rescue of his aged Father.

> *At vero ut vultum vidit morientis, & ora,*
> *Ora modis Anchisiades pallentia miris:*
> *Ingemuit, miserans graviter, dextramque tetendit,* &c.

> *The pious Prince beheld young* Lausus *dead;*
> *He griev'd, he wept; then grasp'd his Hand, and said,*
> *Poor hapless Youth! What Praises can be paid*
> *To Worth so great!* . . .

I shall take another Opportunity to consider the other Parts of this old Song.[2]

ON THE PLEASURES OF THE IMAGINATION

(The Spectator *CDXI, June 21, 1712*)

> *Avia Pieridum peragro loca, nullius ante*
> *Trita solo; juvat integros accedere fonteis;*
> *Atque haurire: . . .*—Lucr.

[I traverse the pathless places of the Muses, trod before by none: it is a joy to draw near untouched springs, and to drink.]

OUR SIGHT IS THE most perfect and most delightful of all our Senses. It fills the Mind with the largest Variety of Ideas, converses with its Objects at the greatest Distance, and continues the longest in Action without being tired or satiated with its proper Enjoyments. The Sense of Feeling can indeed give us a Notion of Extension, Shape, and all other Ideas that enter at the Eye, except Colours; but at the same time it is very much streightned and confined in its Operations, to the Number, Bulk, and Distance of its particular Objects. Our Sight seems designed to supply all these Defects, and may be considered as a more delicate and diffusive Kind of Touch, that spreads its self over

[2] Addison returned to the discussion of this ballad in *Spectator* no. 74.

an infinite Multitude of Bodies, comprehends the largest Figures, and brings into our reach some of the most remote Parts of the Universe.

It is this Sense which furnishes the Imagination with its Ideas; so that by the Pleasures of the Imagination or Fancy (which I shall use promiscuously) I here mean such as arise from visible Objects, either when we have them actually in our View, or when we call up their Ideas into our Minds by Paintings, Statues, Descriptions, or any the like Occasion. We cannot indeed have a single Image in the Fancy that did not make its first Entrance through the Sight; but we have the Power of retaining, altering and compounding those Images, which we have once received, into all the Varieties of Picture and Vision that are most agreeable to the Imagination; for by this Faculty a Man in a Dungeon is capable of entertaining himself with Scenes and Landskips more beautiful than any that can be found in the whole Compass of Nature.

There are few Words in the *English* Language which are employed in a more loose and uncircumscribed Sense than those of the *Fancy* and the *Imagination*. I therefore thought it necessary to fix and determine the Notion of these two Words, as I intend to make use of them in the Thread of my following Speculations, that the Reader may conceive rightly what is the Subject which I proceed upon. I must therefore desire him to remember, that by the Pleasures of the Imagination, I mean only such Pleasures as arise originally from Sight, and that I divide these Pleasures into two Kinds: My Design being first of all to discourse of those Primary Pleasures of the Imagination, which entirely proceed from such Objects as are before our Eyes; and in the next place to speak of those Secondary Pleasures of the Imagination which flow from the Ideas of visible Objects, when the Objects are not actually before the Eye, but are called up into our Memories, or formed into agreeable Visions of Things that are either Absent or Fictitious.

The Pleasures of the Imagination, taken in their full Extent, are not so gross as those of Sense, nor so refined as those of the Understanding. The last are, indeed, more preferable, because they are founded on some new Knowledge or Improvement in the Mind of Man; yet it must be confest, that those of the Imagination are as great and as transporting as the other. A beautiful Prospect delights the Soul, as much as a Demonstration; and a Description in *Homer* has charm'd more Readers than a Chapter in *Aristotle*. Besides, the Pleasures of the Imagination have this Advantage, above those of the Understanding, that they are more obvious, and more easie to be acquired. It is but opening the Eye, and the Scene enters. The Colours paint themselves on the Fancy, with very little Attention of Thought or Application of Mind in the Beholder. We are struck, we know not how, with the Symmetry of any thing we see, and immediately assent to the Beauty of an Object, without enquiring into the particular Causes and Occasions of it.

A Man of a Polite Imagination is let into a great many Pleasures, that the Vulgar are not capable of receiving. He can converse with a Picture, and find an agreeable Companion in a Statue. He meets with a secret Refreshment in a Description, and often feels a greater Satisfaction in the Prospect of Fields and Meadows, than another does in the Possession. It gives him, indeed, a kind of Property in every thing he sees, and makes the most rude uncultivated Parts of Nature administer to his Pleasures: So that he looks upon the World, as it were, in another Light, and discovers in it a Multitude of Charms, that conceal themselves from the generality of Mankind.

There are, indeed, but very few who know how to be idle and innocent, or have a Relish of any Pleasures that are not Criminal; every Diversion they take is at the Expence of some one Virtue or another, and their very first Step out of Business is into Vice or Folly. A Man should endeavour, therefore, to make the Sphere of his innocent Pleasures as wide as possible, that he may retire into them with Safety, and find in them such a Satisfaction as a wise Man would not blush to take. Of this Nature are those of the Imagination, which do not require such a Bent of Thought as is necessary to our more serious Employments, nor at the same Time, suffer the Mind to sink into that Negligence and Remissness, which are apt to accompany our more sensual Delights, but, like a gentle Exercise to the Faculties, awaken them from Sloth and Idleness, without putting them upon any Labour or Difficulty.

We might here add, that the Pleasures of the Fancy are more

conducive to Health, than those of the Understanding, which are worked out by Dint of Thinking, and attended with too violent a Labour of the Brain. Delightful Scenes, whether in Nature, Painting, or Poetry, have a kindly Influence on the Body, as well as the Mind, and not only serve to clear and brighten the Imagination, but are able to disperse Grief and Melancholy, and to set the Animal Spirits in pleasing and agreeable Motions. For this Reason Sir *Francis Bacon,* in his Essay upon Health, has not thought it improper to prescribe to his Reader a Poem or a Prospect, where he particularly dissuades him from knotty and subtle Disquisitions, and advises him to pursue Studies that fill the Mind with splendid and illustrious Objects, as Histories, Fables, and Contemplations of Nature.

I have in this Paper, by way of Introduction, settled the Notion of those Pleasures of the Imagination which are the Subject of my present Undertaking, and endeavoured, by several Considerations, to recommend to my Reader the Pursuit of those Pleasures. I shall, in my next Paper, examine the several Sources from whence these Pleasures are derived.

(The Spectator *CDXVI, June 27, 1712*)

Quatenus hoc simile est oculis, quod mente videmus.—Lucr.

[How like what we see with our eyes is what we see with our minds.]

I AT FIRST DIVIDED the Pleasures of the Imagination, into such as arise from Objects that are actually before our Eyes, or that once entered in at our Eyes, and are afterwards called up into the Mind, either barely by its own Operations, or on occasion of something without us, as Statues or Descriptions. We have already considered the first Division, and shall therefore enter on the other, which, for Distinction sake, I have called the Secondary Pleasures of the Imagination. When I say the Ideas we receive from Statues, Descriptions, or such like Occasions, are the same that were once actually in our View, it must not be understood that we had once seen the very Place, Action, or Person which are carved or described. It is sufficient, that we have seen Places, Persons, or Actions in general, which bear a Resemblance, or at least some remote Analogy with what we find represented. Since it is in the Power of the Imagination, when it is once Stocked with particular Ideas, to enlarge, compound, and vary them at her own Pleasure.

Among the different Kinds of Representation, *Statuary* is the most natural, and shews us something *likest* the Object that is represented. To make use of a common Instance, let one who is born Blind take an Image in his Hands, and trace out with his Fingers the different Furrows and Impressions of the Chissel, and he will easily conceive how the Shape of a Man, or Beast, may be represented by it; but should he draw his Hand over a *Picture*, where all is smooth and uniform, he would never be able to imagine how the several Prominencies and Depressions of a human Body could be shewn on a plain Piece of Canvas, that has in it no Unevenness or Irregularity. *Description* runs yet further from the things it represents than Painting; for a Picture bears a real Resemblance to its Original, which Letters and Syllables are wholly void of. Colours speak all Languages, but Words are understood only by such a People or Nation. For this reason, tho' Men's Necessities quickly put them on finding out Speech, Writing is probably of a later Invention than Painting; particularly we are told, that in *America* when the *Spaniards* first arrived there, Expresses were sent to the Emperor of *Mexico* in Paint, and the News of his Country delineated by the Strokes of a Pencil, which was a more natural Way than that of Writing, tho' at the same time much more imperfect, because it is impossible to draw the little connexions of Speech, or to give the Picture of a Conjunction or an Adverb. It would be yet more strange, to represent visible Objects by Sounds that have no Ideas annexed to them, and to make something like Description in *Musick*. Yet it is certain, there may be confused, imperfect Notions of this Nature raised in the Imagination by an Artificial Composition of Notes; and we find that great Masters in the Art are able, sometimes to set their Hearers in the heat and hurry of a Battel, to overcast their Minds with melancholy Scenes and Apprehensions of Deaths and Funerals, or to lull them into pleasing Dreams of Groves and Elisiums.

In all these Instances, this Secondary Pleasure of the Imagination proceeds from that Action of the Mind, which compares the Ideas arising from the Original Objects, with the Ideas we receive from the Statue, Picture, Description, or Sound that represents them. It is impossible for us to give the necessary Reason, why this Operation of the Mind is attended with so much Pleasure, as I have before observed on the same Occasion; but we find a great variety of Entertainments derived from this single Principle: For it is this that not only gives us a relish of Statuary, Painting and Description, but makes us delight in all the Actions and Arts of Mimickry. It is this that makes the several kinds of Wit pleasant, which consists, as I have formerly shewn, in the Affinity of Ideas: And we may add, it is this also that raises the little Satisfaction we sometimes find in the different Sorts of false Wit; whether it consist in the Affinity of Letters, as an Anagram, Acrostick; or of Syllables, as in Doggerel Rhimes, Ecchos; or of Words, as in Puns, Quibbles; or of a whole Sentence or Poem, to Wings, and Altars. The *final Cause*, probably, of annexing Pleasure to this Operation of the Mind, was to quicken and encourage us in our Searches after Truth, since the distinguishing one thing from another, and the right discerning betwixt our Ideas, depends wholly upon our comparing them together, and observing the Congruity or Disagreement that appears among the several Works of Nature.

But I shall here confine my self to those Pleasures of the Imagination, which proceed from Ideas raised by *Words,* because most of the Observations that agree with Descriptions, are equally Applicable to Painting and Statuary.

Words, when well chosen, have so great a Force in them, that a Description often gives us more lively Ideas than the Sight of Things themselves. The Reader finds a Scene drawn in Stronger Colours, and painted more to the Life in his Imagination, by the help of Words, than by an actual Survey of the Scene which they describe. In this Case the Poet seems to get the better of Nature; he takes, indeed, the Landskip after her, but gives it more vigorous Touches, heightens its Beauty, and so enlivens the whole Piece, that the Images which flow from the Objects themselves appear weak and faint, in Comparison of those that come from the Expressions. The Reason, probably, may be, because in the Survey of any Object, we have only so much of it painted on the Imagination, as comes in at the Eye; but in its Description, the Poet gives us as free a View of it as he pleases, and discovers to us several Parts, that either we did not attend to, or that lay out of our Sight when we first beheld it. As we look on any Object, our Idea of it is, perhaps, made up of two or three simple Ideas; but when the Poet represents it, he may either give us a more complex Idea of it, or only raise in us such Ideas as are most apt to affect the Imagination.

It may be here worth our while to examine, how it comes to pass that several Readers, who are all acquainted with the same Language, and know the Meaning of the Words they read, should nevertheless have a different Relish of the same Descriptions. We find one transported with a Passage, which another runs over with Coldness and Indifference, or finding the Representation extremely natural, where another can perceive nothing of Likeness and Conformity. This different Taste must proceed either from the *Perfection of Imagination* in one more than in another, or from the *different Ideas* that several Readers affix to the same Words. For, to have a true Relish, and form a right Judgment of a Description, a Man should be born with a good Imagination, and must have well weighed the Force and Energy that lye in the several Words of a Language, so as to be able to distinguish which are most significant and expressive of their proper Ideas, and what additional Strength and Beauty they are capable of receiving from Conjunction with others. The Fancy must be warm, to retain the Print of those Images it hath received from outward Objects; and the Judgment discerning, to know what Expressions are most proper to cloath and adorn them to the best Advantage. A Man who is deficient in either of these Respects, tho' he may receive the general Notion of a Description, can never see distinctly all its particular Beauties: As a Person with a weak Sight may have the confused Prospect of a Place that lyes before him, without entering into its several Parts, or discerning the variety of its Colours in their full Glory and Perfection.

(The Spectator *CDXVIII, June 30, 1712*)

> . . . *Ferat & rubus asper amomum.*—Virg.
> [The rough bramble will also bear balm.]

THE PLEASURES OF THESE Secondary Views of the Imagination, are of a wider and more universal Nature than those it has when joined with Sight; for not only what is Great, Strange or Beautiful, but any Thing that is Disagreeable when looked upon, pleases us in an apt Description. Here, therefore, we must enquire after a new Principle of Pleasure, which is nothing else but the Action of the Mind, which *compares* the Ideas that arise from Words, with the Ideas that arise from the Objects themselves; and why this Operation of the Mind is attended with so much Pleasure, we have before considered. For this Reason therefore, the Description of a Dunghill is pleasing to the Imagination, if the Image be represented to our Minds by suitable Expressions; tho', perhaps, this may be more properly called the Pleasure of the Understanding than of the Fancy, because we are not so much delighted with the Image that is contained in the Description, as with the Aptness of the Description to excite the Image.

But if the Description of what is Little, Common or Deformed, be acceptable to the Imagination, the Description of what is Great, Surprising or Beautiful, is much more so; because here we are not only delighted with *comparing* the Representation with the Original, but are highly pleased with the Original it self. Most Readers, I believe, are more charmed with *Milton's* Description of Paradise, than of Hell; they are both, perhaps, equally perfect in their Kind, but in the one the Brimstone and Sulphur are not so refreshing to the Imagination, as the Beds of Flowers and the Wilderness of Sweets in the other.

There is yet another Circumstance which recommends a Description more than all the rest, and that is, if it represents to us such Objects as are apt to raise a secret Ferment in the Mind of the Reader, and to work, with Violence, upon his Passions. For, in this Case, we are at once warmed and enlightened, so that the Pleasure becomes more Universal, and is several ways qualified to entertain us. Thus, in Painting, it is pleasant to look on the Picture of any Face, where the Resemblance is hit, but the Pleasure increases, if it be the Picture of a Face that is beautiful, and is still greater, if the Beauty be softened with an Air of Melancholy or Sorrow. The two leading Passions which the more serious Parts of Poetry endeavour to stir up in us, are Terror and Pity. And here, by the way, one would wonder how it comes to pass, that such Passions as are very unpleasant at all other times, are very agreeable when excited by proper Descriptions.

It is not strange, that we should take Delight in such Passages as
are apt to produce Hope, Joy, Admiration, Love, or the like
Emotions in us, because they never rise in the Mind without an
inward Pleasure which attends them. But how comes it to pass,
that we should take delight in being terrified or dejected by a
Description, when we find so much Uneasiness in the Fear or
Grief which we receive from any other Occasion?

If we consider, therefore, the Nature of this Pleasure, we shall
find that it does not arise so properly from the Description of
what is Terrible, as from the Reflection we make on our selves
at the time of reading it. When we look on such hideous Objects, we are not a little pleased to think we are in no Danger of
them. We consider them at the same time, as Dreadful and
Harmless; so that the more frightful Appearance they make, the
greater is the Pleasure we receive from the Sense of our own
Safety. In short, we look upon the Terrors of a Description, with
the same Curiosity and Satisfaction that we survey a dead Monster.

> . . . *Informe cadaver*
> *Protrahitur, nequeunt expleri corda tuendo*
> *Terribiles oculos: vultum, villosaque setis*
> *Pectora semiferi, atque extinctos faucibus ignes.*—Virg.
> [. . . The monstrous corpse is dragged along: their
> hearts cannot be sated with gazing upon the terrifying
> eyes, the countenance, and the hairy chest of the half-
> wild creature, and the extinct fire from his jaws. *Aeneid*,
> viii. 264]

It is for the same Reason that we are delighted with the reflecting upon Dangers that are past, or in looking on a Precipice at
a distance, which would fill us with a different kind of Horrour,
if we saw it hanging over our Heads.

In the like manner, when we read of Torments, Wounds,
Deaths, and the like dismal Accidents, our Pleasure does not flow
so properly from the Grief which such melancholy Descriptions
give us, as from the secret Comparison which we make between
our selves and the Person who suffers. Such Representations
teach us to set a just Value upon our own Condition, and make
us prize our good Fortune, which exempts us from the like Ca-

lamities. This is, however, such a kind of Pleasure as we are not capable of receiving, when we see a Person actually lying under the Tortures that we meet with in a Description; because, in this Case, the Object presses too close upon our Senses, and bears so hard upon us, that it does not give us Time or Leisure to reflect on our selves. Our Thoughts are so intent upon the Miseries of the Sufferer, that we cannot turn them upon our own Happiness. Whereas, on the contrary, we consider the Misfortunes we read in History or Poetry, either as past, or as fictitious, so that the Reflection upon our selves rises in us insensibly, and over-bears the Sorrow we conceive for the Sufferings of the Afflicted.

But because the Mind of Man requires something more perfect in Matter, than what it finds there, and can never meet with any Sight in Nature which sufficiently answers its highest Ideas of Pleasantness; or, in other Words, because the Imagination can fancy to it self Things more Great, Strange, or Beautiful, than the Eye ever saw, and is still sensible of some Defect in what it has seen; on this account it is the part of a Poet to humour the Imagination in its own Notions, by mending and perfecting Nature where he describes a Reality, and by adding greater Beauties than are put together in Nature, where he describes a Fiction.

He is not obliged to attend her in the slow Advances which she makes from one Season to another, or to observe her Conduct in the successive Production of Plants and Flowers. He may draw into his Description all the Beauties of the Spring and Autumn, and make the whole Year contribute something to render it the more agreeable. His Rose-trees, Wood-bines and Jessamines may flower together, and his Beds be covered at the same time with Lilies, Violets, and Amaranths. His Soil is not restrained to any particular Sett of Plants, but is proper either for Oaks or Mirtles, and adapts it self to the Products of every Climate. Oranges may grow wild in it; Myrrh may be met with in every Hedge, and if he thinks it proper to have a Grove of Spices, he can quickly command Sun enough to raise it. If all this will not furnish out an agreeable Scene, he can make several new Species of Flowers, with richer Scents and higher Colours than any that grow in the Gardens of Nature. His Consorts of

Birds may be as full and harmonious, and his Woods as thick and gloomy as he pleases. He is at no more Expence in a long Vista, than a short one, and can as easily throw his Cascades from a Precipice of half a Mile high, as from one of twenty Yards. He has his Choice of the Winds, and can turn the Course of his Rivers in all the variety of *Meanders,* that are most delightful to the Reader's Imagination. In a Word, he has the modelling of Nature in his own Hands, and may give her what Charms he pleases, provided he does not reform her too much, and run into Absurdities, by endeavouring to excel.

Sir Richard Steele

[1672–1729]

STEELE WAS AT VARIOUS TIMES a playwright, a periodical essayist (he founded the *Tatler,* and contributed to the *Spectator*), and a politician. His essays are not often critical; Steele was more concerned with the correction of manners and morals than with the judgment of literature, and all the important critical essays in the *Spectator* are Addison's.

Steele's moral bias is apparent in his first published work, *The Christian Hero: an Argument proving that no Principles but those of Religion are sufficient to make a great man* (1701). This moral bias also informs his plays—*The Funeral* (1701), *The Lying Lover* (1703), *The Tender Husband* (1705), and *The Conscious Lovers* (1722). These are all comedies, in which Steele uses the comedy-of-manners materials of the Restoration. But they are comedies with a difference; in them tears flow, tender sentiments are admired, and virtue, though it may suffer, is in the end rewarded. They belong to a new dramatic category—what Goldsmith called "Sentimental Comedy" (see below, pp. 285 to 289).

Sentimental comedy is, in part, a reaction to late seventeenth-century criticisms of the "immorality and profaneness" of the English stage (see Collier above, pp. 96 to 130). But it would have appeared even without Collier's assistance, for it expresses a strain of eighteenth-century sensibility which was an increasingly strong one— the middle-class concern with the emotional sources of morality, and the relation of personal goodness to tender and sympathetic feelings. In writing a play which was to be an "innocent performance," with a place for manly tears, Steele was anticipating the novels of Richardson and Sterne, as well as aspects of the Romantic movement.

BIBLIOGRAPHY. *Dramatic Works,* ed. G. A. Aitken (London, 1894); *The Spectator,* ed. Aitken, 8 vols. (London, 1898); *The Tatler,* ed. Aitken, 4 vols. (London, 1898–9).

G. A. Aitken, *Richard Steele,* 2 vols. (London, 1889); Walter

Graham, *English Literary Periodicals* (New York, 1930); J. W. Krutch, *Comedy and Conscience after the Restoration*, 2nd ed. (New York, 1949); John Loftis, *Steele at Drury Lane* (Berkeley, 1952).

TEXT. *The Conscious Lovers. A Comedy* (London, 1723).

preface to

THE CONSCIOUS LOVERS

[1722]

THIS COMEDY HAS BEEN RECEIV'D with universal Acceptance, for it was in every Part excellently perform'd; and there needs no other Applause of the Actors, but that they excell'd according to the Dignity and Difficulty of the Character they represented. But this great Favour done to the Work in Acting, renders the Expectation still the greater from the Author, to keep up the Spirit in the Representation of the Closet, or any other Circumstance of the Reader, whether alone or in Company: To which I can only say, that it must be remember'd a Play is to be Seen, and is made to be Represented with the Advantage of action, nor can appear but with half the Spirit, without it; for the greatest effect of a Play in reading is to excite the Reader to go see it; and when he does so, it is then a Play has the Effect of Example and Precept.

The chief Design of this was to be an innocent Performance, and the Audience have abundantly show'd how ready they are to support what is visibly intended that way; nor do I make any Difficulty to acknowledge, that the whole was writ for the sake of the Scene of the Fourth Act, where in Mr. *Bevill* evades the Quarrel with his Friend, and hope it may have some Effect upon the *Goths* and *Vandals* that frequent the Theatres, or a more polite Audience may supply their Absence.

But this Incident, and the Case of the Father and Daughter, are esteem'd by some People no Subjects of Comedy; but I cannot be of their Mind; for any thing that has its Foundation in Happiness and Success, must be allow'd to be the Object of Comedy; and sure it must be an Improvement of it, to introduce a Joy too exquisite for Laughter, that can have no Spring but in Delight, which is the Case of this young Lady. I must therefore contend, that the Tears which were shed on that Occasion flow'd from Reason and Good Sense, and that Men ought not to be laugh'd at for weeping, till we are come to a more clear Notion of what is to be imputed to the Hardness of the Head, and the Softness of the Heart; and I think it was very politely said of Mr. *Wilks*[1] to one who told him there was a *General* weeping for *Indiana*,[2] I'll warrant he'll fight ne'er the worse for that. To be apt to give way to the Impressions of Humanity is the Excellence of a right Disposition, and the natural Working of a well-turn'd Spirit. But as I have suffer'd by Criticks who are got no farther than to enquire whether they ought to be pleas'd or not, I would willingly find them properer Matter for their employment, and revive here a Song which was omitted for want of a Performer, and design'd for the Entertainment of *Indiana;* Sig. *Carbonelli*[3] instead of it play'd on the Fiddle, and it is for want of a Singer that such advantageous things are said of an Instrument which were design'd for a Voice. The Song is the Distress of a Love-sick Maid, and may be a fit Entertainment for some small Criticks to examine whether the Passion is just, or the Distress Male or Female.

I.
From Place to Place forlorn I go,
*   With downcast Eyes a silent Shade,*
Forbidden to declare my Woe;
*   To speak, till spoken to, afraid.*

II.
My inward Pangs, my secret Grief,
*   My soft consenting Looks betray.*
He Loves, but gives me no Relief;
*   Why speaks not he who may?*

It remains to say a Word concerning *Terence*, and I am extremely surpris'd to find what Mr. *Cibber*[4] told me, prove a

---

[1] Actor who played Myrtle in first performance.
[2] The heroine of the play.
[3] An Italian violinist who performed at Drury Lane.
[4] Colley Cibber (167–1757), actor, dramatist and poet, played the role of Tom in the first performance.

Truth, That what I valued myself so much upon, the Translation of him, should be imputed to me as a Reproach. Mr. *Cibber's*
Zeal for the Work, his Care and Application in instructing the
Actors, and altering the Disposition of the Scenes, when I was,
through Sickness, unable to cultivate such Things my self, has
been a very obliging Favour and Friendship to me. For this Reason, I was very hardly persuaded to throw away *Terence's* celebrated Funeral,[5] and take only the bare Authority of the young
Man's Character; and how I have work'd it into an *Englishman*,
and made Use of the same Circumstances of discovering a
Daughter, when we least hop'd for one, is humbly submitted to
the Learned Reader.

[5] Steele had borrowed the general idea of *The Conscious Lovers* from
Terence's *Andria*.

Henry Fielding

[1707–1754]

FIELDING WAS AT VARIOUS TIMES a playwright, a theater manager, a lawyer, a political journalist, and a police-court magistrate—everything but a professional novelist. Yet he, more than any other writer, is responsible for the fact that in the eighteenth century the novel became a serious literary genre. Both his examples and the precepts which he attached to them contributed to this change: Fielding is the first great English novelist, and he is also the first English critic of fiction.

In his Preface to *Joseph Andrews,* and in the introductory chapters to the various books of *Tom Jones,* Fielding set out to establish prose fiction as a genre within the existing neo-classical categories. The critical principles and terms he employs are those of Dryden, of Pope (whose *Essay on Criticism* he quoted approvingly in *Tom Jones*), and ultimately of Aristotle. The novel is an imitation of nature, subject to the same laws of unity, probability, and decorum as epic or drama; it can be described in the same Aristotelian terms—fable, action, characters, sentiments, and diction—and in fact is related to the general category of Epic in the same way that comedy is related to the general category of Drama. Fielding is careful to distinguish his genre from the more debased forms of prose narrative—from romance on the one hand, and burlesque on the other. The novel is more comic than the one, and more realistic than the other: its ancestors are "those great Masters who have sent their satire . . . laughing into the World"—Lucian, Cervantes, Swift.

Fielding's theory of the "comic epic poem in prose" belongs to the beginning of the history of criticism of the novel, but it also has a place in another, older critical debate—the discussions of the nature of comedy. In his views of the function of comedy, Fielding is in the tradition of Jonson and Dryden, but in his version of the comic character he is notably original. When he rejects burlesque, he is rejecting the seventeenth-century "humor" character, and substituting a more realistic model, the ridiculous character, the Man of Affectations

199

(one side of whom is the Man of Sensibility of sentimental comedy) seen with a satiric eye.

BIBLIOGRAPHY. *Works,* ed. George Saintsbury, 12 vols. (London, 1901); *The Covent Garden Journal,* ed. Gerald E. Jensen, 2 vols. (New Haven, 1915).

Frederick O. Bissell, *Fielding's Theory of the Novel* (Ithaca, 1933); Ethel M. Thornbury, *Henry Fielding's Theory of the Comic Novel* (Madison, 1931); Ian Watts, *Rise of the Novel: Studies in Defoe, Richardson, and Fielding* (Berkeley, 1957).

TEXT. *Works,* 8 vols. (London, 1771).

preface to

JOSEPH ANDREWS

[1742]

As IT IS POSSIBLE the mere English reader may have a different idea of romance from the author of these little volumes; and may consequently expect a kind of entertainment not to be found, nor which was even intended, in the following pages; it may not be improper to premise a few words concerning this kind of writing, which I do not remember to have seen hitherto attempted in our language.

THE EPIC, as well as the DRAMA, is divided into tragedy and comedy. HOMER, who was the father of this species of poetry, gave us a pattern of both these, though that of the latter kind is entirely lost; which Aristotle tells us, bore the same relation to comedy which his Iliad bears to tragedy. And perhaps, that we have no more instances of it among the writers of antiquity, is owing to the loss of this great pattern, which, had it survived, would have found its imitators equally with the other poems of this great original.

AND farther, as this poetry may be tragic or comic, I will not scruple to say it may be likewise either in verse or prose: For thô it wants one particular, which the critic enumerates in the constituent parts of an epic poem, namely metre; yet, when any kind of writing contains all its other parts, such as fable, action, characters, sentiments, and diction, and is deficient in metre only; it seems, I think, reasonable to refer it to the epic; at least, as no critic hath thought proper to range it under any other head, or to assign it a particular name to itself.

THUS the Telemachus of the archbishop of Cambray appears to me of the epic kind, as well as the Odyssey of Homer; indeed, it is much fairer and more reasonable to give it a name common with that species from which it differs only in a single instance, than to confound it with those which it resembles in no other. Such as those voluminous works commonly called Romances, namely, Clelia, Cleopatra, Astræa, Cassandra, the Grand Cyrus, and innumerable others, which contain, as I apprehend, very little instruction or entertainment.

Now a comic romance is a comic epic-poem in prose; differing from comedy, as the serious epic from tragedy: its action being more extended and comprehensive; containing a much larger circle of incidents, and introducing a greater variety of characters. It differs from the serious romance in its fable and action, in this; that as in the one these are grave and solemn, so in the other they are light and ridiculous: it differs in its characters, by introducing persons of inferior rank, and consequently, of inferior manners, whereas the grave romance sets the highest before us; lastly, in its sentiments and diction; by preserving the ludicrous instead of the sublime. In the diction, I think, burlesque itself may be sometimes admitted; of which many instances will occur in this work, as in the description of the battles, and some other places, not necessary to be pointed out to the classical reader; for whose entertainment those parodies or burlesque imitations are chiefly calculated.

BUT tho' we have sometimes admitted this in our diction, we have carefully excluded it from our sentiments and characters: for there it is never properly introduced, unless in writings of the burlesque kind, which this is not intended to be. Indeed, no two species of writing can differ more widely than the comic and the burlesque: for as the latter is ever the exhibition of what is monstrous and unnatural, and where our delight, if we examine it, arises from the surprising absurdity, as in appropriating the manners of the highest to the lowest, or *è converso;* so in the former, we should ever confine ourselves strictly to nature, from the just imitation of which, will flow all the pleasure we can this way convey to a sensible reader. And perhaps there is one reason why a comic writer should of all others be the least excused for deviating from nature, since it may not be always so easy for a serious poet to meet with the great and the admirable; but life every where furnishes an accurate observer with the ridiculous.

I have hinted this little concerning burlesque; because, I have often heard that name given to performances which have been truly of the comic kind, from the author's having sometimes admitted it in his diction only; which, as it is the dress of poetry, doth, like the dress of men, establish characters, (the one of the whole poem, and the other of the whole man) in vulgar opinion, beyond any of their greater excellencies. But surely, a certain drollery in stile, where the characters and sentiments are perfectly natural, no more constitutes the burlesque, than an empty pomp and dignity of words, where every thing else is mean and low, can entitle any performance to the appellation of the true sublime.

And I apprehend, my Lord Shaftesbury's opinion of mere burlesque agrees with mine, when he asserts, There is no such thing to be found in the writings of the ancients. But perhaps, I have less abhorrence than he professes for it: and that not because I have had some little success on the stage this way; but rather, as it contributes more to exquisite mirth and laughter than any other; and these are probably more wholesome physic for the mind, and conduce better to purge away spleen, melancholy and ill affections than is generally imagined. Nay, I will appeal to common observation, whether the same companies are not found more full of good humour and benevolence, after they have been sweetened for two or three hours with entertainments of this kind, than when soured by a tragedy or a grave lecture.

But to illustrate all this by another science, in which, perhaps, we shall see the distinction more clearly and plainly: Let us examine the works of a comic history-painter, with those performances which the Italians call Caricatura; where we shall find the true excellence of the former to consist in the exactest copying of Nature; insomuch that a judicious eye instantly rejects any thing *outré;* any liberty which the painter hath taken with the features of that *alma mater.* Whereas in the Caricatura we allow all licence. Its aim is to exhibit monsters not men; and all distortions and exaggerations whatever are within its proper province.

Now what Caricatura is in painting, Burlesque is in writing; and in the same manner the comic writer and painter correlate to each other. And here I shall observe, that, as in the former the painter seems to have the advantage; so it is in the latter infinitely on the side of the writer: for the Monstrous is much easier to paint than describe, and the Ridiculous to describe than paint.

AND tho' perhaps this latter species doth not in either science so strongly affect and agitate the muscles as the other; yet it will be owned, I believe that a more rational and useful pleasure arises to us from it. He who should call the ingenious Hogarth a burlesque painter, would in my opinion, do him very little honour: for sure it is much easier, much less the subject of admiration, to paint a man with a nose, or any other feature of a preposterous size, or to expose him in some absurd or monstrous attitude, than to express the affections of men on canvas. It hath been thought a vast commendation of a painter, to say his figures seem to breathe, but surely it is a much greater and nobler applause, that they appear to think.

BUT to return—The Ridiculous only, as I have before said, falls within my province in the present work.—Nor will some explanation of this word be thought impertinent by the reader, if he considers how wonderfully it hath been mistaken, even by writers who have profess'd it: for to what but such a mistake, can we attribute the many attempts to ridicule the blackest villanies; and what is yet worse, the most dreadful calamities? What could exceed the absurdity of an author, who should write the comedy of Nero, with the merry incident of ripping up his mother's belly; or what would give a greater shock to humanity, than an attempt to expose the miseries of poverty and distress to ridicule? And yet, the reader will not want much learning to suggest such instances to himself.

BESIDES, it may seem remarkable, that Aristotle, who is so fond and free of definitions, hath not thought proper to define the

Ridiculous. Indeed, where he tells us it is proper to comedy, he hath remarked that villany is not its object: but he hath not, as I remember, positively asserted what is. Nor doth the Abbé Bellegarde, who hath writ a treatise on this subject, tho' he shews us many species of it, once trace it to its fountain.

The only source of the true Ridiculous (as it appears to me) is affectation. But tho' it arises from one spring only; when we consider the infinite streams into which this one branches, we shall presently cease to admire at the copious field it affords to an observer. Now affectation proceeds from one of these two causes; vanity or hypocrisy: For as vanity puts us on affecting false characters, in order to purchase applause; so hypocrisy sets us on an endeavour to avoid censure, by concealing our vices under an appearance of their opposite virtues. And tho' these two causes are often confounded (for there is some difficulty in distinguishing them), yet, as they proceed from very different motives, so they are as clearly distinct in their operations: For indeed, the affectation which arises from vanity is nearer to truth than the other; as it hath not that violent repugnancy of nature to struggle with, which that of the hypocrite hath. It may be likewise noted, that affectation doth not imply an absolute negation of those qualities which are affected: and therefore, tho' when it proceeds from hypocrisy, it be nearly allied to deceit; yet when it comes from vanity only, it partakes of the nature of ostentation: for instance, the affectation of liberality in a vain man differs visibly from the same affectation in the avaricious; for tho' the vain man is not what he would appear, or hath not the virtue he affects, to the degree he would be thought to have it; yet it sits less aukwardly on him than on the avaricious man, who is the very reverse of what he would seem to be.

From the discovery of this affectation arises the Ridiculous—which always strikes the reader with surprize and pleasure; and that in a higher and stronger degree when the affectation arises from hypocrisy, than when from vanity: for to discover any one to be the exact reverse of what he affects, is more surprizing, and consequently more ridiculous, than to find him a little deficient in the quality he desires the reputation of. I might observe, that our Ben Johnson, who of all men understood the Ridiculous the best, hath chiefly used the hypocritical affectation.

Now from affectation only, the misfortunes and calamities of life, or the imperfections of nature, may become the objects of ridicule. Surely he hath a very ill-framed mind, who can look on ugliness, infirmity, or poverty, as ridiculous in themselves: nor do I believe any man living who meets a dirty fellow riding through the streets in a cart, is struck with an idea of the ridiculous from it; but if he should see the same figure descend from his coach and six, or bolt from his chair with his hat under his arm, he would then begin to laugh, and with justice. In the same manner, were we to enter a poor house, and behold a wretched family shivering with cold and languishing with hunger, it would not incline us to laughter (at least we must have very diabolical natures if it would:) but should we discover there a grate, instead of coals, adorned with flowers, empty plate or china dishes on the sideboard, or any other affectation of riches and finery either on their persons or in their furniture; we might then indeed be excused for ridiculing so fantastical an appearance. Much less are natural imperfections the object of derision: but when ugliness aims at the applause of beauty, or lameness endeavours to display agility; it is then that these unfortunate circumstances, which at first moved our compassion, tend only to raise our mirth.

THE poet carries this very far;

> None are for being what they are in fault,
> But for not being what they would be thought.

Where if the metre would suffer the word Ridiculous to close the first line, the thought would be rather more proper. Great vices are the proper objects of our detestation, smaller faults of our pity: but affectation appears to me the only true source of the Ridiculous.

BUT perhaps it may be objected to me, that I have against my own rules introduced vices, and of a very black kind into this work. To which I shall answer: first, that it is very difficult to pursue a series of human actions and keep clear from them. Secondly, that the vices to be found here, are rather the accidental consequences of some human frailty or foible, than causes habitually existing in the mind. Thirdly, that they are never set forth as the objects of ridicule but detestation. Fourthly, that they are never the principal figure at that time on the scene: and lastly, they never produce the intended evil.

Having thus distinguished Joseph Andrews from the productions of romance writers on the one hand, and burlesque writers on the other, and given some few very short hints (for I intended no more) of this species of writing, which I have affirmed to be hitherto unattempted in our language; I shall leave to my good-natur'd reader to apply my piece to my observations, and will detain him no longer than with a word concerning the characters in this work.

And here I solemnly protest, I have no intention to vilify or asperse any one: for tho' every thing is copied from the book of nature, and scarce a character or action produced which I have not taken from my own observations and experience; yet I have used the utmost care to obscure the persons by such different circumstances, degrees and colours, that it will be impossible to guess at them with any degree of certainty; and if it ever happens otherwise, it is only where the failure characterized is so minute, that it is a foible only which the party himself may laugh at as well as any other.

As to the character of Adams, as it is the most glaring in the whole, so I conceive it is not to be found in any book now extant. It is designed a character of perfect simplicity; and as the goodness of his heart will recommend him to the good-natured; so I hope it will excuse me to the gentlemen of his cloth; for whom, while they are worthy of their sacred order, no man can possibly have a greater respect. They will therefore excuse me, notwithstanding the low adventures in which he is engaged, that I have made him a clergyman; since no other office could have given him so many opportunities of displaying his worthy inclinations.

introductory chapters from

TOM JONES

[1749]

BOOK I

I: THE INTRODUCTION TO THE WORK, OR BILL OF FARE TO THE FEAST

AN AUTHOR OUGHT TO consider himself, not as a gentleman who gives a private or eleemosynary treat, but rather as one who keeps a public ordinary, at which all persons are welcome for their money. In the former case, it is well known that the entertainer provides what fare he pleases; and though this should be very indifferent, and utterly disagreeable to the taste of his company, they must not find any fault; nay, on the contrary, good-breeding forces them outwardly to approve and to commend whatever is set before them. Now the contrary of this happens to the master of an ordinary. Men who pay for what they eat will insist on gratifying their palates however nice and whimsical these may prove; and if everything is not agreeable to their taste, will challenge a right to censure, to abuse, and to d—n their dinner without controul.

To prevent therefore giving offence to their customers by any such disappointment, it hath been usual with the honest and well-meaning host, to provide a bill of fare which all persons may peruse at their first entrance into the house; and having thence acquainted themselves with the entertainment which they may expect, may either stay and regale with what is provided for them, or may depart to some other ordinary better accommodated to their taste.

As we do no disdain to borrow wit or wisdom from any man who is capable of lending us either, we have condescended to take a hint from these honest victuallers, and shall prefix not only a general bill of fare to our whole entertainment, but shall like-

wise give the reader particular bills to every course which is to
be served up in this and the ensuing volumes.

The provision, then, which we have here made is no other than
HUMAN NATURE. Nor do I fear that my sensible reader,
though most luxurious in his taste, will start, cavil, or be offended,
because I have named but one article. The tortoise, as the alder-
man of Bristol, well learned in eating, knows by much experience, besides the delicious Calibash and Calipee, contains many
different kinds of food; nor can the learned reader be ignorant,
that in human nature, though here collected under one general
name, is such prodigious variety, that a cook will have sooner
gone through all the several species of animal and vegetable food
in the world, than an author will be able to exhaust so extensive
a subject.

An objection may perhaps be apprehended from the more delicate, that this dish is too common and vulgar; for what else is
the subject of all the romances, novels, plays, and poems, with
which the stalls abound? Many exquisite viands might be rejected by the epicure, if it was a sufficient cause for his con-
temning of them as common and vulgar, that something was to
be found in the most paltry alleys under the same name. In
reality, true nature is as difficult to be met with in authors, as
the Bayonne ham, or Bologna sausage is to be found in the shops.

But the whole, to continue the same metaphor, consists in the
cookery of the author; for, as Mr. Pope tells us,

> 'True wit is nature to advantage drest,
> What oft' was thought, but ne'er so well exprest.'

The same animal which hath the honour to have some part of
his flesh eaten at the table of a duke, may perhaps be degraded
in another part, and some of his limbs gibbeted, as it were, in
the vilest stall in town. Where, then, lies the difference between
the food of the nobleman and the porter, if both are at dinner
on the same ox or calf, but in the seasoning, the dressing, the
garnishing, and the setting forth? Hence the one provokes and
incites the most languid appetite, and the other turns and palls
that which is the sharpest and keenest.

In like manner, the excellence of the mental entertainment
consists less in the subject than in the author's skill in well dress-

ing it up. How pleased therefore will the reader be to find, that we have, in the following work, adhered closely to one of the highest principles of the best cook which the present age, or perhaps that of Heliogabalus, hath produced? This great man, as is well known to all lovers of polite eating, begins at first by setting plain things before his hungry guests, rising afterwards by degrees as their stomachs may be supposed to decrease, to the very quintessence of sauce and spices. In like manner, we shall represent human nature at first to the keen appetite of our reader in that more plain and simple manner in which it is found in the country, and shall hereafter hash and ragoo it with all the high French and Italian seasoning of affectation and vice which courts and cities afford. By these means, we doubt not but our reader may be rendered desirous to read on for ever, as the great person, just above-mentioned, is supposed to have made some persons eat.

Having premised thus much, we will now detain those, who like our bill of fare, no longer from their diet, and shall proceed directly to serve up the first course of our history, for their entertainment.

BOOK V

I: OF THE SERIOUS IN WRITING, AND FOR WHAT PURPOSE IT IS INTRODUCED

PERADVENTURE THERE MAY BE no parts in this prodigious work which will give the reader less pleasure in the perusing, than those which have given the author the greatest pains in composing. Among these probably may be reckoned those initial essays which we have prefixed to the historical matter contained in every book; and which we have determined to be essentially necessary to this kind of writing, of which we have set ourselves at the head.

For this our determination we do not hold ourselves strictly bound to assign any reason; it being abundantly sufficient that we have laid it down as a rule necessary to be observed in all prosai-comi-epic writing. Who ever demanded the reasons of that nice unity of time or place which is now established to be so essential to dramatic poetry? What critic hath been ever asked,

why a play may not contain two days as well as one? Or why
the audience (provided they travel, like electors, without any
expence) may not be wafted fifty miles as well as five? Hath
any commentator well accounted for the limitation which an
ancient critic hath set to the drama, which he will have contain
neither more nor less than five acts? Or hath any one living attempted to explain, what the modern judges of our theatres mean
by that word LOW; by which they have happily succeeded in
banishing all humour from the stage, and have made the theatre
as dull as a drawing-room! Upon all these occasions the world
seems to have embraced a maximum of our law, viz., *cuicunque
in arte suo perito credendum est.* [Each person must trust experience in his own art.] for it seems, perhaps, difficult to conceive that any one should have had enough of impudence to
lay down dogmatical rules in any art of science without the least
foundation. In such cases, therefore, we are apt to conclude
there are sound and good reasons at the bottom, though we are
unfortunately not able to see so far.

Now, in reality, the world have paid too great a compliment
to critics, and have imagined them men of much greater pro-
fundity than they really are. From this complaisance, the critics
have been emboldened to assume a dictatorial power, and have
so far succeeded that they are now become the masters, and
have the assurance to give laws to those authors, from whose
predecessors they originally received them.

The critic, rightly considered, is no more than the clerk, whose
office it is to transcribe the rules and laws laid down by those
great judges, whose vast strength of genius hath placed them
in the light of legislators, in the several sciences over which they
presided. This office was all which the critics of old aspired to,
nor did they ever dare to advance a sentence, without supporting it by the authority of the judge from whence it was borrowed.

But in process of time, and in ages of ignorance, the clerk
began to invade the power, and assume the dignity of his master. The laws of writing were no longer founded on the practice of the author, but on the dictates of the critic. The clerk
became the legislator, and those very peremptorily gave laws,
whose business it was, at first, only to transcribe them.

Hence arose an obvious, and, perhaps, an unavoidable error: for these critics being men of shallow capacities, very easily mistook mere form for substance. They acted as a judge would, who should adhere to the lifeless letter of law, and reject the spirit. Little circumstances which were, perhaps, accidental in a great author, were, by these critics, considered to constitute his chief merit, and transmitted as essentials to be observed by all his successors. To these encroachments, time and ignorance, the two great supporters of imposture, gave authority; and thus many rules for good writing have been established which have not the least foundation in truth or nature; and which commonly serve for no other purpose than to curb and restrain genius, in the same manner as it would have restrained the dancing-master, had the many excellent treatises on that art laid it down as an essential rule, that every man must dance in chains.

To avoid, therefore, all imputation of laying down a rule for posterity, founded only on the authority of *ipse dixit* [He himself spoke]; for which, to say the truth, we have not the profoundest veneration, we shall here waive the privilege above contended for, and proceed to lay before the reader the reasons which have induced us to intersperse these several digressive essays in the course of this work.

And here we shall of necessity be led to open a new vein of knowledge, which, if it hath been discovered, hath not, to our remembrance, been wrought on by any ancient or modern writer. This vein is no other than that of contrast, which runs through all the works of the creation, and may probably have a large share in constituting in us the idea of all beauty, as well natural as artificial: for what demonstrates the beauty and excellence of anything but its reverse? Thus the beauty of day, and that of summer, is set off by the horrors of night and winter. And, I believe, if it was possible for a man to have seen only the two former, he would have a very imperfect idea of their beauty.

But to avoid too serious an air: can it be doubted, but that the finest woman in the world would lose all benefit of her charms in the eye of a man who had never seen one of another cast? The ladies themselves seem so sensible of this, that they are all industrious to procure foils: nay, they will become foils to themselves; for I have observed (at Bath particularly) that they endeavour to appear as ugly as possible in the morning, in order to set off that beauty which they intend to shew you in the evening.

Most artists have this secret in practice, though some, perhaps, have not much studied the theory. The jeweller knows that the finest brilliant requires a foil; and the painter, by the contrast of his figures, often acquires great applause.

A great genius among us will illustrate this matter fully. I cannot, indeed, range him under any general head of common artists, as he hath a title to be placed among those

> *Inventas qui vitam excoluere per artes.*
>
> Who by invented arts have life improv'd.

I mean here the inventor of that most exquisite entertainment, called the English Pantomime.

This entertainment consisted of two parts, which the inventor distinguished by the names of the serious and the comic. The serious exhibited a certain number of heathen gods and heroes, who were certainly the worst and dullest company into which an audience was ever introduced; and (which was a secret known to few) were actually intended so to be, in order to contrast the comic part of the entertainment, and to display the tricks of harlequin to the better advantage.

This was, perhaps, no very civil use of such personages; but the contrivance was, nevertheless, ingenious enough, and had its effect. And this will now plainly appear, if, instead of serious and comic, we supply the words duller and dullest; for the comic was certainly duller than anything before shown on the stage, and could be set off only by that superlative degree of dullness which composed the serious. So intolerably serious, indeed, were these gods and heroes, that harlequin (though the English gentleman of that name is not at all related to the French family, for he is of a much more serious disposition) was always welcome on the stage, as he relieved the audience from worse company.

Judicious writers have always practised this art of contrast with great success. I have been surprized that Horace should

cavil at this art in Homer; but indeed he contradicts himself
in the very next line:

> *Indignor quandoque bonus dormitat Homerus,*
> *Verùm opere in longo fas est obrepere somnum.*
>
> I grieve if e'er great Homer chance to sleep,
> Yet slumbers on long works have right to creep.

For we are not here to understand, as, perhaps, some have,
that an author actually falls asleep while he is writing. It is
true that readers are too apt to be so overtaken; but if the work
was as long as any of Oldmixon,[1] the author himself is too well
entertained to be subject to the least drowsiness. He is, as Mr.
Pope observes,

> Sleepless himself to give his readers sleep.

To say the truth, these soporific parts are so many scenes of
Serious artfully interwoven, in order to contrast and set off the
rest; and this is the true meaning of a late facetious writer, who
told the public, that whenever he was dull, they might be assured there was a design in it.

In this light then, or rather in this darkness, I would have
the reader to consider these initial essays. And after this warning, if he shall be of opinion that he can find enough of serious
in other parts of this history, he may pass over these, in which
we profess to be laboriously dull, and begin the following books
at the second chapter.

BOOK VIII

I: A WONDERFUL LONG CHAPTER CONCERNING THE MARVELLOUS; BEING MUCH THE LONGEST OF ALL OUR INTRODUCTORY CHAPTERS

As WE ARE NOW ENTERING upon a book, in which the course of
our history will oblige us to relate some matters of a more
strange and surprizing kind than any which have hitherto occurred, it may not be amiss, in the prolegomenous or introduc-

---

[1] John Oldmixon (1673–1742), historian and pamphleteer. His works,
written to advance party politics, are of slight merit.

tory chapter, to say something of that species of writing which is called the marvellous. To this we shall, as well for the sake of ourselves, as of others, endeavour to set some certain bounds; and indeed nothing can be more necessary, as critics [2] of different complexions are here apt to run into very different extremes; for while some are, with M. Dacier, ready to allow, that the same thing which is impossible may be yet probable,[3] others have so little historic or poetic faith, that they believe nothing to be either possible or probable the like to which hath not occurred to their own observation.

First then, I think, it may very reasonably be required of every writer, that he keeps within the bounds of possibility; and still remembers that what it is not possible for man to perform, it is scarce possible for man to believe he did perform. This conviction, perhaps, gave birth to many stories of the ancient Heathen deities (for most of them are of poetical original). The poet, being desirous to indulge a wanton and extravagant imagination, took refuge in that power, of the extent of which his readers were no judges, or rather which they imagined to be infinite, and consequently they could not be shocked at any prodigies related of it. This hath been strongly urged in defence of Homer's miracles; and it is perhaps a defence; not, as Mr. Pope would have it, because Ulysses told a set of foolish lies to the Phæacians, who were a very dull nation; but because the poet himself wrote to heathens, to whom poetical fables were articles of faith. For my own part, I must confess, so compassionate is my temper, I wish Polypheme had confined himself to his milk diet, and preserved his eye; nor could Ulysses be much more concerned than myself, when his companions were turned into swine by Circe, who shewed, I think, afterwards, too much regard for man's flesh to be supposed capable of converting it into bacon. I wish, likewise, with all my heart, that Homer could have known the rule prescribed by Horace, to introduce supernatural agents as seldom as possible. We should not then have seen his gods coming on trivial errands, and often behaving

[2] By this word here, and in most other parts of our work, we mean every reader in the world. [Fielding's note.]

[3] It is happy for M. Dacier that he was not an Irishman. [Fielding.] André Dacier (1651–1722) translated Aristotle's *Poetics* into French.

themselves so as not only to forfeit all title to respect, but to become the objects of scorn and derision. A conduct which must have shocked the credulity of a pious and sagacious heathen; and which could never have been defended, unless by agreeing with a supposition to which I have been sometimes almost inclined, that this most glorious poet, as he certainly was, had an intent to burlesque the superstitious faith of his own age and country.

But I have rested too long on a doctrine which can be of no use to a christian writer; for as he cannot introduce into his works any of that heavenly host which make a part of his creed, so it is horrid puerility to search the heathen theology for any of those deities who have been long since dethroned from their immortality. Lord Shaftesbury observes, that nothing is more cold than the invocation of a muse by a modern; he might have added, that nothing can be more absurd. A modern may with much more elegance invoke a ballad, as some have thought Homer did, or a mug of ale with the author of Hudibras; which latter may perhaps have inspired much more poetry as well as prose, than all the liquors of Hippocrene or Helicon.

The only supernatural agents which can in any manner be allowed to us moderns, are ghosts; but of these I would advise an author to be extremely sparing. These are indeed, like arsenic, and other dangerous drugs in physic, to be used with the utmost caution; nor would I advise the introduction of them at all in those works, or by those authors, to which, or to whom, a horse-laugh in the reader would be any great prejudice or mortification.

As for elves and fairies, and other such mummery, I purposely omit the mention of them, as I should be very unwilling to confine within any bounds those suprising imaginations, for whose vast capacity the limits of human nature are too narrow; whose works are to be considered as a new creation; and who have consequently just right to do what they will with their own.

Man therefore is the highest subject (unless on very extraordinary occasions indeed) which presents itself to the pen of our historian, or of our poet; and, in relating his actions, great care is to be taken, that we do not exceed the capacity of the agent we describe.

Nor is possibility alone sufficient to justify us, we must keep
likewise within the rules of probability. It is, I think, the opinion
of Aristotle; or if not, it is the opinion of some wise man,
whose authority will be as weighty when it is as old, 'That it
is no excuse for a poet who relates what is incredible, that the
thing related is really matter of fact.' This may perhaps be allowed true with regard to poetry, but it may be thought impracticable to extend it to the historian; for he is obliged to record
matters as he finds them, though they may be of so extraordinary a nature, as will require no small degree of historical faith
to swallow them. Such was the successless armament of Xerxes,
described by Herodotus, or the successful expedition of Alexander related by Arrian. Such of later years was the victory of
Agincourt obtained by Harry the Fifth, or that of Narva won
by Charles the Twelfth of Sweden. All which instances, the
more we reflect on them, appear still the more astonishing.

Such facts, however, as they occur in the thread of the story;
nay, indeed, as they constitute the essential parts of it, the historian is not only justifiable in recording as they really happened;
but indeed would be unpardonable should he omit or alter them.
But there are other facts not of such consequence nor so necessary, which, though ever so well attested, may nevertheless be
sacrificed to oblivion in complaisance to the scepticism of a
reader. Such is that memorable story of the ghost of George
Villers, which might with more propriety have been made a
present of to Dr. Drelincourt, to have kept the ghost of Mrs.
Veale company, at the head of his discourse upon death, than
have been introduced into so solemn a work as the history of
the rebellion.[4]

To say the truth, if the historian will confine himself to what
really happened, and utterly reject any circumstance, which,
though never so well attested, he must be well assured is false,
he will sometimes fall into the marvellous, but never into the

[4] The Earl of Clarendon tells the story of the ghost of George Villiers,
Duke of Buckingham, in Book I of his *History of the Rebellion and Civil
Wars in England;* Mrs. Veal appears in Defoe's "True Relation of the Ap-
parition of one Mrs. Veal, the next Day after her Death, to one Mrs. Bar-
grave at Canterbury, the 8th of September, 1705," a story first printed as a
part of Peter Drelincourt's *The Christian's Defense against the Fear of
Death* in 1706.

incredible. He will often raise the wonder and surprize of his reader, but never that incredulous hatred mentioned by Horace. It is by falling into fiction, therefore, that we generally offend against this rule, of deserting probability, which the historian seldom, if ever, quits, till he forsakes his character and commences a writer of romance. In this, however, those historians who relate public transactions have the advantage of us who confine ourselves to scenes of private life. The credit of the former is by common notoriety supported for a long time; and public records, with the concurrent testimony of many authors, bear evidence to their truth in future ages. Thus a Trajan and an Antoninus, a Nero and a Caligula, have all met with the belief of posterity; and no one doubts but that men so very good, and so very bad, were once the masters of mankind.

But we who deal in private character, who search into the most retired recesses, and draw forth examples of virtue and vice from holes and corners of the world, are in a more dangerous situation. As we have no public notoriety, no concurrent testimony, no records to support and corroborate what we deliver, it becomes us to keep within the limits not only of possibility, but of probability too; and this more especially in painting what is greatly good and amiable. Knavery and folly, though never so exorbitant, will more easily meet with assent; for ill-nature adds great support and strength to faith.

Thus we may, perhaps, with little danger, relate the history of Fisher, who having long owed his bread to the generosity of Mr. Derby, and having one morning received a considerable bounty from his hands, yet, in order to possess himself of what remained in his friend's scrutoire, concealed himself in a public office of the Temple, through which there was a passage into Mr. Derby's chambers. Here he overheard Mr. Derby for many hours solacing himself at an entertainment which he that evening gave his friends, and to which Fisher had been invited. During all this time, no tender, no grateful reflections arose to restrain his purpose; but when the poor gentleman had let his company out through the office, Fisher came suddenly from his lurking-place and walking softly behind his friend into his chamber, discharged a pistol-ball into his head. This may be believed, when the bones of Fisher are as rotten as his heart. Nay, perhaps,

it will be credited, that the villain went two days afterwards
with some young ladies to the play of Hamlet; and with an un-
altered countenance heard one of the ladies, who little suspected
how near she was to the person, cry out, 'Good God! if the man
that murdered Mr. Derby was now present.' Manifesting in this
a more seared and callous conscience than even Nero himself;
of whom we are told by Suetonius, 'that the consciousness of
his guilt, after the death of his mother, became immediately intolerable, and so continued; nor could all the congratulations
of the soldiers, of the senate, and the people, allay the horrors
of his conscience.'

But now, on the other hand, should I tell my reader, that I
had known a man whose penetrating genius had enabled him
to raise a large fortune in a way where no beginning was chalked
out to him; that he had done this with the most perfect preservation of his integrity, and not only without the least injustice or
injury to any one individual person, but with the highest advantage to trade, and a vast increase of the public revenue; that
he had expended one part of the income of this fortune in discovering a taste superior to most, by works where the highest
dignity was united with the purest simplicity, and another part
in displaying a degree of goodness superior to all men, by acts
of charity to objects whose only recommendations were their
merits, or their wants; that he was most industrious in searching
after merit in distress, most eager to relieve it, and then as careful (perhaps too careful) to conceal what he had done; that
his house, his furniture, his gardens, his table, his private hos-
pitality, and his public beneficence, all denoted the mind from
which they flowed, and were all intrinsically rich and noble,
without tinsel or external ostentation; that he filled every relation in life with the most adequate virtue; that he was most
piously religious to his creator, most zealously loyal to his sov-
ereign; a most tender husband to his wife, a kind relation; a
munificent patron, a warm and firm friend, a knowing and a
cheerful companion, indulgent to his servants, hospitable to
his neighbours, charitable to the poor, and benevolent to all
mankind. Should I add to these the epithets of wise, brave, elegant, and indeed every other amiable epithet in our language,
I might surely say,

—*Quis credet? nemo Hercule! nemo;*
Vel duo, vel nemo;

[Who will believe it? No one, by Hercules, no one;
Well, maybe two; maybe no one.]

And yet I know a man who is all I have here described. But a single instance (and I really know not such another) is not sufficient to justify us, while we are writing to thousands who never heard of the person, nor of anything like him. Such *Raræ Aves* [rare birds] should be remitted to the epitaph writer, or to some poet who may condescend to hitch him in a distich, or to slide him into a rhime with an air of carelessness and neglect, without giving any offence to the reader.

In the last place, the actions should be such as may not only be within the compass of human agency, and which human agents may probably be supposed to do; but they should be likely for the very actors and characters themselves to have performed; for what may be only wonderful and surprizing in one man, may become improbable, or indeed impossible, when related of another.

This last requisite is what the dramatic critics call conservation of character; and it requires a very extraordinary degree of judgment, and a most exact knowledge of human nature. It is admirably remarked by a most excellent writer, that zeal can no more hurry a man to act in direct opposition to itself, than a rapid stream can carry a boat against its own current. I will venture to say, that for a man to act in direct contradiction to the dictates of his nature, is, if not impossible, as improbable and as miraculous as anything which can well be conceived. Should the best parts of the story of M. Antoninus be ascribed to Nero, or should the worst incidents of Nero's life be imputed to Antoninus, what would be more shocking to belief than either instance; whereas both these being related of their proper agent, constitute the truly marvellous.

Our modern authors of comedy have fallen almost universally into the error here hinted at; their heroes generally are notorious rogues, and their heroines abandoned jades, during the first four acts; but in the fifth, the former become very worthy gentlemen, and the latter women of virtue and discretion: nor is the writer often so kind as to give himself the least trouble to reconcile or account for this monstrous change and incongruity. There is, indeed, no other reason to be assigned for it, than because the play is drawing to a conclusion; as if it was no less natural in a rogue to repent in the last act of a play, than in the last of his life; which we perceive to be generally the case at Tyburn, a place which might, indeed, close the scene of some comedies with much propriety, as the heroes in these are most commonly eminent for those very talents which not only bring men to the gallows, but enable them to make an heroic figure when they are there.

Within these few restrictions, I think, every writer may be permitted to deal as much in the wonderful as he pleases; nay, if he thus keeps within the rules of credibility, the more he can surprize the reader the more he will engage his attention, and the more he will charm him. As a genius of the highest rank observes in his fifth chapter of the Bathos, 'The great art of all poetry is to mix truth with fiction; in order to join the credible with the surprizing.'

For though every good author will confine himself within the bounds of probability, it is by no means necessary that his characters, or his incidents, should be trite, common, or vulgar; such as happen in every street, or in every house, or which may be met with in the home articles of a news-paper. Nor must he be inhibited from showing many persons and things, which may possibly have never fallen within the knowledge of great part of his readers. If the writer strictly observes the rules above-mentioned, he hath discharged his part; and is then entitled to some faith from his reader, who is indeed guilty of critical infidelity if he disbelieves him. For want of a portion of such faith, I remember the character of a young lady of quality, which was condemned on the stage for being unnatural, by the unanimous voice of a very large assembly of clerks and apprentices; though it had the previous suffrages of many ladies of the first rank; one of whom, very eminent for her understanding, declared it was the picture of half the young people of her acquaintance.

BOOK IX

I: OF THOSE WHO LAWFULLY MAY, AND OF THOSE WHO MAY NOT, WRITE SUCH HISTORIES AS THIS

AMONG OTHER GOOD USES for which I have thought proper to institute these several introductory chapters, I have considered them as a kind of mark or stamp, which may hereafter enable a very indifferent reader to distinguish what is true and genuine in this historic kind of writing, from what is false and counterfeit. Indeed, it seems likely that some such mark may shortly become necessary, since the favourable reception which two or three authors have lately procured for their works of this nature from the public, will probably serve as an encouragement to many others to undertake the like. Thus a swarm of foolish novels, and monstrous romances will be produced, either to the great impoverishing of booksellers, or to the great loss of time and depravation of morals in the reader; nay, often to the spreading of scandal and calumny, and to the prejudice of the characters of many worthy and honest people.

I question not but the ingenious author of the Spectator was principally induced to prefix Greek and Latin mottos to every paper from the same consideration of guarding against the pursuit of those scribblers, who, having no talents of a writer but what is taught by the writing-master, are yet nowise afraid nor ashamed to assume the same titles with the greatest genius, than their good brother in the fable was of braying in the lion's skin.

By the device therefore of his motto, it became impracticable for any man to presume to imitate the Spectator, without understanding at least one sentence in the learned languages. In the same manner I have now secured myself from the imitation of those who are utterly incapable of any degree of reflection, and whose learning is not equal to an essay.

I would not be here understood to insinuate, that the greatest merit of such historical productions can ever lie in these introductory chapters; but, in fact, those parts which contain mere narrative only, afford much more encouragement to the pen of an imitator, than those which are composed of observation and reflection. Here I mean such imitators as Rowe was of Shakespear, or as Horace hints some of the Romans were of Cato, by bare feet and sour faces.

To invent good stories, and to tell them well, are possibly very rare talents, and yet I have observed few persons who have scrupled to aim at both; and if we examine the romances and novels with which the world abounds, I think we may fairly conclude, that most of the authors would not have attempted to shew their teeth (if the expression may be allowed me) in any other way of writing; nor could indeed have strung together a dozen sentences on any other subject whatever. *Scribimus indocti doctique passim*,[5] may be more truly said of the historian and biographer than of any other species of writing; for all the arts and sciences (even criticism itself) require some little degree of learning and knowledge. Poetry, indeed, may perhaps be thought an exception; but then it demands numbers, or something like numbers: whereas, to the composition of novels and romances, nothing is necessary but paper, pens and ink, with the manual capacity of using them. This, I conceive, their productions shew to be the opinion of the authors themselves: and this must be the opinion of their readers, if indeed there be any such.

Hence we are to derive that universal contempt which the world, who always denominate the whole from the majority, have cast on all historical writers who do not draw their materials from records. And it is the apprehension of this contempt, that hath made us so cautiously avoid the term romance, a name with which we might otherwise have been well enough contented. Though, as we have good authority for all our characters, no less indeed than the vast authentic doomsday-book of nature, as is elsewhere hinted, our labours have sufficient title to the name of history. Certainly they deserve some distinction from those works, which one of the wittiest of men regarded only as proceeding from a Pruritus, [itching] or indeed rather from a looseness of the brain.

[5] —Each desperate blockhead dares to write,
   Verse is the trade of every living wight.—Francis. [Fielding.]

But besides the dishonour which is thus cast on one of the most useful as well as entertaining of all kinds of writing, there is just reason to apprehend, that by encouraging such authors we shall propagate much dishonour of another kind; I mean to the characters of many good and valuable members of society; for the dullest writers, no more than the dullest companions, are always inoffensive. They have both enough of language to be indecent and abusive. And surely, if the opinion just above cited be true, we cannot wonder, that works so nastily derived should be nasty themselves, or have a tendency to make others so.

To prevent therefore, for the future, such intemperate abuses of leisure, of letters, and of the liberty of the press, especially as the world seems at present to be more than usually threatened with them, I shall here venture to mention some qualifications, every one of which are in a pretty high degree necessary to this order of historians.

The first is, genius, without a full vein of which, no study, says Horace, can avail us. By genius I would understand that power, or rather those powers of the mind, which are capable of penetrating into all things within our reach and knowledge, and of distinguishing their essential differences. These are no other than invention and judgment; and they are both called by the collective name of genius, as they are of those gifts of nature which we bring with us into the world. Concerning each of which many seem to have fallen into very great errors; for by invention, I believe, is generally understood a creative faculty, which would indeed prove most romance writers to have the highest pretensions to it; whereas by invention is really meant no more, (and so the word signifies) than discovery, or finding out; or to explain it at large, a quick and sagacious penetration into the true essence of all the objects of our contemplation. This, I think, can rarely exist without the concomitancy of judgment; for how we can be said to have discovered the true essence of two things, without discerning their difference, seems to me hard to conceive. Now this last is the undisputed province of judgment, and yet some few men of wit have agreed with all the dull fellows in the world in representing these two to have been seldom or never the property of one and the same person.

But though they should be so, they are not sufficient for our purpose, without a good share of learning; for which I could again cite the authority of Horace, and of many others, if any was necessary to prove that tools are of no service to a workman, when they are not sharpened by art, or when he wants rules to direct him in his work, or hath no matter to work upon. All these uses are supplied by learning; for nature can only furnish us with capacity; or, as I have chose to illustrate it, with the tools of our profession; learning must fit them for use, must direct them in it, and, lastly, must contribute, part at least of the materials. A competent knowledge of history and of the Belles Lettres is here absolutely necessary; and without this share of knowledge at least, to affect the character of an historian, is as vain as to endeavour at building a house without timber or mortar, or brick or stone. Homer and Milton, who, though they added the ornament of numbers to their works, were both historians of our order, were masters of all the learning of their times.

Again, there is another sort of knowledge, beyond the power of learning to bestow, and this is to be had by conversation. So necessary is this to the understanding the characters of men, that none are more ignorant of them than those learned pedants whose lives have been entirely consumed in colleges and among books; for however exquisitely human nature may have been described by writers, the true practical system can be learnt only in the world. Indeed the like happens in every other kind of knowledge. Neither physic nor law are to be practically known from books. Nay, the farmer, the planter, the gardener, must perfect by experience what he hath acquired the rudiments of by reading. How accurately soever the ingenious Mr. Miller [6] may have described the plant, he himself would advise his disciple to see it in the garden. As we must perceive, that after the nicest strokes of a Shakespeare or a Johnson, of a Wycherly or an Otway, some touches of nature will escape the reader, which

[6] Philip Miller (1691–1771), the leading English horticulturist of his day, author of *The Gardener's Dictionary*.

the judicious action of a Garrick, of a Cibber, or a Clive,[7] can convey to him; so, on the real stage, the character shows himself in a stronger and bolder light than he can be described. And if this be the case in those fine and nervous descriptions which great authors themselves have taken from life, how much more strongly will it hold when the writer himself takes his lines not from nature, but from books? Such characters are only the faint copy of a copy, and can have neither the justness nor spirit of an original.

Now this conversation in our historian must be universal, that is, with all ranks and degrees of men; for the knowledge of what is called high-life will not instruct him in low; nor, *è converso,* will his being acquainted with the inferior part of mankind teach him the manners of the superior. And though it may be thought that the knowledge of either may sufficiently enable him to describe at least that in which he hath been conversant, yet he will ever here fall greatly short of perfection; for the follies of either rank do in reality illustrate each other. For instance, the affectation of high-life appears more glaring and ridiculous from the simplicity of the low; and again, the rudeness and barbarity of this latter, strikes with much stronger ideas of absurdity when contrasted with, and opposed to, the politeness which controls the former. Besides, to say the truth, the manners of our historians will be improved by both these conversations; for in the one he will easily find examples of plainness, honesty, and sincerity; in the other of refinement, elegance, and a liberality of spirits; which last quality I myself have scarce ever seen in men of low birth and education.

Nor will all the qualities I have hitherto given my historian avail him, unless he have what is generally meant by a good heart, and be capable of feeling. The author who will make me weep, says Horace, must first weep himself. In reality, no man can paint a distress well which he doth not feel while he is

---

[7] There is a peculiar propriety in mentioning this great actor, and these two most justly celebrated actresses, in this place, as they have all formed themselves on the study of nature only, and not on the imitation of their predecessors. Hence they have been able to excel all who have gone before them; a degree of merit which the servile herd of imitators can never possibly arrive at. [Fielding.]

painting it; nor do I doubt, but that the most pathetic and affecting scenes have been writ with tears. In the same manner it is with the ridiculous. I am convinced I never make my reader laugh heartily but where I have laughed before him; unless it should happen at any time, that instead of laughing with me, he should be inclined to laugh at me. Perhaps this may have been the case at some passages in this chapter, from which apprehension I will here put an end to it.

BOOK X

I: CONTAINING INSTRUCTIONS VERY NECESSARY TO BE PERUSED BY MODERN CRITICS

READER, it is impossible we should know what sort of person thou wilt be; for, perhaps, thou may'st be as learned in human nature as Shakespeare himself was, and, perhaps, thou may'st be no wiser than some of his editors. Now, lest this latter should be the case, we think proper, before we go any farther together, to give thee a few wholesome admonitions; that thou may'st not as grossly misunderstand and misrepresent us, as some of the said editors have misunderstood and misrepresented their author.

First, then, we warn thee not too hastily to condemn any of the incidents in this our history as impertinent and foreign to our main design, because thou dost not immediately conceive in what manner such incident may conduce to that design. This work may, indeed, be considered as a great creation of our own; and for a little reptile of a critic to presume to find fault with any of its parts, without knowing the manner in which the whole is connected, and before he comes to the final catastrophe, is a most presumptuous absurdity. The allusion and metaphor we have here made use of we must acknowledge to be infinitely too great for our occasion; but there is, indeed, no other which is at all adequate to express the difference between an author of the first rate and a critic of the lowest.

Another caution we would give thee, my good reptile, is, that thou dost not find out too near a resemblance between certain characters here introduced; as, for instance, between the land-lady who appears in the seventh book and her in the ninth. Thou art to know, friend, that there are certain characteristics in which most individuals of every profession and occupation agree. To be able to preserve these characteristics, and at the same time to diversify their operations, is one talent of a good writer. Again, to mark the nice distinction between two persons actuated by the same vice or folly, is another; and, as this last talent is found in very few writers, so is the true discernment of it found in as few readers: though, I believe, the observation of this forms a very principal pleasure in those who are capable of the discovery; every person, for instance, can distinguish between Sir Epicure Mammon, and Sir Fopling Flutter; but to note the difference between Sir Fopling Flutter and Sir Courtly Nice, requires a more exquisite judgment: for want of which, vulgar spectators of plays very often do great injustice in the theatre; where I have sometimes known a poet in danger of being convicted as a thief, upon much worse evidence than the resemblance of hands hath been held to be in the law. In reality, I apprehend every amorous widow on the stage would run the hazard of being condemned as a servile imitation of Dido, but that happily very few of our play-house critics understand enough of Latin to read Virgil.

In the next place, we must admonish thee, my worthy friend, (for, perhaps, thy heart may be better than thy head) not to condemn a character as a bad one because it is not perfectly a good one. If thou dost delight in these models of perfection, there are books enow written to gratify thy taste; but, as we have not, in the course of our conversation, ever happened to meet with any such person, we have not chosen to introduce any such here. To say the truth, I a little question whether mere man ever arrived at this consummate degree of excellence, as well as whether there hath ever existed a monster bad enough to verify that

> ——*nulla virtute redemptum*
> *A vitiis——* [8]

in Juvenal; nor do I, indeed, conceive the good purposes served by inserting characters of such angelic perfection, or such diabolical depravity, in any work of invention; since, from con-

[8] Whose vices are not allayed with a single virtue. [Fielding.]

templating either, the mind of man is more likely to be overwhelmed with sorrow and shame than to draw any good uses
from such patterns; for in the former instance he may be both
concerned and ashamed to see a pattern of excellence in his
nature, which he may reasonably despair of ever arriving at;
and in contemplating the latter he may be no less affected with
those uneasy sensations, at seeing the nature of which he is a
partaker, degraded into so odious and detestable a creature.

In fact, if there be enough of goodness in a character to engage the admiration and affection of a well-disposed mind,
though there should appear some of those little blemishes *quas
humana parum cavit natura,* [which human nature is too little
cautious about] they will raise our compassion rather than our
abhorrence. Indeed, nothing can be of more moral use than the
imperfections which are seen in examples of this kind; since
such form a kind of surprize, more apt to affect and dwell upon
our minds than the faults of very vicious and wicked persons.
The foibles and vices of men, in whom there is great mixture of
good, become more glaring objects from the virtues which contrast them and shew their deformity; and when we find such
vices attended with their evil consequence to our favourite characters, we are not only taught to shun them for our own sake,
but to hate them for the mischiefs they have already brought
on those we love.

And now, my friend, having given you these few admonitions,
we will, if you please, once more set forward with our history.

BOOK XI

I: A CRUST FOR THE CRITICS

IN OUR LAST INITIAL CHAPTER we may be supposed to have
treated that formidable set of men, who are called critics, with
more freedom than becomes us; since they exact, and indeed
generally receive, great condescension from Authors. We shall
in this, therefore, give the reasons of our conduct to this august
body; and here we shall, perhaps, place them in a light, in which
they have not hitherto been seen.

This word critic is of Greek derivation, and signifies judgment.
Hence I presume some persons who have not understood the

original, and have seen the English translation of the primitive, have concluded that it meant judgment in the legal sense, in which it is frequently used as equivalent to condemnation.

I am the rather inclined to be of that opinion, as the greatest number of critics hath of late years been found amongst the lawyers. Many of these gentlemen, from despair, perhaps, of ever rising to the bench in Westminster-Hall, have placed themselves on the benches at the playhouse, where they have exerted their judicial capacity, and have given judgment, *i.e.*, condemned without mercy.

The gentlemen would, perhaps be well enough pleased, if we were to leave them thus compared to one of the most important and honourable offices in the commonwealth, and, if we intended to apply to their favour, we would do so; but, as we design to deal very sincerely and plainly too with them, we must remind them of another officer of justice of a much lower rank; to whom, as they not only pronounce, but execute, their own judgment, they bear likewise some remote resemblance.

But in reality there is another light in which these modern critics may, with great justice and propriety, be seen; and this is that of a common slanderer. If a person who pries into the characters of others, with no other design but to discover their faults and to publish them to the world, deserves the title of a slanderer of the reputations of men, why should not a critic, who reads with the same malevolent view, be as properly styled the slanderer of the reputation of books?

Vice hath not, I believe, a more abject slave; society produces not a more odious vermin; nor can the devil receive a guest more worthy of him, nor possibly more welcome to him, than a slanderer. The world, I am afraid, regards not this monster with half the abhorrence which he deserves; and I am more afraid to assign the reason of this criminal lenity shewn towards him; yet it is certain that the thief looks innocent in the comparison; nay, the murderer himself can seldom stand in competition with his guilt: for slander is a more cruel weapon than a sword, as the wounds which the former gives are always incurable. One method, indeed, there is of killing, and that the basest and most execrable of all, which bears an exact analogy to the vice here disclaimed against, and that is poison. A means of revenge so base, and yet so horrible, that it was once wisely distinguished by our laws from all other murders, in the peculiar severity of the punishment.

Besides the dreadful mischiefs done by slander, and the baseness of the means by which they are effected, there are other circumstances that highly aggravate its atrocious quality: for it often proceeds from no provocation, and seldom promises itself any reward, unless some black and infernal mind may propose a reward in the thoughts of having procured the ruin and misery of another.

Shakespeare hath nobly touched this vice, when he says—

> 'Who steals my purse steals trash, 'tis something, nothing;
> 'Twas mine, 'tis his, and hath been slave to thousands:
> But he that filches from me my good name
> Robs me of that WHICH NOT ENRICHES HIM,
> BUT MAKES ME POOR INDEED.'

With all this my good reader will doubtless agree; but much of it will probably seem too severe, when applied to the slanderer of books. But let it here be considered, that both proceed from the same wicked disposition of mind, and are alike void of the excuse of temptation. Nor shall we conclude the injury done this way to be very slight, when we consider a book as the Author's offspring, and indeed as the child of his brain.

The reader who hath suffered his muse to continue hitherto in a virgin state, can have but a very inadequate idea of this kind of paternal fondness. To such we may parody the tender exclamation of Macduff, 'Alas! Thou hast written no book.' But the Author whose muse hath brought forth, will feel the pathetic strain, perhaps will accompany me with tears (especially if his darling be already no more) while I mention the uneasiness with which the big muse bears about her burden, the painful labour with which she produces it, and, lastly, the care, the fondness, with which the tender father nourishes his favourite, till it be brought to maturity, and produced into the world.

Nor is there any paternal fondness which seems less to savour of absolute instinct, and which may so well be reconciled to worldly wisdom, as this. These children may most truly be called the riches of their father, and many of them have with true filial piety fed their parent in his old age; so that not only the affection, but the interest, of the Author may be highly injured by these slanderers, whose poisonous breath brings his book to an untimely end.

Lastly, the slander of a book is, in truth, the slander of the Author; for, as no one can call another bastard, without calling the mother a whore, so neither can any one give the names of sad stuff, horrid nonsense, etc., to a book, without calling the Author a blockhead; which, though in a moral sense it is a preferable appellation to that of villain, is perhaps rather more injurious to his worldly interest.

Now, however ludicrous all this may appear to some, others, I doubt not, will feel and acknowledge the truth of it; nay, may, perhaps, think I have not treated the subject with decent solemnity; but surely a man may speak truth with a smiling countenance. In reality, to depreciate a book maliciously, or even wantonly, is at least a very ill-natured office; and a morose snarling critic may, I believe, be suspected to be a bad man.

I will therefore endeavour, in the remaining part of this chapter, to explain the marks of this chapter, and to shew what criticism I here intend to obviate; for I can never be understood, unless by the very persons here meant, to insinuate that there are no proper judges of writing, or to endeavour to exclude from the commonwealth of literature any of those noble critics to whose labours the learned world are so greatly indebted. Such were Aristotle, Horace, and Longinus, among the ancients, Dacier and Bossu among the French, and some perhaps among us; who have certainly been duly authorised to execute at least a judicial authority in *Foro Literario* [the literary forum].

But without ascertaining all the proper qualifications of a critic, which I have touched on elsewhere, I think I may very boldly object to the censures of any one passed upon works which he hath not himself read. Such censurers as these, whether they speak from their own guess or suspicion, or from the report and opinion of others, may properly be said to slander the reputation of the book they condemn.

Such may likewise be suspected of deserving this character, who, without assigning any particular faults, condemn the whole in general defamatory terms; such as vile, dull, d—d stuff, etc., and particularly by the use of the monosyllable low; a word which becomes the mouth of no critic who is not RIGHT HONOURABLE.

Again, though there may be some faults justly assigned in the work, yet, if those are not in the most essential parts, or if they are compensated by greater beauties, it will savour rather of the malice of a slanderer, than of the judgment of a true critic, to pass a severe sentence upon the whole merely on account of some vicious part. This is directly contrary to the sentiments of Horace:

> *Verum ubi plura nitent in carmine, non ego paucis*
> *Offendor maculis, quas aut incuria fudit,*
> *Aut humana parum cavit natura——*

> But where the beauties, more in number, shine,
> I am not angry, when a casual line
> (That with some trivial faults unequal flows)
> A careless hand or human frailty shows.
>   MR. FRANCIS.

For, as Martial says, *Aliter non fit, Avite, Liber.* No book can be otherwise composed. All beauty of character, as well as of countenance, and indeed of everything human, is to be tried in this manner. Cruel indeed would it be if such a work as this history, which hath employed some thousands of hours in the composing, should be liable to be condemned because some particular chapter, or perhaps chapters, may be obnoxious to very just and sensible objections. And yet nothing is more common than the most rigorous sentence upon books supported by such objections, which, if they were rightly taken (and that they are not always), do by no means go to the merit of the whole. In the theatre especially, a single expression which doth not coincide with the taste of the audience, or with any individual critic of that audience, is sure to be hissed; and one scene which should be disapproved would hazard the whole piece. To write within such severe rules as these is as impossible as to live up to some splenetic opinions; and if we judge according to the sentiments of some critics, and of some christians, no Author will be saved in this world, and no man in the next.

BOOK XIV

I: AN ESSAY TO PROVE THAT AN AUTHOR WILL WRITE THE BETTER FOR HAVING SOME KNOWLEDGE OF THE SUBJECT ON WHICH HE WRITES

As SEVERAL GENTLEMEN in these times, by the wonderful force of genius only, without the least assistance of learning, perhaps, without being well able to read, have made a considerable figure in the republic of letters, the modern critics, I am told, have lately begun to assert that all kind of learning is entirely useless to a writer; and, indeed, no other than a kind of fetters on the natural sprightliness and activity of the imagination, which is thus weighed down, and prevented from soaring to those high flights which otherwise it would be able to reach.

This doctrine, I am afraid, is at present carried much too far; for why should writing differ so much from all other arts? The nimbleness of a dancing-master is not at all prejudiced by being taught to move; nor doth any mechanic, I believe, exercise his tools the worse by having learnt to use them. For my own part, I cannot conceive that Homer or Virgil would have writ with more fire, if, instead of being masters of all the learning of their times, they had been as ignorant as most of the Authors of the present age. Nor do I believe that all the imagination, fire, and judgment of Pitt, could have produced those orations that have made the senate of England in these our times a rival in eloquence to Greece and Rome, if he had not been so well read in the writings of Demosthenes and Cicero, as have transferred their whole spirit into his speeches, and, with their spirit, their knowledge too.

I would not here be understood to insist on the same fund of learning in any of my brethren, as Cicero persuades us is necessary to the composition of an orator. On the contrary, very little reading is, I conceive, necessary to the poet, less to the critic, and the least of all to the politician. For the first, perhaps, Byshe's Art of Poetry, and a few of our modern poets, may suffice; for the second, a moderate heap of plays; and for the last, an indifferent collection of political journals.

To say the truth, I require no more than that a man should have some little knowledge of the subject on which he treats, according to the old maxim of law, *Quam quisque nôrit artem in eâ se exerceat* [what skill each man knows, this let him practise.]. With this alone a writer may sometimes do tolerably well; and, indeed without this, all the other learning in the world will stand him in little stead.

For instance, let us suppose that Homer and Virgil, Aristotle and Cicero, Thucydides and Livy, could have met all together, and have clubbed their several talents to have composed a treatise on the art of dancing: I believe it will be readily agreed they could not have equalled the excellent treatise which Mr. Essex hath given us on that subject, entitled The Rudiments of genteel Education. And, indeed, should the excellent Mr. Broughton be prevailed on to set fist to paper, and to complete the above-said rudiments, by delivering down the true principles of Athletics, I question whether the world will have any cause to lament that none of the great writers, either ancient or modern, have ever treated about that noble and useful art.

To avoid a multiplicity of examples in so plain a case, and to come at once to my point, I am apt to conceive, that one reason why many English writers have totally failed in describing the manners of upper life, may possibly be that in reality they know nothing of it.

This is a knowledge unhappily not in the power of many Authors to arrive at. Books will give us a very imperfect idea of it; nor will the stage a much better: the fine gentleman formed upon reading the former will almost always turn out a pedant, and he who forms himself upon the latter, a coxcomb.

Nor are the characters drawn from these models better supported. Vanbrugh and Congreve copied nature; but they who copy them draw as unlike the present age as Hogarth would do if he was to paint a rout or a drum in the dresses of Titian and of Vandyke. In short, imitation here will not do the business. The picture must be after nature herself. A true knowledge of the world is gained only by conversation, and the manners of every rank must be seen in order to be known.

Now it happens that this higher order of mortals is not to be seen, like all the rest of the human species, for nothing, in the streets, shops, and coffeehouses; nor are they shewn, like the upper rank of animals, for so much a-piece. In short, this is a sight to which no persons are admitted, without one or other of these qualifications, viz., either birth or fortune, or, what is equivalent to both, the honourable profession of a gamester. And, very unluckily for the world, persons so qualified very seldom care to take upon themselves the bad trade of writing; which is generally entered upon by the lower and poorer sort, as it is a trade which many think requires no kind of stock to set up with.

Hence those strange monsters in lace and embroidery, in silks and brocades, with vast wigs and hoops; which, under the name of lords and ladies, strut the stage, to the great delight of attornies and their clerks in the pit, and of the citizens and their apprentices in the galleries; and which are no more to be found in real life than the centaur, the chimera, or any other creature of mere fiction. But to let my reader into a secret, this knowledge of upper life, though very necessary for preventing mistakes, is no very great resource to a writer whose province is comedy, or that kind of novels which, like this I am writing, is of the comic class.

What Mr. Pope says of women is very applicable to most in this station, who are, indeed, so entirely made up of form and affectation, that they have no character at all, at least none which appears. I will venture to say the highest life is much the dullest, and affords very little humour or entertainment. The various callings in lower spheres produce the great variety of humorous characters; whereas here, except among the few who are engaged in the pursuit of ambition, and the fewer still who have a relish for pleasure, all is vanity and servile imitation. Dressing and cards, eating and drinking, bowing and courtesying, make up the business of their lives.

Some there are, however, of this rank upon whom passion exercises its tyranny, and hurries them far beyond the bounds which decorum prescribes; of these, the ladies are as much distinguished by their noble intrepidity, and a certain superior contempt of reputation, from the frail ones of meaner degree, as a virtuous woman of quality is by the elegance and delicacy of her sentiments from the honest wife of a yeoman and shopkeeper. Lady Bellaston was of this intrepid character; but let not my country readers conclude from her, that this is the general conduct of women of fashion, or that we mean to represent them as such. They might as well suppose that every clergyman was represented by Thwackum, or every soldier by ensign Northerton.[9]

There is not, indeed, a greater error than that which universally prevails among the vulgar, who, borrowing their opinion from some ignorant satirists, have affixed the character of lewdness to these times. On the contrary, I am convinced there never was less of love intrigue carried on among persons of condition than now. Our present women have been taught by their mothers to fix their thoughts only on ambition and vanity, and to despise the pleasures of love as unworthy their regard; and being afterwards, by the care of such mothers, married without having husbands, they seem pretty well confirmed in the justness of those sentiments; whence they content themselves, for the dull remainder of life, with the pursuit of more innocent, but I am afraid more childish amusements, the bare mention of which would ill suit with the dignity of this history. In my humble opinion, the true characteristic of the present Beau Monde, is rather folly than vice, and the only epithet which it deserves is that of frivolous.

[9] Two undesirable characters in Fielding's *Tom Jones.*

THE PURPOSE OF LETTERS *

[1752]

At nostri Proavi Plautinos et numeros, et
Laudavére Sales, nimium patienter utrumque,
Ne dicam Stulte, mirati.   Hor.

Modernized.

In former Times this tasteless, silly Town
Too fondly prais'd Tom D'Urfey and Tom Brown.

THE PRESENT AGE SEEMS pretty well agreed in an opinion, that the utmost scope and end of reading is amusement only; and

* FROM the *Covent Garden Journal,* Number X Feb. 4, 1752.

such, indeed, are now the fashionable books, that a reader can propose no more than mere entertainment, and it is sometimes very well for him if he finds even this in his studies.

Letters, however, were surely intended for a much more noble and profitable Purpose than this. Writers are not, I presume, to be considered as mere jack puddings, whose business it is only to excite laughter: This, indeed, may sometimes be intermixed, and served up, with graver matters, in order to titilate the palate, and to recommend wholesome Food to the Mind; and, for this Purpose, it hath been used by many excellent authors: "for why (as Horace says) should not any one promulgate truth with a smile on his countenance? Ridicule, indeed, as he again intimates, is commonly a stronger and better Method of attacking Vice, than the severer kind of Satire."

When wit and humour are introduced for such good purposes, when the agreeable is blended with the useful, then is the Writer said to have succeeded in every Point. Pleasantry, (as the ingenious author of Clarissa says of a story) should be made only the vehicle of instruction; and thus romances themselves, as well as Epic Poems, may become worthy the perusal of the greatest of men: but when no moral, no lesson, no instruction is conveyed to the reader, where the whole design of the composition is no more than to make us laugh, the writer comes very near to the character of a buffoon; and his admirers, if an old Latin proverb be true, deserve no great compliments to be paid to their wisdom.

After what I have here advanced, I cannot fairly, I think, be represented as an enemy to laughter, or to all those kinds of writing that are apt to promote it. On the contrary, few men, I believe, do more admire the works of those great masters who have sent their satire (if I may use the expression) laughing into the world. Such are that great Triumvirate, Lucian, Cervantes, and Swift. These authors I shall ever hold in the highest degree of esteem; not indeed for that wit and humour alone which they all so eminently possest, but because they all endeavoured, with the utmost force of their wit and humour, to expose and extirpate those follies and vices which chiefly prevailed in their several countries.

I would not be thought to confine wit and humour to these writers. Shakespeare, Moliere, and some other authors, have been blessed with the same talents, and have employed them to the same purposes. There are some, however, who tho' not void of these talents have made so wretched a use of them, that had the consecration of their labours been committed to the hands of the hangman, no good man would have regretted their loss: Nor am I afraid to mention Rabelais, and Aristophanes himself in this number. For if I may speak my opinion freely of these two last writers, and of their works, their design appears to me very plainly to have been to ridicule all sobriety, modesty, decency, virtue and religion, out of the world. Now whoever reads over the five great writers first mentioned in this paragraph, must either have a very bad head, or a very bad heart, if he doth not become both a wiser and a better man.

In the exercise of the mind, as well as in the exercise of the body, diversion is a secondary consideration, and designed only to make that agreeable, which is at the same time useful, to such noble purposes as health and wisdom. But what should we say to a man who mounted his chamber hobby, or fought with his own shadow for his amusement only? How much more absurd and weak would he appear, who swallowed poison because it was sweet?

How differently did Horace think of study from our modern Readers?

Quid verum atque decens curo et rogo, et omnis in hoc sum:
Condo et compono, quae mox depromere possim.

"Truth and decency are my whole care and enquiry. In this study I am entirely occupied; these I am always laying up, and so disposing, that I can at any time draw forth my stores for my immediate use." The whole epistle indeed, from which I have paraphrased this passage, is a comment upon it, and affords many useful lessons of philosophy.

When we are employed in reading a great and good author, we ought to consider ourselves as searching after treasures, which, if well and regularly laid up in the mind, will be of use to us on sundry occasions in our lives. If a man, for instance, should be overloaded with prosperity, or adversity, (both of which cases are liable to happen to us) who is there so very wise, or so very foolish, that, if he was a master of Seneca and Plutarch, could not find great matter of comfort and utility from their doctrines? I mention these rather than Plato and Aristotle, as the works of the latter are not, I think, yet completely made English; and, consequently, are less within the reach of most of my countrymen.

But, perhaps, it may be asked, will Seneca or Plutarch make us laugh? Perhaps not; but if you are not a fool, my worthy friend, which I can hardly with civility suspect, they will both, (the latter especially) please you more than if they did. For my own part, I declare, I have not read even Lucian himself with more delight than I have Plutarch; but surely it is astonishing, that such scriblers as Tom Brown, Tom D'Urfey, and the wits of our age should find readers, whilst the writing of so excellent, so entertaining, and so voluminous an author as Plutarch remain in the world, and, as I apprehend, are very little known.

The truth I am afraid is, that real taste is a quality with which human nature is very slenderly gifted. It is indeed so very rare, and so little known, that scarce two authors have agreed in their notions of it; and those who have endeavoured to explain it to others, seem to have succeeded only in shewing us that they knew it not themselves. If I might be allowed to give my own sentiments, I should derive it from a nice harmony between the imagination and the judgment; and hence perhaps it is, that so few have ever possessed this talent in any eminent degree. Neither of these will alone bestow it; nothing is indeed more common than to see men of very bright imaginations, and of very accurate learning (which can hardly be acquired without judgment) who are entirely devoid of taste; and Longinus, who of all men seems most exquisitely to have possessed it, will puzzle his reader very much if he should attempt to decide, whether imagination or judgment shine the brighter in that inimitable critic.

But as for the bulk of mankind, they are clearly void of any degree of taste. It is a quality in which they advance very little beyond a state of infancy. The first thing a child is fond of in a book, is a picture; the second is a story; and the third a jest. Here then is the true Pons Asinorum, which very few readers ever get over.

From what I have said, it may perhaps be thought to appear, that true taste is the real gift of nature only; and if so, some may ask, to what purpose have I endeavoured to show men that they are without a blessing, which it is impossible for them to attain?

Now, tho' it is certain that to the highest consummation of taste, as well as of every other excellence, nature must lend much assistance; yet great is the power of art almost of itself, or at best with only slender aids from nature; and to say the truth, there are very few who have not in their minds some small seeds of taste. "All men (says Cicero) have a sort of tacit sense of what is right or wrong in arts and sciences, even without the help of arts." This surely it is in the power of art very greatly to improve. That most men therefore proceed no farther than as I have above declared, is owing either to the want of any, or (which is perhaps yet worse) to an improper education.

I shall, probably, therefore, in a future paper, endeavour to lay down some rules by which all men may acquire, at least some degree of taste. In the mean while, I shall, (according to the method observed in inoculation) recommend to my readers, as a preparative for their receiving my instructions, a total abstinence from all bad books; I do therefore most earnestly intreat all my young readers, that they would cautiously avoid the perusal of any modern book till it hath first had the sanction of some wise and learned man; and the same caution I propose to all fathers, mothers, and guardians.

"Evil communications corrupt good manners," is a quotation of St. Paul from Menander. *Evil books corrupt at once both our manners and our taste.* c.

Edmund Burke

[1729–1797]

❧❦❧

BURKE's *Philosophical Inquiry into the Origin of our Ideas of the Sublime and Beautiful* is his single work of critical theory in a long career otherwise devoted to politics and to philosophical and political writing. Soon after this work was published, in his twenty-ninth year, Burke entered the political world, first as a journalist, then as secretary to the Prime Minister, and finally, in 1785, as a Member of Parliament, where he remained as a leading figure in the Whig party for almost thirty years.

Burke's *Inquiry* is the most important and influential of many Augustan critical works based on Longinus' *On the Sublime*. But, as Burke's title suggests, it also has roots in the empirical psychology of Locke, and belongs to the line of psychological thought which was an important dimension of eigtheenth-century criticism. Burke set out to clarify the ideas of Sublimity and Beauty by examining the subjective origins of aesthetic experience. He begins with a discussion of Taste, in order to establish the principle that there is a faculty of the mind, based on sensory perceptions and imagination, which is uniform in all minds. If this is true, then the theorist can confidently analyze those properties in experience which produce the passions which are "sublime." Sublimity depends on certain external causes—Burke lists vastness, ruggedness, darkness and gloom, massiveness—but its existence is pychological; it is "the strongest emotion which the mind is capable of feeling."

In his treatment of tragedy, Burke rejects both the "unreality" theory (that we feel pleasure in the fact that the tragic action is *only* an imitation of reality) and the "separation" theory (that we feel relief because the tragedy is not ours); what we feel, he says, is a sympathy with suffering which, since it involves pain, is an aspect of the sublime, and which will increase as our sense of the reality of the suffering increases. In this sympathetic theory, Burke is in the sentimental tradition of Steele (see above, pp. 195 to 198); but he is also anticipating the realist aesthetics of the nineteenth century.

BIBLIOGRAPHY. *Works*, 6 vols., with a general introduction by William
Willis (Oxford, 1936).

Walter John Hipple, Jr., *The Beautiful, The Sublime, and The
Picturesque in Eighteenth-Century British Aesthetic Theory* (Carbondale, Illinois, 1957); Samuel H. Monk, *The Sublime* (New York,
1938); T. M. Moore, *The Background of Burke's Theory of the Sublime* (Ithaca, New York, 1938).

TEXT. *Works* (London, 1803), vol. I.

from

A PHILOSOPHICAL INQUIRY INTO THE ORIGIN OF OUR IDEAS OF THE SUBLIME AND BEAUTIFUL

[1757]

INTRODUCTION: OF TASTE

ON A SUPERFICIAL VIEW we may seem to differ very widely from
each other in our reasonings, and no less in our pleasures: but,
notwithstanding this difference, which I think to be rather apparent than real, it is probable that the standard both of reason
and taste is the same in all human creatures. For if there were
not some principles of judgment as well as of sentiment common
to all mankind, no hold could possibly be taken either on their
reason or their passions, sufficient to maintain the ordinary correspondence of life. It appears indeed to be generally acknowledged, that with regard to truth and falsehood there is something
fixed. We find people in their disputes continually appealing to
certain tests and standards, which are allowed on all sides, and
are supposed to be established in our common nature. But there
is not the same obvious concurrence in any uniform or settled
principles which relate to taste. It is even commonly supposed
that this delicate and aërial faculty, which seems too volatile to
endure even the chains of a definition, cannot be properly tried
by any test, nor regulated by any standard. There is so continual
a call for the exercise of the reasoning faculty; and it is so much

strengthened by perpetual contention, that certain maxims of right reason seem to be tacitly settled amongst the most ignorant. The learned have improved on this rude science, and reduced those maxims into a system. If taste has not been so happily cultivated, it was not that the subject was barren, but that the laborers were few or negligent; for to say the truth, there are not the same interesting motives to impel us to fix the one, which urge us to ascertain the other. And, after all, if men differ in their opinions concerning such matters, their difference is not attended with the same important consequences; else I make no doubt but that the logic of taste, if I may be allowed the expression, might very possibly be as well digested, and we might come to discuss matters of this nature with as much certainty, as those which seem more immediately within the province of mere reason. And, indeed, it is very necessary, at the entrance into such an inquiry as our present, to make this point as clear as possible; for if taste has no fixed principles, if the imagination is not affected according to some invariable and certain laws, our labor is likely to be employed to very little purpose; as it must be judged an useless, if not an absurd undertaking, to lay down rules for caprice, and to set up for a legislator of whims and fancies.

The term taste, like all other figurative terms, is not extremely accurate; the thing which we understand by it is far from a simple and determinate idea in the minds of most men, and it is therefore liable to uncertainty and confusion. I have no great opinion of a definition, the celebrated remedy for the cure of this disorder. For, when we define, we seem in danger of circumscribing nature within the bounds of our own notions, which we often take up by hazard or embrace on trust, or form out of a limited and partial consideration of the object before us; instead of extending our ideas to take in all that nature comprehends, according to her manner of combining. We are limited in our inquiry by the strict laws to which we have submitted at our setting out.

> *Circa vilem patulumque morabimur orbem,*
> *Unde pudor proferre pedem vetat aut operis lex.*
> [We shall tarry about the lowly and extensive world, whence a sense of modesty or the law of work keeps us from moving forward.]

A definition may be very exact, and yet go but a very little way towards informing us of the nature of the thing defined; but let the virtue of a definition be what it will, in the order of things, it seems rather to follow than to precede our inquiry, of which it ought to be considered as the result. It must be acknowledged that the methods of disquisition and teaching may be sometimes different, and on very good reason undoubtedly; but, for my part, I am convinced that the method of teaching which approaches most nearly to the method of investigation is incomparably the best; since, not content with serving up a few barren and lifeless truths, it leads to the stock on which they grew; it tends to set the reader himself in the track of invention, and to direct him into those paths in which the author has made his own discoveries, if he should be so happy as to have made any that are valuable.

But to cut off all pretence for cavilling, I mean by the word Taste, no more than that faculty or those faculties of the mind, which are affected with, or which form a judgment of, the works of imagination and the elegant arts. This is, I think, the most general idea of that word, and what is the least connected with any particular theory. And my point in this inquiry is, to find whether there are any principles, on which the imagination is affected, so common to all, so grounded and certain, as to supply the means of reasoning satisfactorily about them. And such principles of taste I fancy there are; however paradoxical it may seem to those, who on a superficial view imagine that there is so great a diversity of tastes, both in kind and degree, that nothing can be more indeterminate.

All the natural powers in man, which I know, that are conversant about external objects, are the senses; the imagination; and the judgment. And first with regard to the senses. We do and we must suppose, that as the conformation of their organs are nearly or altogether the same in all men, so the manner of perceiving external objects is in all men the same, or with little difference. We are satisfied that what appears to be light to one eye, appears light to another; that what seems sweet to one palate, is sweet to another; that what is dark and bitter to this man, is likewise dark and bitter to that; and we conclude in the same manner of great and little, hard and soft, hot and cold, rough and smooth; and indeed of all the natural qualities and affections of bodies. If we suffer ourselves to imagine, that their senses present to different men different images of things, this sceptical proceeding will make every sort of reasoning on every subject vain and frivolous, even that sceptical reasoning itself which had persuaded us to entertain a doubt concerning the agreement of our perceptions. But as there will be little doubt that bodies present similar images to the whole species, it must necessarily be allowed, that the pleasures and the pains which every object excites in one man, it must raise in all mankind, whilst it operates naturally, simply, and by its proper powers only: for if we deny this, we must imagine that the same cause, operating in the same manner, and on subjects of the same kind, will produce different effects; which would be highly absurd. Let us first consider this point in the sense of taste, and the rather as the faculty in question has taken its name from that sense. All men are agreed to call vinegar sour, honey sweet, and aloes bitter; and as they are all agreed in finding these qualities in those objects, they do not in the least differ concerning their effects with regard to pleasure and pain. They all concur in calling sweetness pleasant, and sourness and bitterness unpleasant. Here there is no diversity in their sentiments; and that there is not, appears fully from the consent of all men in the metaphors which are taken from the sense of taste. A sour temper, bitter expressions, bitter curses, a bitter fate, are terms well and strongly understood by all. And we are altogether as well understood when we say, a sweet disposition, a sweet person, a sweet condition and the like. It is confessed, that custom and some other causes have made many deviations from the natural pleasures or pains which belong to these several tastes; but then the power of distinguishing between the natural and the acquired relish remains to the very last. A man frequently comes to prefer the taste of tobacco to that of sugar, and the flavor of vinegar to that of milk; but this makes no confusion in tastes, whilst he is sensible that the tobacco and vinegar are not sweet, and whilst he knows that habit alone has reconciled his palate to these alien pleasures. Even with such a person we may speak, and with sufficient precision, concerning tastes. But should any man be found who declares, that to him tobacco has a taste like sugar, and that he cannot distinguish between milk and vinegar; or that tobacco and vinegar are sweet, milk bitter, and sugar sour; we immediately conclude that the organs of this man are out of order, and that his palate is utterly vitiated. We are as far from conferring with such a person upon tastes, as from reasoning concerning the relations of quantity with one who should deny that all the parts together were equal to the whole. We do not call a man of this kind wrong in his notions, but absolutely mad. Exceptions of this sort, in either way, do not at all impeach our general rule, nor make us conclude that men have various principles concerning the relations of quantity or the taste of things. So that when it is said, taste cannot be disputed, it can only mean, that no one can strictly answer what pleasure or pain some particular man may find from the taste of some particular thing. This indeed cannot be disputed; but we may dispute, and with sufficient clearness too, concerning the things which are naturally pleasing or disagreeable to the sense. But when we talk of any peculiar or acquired relish, then we must know the habits, the prejudices, or the distempers of this particular man, and we must draw our conclusion from those.

This agreement of mankind is not confined to the taste solely. The principle of pleasure derived from sight is the same in all. Light is more pleasing than darkness. Summer, when the earth is clad in green, when the heavens are serene and bright, is more agreeable than winter, when everything make a different appearance. I never remember that anything beautiful, whether a man, a beast, a bird, or a plant, was ever shown, though it were to a hundred people, that they did not all immediately agree that it was beautiful, though some might have thought that it fell short of their expectation, or that other things were still finer. I believe no man thinks a goose to be more beautiful than a swan, or images that what they call a Friesland hen excels a peacock. It must be observed too, that the pleasures of the sight are not near so complicated, and confused, and altered by unnatural habits and associations, as the pleasures of the taste are; because the pleasures of the sight more commonly acquiesce in themselves; and are not so often altered by considerations which are independent of the sight itself. But things do not spontaneously present themselves to the palate as they do to the sight; they are generally applied to it, either as food or as medicine; and from the qualities which they possess for nutritive or medicinal purposes they often form the palate by degrees, and by force of these associations. Thus opium is pleasing to Turks, on account of the agreeable delirium it produces. Tobacco is the delight of Dutchmen, as it diffuses a torpor and pleasing stupefaction. Fermented spirits please our common people, because they banish care, and all consideration of future or present evils. All of these, together with tea and coffee, and some other things, have passed from the apothecary's shop to our tables, and were taken for health long before they were thought of for pleasure. The effect of the drug has made us use it frequently; and frequent use, combined with the agreeable effect, has made the taste itself at last agreeable. But this does not in the least perplex our reasoning; because we distinguish to the last the acquired from the natural relish. In describing the taste of an unknown fruit, you would scarcely say that it had a sweet and pleasant flavor like tobacco, opium, or garlic, although you spoke to those who were in the constant use of these drugs, and had great pleasure in them. There is in all men a sufficient remembrance of the original natural causes of pleasure, to enable them to bring all things offered to their senses to that standard, and to regulate their feelings and opinions by it. Suppose one who had so vitiated his palate as to take more pleasure in the taste of opium than in that of butter or honey, to be presented with a bolus of squills; there is hardly any doubt but that he would prefer the butter or honey to this nauseous morsel, or to any other bitter drug to which he had not been accustomed; which proves that his palate was naturally like that of other men in all things, that it is still like the palate of other men in many things, and only vitiated in some particular points. For in judging of any new thing, even of a taste similar to that which he had been formed by habit to like, he finds his palate affected in the natural manner, and on the common principles. Thus the pleasure of all the senses, of the sight, and even of the taste, that most ambiguous of the senses, is the same in all, high and low, learned and unlearned.

Besides the ideas, with their annexed pains and pleasures, which are presented by the sense; the mind of man possesses a sort of creative power of its own; either in representing at pleasure the images of things in the order and manner in which they were received by the senses, or in combining those images in a new manner, and according to a different order. This power is called imagination; and to this belongs whatever is called wit, fancy, invention, and the like. But it must be observed, that this power of the imagination is incapable of producing anything absolutely new; it can only vary the disposition of those ideas which it has received from the senses. Now the imagination is the most extensive province of pleasure and pain, as it is the region of our fears and our hopes, and of all our passions that are connected with them; and whatever is calculated to affect the imagination with these commanding ideas, by force of any original natural impression, must have the same power pretty equally over all men. For since the imagination is only the representation of the senses, it can only be pleased or displeased with the images, from the same principle on which the sense is pleased or displeased with the realities; and consequently there must be just as close an agreement in the imaginations as in the senses of men. A little attention will convince us that this must of necessity be the case.

But in the imagination, besides the pain or pleasure arising from the properties of the natural object, a pleasure is perceived from the resemblance which the imitation has to the original: the imagination, I conceive, can have no pleasure but what results from one or other of these causes. And these causes operate pretty uniformly upon all men, because they operate by principles in nature, and which are not derived from any particular habits or advantages. Mr. Locke very justly and finely observes of wit, that it is chiefly conversant in tracing resemblances; he remarks, at the same time, that the business of judgment is rather in finding differences. It may perhaps appear, on this supposition, that there is no material distinction between the wit and the judgment, as they both seem to result from different operations of the same faculty of *comparing*. But in reality, whether they are or are not dependent on the same power of the mind, they differ so very materially in many respects, that a perfect union of wit and judgment is one of the rarest things in the world. When two distinct objects are unlike to each other, it is only what we expect; things are in their common way; and therefore they make no impression on the imagination: but when two distinct objects have a resemblance, we are struck, we attend to them, and we are pleased. The mind of man has naturally a far greater alacrity and satisfaction in tracing resemblances than in searching for differences: because by making resemblances we produce *new images;* we unite, we create, we enlarge our stock; but in making distinctions we offer no food at all to the imagination; the task itself is more severe and irksome, and what pleasure we derive from it is something of a negative and indirect nature. A piece of news is told me in the morning; this, merely as a piece of news, as a fact added to my stock, gives me some pleasure. In the evening I find there was nothing in it. What do I gain by this, but the dissatisfaction to find that I had been imposed upon? Hence it is that men are much more naturally inclined to belief than to incredulity. And it is upon this principle, that the most ignorant and barbarous nations have frequently excelled in similitudes, comparisons, metaphors, and allegories, who have been weak and backward in distinguishing and sorting their ideas. And it is for a reason of this kind, that Homer and the oriental writers, though very fond of similitudes, and though they often strike out such as are truly admirable, seldom take care to have them exact; that is, they are taken with the general resemblance, they paint it strongly, and they take no notice of the difference which may be found between the things compared.

Now as the pleasure of resemblance is that which principally flatters the imagination, all men are nearly equal in this point, as far as their knowledge of the things represented or compared extends. The principle of this knowledge is very much accidental, as it depends upon experience and observation, and not on the strength or weakness of any natural faculty; and it is from this difference in knowledge, that what we commonly, though with no great exactness, call a difference in taste proceeds. A man to whom sculpture is new, sees a barber's block, or some ordinary piece of statuary; he is immediately struck and pleased, because he sees something like a human figure; and, entirely taken up with this likeness, he does not at all attend to its defects. No person, I believe, at the first time of seeing a piece of imitation ever did. Some time after, we suppose that this novice lights upon a more artificial work of the same nature; he now begins to look with contempt on what he admired at first; not that he admired it even then for its unlikeness to a man, but for that general though inaccurate resemblance which it bore to the human figure. What he admired at different times in these so different figures, is strictly the same; and though his knowledge is improved, his taste is not altered. Hitherto his mistake was from a want of knowledge in art, and this arose from his inexperience; but he may be still deficient from a want of knowledge in nature. For it is possible that the man in question may stop here, and that the masterpiece of a great hand may please him no more than the middling performance of a vulgar artist; and this not for want of better or higher relish, but because all men do not observe with sufficient accuracy on the human figure to enable them to judge properly of an imitation of it. And that the critical taste does not depend upon a superior principle in men, but upon superior knowledge, may appear from several instances. The story of the ancient painter and the shoemaker is very well known. The shoemaker set the painter right with regard to some mistakes he had made in the shoe of one of his figures, which the painter, who had not made such accurate observations on shoes, and was content with a general resemblance, had never observed. But this was no impeachment to the taste of the painter; it only showed some want of knowledge in the art of making shoes. Let us imagine, that an anatomist had come into the painter's working-room. His piece is in general well done, the figure in question in a good attitude, and the parts well adjusted to their various movements; yet the anatomist, critical in his art, may observe the swell of some muscle not quite just in the peculiar action of the figure. Here the anatomist observes what the painter had not observed; and he passes by what the shoemaker had remarked. But a want of the last critical knowledge in anatomy no more reflected on the natural good taste of the painter, or of any common observer of his piece, than the want of an exact knowledge in the formation of a shoe. A fine piece of a decollated head of St. John the Baptist was shown to a Turkish emperor: he praised many things, but he observed one defect: he observed that the skin did not shrink from the wounded part of the neck. The sultan on this occasion, though his observation was very just, discovered no more natural taste than the painter

who executed this piece, or than a thousand European connois-
seurs, who probably would have made the same observation. His
Turkish majesty had indeed been well acquainted with that terrible spectacle, which the others could only have represented in
their imagination. On the subject of their dislike there is a difference between all these people, arising from the different kinds
and degrees of their knowledge; but there is something in common to the painter, the shoemaker, the anatomist, and the Turkish
emperor, the pleasure arising from a natural object, so far as each
perceives it justly imitated; the satisfaction in seeing an agreeable figure; the sympathy proceeding from a striking and affecting incident. So far as taste is natural, it is nearly common to all.

In poetry, and other pieces of imagination, the same parity
may be observed. It is true, that one man is charmed with Don
Bellianis,[1] and reads Virgil coldly; whilst another is transported
with the Aeneid, and leaves Don Bellianis to children. These two
men seem to have a taste very different from each other; but in
fact they differ very little. In both these pieces, which inspire
such opposite sentiments, a tale exciting admiration is told; both
are full of action, both are passionate; in both are voyages,
battles, triumphs, and continual changes of fortune. The admirer
of Don Bellianis perhaps does not understand the refined language of the Aeneid, who, if it was degraded into the style of
the "Pilgrim's Progress," might feel it in all its energy, on the
same principle which made him an admirer of Don Bellianis.

In his favorite author he is not shocked with the continual
breaches of probability, the confusion of times, the offenses
against manners, the trampling upon geography; for he knows
nothing of geography and chronology, and he has never examined the grounds of probability. He perhaps reads of a shipwreck on the coast of Bohemia; wholly taken up with so interesting an event, and only solicitous for the fate of his hero, he is not
in the least troubled at this extravagant blunder. For why should
he be shocked at a shipwreck on the coast of Bohemia, who does
not know but that Bohemia may be an island in the Atlantic

[1] Probably a reference to *The History of Don Belianis of Greece; containing an account of his many wonderful exploits, and his obtaining the Soldan
of Babylon's Daughter in marriage,* an anonymous chapbook published in
London at about the time Burke was writing.

ocean? and after all, what reflection is this on the natural good taste of the person here supposed?

So far then as taste belongs to the imagination, its principle is the same in all men; there is no difference in the manner of their being affected, nor in the causes of the affection; but in the *degree* there is a difference, which arises from two causes principally; either from a greater degree of natural sensibility, or from a closer and longer attention to the object. To illustrate this by the procedure of the senses, in which the same difference is found, let us suppose a very smooth marble table to be set before two men; they both perceive it to be smooth, and they are both pleased with it because of this quality. So far they agree. But suppose another, and after that another table, the latter still smoother than the former, to be set before them. It is now very probable that these men, who are so agreed upon what is smooth, and in the pleasure from thence, will disagree when they come to settle which table has the advantage in point of polish. Here is indeed the great difference between tastes, when men come to compare the excess or diminution of things which are judged by degree and not by measure. Nor is it easy, when such a difference arises, to settle the point, if the excess or diminution be not glaring. If we differ in opinion about two quantities, we can recourse to a common measure, which may decide the question with the utmost exactness; and this, I take it, is what gives mathematical knowledge a greater certainty than any other. But in things whose excess is not judged by greater or smaller, as smoothness and roughness, hardness and softness, darkness and light, the shades of colors, all these are very easily distinguished when the difference is any way considerable, but not when it is minute, for want of some common measures, which perhaps may never come to be discovered. In these nice cases, supposing the acuteness of the sense equal, the greater attention and habit in such things will have the advantage. In the question about the tables, the marble-polisher will unquestionably determine the most accurately. But notwithstanding this want of a common measure for settling many disputes relative to the senses, and their representative the imagination, we find that the principles are the same in all, and that there is no disagreement until we come to examine into the pre-eminence or difference of things, which brings us within the province of the judgment.

So long as we are conversant with the sensible qualities of things, hardly any more than the imagination seems concerned; little more also than the imagination seems concerned when the passions are represented, because by the force of natural sympathy they are felt in all men without any recourse to reasoning, and their justness recognized in every breast. Love, grief, fear, anger, joy, all these passions have, in their turns, affected every mind; and they do not affect it in an arbitrary or casual manner, but upon certain, natural, and uniform principles. But as many of the works of imagination are not confined to the representation of sensible objects, nor to efforts upon the passions, but extend themselves to the manners, the characters, the actions, and designs of men, their relations, their virtues and vices, they come within the province of the judgment, which is improved by attention, and by the habit of reasoning. All these make a very considerable part of what are considered as the objects of taste; and Horace sends us to the schools of philosophy and the world for our instruction in them. Whatever certainty is to be acquired in morality and the science of life; just the same degree of certainty have we in what relates to them in works of imitation. Indeed it is for the most part in our skill in manners, and in the observances of time and place, and of decency in general, which is only to be learned in those schools to which Horace recommends us, that what is called taste, by way of distinction, consists: and which is in reality no other than a more refined judgment. On the whole, it appears to me, that what is called taste, in its most general acceptation, is not a simple idea, but is partly made up of a perception of the primary pleasures of sense, of the secondary pleasures of the imagination, and of the conclusions of the reasoning faculty, concerning the various relations of these, and concerning the human passions, manners, and actions. All this is requisite to form taste, and the groundwork of all these is the same in the human mind; for as the senses are the great originals of all our ideas, and consequently of all our pleasures, if they are not uncertain and arbitrary, the whole groundwork of taste is common to all, and therefore there is a sufficient foundation for a conclusive reasoning on these matters.

Whilst we consider taste merely according to its nature and species, we shall find its principles entirely uniform; but the degree in which these principles prevail, in the several individuals

of mankind, is altogether as different as the principles themselves are similar. For sensibility and judgment, which are the
qualities that compose what we commonly call a *taste,* vary exceedingly in various people. From a defect in the former of these
qualities arises a want of taste; a weakness in the latter constitutes a wrong or a bad one. There are some men formed with
feelings so blunt, with tempers so cold and phlegmatic, that they
can hardly be said to be awake during the whole course of their
lives. Upon such persons the most striking objects make but a
faint and obscure impression. There are others so continually in
the agitation of gross and merely sensual pleasures, or so occupied in the low drudgery of avarice, or so heated in the chase
of honors and distinction, that their minds, which had been used
continually to the storms of these violent and tempestuous passions, can hardly be put in motion by the delicate and refined
play of the imagination. These men, though from a different
cause, become as stupid and insensible as the former; but whenever either of these happen to be struck with any natural elegance
or greatness, or with these qualities in any work of art, they are
moved upon the same principle.

The cause of a wrong taste is a defect of judgment. And this
may arise from a natural weakness of understanding (in whatever the strength of that faculty may consist), or, which is much
more commonly the case, it may arise from a want of a proper
and well-directed exercise, which alone can make it strong and
ready. Besides, that ignorance, inattention, prejudice, rashness,
levity, obstinacy, in short, all those passions, and all those vices,
which pervert the judgment in other matters, prejudice it no less
in this its more refined and elegant province. These causes produce different opinions upon everything which is an object of
the understanding, without inducing us to suppose that there are
no settled principles of reason. And indeed, on the whole, one
may observe, that there is rather less difference upon matters of
taste among mankind, than upon most of those which depend
upon the naked reason; and that men are far better agreed on
the excellence of a description in Virgil, than on the truth or
falsehood of a theory of Aristotle.

A rectitude of judgment in the arts, which may be called a
good taste, does in a great measure depend upon sensibility; be-

cause if the mind has no bent to the pleasures of the imagination, it will never apply itself sufficiently to works of that species to acquire a competent knowledge of them. But though a degree of sensibility is requisite to form a good judgment, yet a good judgment does not necessarily arise from a quick sensibility to pleasure; it frequently happens that a very poor judge, merely by force of a greater complexional sensibility, is more affected by a very poor piece, than the best judge by the most perfect; for as everything new, extraordinary, grand, or passionate, is well calculated to affect such a person, and that the faults do not affect him, his pleasure is more pure and unmixed; and as it is merely a pleasure of the imagination, it is much higher than any which is derived from a rectitude of judgment; the judgment is for the greater part employed in throwing stumbling-blocks in the way of the imagination, in dissipating the scenes of its enchantment, and in tying us down to the disagreeable yoke of our reason: for almost the only pleasure that men have in judging better than others, consists in a sort of conscious pride and superiority, which arises from thinking rightly; but then this is an indirect pleasure, a pleasure which does not immediately result from the object which is under contemplation. In the morning of our days, when the senses are unworn and tender, when the whole man is awake in every part, and the gloss of novelty fresh upon all the objects that surround us, how lively at that time are our sensations, but how false and inaccurate the judgments we form of things! I despair of ever receiving the same degree of pleasure from the most excellent performances of genius, which I felt at that age from pieces which my present judgment regards as trifling and contemptible. Every trivial cause of pleasure is apt to affect the man of too sanguine a complexion: his appetite is too keen to suffer his taste to be delicate; and he is in all re-spects what Ovid says of himself in love,

> *Molle meum levibus cor est violabile telis,*
> *Et semper causa est, cur ego semper amem.*
> [My soft heart is susceptible to light weapons,
> And there is always a reason why I am always in love.]

One of this character can never be a refined judge; never what the comic poet calls *elegans formarum spectator.* [a refined observer of forms] The excellence and force of a composition must always be imperfectly estimated from its effect on the minds of any, except we know the temper and character of those minds. The most powerful effects of poetry and music have been displayed, and perhaps are still displayed, where these arts are but in a very low and imperfect state. The rude hearer is affected by the principles which operate in these arts even in their rudest condition; and he is not skilful enough to perceive the defects. But as the arts advance toward their perfection, the science of criticism advances with equal pace, and the pleasure of judges is frequently interrupted by the faults which are discovered in the most finished compositions.

Before I leave this subject, I cannot help taking notice of an opinion which many persons entertain, as if the taste were a separate faculty of the mind, and distinct from the judgment and imagination; a species of instinct, by which we are struck naturally, and at first glance, without any previous reasoning, with the excellences or the defects of a composition. So far as the imagination and the passions are concerned, I believe it true, that the reason is little consulted; but where disposition, where decorum, where congruity are concerned, in short, wherever the best taste differs from the worst, I am convinced that the understanding operates, and nothing else; and its operation is in reality far from being always sudden, or, when it is sudden, it is often far from being right. Men of the best taste by consideration come frequently to change these early and precipitate judgments, which the mind, from its aversion to neutrality and doubt loves to form on the spot. It is known that the taste (whatever it is) is improved exactly as we improve our judgment, by extending our knowledge, by a steady attention to our object, and by frequent exercise. They who have not taken these methods, if their taste decides quickly, it is always uncertainly; and their quickness is owing to their presumption and rashness, and not to any sudden irradiation, that in a moment dispels all darkness from their minds. But they who have cultivated that species of knowledge which makes the object of taste, by degrees and habitually attain not only a soundness but a readiness of judgment, as men do by the same methods on all other occasions. At first they are obliged to spell, but at last they read with ease and with celerity; but this celerity of its operation is no proof that the taste is a distinct faculty. Nobody, I believe, has attended the course of a discussion which turned upon matters within the sphere of mere naked reason, but must have observed the extreme readiness with which the whole process of the argument is carried on, the grounds discovered, the objections raised and answered, and the conclusions drawn from premises, with a quickness altogether as great as the taste can be supposed to work with; and yet where nothing but plain reason either is or can be suspected to operate. To multiply principles for every different appearance is useless, and unphilosophical too in a high degree.

This matter might be pursued much farther; but it is not the extent of the subject which must prescribe our bounds, for what subject does not branch out to infinity? It is the nature of our particular scheme, and the single point of view in which we consider it, which ought to put a stop to our researches.

PART I, SECTION VII: OF THE SUBLIME

WHATEVER IS FITTED in any sort to excite the ideas of pain and danger, that is to say, whatever is in any sort terrible, or is conversant about terrible objects, or operates in a manner analogous to terror, is a source of the *sublime;* that is, it is productive of the strongest emotion which the mind is capable of feeling. I say the strongest emotion, because I am satisfied the ideas of pain are much more powerful than those which enter on the part of pleasure. Without all doubt, the torments which we may be made to suffer, are much greater in their effect on the body and mind, than any pleasures which the most learned voluptuary could suggest, or than the liveliest imagination, and the most sound and exquisitely sensible body, could enjoy. Nay, I am in great doubt whether any man could be found, who would earn a life of the most perfect satisfaction at the price of ending it in the torments, which justice inflicted in a few hours on the late unfortunate regicide in France. But as pain is stronger in its operation than pleasure, so death is in general a much more affecting idea than pain; because there are very few pains, however exquisite, which are not preferred to death: nay, what generally makes pain itself, if I may say so, more painful, is, that it is considered as an emissary of this king of terrors. When danger or pain press too nearly, they are incapable of giving any delight, and are simply terrible; but at certain distances, and with certain modifications, they may be, and they are, delightful, as we every day experience. The cause of this I shall endeavor to investigate hereafter.

PART I, SECTION XIII: SYMPATHY

IT IS BY THE FIRST of these passions [sympathy] that we enter into the concerns of others; that we are moved as they are moved, and are never suffered to be indifferent spectators of almost anything which men can do or suffer. For sympathy must be considered as a sort of substitution, by which we are put into the place of another man, and affected in many respects as he is affected: so that this passion may either partake of the nature of those which regard self-preservation, and turning upon pain may be a source of the sublime; or it may turn upon ideas of pleasure; and then whatever has been said of the social affections, whether they regard society in general, or only some particular modes of it, may be applicable here. It is by this principle chiefly that poetry, painting, and other affecting arts, transfuse their passions from one breast to another, and are often capable of grafting a delight upon wretchedness, misery, and death itself. It is a common observation, that objects which in the reality would shock, are in tragical, and such like representations, the source of a very high species of pleasure. This taken as a fact, has been the cause of much reasoning. The satisfaction has been commonly attributed, first, to the comfort we receive in considering that so melancholy a story is no more than a fiction; and, next, to the contemplation of our own freedom from the evils which we see represented. I am afraid it is a practice much too common in inquiries of this nature, to attribute the cause of feelings which merely arise from the mechanical structure of our bodies, or from the natural frame and constitution of our minds, to certain conclusions of the reasoning faculty on the objects presented to us; for I should imagine, that the influence of reason in producing our passions is nothing near so extensive as it is commonly believed.

PART I, SECTION XIV: THE EFFECTS OF SYMPATHY IN THE DISTRESSES OF OTHERS

To EXAMINE THIS POINT concerning the effect of tragedy in a proper manner, we must previously consider how we are affected by the feelings of our fellow-creatures in circumstances of real distress. I am convinced that we have a degree of delight, and that no small one, in the real misfortunes and pains of others; for let the affection be what it will in appearance, if it does not make us shun such objects, if on the contrary it induces us to approach them, if it makes us dwell upon them, in this case I conceive we must have a delight or pleasure of some species or other in contemplating objects of this kind. Do we not read the authentic histories of scenes of this nature with as much pleasure as romances or poems, where the incidents are fictitious? The prosperity of no empire, nor the grandeur of no king, can so agreeably affect in the reading, as the ruin of the state of Macedon, and the distress of its unhappy prince. Such a catastrophe touches us in history as much as the destruction of Troy does in fable. Our delight, in cases of this kind, is very greatly heightened, if the sufferer be some excellent person who sinks under an unworthy fortune. Scipio and Cato are both virtuous characters; but we are more deeply affected by the violent death of the one, and the ruin of the great cause he adhered to, than with the deserved triumphs and uninterrupted prosperity of the other: for terror is a passion which always produces delight when it does not press too closely; and pity is a passion accompanied with pleasure, because it arises from love and social affection. Whenever we are formed by nature to any active purpose, the passion which animates us to it is attended with delight, or a pleasure of some kind, let the subject-matter be what it will; and as our Creator has designed that we should be united by the bond of sympathy, he has strengthened that bond by a proportionable delight; and there most where our sympathy is most wanted,— in the distresses of others. If this passion was simply painful, we would shun with the greatest care all persons and places that could excite such a passion; as some, who are so far gone in indolence as not to endure any strong impression, actually do. But the case is widely different with the greater part of mankind; there is no spectacle we so eagerly pursue, as that of some uncommon and grievous calamity; so that whether the misfortune is before our eyes, or whether they are turned back to it in history, it always touches with delight. This is not an unmixed delight, but blended with no small uneasiness. The delight we have in such things hinders us from shunning scenes of misery; and the pain we feel prompts us to relieve ourselves in relieving those who suffer; and all this antecedent to any reasoning, by an instinct that works us to its own purposes without our concurrence.

PART I, SECTION XV: OF THE
EFFECTS OF TRAGEDY

IT IS THUS IN REAL calamities. In imitated distresses the only difference is the pleasure resulting from the effects of imitation; for it is never so perfect, but we can perceive it is imitation, and on that principle are somewhat pleased with it. And indeed in some cases we derive as much or more pleasure from that source than from the thing itself. But then I imagine we shall be much mistaken if we attribute any considerable part of our satisfaction in tragedy to the consideration that tragedy is a deceit, and its representations no realities. The nearer it approaches the reality, and the further it removes us from all idea of fiction, the more perfect is its power. But be its power of what kind it will, it never approaches to what it represents. Choose a day on which to represent the most sublime and affecting tragedy we have; appoint the most favorite actors; spare no cost upon the scenes and decorations; unite the greatest efforts of poetry, painting, and music; and when you have collected your audience, just at the moment when their minds are erect with expectation, let it be reported that a state criminal of high rank is on the point of being executed in the adjoining square; in a moment the emptiness of the theatre would demonstrate the comparative weakness of the imitative arts, and proclaim the triumph of the real sympathy. I believe that this notion of our having a simple pain in the reality, yet a delight in the representation, arises from hence, that we do not sufficiently distinguish what we would by no means choose to do, from what we should be eager enough to see if it was once done. We delight in seeing things, which so far from doing, our heartiest wishes would be to see redressed. This noble capital, the pride of England and of Europe, I believe no man is so strangely wicked as to desire to see destroyed by a conflagration or an earthquake, though he should be removed himself to the greatest distance from the danger. But suppose such a fatal accident to have happened, what numbers from all parts would crowd to behold the ruins, and amongst them many who would have been content never to have seen London in its glory! Nor is it, either in real or fictitious distresses, our immunity from them which produces our delight; in my own mind I can discover nothing like it. I apprehend that this mistake is owing to a sort of sophism, by which we are frequently imposed upon; it arises from our not distinguishing between what is indeed a necessary condition to our doing or suffering anything in general, and what is the cause of some particular act. If a man kills me with a sword, it is a necessary condition to this that we should have been both of us alive before the fact; and yet it would be absurd to say that our being both living creatures was the cause of his crime and my death. So it is certain that it is absolutely necessary my life should be out of any imminent hazard, before I can take a delight in the sufferings of others, real or imaginary, or indeed in anything else from any cause whatsoever. But then it is a sophism to argue from thence that this immunity is the cause of my delight either on these or on any occasions. No one can distinguish such a cause of satisfaction in his own mind, I believe; nay, when we do not suffer any very acute pain, nor are exposed to any imminent danger of our lives, we can feel for others, whilst we suffer ourselves; and often then most when we are softened by affliction; we see with pity even distresses which we would accept in the place of our own.

PART III, SECTION XXVII: THE SUBLIME AND BEAUTIFUL COMPARED

ON CLOSING THIS GENERAL view of beauty, it naturally occurs that we should compare it with the sublime; and in this comparison there appears a remarkable contrast. For sublime objects are vast in their dimensions, beautiful ones comparatively small: beauty should be smooth and polished; the great, rugged and negligent: beauty should shun the right line, yet deviate from it insensibly; the great in many cases loves the right line; and when it deviates, it often makes a strong deviation: beauty should not be obscure; the great ought to be dark and gloomy: beauty should be light and delicate; and great ought to be solid, and even massive. They are indeed ideas of a very different nature, one being founded on pain, the other on pleasure; and, however they may vary afterwards from the direct nature of their causes, yet these causes keep up an eternal distinction between them, a distinction never to be forgotten by any whose business it is to affect the passions. In the infinite variety of natural combinations, we must expect to find the qualities of things the most remote imaginable from each other united in the same object. We must expect also to find combinations of the same kind in the works of art. But when we consider the power of an object upon our passions, we must know that when anything is intended to affect the mind by the force of some predominant property, the affection produced is like to be the more uniform and perfect, if all the other properties or qualities of the object be of the same nature, and tending to the same design as the principal.

"If black and white blend, soften, and unite
    A thousand ways, are there no black and white?"
If the qualities of the sublime and beautiful are sometimes found united, does this prove that they are the same; does it prove that they are any way allied; does it prove even that they are not opposite and contradictory? Black and white may soften, may blend; but they are not therefore the same. Nor, when they are so softened and blended with each other, or with different colors, is the power of black as black, or of white as white, so strong as when each stands uniform and distinguished.

David Hume

[1711–1776]

HUME'S PRINCIPAL IMPORTANCE in eighteenth-century thought is, of course, in his contributions to the development of empirical philosophy. His formulation of the doctrine of association—that what we call knowledge is derived neither from direct experience of a substantial, external world, nor from the logical operations of the mind, but rather from accidental combinations of sense-data—effectively undermined the foundations of classical rationalism, and thus of neoclassical theory. In his critical writings, which were few and informal, Hume tried, as Addison and Burke had tried, to salvage the classical literary genres and the classical assumption of the uniformity of taste, by re-establishing them in the terms of the new philosophy. Like Addison and Burke, Hume concentrated on the psychology of aesthetic experience, and like them he took the nature of tragedy as his test case.

Hume treats tragedy not as a formalistic or philosophical problem, but as a problem of perception: what is there about our experience of the catastrophes of tragedy that makes it pleasurable? His answer, probably the most satisfactory of eighteenth-century answers, combines several points: man would rather be excited by any passion than bored by none; we know that the tragic action is a fiction; our pleasure in the eloquence and expression of the passions alters our painful emotions; and tragedy is an imitation, and imitation is always of itself agreeable.

BIBLIOGRAPHY. *Essays Moral, Political, and Literary,* ed. T. H. Green and T. H. Grose, 2 vols. (London, 1874).

Teddy Brunius, *David Hume on Criticism* (Stockholm, 1952); Walter John Hipple, Jr., *The Beautiful, The Sublime, and The Picturesque in Eighteenth-Century British Aesthetic Theory* (Carbondale, Illinois, 1957); F. L. Lucas, *Art of Living: Four Eighteenth-Century Minds* (New York, 1959); Norman Kemp Smith, *The Philosophy of David Hume* (New York, 1941).

TEXT. *Four Dissertations* (London, 1757).

OF TRAGEDY

[1757]

IT SEEMS AN UNACCOUNTABLE PLEASURE, which the spectators of a well-wrote tragedy receive from sorrow, terror, anxiety, and other passions, that are in themselves disagreeable and uneasy. The more they are touched and affected, the more are they delighted with the spectacle; and as soon as the uneasy passions cease to operate, the piece is at an end. One scene of full joy and contentment and security is the utmost, that any composition of this kind can bear; and it is sure always to be the concluding one. If in the texture of the piece, there be interwoven any scenes of satisfaction, they afford only faint gleams of pleasure, which are thrown in by way of variety, and in order to plunge the actors into deeper distress, by means of that contrast and disappointment. The whole art of the poet is employed in rouzing and supporting the compassion and indignation, the anxiety and resentment of his audience. They are pleased in proportion as they are afflicted, and never are so happy as when they employ tears, sobs, and cries to give vent to their sorrow, and relieve their heart, swoln with the tenderest sympathy and compassion.

The few critics, who have had some tincture of philosophy, have remarked this singular phænomenon, and have endeavoured to account for it.

L'Abbé *Dubos*,[1] in his reflections on poetry and painting, asserts, that nothing is in general so disagreeable to the mind as the languid, listless state of indolence, into which it falls upon the removal of every passion and occupation. To get rid of this painful situation, it seeks every amusement and pursuit: business, gaming, shows, executions; whatever will rouze the passions, and take its attention from itself. No matter, what the

---

[1] Jean-Baptiste Dubos (1670–1742), author of *Réflexions critiques sur la poésie et sur la peinture* (1719).

passion is: Let it be disagreeable, afflicting, melancholy, disordered; it is still better, than that insipid languor, which arises from perfect tranquillity and repose.

It is impossible not to admit this account, as being, at least in part, satisfactory. You may observe, when there are several tables of gaming, that all the company run to those, where the deepest play is, even tho' they find not there the finest players. The view, or, at least, imagination of high passions, arising from great loss or gain, affects the spectator by sympathy, gives him some touches of the same passions, and serves him for a momentary entertainment. It makes the time pass the easier with them, and is some relief to that oppression, under which men commonly labour, when left entirely to their own thoughts and meditations.

We find that common lyars always magnify, in their narrations, all kinds of danger, pain, distress, sickness, deaths, murders, and cruelties; as well as joy, beauty, mirth, and magnificence. It is an absurd secret, which they have for pleasing their company, fixing their attention, and attaching them to such marvellous relations, by the passions and emotions, which they excite.

There is, however, a difficulty of applying to the present subject, in its full extent, this solution, however ingenious and satisfactory it may appear. It is certain, that the same object of distress which pleases in a tragedy, were it really set before us, would give the most unfeigned uneasiness, tho' it be then the most effectual cure to languor and indolence. Monsieur *Fontenelle*[2] seems to have been sensible of this difficulty; and accordingly attempts another solution of the phænomenon; at least, makes some addition to the theory abovementioned.

"Pleasure and pain," says he, "which are two sentiments so different in themselves, differ not so much in their cause. From the instance of tickling, it appears, that the movement of pleasure pushed a little too far, becomes pain; and that the movement of pain, a little moderated, becomes pleasure. Hence it proceeds, that there is such a thing as a sorrow, soft and agreeable: It is a pain weakened and diminished. The heart likes naturally to be moved and affected. Melancholy objects suit it,

---

[2] Bernard Le Bovier, sieur de Fontenelle (1657–1757). Hume quotes from the 36th section of his *Réflexions sur la Poétique* (1691).

and even disastrous and sorrowful, provided they are softened by some circumstance. It is certain, that on the theatre the representation has almost the effect of reality; but yet it has not altogether that effect. However we may be hurried away by the spectacle; whatever dominion the senses and imagination may usurp over the reason, there still lurks at the bottom a certain idea of falshood in the whole of what we see. This idea, tho' weak and disguised, suffices to diminish the pain which we suffer from the misfortunes of those whom we love, and to reduce that affliction to such a pitch as converts it into a pleasure. We weep for the misfortune of a hero, to whom we are attached: In the same instant we comfort ourselves, by reflecting, that it is nothing but a fiction: And it is precisely, that mixture of sentiments, which composes an agreeable sorrow, and tears that delight us. But as that affliction, which is caused by exterior and sensible objects, is stronger than the consolation, which arises from an internal reflection, they are the effects and symptoms of sorrow, that ought to predominate in the composition."

This solution seems just and convincing; but perhaps it wants still some new addition, in order to make it answer fully the phænomenon, which we here examine. All the passions, excited by eloquence, are agreeable in the highest degree, as well as those which are moved by painting and the theatre. The epilogues of *Cicero* are, on this account chiefly, the delight of every reader of taste; and it is difficult to read some of them without the deepest sympathy and sorrow. His merit as an orator, no doubt, depends much on his success in this particular. When he had raised tears in his judges and all his audience, they were then the most highly delighted, and expressed the greatest satisfaction with the pleader. The pathetic description of the butchery made by *Verres* of the *Sicilian* captains, is a master-piece of this kind: But I believe none will affirm, that the being present at a melancholy scene of that nature would afford any entertainment. Neither is the sorrow here softened by fiction: For the audience were convinced of the reality of every circumstance. What is it then, which in this case raises a pleasure from the bosom of uneasiness, so to speak; and a pleasure which still retains all the features and outward symptoms of distress and sorrow?

I answer: This extraordinary effect proceeds from that very eloquence, with which the melancholy scene is represented. The genius required to paint objects in a lively manner, the art employed in collecting all the pathetic circumstances, the judgment displayed in disposing them; the exercise, I say, of these noble talents, together with the force of expression, and beauty of oratorial numbers, diffuse the highest satisfaction on the audience, and excite the most delightful movements. By this means, the uneasiness of the melancholy passions is not only overpowered and effaced by something stronger of an opposite kind; but the whole impulse of those passions is converted into pleasure, and swells the delight, which the eloquence raises in us. The same force of oratory, employed on an uninteresting subject, would not please half so much, or rather would appear altogether ridiculous; and the mind, being left in absolute calmness and indifference, would relish none of those beauties of imagination or expression, which, if joined to passion, give it such exquisite entertainment. The impulse or vehemence, arising from sorrow, compassion, indignation, receives a new direction from the sentiments of beauty. The latter, being the predominant emotion, seize the whole mind, and convert the former into themselves, or at least, tincture them so strongly as totally to alter their nature: And the soul, being, at the same time, rouzed by passion, and charmed by eloquence, feels on the whole a strong movement, which is altogether delightful.

The same principle takes place in tragedy; along with this addition, that tragedy is an imitation, and imitation is always of itself agreeable. This circumstance serves still farther to smooth the motions of passion, and convert the whole feeling into one uniform and strong enjoyment. Objects of the greatest terror and distress please in painting, and please more than the most beautiful objects, that appear calm and indifferent.³ The

---

³ Painters make no scruple of representing distress and sorrow, as well as any other passion: But they seem not to dwell so much on these melancholy affections as the poets, who, though they copy every emotion of the human breast, yet pass very quickly over the agreeable sentiments. A painter represents only one instant; and if that be passionate enough, it is sure to affect and delight the spectator: But nothing can furnish to the poet a variety of scenes and incidents and sentiments, except distress, terror, or anxiety. Compleat joy and satisfaction is attended with a security, and leaves no farther room for action. [Hume's note.]

affection, rouzing the mind, excites a large stock of spirit and vehemence; which is all transformed into pleasure by the force of the prevailing movement. It is thus the fiction of tragedy softens the passion, by an infusion of a new feeling, not merely by weakening or diminishing the sorrow. You may by degrees weaken a real sorrow, till it totally disappears; yet in none of its gradations will it ever give pleasure; except, perhaps, by accident, to a man sunk under lethargic indolence, whom it rouzes from that languid state.

To confirm this theory, it will be sufficient to produce other instances, where the subordinate movement is converted into the predominant, and gives force to it, tho' of a different, and even sometimes tho' of a contrary nature.

Novelty naturally rouzes the mind and attracts our attention; and the movements, which it causes, are always converted into any passion, belonging to the object, and join their force to it. Whether an event excites joy or sorrow, pride or shame, anger or good-will, it is sure to produce a stronger affection, when new or unusual. And tho' novelty, of itself, be agreeable, it enforces the painful, as well as agreeable passions.

Had you any intention to move a person extremely by the narration of any event, the best method of increasing its effect would be artfully to delay informing him of it, and first excite his curiosity and impatience before you let him into the secret. This is the artifice practised by *Iago* in the famous scene of *Shakespeare;* and every spectator is sensible that *Othello's* jealousy acquires additional force from his preceding impatience, and that the subordinate passion is here readily transformed into the predominant.

Difficulties encrease passions of every kind; and by rouzing our attention, and exciting our active powers, they produce an emotion, which nourishes the prevailing affection.

Parents commonly love that child most, whose sickly infirm frame of body has occasioned them the greatest pains, trouble, and anxiety in rearing him. The agreeable sentiment of affection here acquires force from sentiments of uneasiness.

Nothing endears so much a friend as sorrow for his death. The pleasure of his company has not so powerful an influence.

Jealousy is a painful passion, yet without some share of it, the agreeable affection of love has difficulty to subsist in its full force and violence. Absence is also a great source of complaint among lovers, and gives them the greatest uneasiness: Yet nothing is more favorable to their mutual passion than short intervals of that kind. And if long intervals be pernicious, it is only because, thro' time, men are accustomed to them, and they cease to give uneasiness. Jealousy and absence in love compose the *dolce piccante* [sweet sinning] of the *Italians,* which they suppose so essential to all pleasure.

There is a fine observation of the elder *Pliny,* which illustrates the principle here insisted on. *It is very remarkable,* says he, *that the last works of celebrated artists, which they left imperfect, are always the most prized, such as the* Iris *of* Aristides, *the* Tyndarides *of* Nicomachus, *the* Medea *of* Timomachus, *and the* Venus *of* Apelles. *These are valued even above their finished productions: The broken lineaments of the piece and the half formed idea of the painter are carefully studied; and our very grief for that curious hand, which had been stoped by death, is an additional encrease to our pleasure.*[4]

These instances (and many more might be collected) are sufficient to afford us some insight into the analogy of nature, and to show us, that the pleasure, which poets, orators, and musicians give us, by exciting grief, sorrow, indignation, compassion, is not so extraordinary nor paradoxical, as it may at first sight appear. The force of imagination, the energy of expression, the power of numbers, the charms of imitation; all these are naturally, of themselves, delightful to the mind; and when the object presented lays also hold of some affection, the pleasure still rises upon us, by the conversion of this subordinate movement, into that which is predominant. The passion, tho', perhaps, naturally, and when excited by the simple appearance of a real object, it may be painful; yet is so smoothed, and softened, and mollified, when raised by the finer arts, that it affords the highest entertainment.

To confirm this reasoning, we may observe, that if the movements of the imagination be not predominant above those of the passion, a contrary effect follows; and the former, being

[4] *Natural History,* Book XXXV, Ch. 40, sec. 20.

now subordinate, is converted into the latter, and still farther encreases the pain and affliction of the sufferer.

Who could ever think of it as a good expedient for comforting an afflicted parent, to exaggerate, with all the force of oratory, the irreparable loss, which he has met with by the death of a favorite child? The more power of imagination and expression you here employ, the more you encrease his despair and affliction.

The shame, confusion, and terror of *Verres*, no doubt, rose in proportion to the noble eloquence and vehemence of *Cicero:* So also did his pain and uneasiness. These former passions were too strong for the pleasure arising from the beauties of elocution; and operated, tho' from the same principle, yet in a contrary manner, to the sympathy, compassion, and indignation of the audience.

Lord *Clarendon*,[5] when he approaches towards the catastrophe of the royal party, supposes, that his narration must then become infinitely disagreeable; and he hurries over the king's death, without giving us one circumstance of it. He considers it as too horrid a scene to be contemplated with any satisfaction, or even without the utmost pain and aversion. He himself, as well as the readers of that age, were too deeply concerned in the events, and felt a pain from subjects, which an historian and a reader of another age would regard as the most pathetic and most interesting, and, by consequence, the most agreeable.

An action, represented in tragedy, may be too bloody and atrocious. It may excite such movements of horror as will not soften into pleasure; and the greatest energy of expression bestowed on descriptions of that nature serves only to augment our uneasiness. Such is that action represented in the *Ambitious Stepmother*,[6] where a venerable old man, raised to the height of fury and despair, rushes against a pillar, and striking his head upon it, besmears it all over with mingled brains and gore. The *English* theater abounds too much with such shocking images.

Even the common sentiments of compassion require to be

[5] Edward Hyde, Earl of Clarendon (1608–74), author of *The History of the Rebellion and Civil Wars in England* (1702–04).

[6] A tragedy by Nicholas Rowe (1647–1718), produced in 1700.

softened by some agreeable affection, in order to give a thorough satisfaction to the audience. The mere suffering of plaintive virtue, under the triumphant tyranny and oppression of vice, forms a disagreeable spectacle, and is carefully avoided by all masters of the drama. In order to dismiss the audience with entire satisfaction and contentment, the virtue must either convert itself into a noble courageous despair, or the vice receive its proper punishment.

Most painters appear in this light to have been very unhappy in their subjects. As they wrought much for churches and convents, they have chiefly represented such horrible subjects as crucifixions and martyrdoms, where nothing appears but tortures, wounds, executions, and passive suffering, without any action or affection. When they turned their pencil from this ghastly mythology, they had recourse commonly to *Ovid*, whose fictions, tho' passionate and agreeable, are scarcely natural or probable enough for painting.

The same inversion of that principle, which is here insisted on, displays itself in common life, as in the effects of oratory and poetry. Raise so the subordinate passion that it becomes the predominant, it swallows up that affection which it before nourished and encreased. Too much jealousy extinguishes love: too much difficulty renders us indifferent: too much sickness and infirmity disgusts a selfish and unkind parent.

What so disagreeable as the dismal, gloomy, disastrous stories, with which melancholy people entertain their companions? The uneasy passion, being there raised alone, unaccompanied with any spirit, genius, or eloquence, conveys a pure uneasiness, and is attended with nothing that can soften it into pleasure or satisfaction.

Sir Joshua Reynolds

[1723–1792]

REYNOLDS WAS A SUCCESSFUL portrait painter who was the friend of many of the distinguished men of his day, including Burke, Goldsmith, and Johnson; he was a member of Johnson's famous Club, and contributed essays to the *Idler*. When the Royal Academy was founded in 1768, Reynolds was made its first president, and held this post until his death.

Reynolds' critical principles are set forth in his *Discourses,* a series of addresses delivered to the students and members of the Academy at its annual meetings. In the *Discourses* Reynolds applies neo-classical ideas to the art of painting, arguing that the artist should aspire to imitate ideal beauty, that perfection in "the general forms of things" which is "superior to what is to be found in individual nature." The artist may find ideal beauty in the works of the great ancients, or he may find it, as the ancients did, in nature itself, if he will learn to abstract from individual and imperfect things their ideal forms. The proper mode of expression of ideal beauty is the "grand style"; its function is the ethical improvement of mankind.

The *Discourses* are discussions of the visual arts, a painter talking to painters, but they are characteristically neo-classical in being conducted on a level of abstraction which makes them applicable to the arts in general; and in fact the principles involved may be found in Pope and in Johnson. They are also characteristic of their time in the way that the psychological-emotional bias of Longinus becomes increasingly more apparent, shifting Reynolds' admiration from the "correct" Raphael to the "sublime" Michelangelo. In their entirety, the *Discourses* comprise, as Walter Jackson Bate has observed, "the most representative single embodiment in English of eighteenth-century aesthetic principles."

BIBLIOGRAPHY. *Literary Works,* ed. H. W. Beechey, 2 vols. (London, 1852); *Discourses on Art,* ed. Robert R. Wark (San Marino, Calif., 1959).

Walter Jackson Bate, *From Classic to Romantic* (Cambridge, 1946); F. W. Hilles, *The Literary Career of Sir Joshua Reynolds* (Cambridge and New York, 1936); Samual H. Monk, *The Sublime* (New York, 1938); James Northcote, *Memoirs of Sir Joshua Reynolds,* 2 vols. (London, 1818); Elder Olson, "Introduction" to *Discourses* [published with Longinus' *On the Sublime*] (Chicago, 1945).

TEXT. *Works,* ed. Edmund Malone (3rd edition, London, 1801), vol. I.

THIRD DISCOURSE ON ART

[1770]

GENTLEMEN,

It is not easy to speak with propriety to so many Students of different ages and different degrees of advancement. The mind requires nourishment adapted to its growth; and what may have promoted our earlier efforts might retard us in our nearer approaches to perfection.

The first endeavours of a young Painter, as I have remarked in a former discourse, must be employed in the attainment of mechanical dexterity, and confined to the mere imitation of the object before him. Those who have advanced beyond the rudiments, may, perhaps, find advantage in reflecting on the advice which I have likewise given them, when I recommended the diligent study of the works of our great predecessors; but I at the same time endeavoured to guard them against an implicit submission to the authority of any one master however excellent: or by a strict imitation of his manner, precluding themselves from the abundance and variety of Nature. I will now add that Nature herself is not to be too closely copied. There are excellencies in the art of painting beyond what is commonly called the imitation of nature: and these excellencies I wish to point out. The students who, having passed through the initiatory exercises, are more advanced in the art, and who, sure of their hand, have leisure to exert their understanding, must now be told, that a mere copier of nature can never produce any thing great; can never raise and enlarge the conceptions, or warm the heart of the spectator.

The wish of the genuine painter must be more extensive: instead of endeavouring to amuse mankind with the minute neatness of his imitations, he must endeavour to improve them by the grandeur of his ideas; instead of seeking praise by deceiving the superficial sense of the spectator, he must strive for fame by captivating the imagination.

The principle now laid down, that the perfection of this art does not consist in mere imitation, is far from being new or singular. It is, indeed, supported by the general opinion of the enlightened part of mankind. The poets, orators, and rhetoricians of antiquity are continually enforcing this position: that all the arts receive their perfection from an ideal beauty, superior to what is to be found in individual nature. They are ever referring to the practice of the painters and sculptors of their times, particularly Phidias, (the favourite artist of antiquity), to illustrate their assertions. As if they could not sufficiently express their admiration of his genius by what they knew, they have recourse to poetical enthusiasm. They call it inspiration; a gift from heaven. The artist is supposed to have ascended the celestial regions, to furnish his mind with this perfect idea of beauty. "He," says Proclus,[1] "who takes for his model such forms as nature produces, and confines himself to an exact imitation of them, will never attain to what is perfectly beautiful. For the works of nature are full of disproportion, and fall very short of the true standard of beauty. So that Phidias, when he formed his Jupiter, did not copy any object ever presented to his sight; but contemplated only that image which he had conceived in his mind from Homer's description." And thus Cicero, speaking of the same Phidias: "Neither did this artist," says he, "when he carved the image of Jupiter or Minerva, set before him any one human figure, as a pattern, which he was to copy; but having a more perfect idea of beauty fixed in his mind, this he steadily contemplated, and to the imitation of this all his skill and labour were directed."

[1] Lib. 2, in Timaeum Platonis, as cited by Junius de Pictura Veterum. [Note added by Reynolds and Edmund Malone for edition published posthumously in 1797].

The Moderns are not less convinced than the Ancients of this superior power existing in the art; nor less sensible of its effects. Every language has adopted terms expressive of this excellence. The *gusto grande* of the Italians, the *beau ideal* of the French, and the *great style, genius,* and *taste* among the English, are but different appellations of the same thing. It is this intellectual dignity, they say, that ennobles the painter's art; that lays the line between him and the mere mechanick; and produces those great effects in an instant, which eloquence and poetry, by slow and repeated efforts, are scarcely able to attain.

Such is the warmth with which both the Ancients and Moderns speak of this divine principle of the art; but, as I have formerly observed, enthusiastick admiration seldom promotes knowledge. Though a student by such praise may have his attention roused, and a desire excited of running in this great career, yet it is possible that what has been said to excite, may only serve to deter him. He examines his own mind, and perceives there nothing of that divine inspiration with which, he is told, so many others have been favoured. He never travelled to heaven to gather new ideas; and he finds himself possessed of no other qualifications than what mere common observation and a plain understanding can confer. Thus he becomes gloomy amidst the splendour of figurative declamation, and thinks it hopeless to pursue an object which he supposes out of reach of human industry.

But on this, as upon many other occasions, we ought to distinguish how much is to be given to enthusiasm, and how much to reason. We ought to allow for, and we ought to commend, that strength of vivid expression which is necessary to convey, in its full force, the highest sense of the most complete effect of art; taking care at the same time, not to lose in terms of vague admiration, that solidity and truth of principle, upon which alone we can reason, and may be enabled to practise.

It is not easy to define in which this great style consists; nor to describe, by words, the proper means of acquiring it, if the mind of the student should be at all capable of such an acquisition. Could we teach taste or genius by rules, they would be no longer taste and genius. But though there neither are, nor can be, any precise invariable rules for the exercise, or the acquisition, of these great qualities, yet we may truly say that they always operate in proportion to our attention in observing the works of nature, to our skill in selecting, and to our care in digesting, methodizing, and comparing our observations. There are many beauties in our art that seem, at first, to lie without the reach of precept, and yet may easily be reduced to practical principles. Experience is all in all; but it is not every one who profits by experience; and most people err, not so much from want of capacity to find their object, as from not knowing what object to pursue. This great ideal perfection and beauty are not to be sought in the heavens, but upon the earth. They are about us, and upon every side of us. But the power of discovering what is deformed in nature, or in other words, what is particular and uncommon, can be acquired only by experience; and the whole beauty and grandeur of the art consists, in my opinion, in being able to get above all singular forms, local customs, particularities, and details of every kind.

All the objects which are exhibited to our view by nature, upon close examination will be found to have their blemishes and defects. The most beautiful forms have something about them like weakness, minuteness, or imperfection. But it is not every eye that perceives these blemishes. It must be an eye long used to the contemplation and comparison of these forms; and which, by a long habit of observing what any set of objects of the same kind have in common, has acquired the power of discerning what each wants in particular. This long laborious comparison should be the first study of the painter who aims at the greatest style. By this means, he acquires a just idea of beautiful forms; he corrects nature by herself, her imperfect state by her more perfect. His eye being enabled to distinguish the accidental deficiencies, excrescences, and deformities of things, from their general figures, he makes out an abstract idea of their forms more perfect than any one original; and, what may seem a paradox, he learns to design naturally by drawing his figures unlike to any one object. This idea of the perfect state of nature, which the artist calls the Ideal Beauty, is the great leading principle, by which works of genius are conducted. By this Phidias acquired his fame. He wrought upon a sober principle, what has so much excited the enthusiasm of the world; and by this method you, who have courage to tread the same path, may acquire equal reputation.

This is the idea which has acquired, and which seems to have a right to, the epithet of *divine;* as it may be said to preside, like a supreme judge, over all the productions of nature; appearing to be possessed of the will and intention of the Creator, as far as they regard the external form of living beings. When a man once possesses this idea in its perfection, there is no danger but that he will be sufficiently warmed by it himself, and be able to warm and ravish every one else.

Thus it is from a reiterated experience, and a close comparison of the objects in nature, that an artist becomes possessed of the idea of that central form, if I may so express it, from which every deviation is deformity. But the investigation of this form, I grant, is painful, and I know but of one method of shortening the road; this is, by a careful study of the works of the ancient sculptors; who, being indefatigable in the school of nature, have left models of that perfect form behind them, which an artist would prefer as supremely beautiful, who had spent his whole life in that single contemplation. But if industry carried them thus far, may not you also hope for the same reward from the same labour? We have the same school opened to us that was opened to them; for nature denies her instructions to none who desire to become her pupils.

This laborious investigation, I am aware, must appear superfluous to those who think everything is to be done by felicity, and the powers of native genius. Even the great Bacon treats with ridicule the idea of confining proportion to rules, or of producing beauty by selection. "A man cannot tell," says he, "whether Apelles or Albert Durer were the more trifler: whereof the one would make a personage by geometrical proportions; the other, by taking the best parts out of divers faces, to make one excellent. . .The painter," he adds, "must do it by a kind of felicity. . .and not by rule." [2]

It is not safe to question any opinion of so great a writer, and so profound a thinker, as undoubtedly Bacon was. But he studies

[2] Essays, p. 252, edit. 1625 [Reynolds and Malone].

brevity to excess; and therefore his meaning is sometimes doubtful. If he means that beauty has nothing to do with rule, he is mistaken. There is a rule, obtained out of general nature, to contradict which is to fall into deformity. Whenever anything is done beyond this rule, it is in virtue of some other rule which is followed along with it, but which does not contradict it. Everything which is wrought with certainty is wrought upon some principle. If it is not, it cannot be repeated. If by felicity is meant any thing of chance or hazard, or something born with a man, and not earned, I cannot agree with this great philosopher. Every object which pleases must give us pleasure upon some certain principles; but as the objects of pleasure are almost infinite, so their principles vary without end, and every man finds them out, not by felicity or successful hazard, but by care and sagacity.

To the principle I have laid down, that the idea of beauty in each species of beings is an invariable one, it may be objected that in every particular species there are various central forms, which are separate and distinct from each other, and yet are undeniably beautiful; that in the human figure, for instance, the beauty of Hercules is one, of the Gladiator another, of the Apollo another; which makes so many different ideas of beauty.

It is true, indeed, that these figures are each perfect in their kind, though of different characters and proportions; but still none of them is the representation of an individual, but of a class. And as there is one general form, which, as I have said, belongs to the human kind at large, so in each of these classes there is one common idea and central form, which is the abtract of the various individual forms belonging to that class. Thus, though the forms of childhood and age differ exceedingly, there is a common form in childhood, and a common form in age, which is the more perfect as it is more remote from all peculiarities. But I must add further, that though the most perfect forms of each of the general divisions of the human figure are ideal, and superior to any individual form of that class; yet the highest perfection of the human figure is not to be found in any one of them. It is not in the Hercules, nor in the Gladiator, nor in the Apollo; but in that form which is taken from all, and which partakes equally of the activity of the Gladiator, of the delicacy of the Apollo, and of the muscular strength of the Hercules. For perfect beauty in any species must combine all the characters which are beautiful in that species. It cannot consist in any one to the exclusion of the rest: no one, therefore, must be predominant, that no one may be deficient.

The knowledge of these different characters, and the power of separating and distinguishing them, are undoubtedly necessary to the painter, who is to vary his compositions with figures of various forms and proportions, though he is never to lose sight of the general idea of perfection in each kind.

There is, likewise, a kind of symmetry, or proportion, which may properly be said to belong to deformity. A figure lean or corpulent, tall or short, though deviating from beauty, may still have a certain union of the various parts, which may contribute to make them on the whole not unpleasing.

When the Artist has by diligent attention acquired a clear and distinct idea of beauty and symmetry; when he has reduced the variety of nature to the abstract idea; his next task will be to become acquainted with the genuine habits of nature, as distinguished from those of fashion. For in the same manner, and on the same principles, as he has acquired the knowledge of the real forms of nature, distinct from accidental deformity, he must endeavour to separate simple chaste nature from those adventitious, those affected and forced airs or actions with which she is loaded by modern education.

Perhaps I cannot better explain what I mean, than by reminding you of what was taught us by the Professor of Anatomy, in respect to the natural position and movement of the feet. He observed, that the fashion of turning them outwards was contrary to the intent of nature, as might be seen from the structure of the bones, and from the weakness that proceeded from that manner of standing. To this we may add the erect position of the head, the projection of the chest, the walking with straight knees, and many such actions, which we know to be merely the result of fashion, and what nature never warranted, as we are sure that we have been taught them when children.

I have mentioned but a few of those instances, in which

vanity or caprice have contrived to distort and disfigure the
human form: your own recollection will add to these a thousand
more of ill-understood methods, which have been practised to
disguise nature among our dancing-masters, hair-dressers, and
tailors, in their various schools of deformity.[3]

However the mechanick and ornamental arts may sacrifice
to fashion, she must be entirely excluded from the Art of Painting; the painter must never mistake this capricious changeling
for the genuine offspring of nature; he must divest himself of
all prejudices in favour of his age or country; he must disregard
all local and temporary ornaments, and look only on those general habits which are every where and always the same, he
addresses his works to the people of every country and every
age, he calls upon posterity to be his spectators, and says with
Zeuxis, *in aeternitatem pingo* [I paint for eternity].

The neglect of separating modern fashions from the habits
of nature leads to that ridiculous style which has been practised
by some painters, who have given to Grecian Heroes the airs
and graces practised in the court of Lewis the Fourteenth; an
absurdity almost as great as it would have been to have dressed
them after the fashion of that court.

To avoid this error, however, and to retain the true simplicity
of nature, is a task more difficult than at first sight it may appear.
The prejudices in favour of the fashions and customs that we
have been used to, and which are justly called a second nature,
make it too often difficult to distinguish that which is natural,
from that which is the result of education; they frequently even
give a predilection in favour of the artificial mode; and almost
everyone is apt to be guided by those local prejudices, who has
not chastised his mind and regulated the instability of his affections by the eternal invariable idea of nature.

Here then, as before, we must have recourse to the Ancients
as instructors. It is from a careful study of their works that you
will be enabled to attain to the real simplicity of nature; they
will suggest many observations which would probably escape

---

[3] "Those," says Quintilian, "who are taken with the outward show of
things, think that there is more beauty in persons, who are trimmed, curled,
and painted, than uncorrupt nature can give; as if beauty were merely the
effect of the corruption of manners." [Reynolds and Malone].

you, if your study were confined to nature alone. And, indeed, I cannot help suspecting that in this instance the ancients had an easier task than the moderns. They had, probably, little or nothing to unlearn, as their manners were nearly approaching to this desirable simplicity; while the modern artist, before he can see the truth of things, is obliged to remove a veil, with which the fashion of the times has thought proper to cover her.

Having gone thus far in our investigation of the great style in painting; if we now should suppose that the artist has found the true idea of beauty, which enables him to give his works a correct and perfect design; if we should suppose also, that he has acquired a knowledge of the unadulterated habits of nature, which gives him simplicity; the rest of his task is, perhaps, less than is generally imagined. Beauty and simplicity have so great a share in the composition of a great style, that he who has acquired them has little else to learn. It must not, indeed, be forgotten, that there is a nobleness of conception, which goes beyond anything in the mere exhibition even of perfect form; there is an art of animating and dignifying the figures with intellectual grandeur, of impressing the appearance of philosophick wisdom or heroick virtue. This can only be acquired by him that enlarges the sphere of his understanding by a variety of knowledge, and warms his imagination with the best productions of ancient and modern poetry.

A hand thus exercised, and a mind thus instructed, will bring the art to a higher degree of excellence than, perhaps, it has hitherto attained in this country. Such a student will disdain the humbler walks of painting, which, however profitable, can never assure him a permanent reputation. He will leave the meaner artist servilely to suppose that those are the best pictures, which are most likely to deceive the spectator. He will permit the lower painter, like the florist or collector of shells to exhibit the minute discriminations, which distinguish one object of the same species from another; while he, like the philosopher, will consider nature in the abstract, and represent in every one of his figures the character of its species.

If deceiving the eye were the only business of the art, there is no doubt, indeed, but the minute painter would be more apt to succeed: but it is not the eye, it is the mind, which the painter of genius desires to address; nor will he waste a moment upon those smaller objects, which only serve to catch the sense, to divide the attention, and to counteract his great design of speaking to the heart.

This is the ambition which I wish to excite in your minds; and the object I have had in my view, throughout this discourse, is that one great idea, which gives to painting its true dignity, which entitles it to the name of a Liberal Art, and ranks it as a sister of poetry.

It may possibly have happened to many young students, whose application was sufficient to overcome all difficulties, and whose minds were capable of embracing the most extensive views, that they have, by a wrong direction originally given, spent their lives in the meaner walks of painting, without ever knowing there was a nobler to pursue. Albert Durer, as Vasari has justly remarked, would, probably, have been one of the first painters of his age, (and he lived in an era of great artists,) had he been initiated into those great principles of the art, which were so well understood and practised by his contemporaries in Italy. But unluckily having never seen or heard of any other manner, he, without doubt, considered his own as perfect.

As for the various departments of painting, which do not presume to make such high pretensions, they are many. None of them are without their merit, though none enter into competition with this universal presiding idea of the art. The painters who have applied themselves more particularly to low and vulgar characters, and who express with precision the various shades of passion, as they are exhibited by vulgar minds, (such as we see in the works of Hogarth,) deserve great praise; but as their genius has been employed on low and confined subjects, the praise which we give must be as limited as its object. The merry-making or quarrelling of the Boors of Teniers; the same sort of productions of Brouwer, or Ostade,[4] are excellent in their kind; and the excellence and its praise will be in proportion as, in those limited subjects and peculiar forms, they introduce more or less of the expression of those passions as they appear in general and more enlarged nature. This principle

---

[4] Teniers, Brouwer, Ostade: 17th-century Dutch and Flemish genre painters.

may be applied to the Battle-pieces of Bourgognone, the French Gallantries of Watteau, and even beyond the exhibition of animal life, to the Landscapes of Claude Lorraine, and the Sea-Views of Vandervelde.[5] All these painters have, in general, the same right, in different degrees, to the name of a painter, which a satirist, an epigrammatist, a sonneteer, a writer of pastorals, or descriptive poetry, has to that of a poet.

In the same rank, and perhaps of not so great merit, is the cold painter of portraits. But his correct and just imitation of his object has its merits. Even the painter of still life, whose highest ambition is to give a minute representation of every part of those low objects which he sets before him, deserves the praise in proportion to his attainment; because no part of this excellent art, so much the ornament of polished life, is destitute of value and use. These, however, are by no means the views to which the mind of the student ought to be *primarily* directed. Having begun by aiming at better things, if from particular inclination, or from the taste of the time and place he lives in, or from necessity, or from failure in the highest attempts, he is obliged to descend lower, he will bring into the lower sphere or art a grandeur of composition and character that will raise and ennoble his works far above their natural rank.

A man is not weak, though he may not be able to wield the club of Hercules; nor does a man always practise that which he esteems the best; but does that which he can best do. In moderate attempts, there are many walks open to the artist. But as the idea of beauty is of necessity but one, so there can be but one great mode of painting, the leading principle of which I have endeavoured to explain.

I should be sorry, if what is here recommended, should be at all understood to countenance a careless or indetermined manner of painting. For though the painter is to overlook the accidental discriminations of nature, he is to exhibit distinctly, and with precision, the general forms of things. A firm and determined outline is one of the characteristics of the great style in

[5] Bourgognone, Watteau, Claude Lorraine: 17th-century French painters; Vandervelde (Van de Velde): any of several 17th-century Dutch painters of this name.

painting; and let me add, that he who possesses the knowledge of the exact form which every part of nature ought to have, will be fond of expressing that knowledge with correctness and precision in all his works.

To conclude; I have endeavoured to reduce the idea of beauty to general principles; and I had the pleasure to observe that the Professor of Painting proceeded in the same method, when he showed you that the artifice of contrast was founded but on one principle. I am convinced that this is the only means of advancing science; of clearing the mind from a confused heap of contradictory observations, that do but perplex and puzzle the student when he compares them, or misguide him if he gives himself up to their authority: bringing them under one general head, can alone give rest and satisfaction to an inquisitive mind.

Oliver Goldsmith

[1730–1774]

FOR MOST OF HIS MATURE LIFE Goldsmith was an overworked literary hack. He wrote prolifically in a wide variety of forms: informal essays, translations, histories (including one of "The Earth and Animated Nature"), poems, plays, and one novel in a career that lasted only fifteen years. Much of what he wrote is ephemeral, but the range of his genuine talent is indicated by the fact that his reputation is equally secure in the histories of a number of literary forms: the didactic poem (*The Deserted Village*); the novel (*The Vicar of Wakefield*); the play (*She Stoops to Conquer*); the epistolary essay (*The Citizen of the World*).

Goldsmith belongs, with Reynolds and Johnson, to the last great generation of neo-classical critics. His "Sentimental and Laughing Comedy" is in the classical tradition of genre criticism; that is, it defines the genre of comedy in formal terms, supported by classical authority, rather than in the affective terms which were already providing genre definitions for empirical critics like Burke and Hume.

Goldsmith's essay is best seen in the light of the discussion of comedy which runs through the neo-classical period (and through this volume—see Dryden, Congreve, Collier, Steele, and Fielding above). Like his fellow-playwrights of the preceding century, Goldsmith sees the primary function of comedy to be the correction of human vices and follies through ridicule; his principal objection to sentimental comedy is that, in providing virtues and distresses instead of vices and follies, it fails in its moral function—it may be sad, but it is not serious. But, as Goldsmith recognized, popular taste was on the side of sentiment, and laughing comedy was already drowning in a flood of tears.

BIBLIOGRAPHY. *Works,* ed. J. W. M. Gibbs, 5 vols. (London, 1884–86); *New Essays by Oliver Goldsmith,* ed. R. S. Crane (Chicago, 1927).

R. M. Wardle, *Oliver Goldsmith* (Lawrence, Kansas, 1957); F. L.

Lucas, *The Search for Good Sense: Four Eighteenth-Century Characters* (New York, 1959).

TEXT. *Works,* ed. Gibbs, vol. I.

ESSAY ON THE THEATRE; OR, A COMPARISON BETWEEN SENTIMENTAL AND LAUGHING COMEDY [1]

[1773]

THE THEATRE, LIKE ALL other amusements, has its fashions and its prejudices; and when satiated with its excellence, mankind begin to mistake change for improvement. For some years tragedy was the reigning entertainment; but of late it has entirely given way to comedy, and our best efforts are now exerted in these lighter kinds of composition. The pompous train, the swelling phrase, and the unnatural rant, are displaced for that natural portrait of human folly and frailty, of which all are judges, because all have sat for the picture.

But, as in describing nature, it is presented with a double face, either of mirth or sadness, our modern writers find themselves at a loss which chiefly to copy from; and it is now debated, whether the exhibition of human distress is likely to afford the mind more entertainment than that of human absurdity?

Comedy is defined by Aristotle to be a picture of the frailties of the lower part of mankind, to distinguish it from tragedy, which is an exhibition of the misfortunes of the great. When comedy therefore ascends to produce the characters of princes or generals upon the stage, it is out of its walk, since low and middle life are entirely its object. The principal question therefore is, whether in describing low or middle life, an exhibition of its follies be not preferable to a detail of its calamities? Or, in other words, which deserves the preference, the weeping sentimental comedy, so much in fashion at present, or the laughing

[1] First published in the *Westminster Magazine,* January, 1773.

and even low comedy, which seems to have been last exhibited by Vanbrugh and Cibber?

If we apply to authorities, all the great masters in the dramatic art have but one opinion. Their rule is, that as tragedy displays the calamities of the great, so comedy should excite our laughter, by ridiculously exhibiting the follies of the lower part of mankind. Boileau, one of the best modern critics, asserts, that comedy will not admit of tragic distress:

> *Le Comique, ennemi des soupirs et des pleurs,*
> *N'admet point dans ses vers de tragiques douleurs.*
> [Comedy, the foe of sighs and tears,
> Forbids all tragic sorrows to its lines.]

Nor is this rule without the strongest foundation in nature, as the distresses of the mean by no means affect us so strongly as the calamities of the great. When tragedy exhibits to us some great man fallen from his height, and struggling with want and adversity, we feel his situation in the same manner as we suppose he himself must feel, and our pity is increased in proportion to the height from which he fell. On the contrary, we do not so strongly sympathize with one born in humbler circumstances, and encountering accidental distress: so that while we melt for Belisarius,[2] we scarcely give halfpence to the beggar, who accosts us in the street. The one has our pity, the other our contempt. Distress therefore is the proper object of tragedy, since the great excite our pity by their fall; but not equally so of comedy, since the actors employed in it are originally so mean, that they sink but little by their fall.

Since the first origin of the stage, tragedy and comedy have run in distinct channels, and never till of late encroached upon the provinces of each other. Terence, who seems to have made the nearest approaches, always judiciously stops short before he comes to the downright pathetic; and yet he is even reproached by Caesar for wanting the *vis comica*. All the other comic writers of antiquity aim only at rendering folly or vice ridiculous, but never exalt their characters into buskined pomp,

---

[2] According to popular legend, Belisarius, a Roman general, was blinded by Justinian, and wandered the streets of Constantinople as a beggar.

or make what Voltaire humourously calls a *tradesman's tragedy*.

Yet notwithstanding this weight of authority, and the universal practice of former ages, a new species of dramatic composition has been introduced under the name of *sentimental* comedy, in which the virtues of private life are exhibited, rather than the vices exposed; and the distresses rather than the faults of mankind make our interest in the piece. These comedies have had of late great success, perhaps from their novelty, and also from their flattering every man in his favourite foible. In these plays almost all the characters are good, and exceedingly generous; they are lavish enough of their *tin* money on the stage; and though they want humour, have abundance of sentiment and feeling. If they happen to have faults or foibles, the spectator is taught not only to pardon, but to applaud them, in consideration of the goodness of their hearts; so that folly, instead of being ridiculed, is commended, and the comedy aims at touching our passions without the power of being truly pathetic. In this manner we are likely to lose one great source of entertainment on the stage; for while the comic poet is invading the province of the tragic muse, he leaves her lovely sister quite neglected. Of this, however, he is no way solicitous, as he measures his fame by his profits.

But it will be said, that the theatre is formed to amuse mankind, and that it matters little, if this end be answered, by what means it is obtained. If mankind find delight in weeping at comedy, it would be cruel to abridge them in that or any other innocent pleasure. If those pieces are denied the name of comedies, yet call them by any other name, and if they are delightful, they are good. Their success, it will be said, is a mark of their merit, and it is only abridging our happiness to deny us an inlet to amusement.

These objections, however, are rather specious than solid. It is true, that amusement is a great object of the theatre; and it will be allowed, that these sentimental pieces do often amuse us; but the question is, whether the true comedy would not amuse us more? The question is, whether a character supported throughout a piece with its ridicule still attending, would not give us more delight than this species of bastard tragedy, which only is applauded because it is new?

A friend of mine, who was sitting unmoved at one of these sentimental pieces, was asked how he could be so indifferent? "Why, truly," says he, "as the hero is but a tradesman, it is indifferent to me whether he be turned out of his counting-house on Fish-Street Hill, since he will still have enough left to open shop in St. Giles's."

The other objection is as ill-grounded; for though we should give these pieces another name, it will not mend their efficacy. It will continue a kind of *mulish* production, with all the defects of its opposite parents, and marked with sterility. If we are permitted to make comedy weep, we have an equal right to make tragedy laugh, and to set down in blank verse the jests and repartees of all the attendants in a funeral procession.

But there is one argument in favour of sentimental comedy which will keep it on the stage, in spite of all that can be said against it. It is of all others the most easily written. Those abilities that can hammer out a novel, are fully sufficient for the production of a sentimental comedy. It is only sufficient to raise the characters a little; to deck out the hero with a riband, or give the heroine a title; then to put an insipid dialogue, without character or humour, into their mouths, give them mighty good hearts, very fine clothes, furnish a new set of scenes, make a pathetic scene or two, with a sprinkling of tender melancholy conversation through the whole; and there is no doubt but all the ladies will cry and all the gentlemen applaud.

Humour at present seems to be departing from the stage, and it will soon happen that our comic players will have nothing left for it but a fine coat and a song. It depends upon the audience whether they will actually drive those poor merry creatures from the stage, or sit at a play as gloomy as at the tabernacle. It is not easy to recover an art when once lost; and it will be a just punishment, that when, by our being too fastidious, we have banished humour from the stage, we should ourselves be deprived of the art of laughing.

Samuel Johnson

[1709–1784]

BORN IN LICHFIELD, the son of a bookseller, Johnson spent a few terms at Oxford, returned to Lichfield to open a school (which failed), and finally moved to London, determined to become an author. His first literary work was hack journalism, but gradually his poems, his play *Irene,* and his *Rambler* essays established his reputation as a man of letters. The success of two great editorial labors, his *Dictionary* (1755) and his edition of Shakespeare (1765) made Johnson the undisputed literary dictator of his age. He surrounded himself with a circle of friends that included Burke, Goldsmith, and Reynolds, and indulged in that commodity which he valued so highly, conversation. It is this circle, and this conversation, that Boswell recorded in the biography that made Johnson more famous than his own writings.

Johnson stands at the end of the neo-classical tradition in England, its last and greatest spokesman. In his criticism one finds the best and most characteristic qualities of English neo-classicism: its rationality, its will to order and define, its empirical flexibility, and above all its concern for the moral function of art. It is this last quality which defines Johnson as a critic. He recognized, as later critics have not always done, the power of art to influence and persuade, and he was therefore concerned above all that the power of art should be used in the cause of truth and virtue. To perform its moral function, art must express general truth, and Johnson, like Reynolds, argues that it must therefore "remark general properties and large appearances" of things rather than particular details; his criticism of the metaphysical poets is primarily that they are too particular: "great thoughts," he says, "are always general."

To test the truth of generalities, Johnson appeals to nature and to reason; he shows, in his careful judgments of individual cases, that empirical bias which gives English neo-classicism its amiable flexibility. In general he is hostile to rules and conventions: he dismisses the classical unities in drama, and ridicules artificial pastorals which are not based in nature and human experience. It is from experience and not from books that the artist learns what is most valuable to him, and experience comes "from general converse, and accurate observation of the living world."

"The task of an author," Johnson wrote, "is, either to teach what is not known, or to recommend known truths by his manner of adorning them." The task of the critic is to evaluate and judge the author's work, distinguishing right from wrong and truth from falsehood. Johnson is notable, in a century of Shakespeare and Milton worship, for the scrupulousness with which he divides the faulty from the fine, praising what merits praise, and condemning what does not. The fact that his judgments are not always ours, and that he sometimes seems insensitive to obvious excellences, should not blind us to the greatness of his critical achievement.

BIBLIOGRAPHY. *Works,* 12 vols. (London, 1806); *Works,* ed. E. L. McAdam Jr. and others (New Haven, 1959—[in progress]); *Lives of the English Poets,* ed. G. Birkbeck Hill, 3 vols. (Oxford, 1905).

Walter Jackson Bate, *The Achievement of Samuel Johnson* (Oxford, 1955); Jean H. Hagstrum, *Samuel Johnson's Literary Criticism* (Minneapolis, 1952); W. R. Keast, "The Theoretical Foundations of Johnson's Criticism," in *Critics and Criticism,* ed. R. S. Crane (Chicago, 1952); W. B. C. Watkins, *Johnson and English Poetry before 1660* (Princeton, 1936).

TEXT. *Works* (1806), vols. III, IV, IX.

ON THE NOVEL *

[1750]

Simul et jucunda et idonea dicere Vitæ.   HOR. [*Ars. Poet.* 334.]
And join both profit and delight in one.   CREECH.

THE WORKS OF FICTION, with which the present generation seems more particularly delighted, are such as exhibit life in its true state, diversified only by accidents that daily happen in the world, and influenced by passions and qualities which are really to be found in conversing with mankind.

* FROM the *Rambler,* Number 4, March 31, 1750.

This kind of writing may be termed not improperly the comedy of romance, and is to be conducted nearly by the rules of comick poetry. Its province is to bring about natural events by easy means, and to keep up curiosity without the help of wonder: it is therefore precluded from the machines and expedients of the heroick romance, and can neither employ giants to snatch away a lady from the nuptial rites, nor knights to bring her back from captivity; it can neither bewilder its personages in deserts, nor lodge them in imaginary castles.

I remember a remark made by Scaliger upon Pontanus, that all his writings are filled with the same images; and that if you take from him his lillies and his roses, his satyrs and his dryads, he will have nothing left that can be called poetry. In like manner almost all the fictions of the last age will vanish, if you deprive them of a hermit and a wood, a battle and a shipwreck.

Why this wild strain of imagination found reception so long, in polite and learned ages, it is not easy to conceive; but we cannot wonder that while readers could be procured, the authors were willing to continue it; for when a man had by practice gained some fluency of language, he had no further care than to retire to his closet, let loose his invention, and heat his mind with incredibilities; a book was thus produced without fear of criticism, without the toil of study, without knowledge of nature, or acquaintance with life.

The task of our present writers is very different; it requires, together with that learning which is to be gained from books, that experience which can never be attained by solitary diligence, but must arise from general converse, and accurate observation of the living world. Their performances have, as Horace expresses it, *plus oneris quantum veniæ minus*, little indulgence, and therefore more difficulty. They are engaged in portraits of which every one knows the original, and can detect any deviation from exactness of resemblance. Other writings are safe, except from the malice of learning, but these are in danger from every common reader; as the slipper ill executed was censured by a shoemaker who happened to stop in his way at the Venus of Apelles.

But the fear of not being approved as just copiers of human manners, is not the most important concern that an author of this sort ought to have before him. These books are written chiefly to the young, the ignorant, and the idle, to whom they serve as lectures of conduct, and introductions into life. They are the entertainment of minds unfurnished with ideas, and therefore easily susceptible of impressions; not fixed by principles, and therefore easily following the current of fancy; not informed by experience, and consequently open to every false suggestion and partial account.

That the highest degree of reverence should be paid to youth, and that nothing indecent should be suffered to approach their eyes or ears; are precepts extorted by sense and virtue from an ancient writer, by no means eminent for chastity of thought. The same kind, though not the same degree of caution, is required to every thing which is laid before them, to secure them from unjust prejudices, perverse opinions, and incongruous combinations of images.

In the romances formerly written, every transaction and sentiment was so remote from all that passes among men, that the reader was in very little danger of making any applications to himself; the virtues and crimes were equally beyond his sphere of activity; and he amused himself with heroes and with traitors, deliverers and persecutors, as with beings of another species, whose actions were regulated upon motives of their own, and who had neither faults nor excellencies in common with himself.

But when an adventurer is levelled with the rest of the world, and acts in such scenes of the universal drama, as may be the lot of any other man; young spectators fix their eyes upon him with closer attention, and hope, by observing his behaviour and success, to regulate their own practices, when they shall be engaged in the like part.

For this reason these familiar histories may perhaps be made of greater use than the solemnities of professed morality, and convey the knowledge of vice and virtue with more efficacy than axioms and definitions. But if the power of example is so great, as to take possession of the memory by a kind of violence, and produce effects almost without the intervention of the will, care ought to be taken, that, when the choice is unrestrained, the best examples only should be exhibited; and that which is likely to operate so strongly, should not be mischievous or uncertain in its effects.

The chief advantage which these fictions have over real life is, that their authors are at liberty, though not to invent, yet to select objects, and to cull from the mass of mankind, those individuals upon which the attention ought most to be employed; as a diamond, though it cannot be made, may be polished by art, and placed in such a situation, as to display that lustre which before was buried among common stones.

It is justly considered as the greatest excellency of art, to imitate nature; but it is necessary to distinguish those parts of nature, which are most proper for imitation: greater care is still required in representing life, which is so often discoloured by passion, or deformed by wickedness. If the world be promiscuously described, I cannot see of what use it can be to read the account; or why it may not be as safe to turn the eye immediately upon mankind as upon a mirror which shows all that presents itself without discrimination.

It is therefore not a sufficient vindication of a character, that it is drawn as it appears; for many characters ought never to be drawn: nor of a narrative, that the train of events is agreeable to observation and experience; for that observation which is called knowledge of the world, will be found much more frequently to make men cunning than good. The purpose of these writings is surely not only to show mankind, but to provide that they may be seen hereafter with less hazard; to teach the means of avoiding the snares which are laid by TREACHERY for INNOCENCE, without infusing any wish for that superiority with which the betrayer flatters his vanity; to give the power of counteracting fraud, without the temptation to practise it; to initiate youth by mock encounters in the art of necessary defence, and to encrease prudence without impairing virtue.

Many writers, for the sake of following nature, so mingle good and bad qualities in their principal personages, that they are both equally conspicuous; and as we accompany them through their adventures with delight, and are led by degrees to interest ourselves in their favour, we lose the abhorrence of their faults, because they do not hinder our pleasure, or, perhaps, regard them with some kindness, for being united with so much merit.

There have been men indeed splendidly wicked, whose endowments threw a brightness on their crimes, and whom scarce any villainy made perfectly detestable, because they never could be wholly divested of their excellencies; but such have been in all ages the great corrupters of the world, and their resemblance ought no more to be preserved, than the art of murdering without pain.

Some have advanced, without due attention to the consequences of this notion, that certain virtues have their correspondent faults, and therefore that to exhibit either apart is to deviate from probability. Thus men are observed by Swift to be "grateful in the same degree as they are resentful." This principle, with others of the same kind, supposes man to act from a brute impulse, and pursue a certain degree of inclination, without any choice of the object; for, otherwise, though it should be allowed that gratitude and resentment arise from the same constitution of the passions, it follows not that they will be equally indulged when reason is consulted; yet, unless that consequence be admitted, this sagacious maxim becomes an empty sound, without any relation to practice or to life.

Nor is it evident, that even the first motions to these effects are always in the same proportion. For pride, which produces quickness of resentment, will obstruct gratitude, by unwillingness to admit that inferiority which obligation implies; and it is very unlikely that he who cannot think he receives a favour, will acknowledge or repay it.

It is of the utmost importance to mankind, that positions of this tendency should be laid open and confuted; for while men consider good and evil as springing from the same root, they will spare the one for the sake of the other, and in judging, if not of others at least of themselves, will be apt to estimate their virtues by their vices. To this fatal errour all those will contribute, who confound the colours of right and wrong, and instead of helping to settle their boundaries, mix them with so much art, that no common mind is able to disunite them.

In narratives, where historical veracity has no place, I cannot discover why there should not be exhibited the most perfect idea of virtue; of virtue not angelical, nor above probability, for what we cannot credit we shall never imitate, but the highest and purest that humanity can reach, which, exercised in such trials as the various revolutions of things shall bring upon it, may, by conquering some calamities, and enduring others, teach us what we may hope, and what we can perform. Vice, for vice is necessary to be shewn, should always disgust; nor should the graces of gaiety, or the dignity of courage, be so united with it, as to reconcile it to the mind. Wherever it appears, it should raise hatred by the malignity of its practices, and contempt by the meanness of its stratagems: for while it is supported by either parts or spirit, it will be seldom heartily abhorred. The Roman tyrant was content to be hated, if he was but feared; and there are thousands of the readers of romances willing to be thought wicked, if they may be allowed to be wits. It is therefore to be steadily inculcated, that virtue is the highest proof of understanding, and the only solid basis of greatness; and that vice is the natural consequence of narrow thoughts; that it begins in mistake, and ends in ignominy.

ON PASTORAL POETRY *

[1750]

Canto quae solitus, si quando armenta vocabat,
Amphion Dircaeus.   VIRG.

Such strains I sing as once *Amphion* play'd,
When list'ning flocks the powerful call obey'd.
                              ELPHINSTON.

IN WRITING OR JUDGING OF pastoral poetry, neither the authors nor criticks of latter times seem to have paid sufficient regard to the originals left us by antiquity, but have entangled themselves with unnecessary difficulties, by advancing principles, which, having no foundation in the nature of things, are wholly to be rejected from a species of composition, in which, above all others, mere nature is to be regarded.

It is therefore necessary to inquire after some more distinct

* FROM the *Rambler,* Number 37, July 24, 1750.

and exact idea of this kind of writing. This may, I think, be easily found in the pastorals of Virgil, from whose opinion it will not appear very safe to depart, if we consider that every advantage of nature, and of fortune, concurred to complete his productions; that he was born with great accuracy and severity of judgment, enlightened with all the learning of one of the brightest ages, and embellished with the elegance of the Roman court; that he employed his powers rather in improving, than inventing, and therefore must have endeavoured to recompence the want of novelty by exactness; that taking Theocritus for his original, he found pastoral far advanced towards perfection, and that having so great a rival, he must have proceeded with uncommon caution.

If we search the writings of Virgil, for the true definition of a pastoral, it will be found *a poem in which any action or passion is represented by its effects upon a country life.* Whatsoever therefore may, according to the common course of things, happen in the country, may afford a subject for a pastoral poet.

In this definition, it will immediately occur to those who are versed in the writings of the modern criticks, that there is no mention of the golden age. I cannot indeed easily discover why it is thought necessary to refer descriptions of a rural state to remote times, nor can I perceive that any writer has consistently preserved the Arcadian manners and sentiments. The only reason, that I have read, on which this rule has been founded, is, that, according to the customs of modern life, it is improbable that shepherds should be capable of harmonious numbers, or delicate sentiments; and therefore the reader must exalt his ideas of the pastoral character, by carrying his thoughts back to the age in which the care of herds and flocks was the employment of the wisest and greatest men.

These reasoners seem to have been led into their hypothesis, by considering pastoral, not in general, as a representation of rural nature, and consequently as exhibiting the ideas and sentiments of those, whoever they are, to whom the country affords pleasure or employment, but simply as a dialogue, or narrative of men actually tending sheep, and busied in the lowest and most laborious offices; from whence they very readily concluded, since characters must necessarily be preserved, that either the sentiments must sink to the level of the speakers, or the speakers must be raised to the height of the sentiments.

In consequence of these original errours, a thousand precepts have been given, which have only contributed to perplex and confound. Some have thought it necessary that the imaginary manners of the golden age should be universally preserved, and have therefore believed, that nothing more could be admitted in pastoral, than lilies and roses, and rocks and streams, among which are heard the gentle whispers of chaste fondness, or the soft complaints of amorous impatience. In pastoral, as in other writings, chastity of sentiment ought doubtless to be observed, and purity of manners to be represented; not because the poet is confined to the images of the golden age, but because, having the subject in his own choice, he ought always to consult the interest of virtue.

These advocates for the golden age lay down other principles, not very consistent with their general plan; for they tell us, that, to support the character of the shepherd, it is proper that all refinement should be avoided, and that some slight instances of ignorance should be interspersed. Thus the shepherd in Virgil is supposed to have forgot the name of Anaximander, and in Pope the term Zodiack is too hard for a rustick apprehension. But if we place our shepherds in their primitive condition, we may give them learning among their other qualifications; and if we suffer them to allude at all to things of later existence, which, perhaps, cannot with any great propriety be allowed, there can be no danger of making them speak with too much accuracy, since they conversed with divinities, and transmitted to succeeding ages the arts of life.

Other writers, having the mean and despicable condition of a shepherd always before them, conceive it necessary to degrade the language of pastoral by obsolete terms and rustick words, which they very learnedly call Dorick, without reflecting, that they thus became authors of a mangled dialect, which may as well refine the speech as the sentiments of their personage, and that none of the inconsistencies which they endeavour to avoid, is greater than that of joining elegance of thought with coarseness of diction. Spenser begins one of his pastorals with studied barbarity;

> *Diggon Davie,* I bid her good-day:
> Or, *Diggon* her is, or I missay.
> *Dig.* Her was her while it was day-light,
> But now her is a most wretched wight.

What will the reader imagine to be the subject on which speakers like these exercise their eloquence? Will he not be somewhat disappointed, when he finds them met together to condemn the corruptions of the church of Rome? Surely, at the same time that a shepherd learns theology, he may gain some acquaintance with his native language.

Pastoral admits of all ranks of persons, because persons of all ranks inhabit the country. It excludes not, therefore, on account of the characters necessary to be introduced, any elevation or delicacy of sentiment; those ideas only are improper, which, not owing their original to rural objects, are not pastoral. Such is the exclamation in Virgil,

> *Nunc scio quid sit Amor, duris in cautibus illum,*
> *Ismarus, aut Rhodope, aut extremi Garamantes,*
> *Nec generis nostri puerum, nec sanguinis, edunt.*

> I know thee, Love, in deserts thou wert bred,
> And at the dugs of savage tygers fed;
> Alien of birth, usurper of the plains.   DRYDEN

which Pope, endeavouring to copy, was carried to still greater impropriety:

> I know thee, Love, wild as the raging main,
> More fierce than tygers on the Libyan plain;
> Thou wert from Aetna's burning entrails torn;
> Begot in tempests, and in thunders born!

Sentiments like these, as they have no ground in nature, are indeed of little value in any poem; but in pastoral they are particularly liable to censure, because it wants that exaltation above common life, which in tragick or heroick writings often reconciles us to bold flights and daring figures.

Pastoral being the *representation of an action or passion, by its effects upon a country life,* has nothing peculiar but its confinement to rural imagery, without which it ceases to be pastoral. This is its true characteristick, and this it cannot lose by any dignity of sentiment, or beauty of diction. The Pollio of Virgil, with all its elevation, is a composition truly bucolick, though rejected by the criticks; for all the images are either taken from the country, or from the religion of the age common to all parts of the empire.

The Silenus is indeed of a more disputable kind, because though the scene lies in the country, the song being religious and historical, had been no less adapted to any other audience or place. Neither can it well be defended as a fiction; for the introduction of a god seems to imply the golden age, and yet he alludes to many subsequent transactions, and mentions Gallus the poet's contemporary.

It seems necessary to the perfection of this poem, that the occasion which is supposed to produce it, be at least not inconsistent with a country life, or less likely to interest those who have retired into places of solitude and quiet, than the more busy part of mankind. It is therefore improper to give the title of a pastoral to verses, in which the speakers, after the slight mention of their flocks, fall to complaints of errours in the church, and corruptions in the government, or to lamentations of the death of some illustrious person, whom, when once the poet has called a shepherd, he has no longer any labour upon his hands, but can make the clouds weep, and lilies wither, and the sheep hang their heads, without art or learning, genius or study.

It is part of Claudian's character of his rustick, that he computes his time not by the succession of consuls, but of harvests. Those who pass their days in retreats distant from the theatres of business, are always least likely to hurry their imagination with publick affairs.

The facility of treating actions or events in the pastoral style, has incited many writers, from whom more judgment might have been expected, to put the sorrow or the joy which the occasion required into the mouth of Daphne or of Thyrsis, and as one absurdity must naturally be expected to make way for another, they have written with an utter disregard both of life and nature, and filled their productions with mythological allusions, with incredible fictions, and with sentiments which neither passion nor reason could have dictated, since the change which religion has made in the whole system of the world.

from

THE HISTORY OF RASSELAS, PRINCE OF ABISSINIA

[1759]

CHAPTER X

IMLAC'S HISTORY CONTINUED. A DISSERTATION UPON POETRY

"Wherever I went, I found that poetry was considered as the highest learning, and regarded with a veneration somewhat approaching to that which man would pay to the Angelick Nature. And it yet fills me with wonder, that, in almost all countries, the most ancient poets are considered as the best: whether it be that every other kind of knowledge is an acquisition gradually attained, and poetry is a gift conferred at once; or that the first poetry of every nation surprised them as a novelty, and retained the credit by consent which it received by accident at first: or whether, as the province of poetry is to describe Nature and Passion, which are always the same, the first writers took possession of the most striking objects for description, and the most probable occurrences for fiction, and left nothing to those that followed them, but transcription of the same events, and new combinations of the same images. Whatever be the reason, it is commonly observed that the early writers are in possession of nature, and their followers of art: that the first excel in strength and invention, and the latter in elegance and refinement.

"I was desirous to add my name to this illustrious fraternity. I read all the poets of Persia and Arabia, and was able to repeat by memory the volumes that are suspended in the mosque of Mecca. But I soon found that no man was ever great by imitation. My desire of excellence impelled me to transfer my attention to nature and to life. Nature was to be my subject, and men to be my auditors: I could never describe what I had not seen: I could not hope to move those with delight or terrour, whose interests and opinions I did not understand.

"Being now resolved to be a poet, I saw every thing with a new purpose; my sphere of attention was suddenly magnified: no kind of knowledge was to be overlooked. I ranged mountains and deserts for images and resemblances, and pictured upon my mind every tree of the forest and flower of the valley. I observed with equal care the crags of the rock and the pinnacles of the palace. Sometimes I wandered along the mazes of the rivulet, and sometimes watched the changes of the summer clouds. To a poet nothing can be useless. Whatever is beautiful, and whatever is dreadful, must be familiar to his imagination: he must be conversant with all that is awfully vast or elegantly little. The plants of the garden, the animals of the wood, the minerals of the earth, and meteors of the sky, must all concur to store his mind with inexhaustible variety: for every idea is useful for the inforcement or decoration of moral or religious truth; and he, who knows most, will have most power of diversifying his scenes, and of gratifying his reader with remote allusions and unexpected instruction.

"All the appearances of nature I was therefore careful to study, and every country which I have surveyed has contributed something to my poetical powers."

"In so wide a survey, said the prince, you must surely have left much unobserved. I have lived, till now, within the circuit of these mountains, and yet cannot walk abroad without the sight of something which I had never beheld before, or never heeded."

"The business of a poet, said Imlac, is to examine, not the individual, but the species; to remark general properties and large appearances: he does not number the streaks of the tulip, or describe the different shades in the verdure of the forest. He is to exhibit in his portraits of nature such prominent and striking features, as recal the original to every mind; and must neglect the minuter discriminations, which one may have remarked, and another have neglected, for those characteristicks which are alike obvious to vigilance and carelessness.

"But the knowledge of nature is only half the task of a poet; he must be acquainted likewise with all the modes of life. His character requires that he estimate the happiness and misery of every condition; observe the power of all the passions in all their combinations, and trace the changes of the human mind as they are modified by various institutions and accidental influences of climate or custom, from the spriteliness of infancy to the despondence of decrepitude. He must divest himself of the prejudices of his age or country; he must consider right and wrong in their abstracted and invariable state; he must disregard present laws and opinions, and rise to general and transcendental truths, which will always be the same: he must therefore content himself with the slow progress of his name; contemn the applause of his own time, and commit his claims to the justice of posterity. He must write as the interpreter of nature, and the legislator of mankind, and consider himself as presiding over the thoughts and manners of future generations; as a being superiour to time and place.

"His labour is not yet at an end: he must know many languages and many sciences; and, that his style may be worthy of his thoughts, must, by incessant practice, familiarize to himself every delicacy of speech and grace of harmony."

from

LIVES OF THE POETS

[1779–1781]

from

COWLEY

WIT, LIKE ALL OTHER THINGS subject by their nature to the choice of man, has its changes and fashions, and at different times takes different forms. About the beginning of the seventeenth century appeared a race of writers that may be termed the metaphysical poets, of whom, in a criticism on the works of Cowley, it is not improper to give some account.

The metaphysical poets were men of learning, and to shew their learning was their whole endeavour; but, unluckily resolving to shew it in rhyme, instead of writing poetry they only wrote verses, and very often such verses as stood the trial of the finger better than of the ear; for the modulation was so imperfect that they were only found to be verses by counting the syllables.

If the father of criticism has rightly denominated poetry τέχνη μιμητικὴ *an imitative art,* these writers will, without great wrong, lose their right to the name of poets, for they cannot be said to have imitated any thing; they neither copied nature nor life; neither painted the forms of matter, nor represented the operations of intellect.

Those however who deny them to be poets, allow them to be wits. Dryden confesses of himself and his contemporaries, that they fall below Donne in wit; but maintains, that they surpass him in poetry.[1]

If Wit be well described by Pope as being "that which has been often thought, but was never before so well expressed," [2] they certainly never attained, nor ever sought it; for they endeavoured to be singular in their thoughts, and were careless of their diction. But Pope's account of wit is undoubtedly erroneous; he depresses it below its natural dignity, and reduces it from strength of thought to happiness of language.

If by a more noble and more adequate conception that be considered as wit which is at once natural and new, that which, though not obvious, is, upon its first production, acknowledged to be just; if it be that which he that never found it wonders how he missed; to wit of this kind the metaphysical poets have seldom risen. Their thoughts are often new, but seldom natural; they are not obvious, but neither are they just; and the reader, far from wondering that he missed them, wonders more frequently by what perverseness of industry they were ever found.

But wit, abstracted from its effects upon the hearer, may be more rigorously and philosophically considered as a kind of *discordia concors;* a combination of dissimilar images, or discovery of occult resemblances in things apparently unlike. Of wit, thus defined, they have more than enough. The most heterogeneous ideas are yoked by violence together; nature and art are ransacked for illustrations, comparisons, and allusions; their learning instructs, and their subtlety surprises; but the reader

---

[1] In "A Discourse Concerning the Original and Progress of Satire" (Ker, *Essays of John Dryden,* vol. II, p. 102).

[2] *Essay on Criticism* (see above, p. 164).

commonly thinks his improvement dearly bought, and, though he sometimes admires, is seldom pleased.

From this account of their compositions it will be readily inferred, that they were not successful in representing or moving the affections. As they were wholly employed on something unexpected and surprising, they had no regard to that uniformity of sentiment which enables us to conceive and to excite the pains and the pleasure of other minds: they never inquired what, on any occasion, they should have said or done; but wrote rather as beholders than partakers of human nature; as Beings looking upon good and evil, impassive and at leisure; as Epicurean deities, making remarks on the actions of men, and the vicissitudes of life, without interest and without emotion. Their courtship was void of fondness, and their lamentation of sorrow. Their wish was only to say what they hoped had been never said before.

Nor was the sublime more within their reach than the pathetick; for they never attempted that comprehension and expanse of thought which at once fills the whole mind, and of which the first effect is sudden astonishment, and the second rational admiration. Sublimity is produced by aggregation, and littleness by dispersion. Great thoughts are always general, and consist in positions not limited by exceptions, and in descriptions not descending to minuteness. It is with great propriety that subtlety, which in its original import means exility of particles, is taken in its metaphorical meaning for nicety of distinction. Those writers who lay on the watch for novelty could have little hope of greatness; for great things cannot have escaped former observation. Their attempts were always analytick: they broke every image into fragments, and could no more represent by their slender conceits and laboured particularities the prospects of nature, or the scenes of life, than he who dissects a sun-beam with a prism can exhibit the wide effulgence of a summer noon.

What they wanted however of the sublime they endeavoured to supply by hyperbole; their amplification had no limits: they left not only reason but fancy behind them; and produced combinations of confused magnificence, that not only could not be credited, but could not be imagined.

Yet great labour, directed by great abilities, is never wholly lost: if they frequently threw away their wit upon false conceits, they likewise sometimes struck out unexpected truth: if their conceits were far-fetched, they were often worth the carriage. To write on their plan it was at least necessary to read and think. No man could be born a metaphysical poet, nor assume the dignity of a writer, by descriptions copied from descriptions, by imitations borrowed from imitations, by traditional imagery, and hereditary similes, by readiness of rhyme, and volubility of syllables.

In perusing the works of this race of authors, the mind is exercised either by recollection or enquiry: either something already learned is to be retrieved, or something new is to be examined. If their greatness seldom elevates, their acuteness often surprises; if the imagination is not always gratified, at least the powers of reflection and comparison are employed; and in the mass of materials which ingenious absurdity has thrown together, genuine wit and useful knowledge may be sometimes found, buried perhaps in grossness of expression, but useful to those who know their value; and such as, when they are expanded to perspicuity, and polished to elegance, may give lustre to works which have more propriety though less copiousness of sentiment.

from

MILTON

I am now to examine *Paradise Lost;* a poem, which, considered with respect to design, may claim the first place, and with respect to performance, the second, among the productions of the human mind.

By the general consent of criticks the first praise of genius is due to the writer of an epick poem, as it requires an assemblage of all the powers which are singly sufficient for other compositions. Poetry is the art of uniting pleasure with truth, by calling imagination to the help of reason. Epick poetry undertakes to teach the most important truths by the most pleasing precepts, and therefore relates some great event in the most affecting manner. History must supply the writer with the rudiments of narration, which he must improve and exalt by a nobler art, must animate by dramatick energy, and diversify by retrospection and anticipation; morality must teach him the exact bounds, and different shades, of vice and virtue; from policy, and the practice of life, he has to learn the discriminations of character, and the tendency of the passions, either single or combined; and physiology must supply him with illustrations and images. To put these materials to poetical use, is required an imagination capable of painting nature, and realizing fiction. Nor is he yet a poet till he has attained the whole extension of his language, distinguished all the delicacies of phrase, and all the colours of words, and learned to adjust their different sounds to all the varieties of metrical modulation.

Bossu is of opinion, that the poet's first work is to find a *moral*, which his fable is afterwards to illustrate and establish.[3] This seems to have been the process only of Milton: the moral of other poems is incidental and consequent; in Milton's only it is essential and intrinsick. His purpose was the most useful and the most arduous: *to vindicate the ways of God to man;* to show the reasonableness of Religion, and the necessity of obedience to the Divine Law.

To convey this moral, there must be a *fable,* a narration artfully constructed, so as to excite curiosity and surprise expectation. In this part of his work, Milton must be confessed to have equalled every other poet. He has involved in his account of the Fall of Man the events which preceded, and those that were to follow it: he has interwoven the whole system of theology with such propriety, that every part appears to be necessary; and scarcely any recital is wished shorter for the sake of quickening the progress of the main action.

The subject of an epick poem is naturally an event of great importance. That of Milton is not the destruction of a city, the conduct of a colony, or the foundation of an empire. His subject is the fate of worlds, the revolutions of Heaven and of Earth; rebellion against the supreme King, raised by the highest order of created beings; the overthrow of their host, and the punishment of their crime; the creation of a new race of reasonable creatures; their original happiness and innocence, their forfeiture of immortality, and their restoration to hope and peace.

Great events can be hastened or retarded only by persons of

[3] René le Bossu (French critic, 1631–1680) in *Traité du Poème Epique,* I, 7.

elevated dignity. Before the greatness displayed in Milton's poem, all other greatness shrinks away. The weakest of his agents are the highest and noblest of human beings, the original parents of mankind; with whose actions the elements consented; on whose rectitude, or deviation of will, depended the state of terrestrial nature, and the condition of all the future inhabitants of the globe.

Of the other agents in the poem, the chief are such as it is irreverence to name on slight occasions. The rest were lower powers;

> of which the least could wield
> Those elements, and arm him with the force
> Of all their regions; [Par. Lost, IV, 221–223]

powers, which only the controul of Omnipotence restrains from laying creation waste, and filling the vast expanse of space with ruin and confusion. To display the motives and actions of beings thus superiour, so far as human reason can examine them, or human imagination represent them, is the task which this mighty poet has undertaken and performed.

In the examination of epick poems much speculation is commonly employed upon the *characters*. The characters in the *Paradise Lost* which admit of examination are those of angels and of man; of angels good and evil; of man in his innocent and sinful state.

Among the angels the virtue of Raphael is mild and placid, of easy condescension and free communication; that of Michael is regal and lofty, and, as may seem, attentive to the dignity of his own nature. Abdiel and Gabriel appear occasionally, and act as every incident requires; the solitary fidelity of Abdiel is very amiably painted.

Of the evil angels the characters are more diversified. To Satan, as Addison observes, such sentiments are given as suit *the most exalted and most depraved being*.[4] Milton has been censured by Clarke [5] for the impiety which sometimes breaks from Satan's mouth; for there are thoughts, as he justly remarks, which no observation of character can justify, because no good man

---

4 *Spectator* no. 303.
5 Author of the "Essay on Study." [Johnson's note.]

would willingly permit them to pass, however transiently, through his own mind. To make Satan speak as a rebel, without any such expressions as might taint the reader's imagination, was indeed one of the great difficulties in Milton's undertaking; and I cannot but think that he has extricated himself with great happiness. There is in Satan's speeches little that can give pain to a pious ear. The language of rebellion cannot be the same with that of obedience. The malignity of Satan foams in haughtiness and obstinacy; but his expressions are commonly general, and no otherwise offensive than as they are wicked.

The other chiefs of the celestial rebellion are very judiciously discriminated in the first and second books; and the ferocious character of Moloch appears, both in the battle and the council, with exact consistency.

To Adam and to Eve are given, during their innocence, such sentiments as innocence can generate and utter. Their love is pure benevolence and mutual veneration; their repasts are without luxury and their diligence without toil. Their addresses to their Maker have little more than the voice of admiration and gratitude. Fruition left them nothing to ask; and Innocence left them nothing to fear.

But with guilt enter distrust and discord, mutual accusation, and stubborn self-defence; they regard each other with alienated minds, and dread their Creator as the avenger of their transgression. At last they seek shelter in his mercy, soften to repentance, and melt in supplication. Both before and after the Fall, the superiority of Adam is diligently sustained.

Of the *probable* and the *marvellous*, two parts of a vulgar epick poem, which immerge the critick in deep consideration, the *Paradise Lost* requires little to be said. It contains the history of a miracle, of Creation and Redemption; it displays the power and the mercy of the Supreme Being: the probable therefore is marvellous, and the marvellous is probable. The substance of the narrative is truth; and as truth allows no choice, it is, like necessity, superior to rule. To the accidental or adventitious parts, as to every thing human, some slight exceptions may be made; but the main fabrick is immovably supported.

It is justly remarked by Addison [6] that this poem has, by the

---

[6] *Spectator* no. 273.

nature of its subject, the advantage above all others, that it is universally and perpetually interesting. All mankind will, through all ages, bear the same relation to Adam and to Eve, and must partake of that good and evil which extend to themselves.

Of the *machinery,* so called from θεὸς ἀπὸ μηχανῆς [Deus ex machina] by which is meant the occasional interposition of supernatural power, another fertile topic of critical remarks, here is no room to speak, because every thing is done under the immediate and visible direction of Heaven; but the rule is so far observed, that no part of the action could have been accomplished by any other means.

Of *episodes,* I think there are only two, contained in Raphael's relation of the war in Heaven and Michael's prophetick account of the changes to happen in this world. Both are closely connected with the great action; one was necessary to Adam as a warning, the other as a consolation.

To the completeness or *integrity* of the design nothing can be objected; it has distinctly and clearly what Aristotle requires, a beginning, a middle, and an end. There is perhaps no poem, of the same length, from which so little can be taken without apparent mutilation. Here are no funeral games, nor is there any long description of a shield. The short digressions at the beginning of the third, seventh, and ninth books might doubtless be spared; but superfluities so beautiful who would take away? or who does not wish that the author of the *Iliad* had gratified succeeding ages with a little knowledge of himself? Perhaps no passages are more frequently or more attentively read than those extrinsick paragraphs; and, since the end of poetry is pleasure, that cannot be unpoetical with which all are pleased.

The questions, whether the action of the poem be strictly *one,* whether the poem can be properly termed *heroick,* and who is the hero, are raised by such readers as draw their principles of judgement rather from books than from reason. Milton, though he intituled [entitled] *Paradise Lost* only a *poem,* yet calls it himself *heroick song.* Dryden petulantly and indecently denies the heroism of Adam, because he was overcome: but there is no reason why the hero should not be unfortunate, except established practice, since success and virtue do not go necessarily together. Cato is the hero of Lucan, but Lucan's authority will not be suffered by Quintilian to decide. However, if success be necessary, Adam's deceiver was at last crushed; Adam was restored to his Maker's favour, and therefore may securely resume his human rank.

After the scheme and fabrick of the poem, must be considered its component parts, the sentiments and the diction.

The *sentiments,* as expressive of manners, or appropriated to characters, are, for the greater part, unexceptionably just.

Splendid passages, containing lessons of morality, or precepts of prudence, occur seldom. Such is the original formation of this poem that, as it admits no human manners till the Fall, it can give little assistance to human conduct. Its end is to raise the thoughts above sublunary cares or pleasures. Yet the praise of that fortitude, with which Abdiel maintained his singularity of virtue against the scorn of multitudes, may be accommodated to all times; and Raphael's reproof of Adam's curiosity after the planetary motions, with the answer returned by Adam, may be confidently opposed to any rule of life which any poet has delivered.

The thoughts which are occasionally called forth in the progress, are such as could only be produced by an imagination in the highest degree fervid and active, to which materials were supplied by incessant study and unlimited curiosity. The heat of Milton's mind might be said to sublimate his learning, to throw off into his work the spirit of science, unmingled with its grosser parts.

He had considered creation in its whole extent, and his descriptions are therefore learned. He had accustomed his imagination to unrestrained indulgence, and his conceptions therefore were extensive. The characteristick quality of his poem is sublimity. He sometimes descends to the elegant, but his element is the great. He can occasionally invest himself with grace; but his natural port is gigantick loftiness. He can please when pleasure is required; but it is his peculiar power to astonish.

He seems to have been well acquainted with his own genius, and to know what it was that Nature had bestowed upon him more bountifully than upon others; the power of displaying the vast, illuminating the splendid, enforcing the awful, darkening the gloomy, and aggravating the dreadful: he therefore chose a subject on which too much could not be said, on which he might tire his fancy without the censure of extravagance.

The appearances of nature, and the occurrences of life did not satiate his appetite of greatness. To paint things as they are requires a minute attention, and employs the memory rather than the fancy. Milton's delight was to sport in the wide regions of possibility; reality was a scene too narrow for his mind. He sent his faculties out upon discovery, into worlds where only imagination can travel, and delighted to form new modes of existence, and furnish sentiment and action to superior beings, to trace the counsels of Hell, or accompany the choirs of Heaven.

But he could not be always in other worlds: he must sometimes revisit earth, and tell of things visible and known. When he cannot raise wonder by the sublimity of his mind, he gives delight by its fertility.

Whatever be his subject he never fails to fill the imagination. But his images and descriptions of the scenes or operations of Nature do not seem to be always copied from original form, nor to have the freshness, raciness, and energy, of immediate observation. He saw Nature, as Dryden expresses it, *through the spectacles of books;* and on most occasions calls learning to his assistance. The garden of Eden brings to his mind the vale of *Enna,* where Proserpine was gathering flowers. Satan makes his way through fighting elements, like *Argo* between the *Cyanean* rocks; or *Ulysses* between the two *Sicilian* whirlpools, when he shunned *Charybdis* on the *larboard.* The mythological allusions have been justly censured, as not being always used with notice of their vanity; but they contribute variety to the narration, and produce an alternate exercise of the memory and the fancy.

His similes are less numerous, and more various, than those of his predecessors. But he does not confine himself within the limits of rigorous comparison: his great excellence is amplitude; and he expands the adventitious image beyond the dimensions which the occasion required. Thus, comparing the shield of Satan to the orb of the Moon, he crowds the imagination with the discovery of the telescope, and all the wonders which the telescope discovers.

Of his moral sentiments it is hardly praise to affirm that they excel those of all other poets; for this supcriority he was indebted to his acquaintance with the sacred writings. The antient epick poets, wanting the light of Revelation, were very unskilful teachers of virtue; their principal characters may be great, but they are not amiable. The reader may rise from their works with a greater degree of active or passive fortitude, and sometimes of prudence; but he will be able to carry away few precepts of justice, and none of mercy.

From the Italian writers it appears, that the advantages of even Christian knowledge may be possessed in vain. Ariosto's pravity is generally known; and, though the *Deliverance of Jerusalem* may be considered as a sacred subject, the poet [7] has been very sparing of moral instruction.

In Milton every line breathes sanctity of thought and purity of manners, except when the train of the narration requires the introduction of the rebellious spirits; and even they are compelled to acknowledge their subjection to God, in such a manner as excites reverence and confirms piety.

Of human beings there are but two; but those two are the parents of mankind, venerable before their fall for dignity and innocence, and amiable after it for repentance and submission. In their first state their affection is tender without weakness, and their piety sublime without presumption. When they have sinned they shew how discord begins in mutual frailty, and how it ought to cease in mutual forbearance; how confidence of the divine favour is forfeited by sin, and how hope of pardon may be obtained by penitence and prayer. A state of innocence we can only conceive, if indeed, in our present misery, it be possible to conceive it; but the sentiments and worship proper to a fallen and offending Being we have all to learn, as we have all to practise.

The poet, whatever be done, is always great. Our progenitors in their first state conversed with angels; even when folly and sin had degraded them, they had not in their humiliation *the port of mean suitors;* and they rise again to reverential regard, when we find that their prayers were heard.

As human passions did not enter the world before the Fall, there is in the *Paradise Lost* little opportunity for the pathetick;

[7] Torquato Tasso (Italian poet, 1544–95).

but what little there is has not been lost. That passion which is peculiar to rational nature, the anguish arising from the consciousness of transgression, and the horrours attending the sense of the Divine displeasure, are very justly described and forcibly impressed. But the passions are moved only on one occasion; sublimity is the general and prevailing quality in this poem; sublimity variously modified, sometimes descriptive, sometimes argumentative.

The defects and faults of *Paradise Lost*, for faults and defects every work of man must have, it is the business of impartial criticism to discover. As in displaying the excellence of Milton, I have not made long quotations, because of selecting beauties there had been no end, I shall in the same general manner mention that which seems to deserve censure; for what Englishman can take delight in transcribing passages, which, if they lessen the reputation of Milton, diminish in some degree the honour of our country?

The generality of my scheme does not admit the frequent notice of verbal inaccuracies; which Bentley,[8] perhaps better skilled in grammar than in poetry, has often found, though he sometimes made them, and which he imputed to the obtrusions of a reviser, whom the author's blindness obliged him to employ; a supposition rash and groundless, if he thought it true; and vile and pernicious if, as is said, he in private allowed it to be false.

The plan of *Paradise Lost* has this inconvenience, that it comprises neither human actions nor human manners. The man and woman who act and suffer are in a state which no other man or woman can ever know. The reader finds no transaction in which he can be engaged; beholds no condition in which he can by any effort of imagination place himself; he has, therefore, little natural curiosity or sympathy.

We all, indeed, feel the effects of Adam's disobedience; we all sin like Adam, and like him must all bewail our offences; we have restless and insidious enemies in the fallen angels: and in the blessed spirits we have guardians and friends; in the Re-

---

[8] In Preface to his edition of *Paradise Lost* (1732).

demption of mankind we hope to be included: in the description of Heaven and Hell we are surely interested, as we are all to reside hereafter either in the regions of horrour or of bliss.

But these truths are too important to be new; they have been taught to our infancy; they have mingled with our solitary thoughts and familiar conversation, and are habitually interwoven with the whole texture of life. Being therefore not new, they raise no unaccustomed emotion in the mind; what we knew before, we cannot learn; what is not unexpected, cannot surprise.

Of the ideas suggested by these awful scenes, from some we recede with reverence, except when stated hours require their association; and from others we shrink with horrour, or admit them only as salutary inflictions, as counterpoises to our interests and passions. Such images rather obstruct the career of fancy than incite it.

Pleasure and terrour are indeed the genuine sources of poetry; but poetical pleasure must be such as human imagination can at least conceive; and poetical terrour such as human strength and fortitude may combat. The good and evil of Eternity are too ponderous for the wings of wit; the mind sinks under them in passive helplessness, content with calm belief and humble adoration.

Known truths, however, may take a different appearance, and be conveyed to the mind by a new train of intermediate images. This Milton has undertaken, and performed with pregnancy and vigour of mind peculiar to himself. Whoever considers the few radical positions which the Scriptures afforded him, will wonder by what energetic operation he expanded them to such extent, and ramified them to so much variety, restrained as he was by religious reverence from licentiousness of fiction.

Here is a full display of the united force of study and genius; of a great accumulation of materials, with judgment to digest, and fancy to combine them: Milton was able to select from nature, or from story, from ancient fable, or from modern science, whatever could illustrate or adorn his thoughts. An accumulation of knowledge impregnated his mind, fermented by study and exalted by imagination.

It has been therefore said, without an indecent hyperbole, by one of his encomiasts, that in reading *Paradise Lost* we read a book of universal knowledge.

But original deficience cannot be supplied. The want of human interest is always felt. *Paradise Lost* is one of the books which the reader admires and lays down, and forgets to take up again. None ever wished it longer than it is. Its perusal is a duty rather than a pleasure. We read Milton for instruction, retire harassed and overburdened, and look elsewhere for recreation; we desert our master, and seek for companions.

Another inconvenience of Milton's design is, that it requires the description of what cannot be described, the agency of spirits. He saw that immateriality supplied no images, and that he could not shew angels acting but by instruments of action; he therefore invested them with form and matter. This, being necessary, was therefore defensible; and he should have secured the consistency of his system, by keeping immateriality out of sight, and enticing his reader to drop it from his thoughts. But he has unhappily perplexed his poetry with his philosophy. His infernal and celestial powers are sometimes pure spirit, and sometimes animated body. When Satan walks with his lance upon the *burning marle* he has a body; when in his passage between Hell and the new world he is in danger of sinking in the vacuity, and is supported by a gust of rising vapours, he has a body; when he animates the toad, he seems to be mere spirit that can penetrate matter at pleasure; when he *starts up in his own shape*, he has at least a determined form; and when he is brought before Gabriel, he has *a spear and a shield*, which he had the power of hiding in the toad, though the arms of the contending angels are evidently material.

The vulgar inhabitants of Pandæmonium, being *incorporeal spirits*, are *at large though without number*, in a limited space: yet in the battle, when they were overwhelmed by mountains, their armour hurt them, *crushed in upon their substance, now grown gross by sinning*. This likewise happened to the uncorrupted angels, who were overthrown *the sooner for their arms*, *for unarmed they might easily as spirits have evaded by contraction or remove*. Even as spirits they are hardly spiritual; for *con-*

traction and *remove* are images of matter; but if they could have escaped without their armour, they might have escaped from it and left only the empty cover to be battered. Uriel, when he rides on a sunbeam, is material; Satan is material when he is afraid of the prowess of Adam.

The confusion of spirit and matter, which pervades the whole narration of the war of Heaven, fills it with incongruity; and the book in which it is related is, I believe, the favourite of children, and gradually neglected as knowledge is increased.

After the operation of immaterial agents which cannot be explained, may be considered that of allegorical persons which have no real existence. To exalt causes into agents, to invest abstract ideas with form, and animate them with activity, has always been the right of poetry. But such airy beings are, for the most part, suffered only to do their natural office, and retire. Thus Fame tells a tale, and Victory hovers over a general, or perches on a standard; but Fame and Victory can do no more. To give them any real employment, or ascribe to them any material agency, is to make them allegorical no longer, but to shock the mind by ascribing effects to non-entity. In the *Prometheus* of Æschylus we see *Violence* and *Strength*, and in the *Alcestis* of Euripides we see *Death*, brought upon the stage, all as active persons of the drama; but no precedents can justify absurdity.

Milton's allegory of Sin and Death is undoubtedly faulty. Sin is indeed the mother of Death, and may be allowed to be the portress of Hell; but when they stop the journey of Satan, a journey described as real, and when Death offers him battle, the allegory is broken. That Sin and Death should have shewn the way to Hell might have been allowed; but they cannot facilitate the passage by building a bridge, because the difficulty of Satan's passage is described as real and sensible, and the bridge ought to be only figurative. The Hell assigned to the rebellious spirits is described as not less local than the residence of man. It is placed in some distant part of space, separated from the regions of harmony and order by a chaotic waste and an unoccupied vacuity; but *Sin* and *Death* worked up a *mole of aggravated soil*, cemented with *asphaltus;* a work too bulky for ideal architects.

This unskilful allegory appears to me one of the greatest

faults of the poem; and to this there was no temptation but the author's opinion of its beauty.

To the conduct of the narrative some objections may be made. Satan is with great expectation brought before Gabriel in Paradise, and is suffered to go away unmolested. The Creation of man is represented as the consequence of the vacuity left in Heaven by the expulsion of the rebels; yet Satan mentions it as a report *rife in heaven* before his departure.

To find sentiments for the state of innocence was very difficult; and something of anticipation perhaps is now and then discovered. Adam's discourse of dreams seems not to be the speculation of a new-created being. I know not whether his answer to the angel's reproof for curiosity does not want something of propriety; it is the speech of a man acquainted with many other men. Some philosophical notions, especially when the philosophy is false, might have been better omitted. The angel, in a comparison, speaks of *timorous deer*, before deer were yet timorous, and before Adam could understand the comparison.

Dryden remarks that Milton has some flats among his elevations.[9] This is only to say, that all the parts are not equal. In every work one part must be for the sake of others; a palace must have passages, a poem must have transitions. It is no more to be required that wit should always be blazing, than that the sun should always stand at noon. In a great work there is a vicissitude of luminous and opaque parts, as there is in the world a succession of day and night. Milton, when he has expatiated in the sky, may be allowed sometimes to revist earth; for what other author ever soared so high, or sustained his flight so long?

Milton, being well versed in the Italian poets, appears to have borrowed often from them; and, as every man catches something from his companions, his desire of imitating Ariosto's levity has disgraced his work with the *Paradise of Fools;* a fiction not in itself ill-imagined, but too ludicrous for its place.

His play on words, in which he delights too often; his equivocations, which Bentley endeavours to defend by the example of the ancients; his unnecessary and ungraceful use of terms of art; it is not necessary to mention, because they are easily re-

[9] In "Preface to Sylvae," (Ker, *Essays,* I, 268).

marked and generally censured; and at last bear so little proportion to the whole, that they scarcely deserve the attention of a
critick.

Such are the faults of that wonderful performance *Paradise
Lost;* which he who can put in balance with its beauties must be
considered not as nice but as dull, as less to be censured for want
of candour than pitied for want of sensibility.

. . . Of *Paradise Regained,* the general judgment seems now to
be right, that it is in many parts elegant, and everywhere instructive. It was not to be supposed that the writer of *Paradise Lost*
could ever write without great effusions of fancy, and exalted precepts of wisdom. The basis of *Paradise Regained* is narrow; a
dialogue without action can never please like an union of the
narrative and dramatick powers. Had this poem been written not
by Milton, but by some imitator, it would have claimed and received universal praise.

If *Paradise Regained* has been too much depreciated, *Samson
Agonistes* has in requital been too much admired. It could only
be by long prejudice, and the bigotry of learning, that Milton
could prefer the ancient tragedies, with their encumbrance of
a chorus, to the exhibitions of the French and English stages; and
it is only by a blind confidence in the reputation of Milton, that
a drama can be praised in which the intermediate parts have
neither cause nor consequence, neither hasten nor retard the
catastrophe.

In this tragedy are however many particular beauties, many
just sentiments and striking lines; but it wants that power of at-
tracting the attention which a well-connected plan produces.

Milton would not have excelled in dramatic writing; he knew
human nature only in the gross, and had never studied the shades
of character, nor the combinations of concurring, or the per-
plexity of contending passions. He had read much, and knew
what books could teach; but had mingled little in the world, and
was deficient in the knowledge which experience must confer.

Through all his greater works there prevails an uniform peculiarity of *Diction,* a mode and cast of expression which bears
little resemblance to that of any former writer; and which is so
far removed from common use, that an unlearned reader, when
he first opens his book, finds himself surprised by a new language.

This novelty has been, by those who can find nothing wrong in Milton, imputed to his laborious endeavours after words suitable to the grandeur of his ideas. *Our language,* says Addison, *sunk under him.*[10] But the truth is, that, both in prose and verse, he had formed his style by a perverse and pedantick principle. He was desirous to use English words with a foreign idiom. This in all his prose is discovered and condemned; for there judgment operates freely, neither softened by the beauty, nor awed by the dignity of his thoughts; but such is the power of his poetry, that his call is obeyed without resistance, the reader feels himself in captivity to a higher and nobler mind, and criticism sinks in admiration.

Milton's style was not modified by his subject; what is shown with greater extent in *Paradise Lost,* may be found in *Comus.* One source of his peculiarity was his familiarity with the Tuscan poets; the disposition of his words is, I think, frequently Italian, perhaps sometimes combined with other tongues. Of him, at last, may be said what Jonson says of Spenser, that *he wrote no language,* but has formed what *Butler* calls a *Babylonish dialect,* in itself harsh and barbarous, but made by exalted genius and extensive learning the vehicle of so much instruction and so much pleasure, that, like other lovers, we find grace in its deformity.

Whatever be the faults of his diction, he cannot want the praise of copiousness and variety: he was master of his language in its full extent; and has selected the melodious words with such diligence, that from his book alone the Art of English Poetry might be learned.

After his diction, something must be said of his *versification.* The *measure,* he says, *is the English heroick verse without rhyme.* Of this mode he had many examples among the Italians, and some in his own country. The Earl of Surrey is said to have translated one of Virgil's books without rhyme; and, beside our tragedies, a few short poems had appeared in blank verse, particularly one tending to reconcile the nation to Raleigh's wild attempt upon Guiana, and probably written by Raleigh himself. These petty performances cannot be supposed to have much influenced Milton, who more probably took his hint from Trissino's

[10] *Spectator* no. 297.

Italia Liberata; and, finding blank verse easier than rhyme, was desirous of persuading himself that it is better.

Rhyme, he says, and says truly, *is no necessary adjunct of true poetry.* But, perhaps, of poetry, as a mental operation, metre or musick is no necessary adjunct: it is however by the musick of metre that poetry has been discriminated in all languages; and, in language melodiously constructed with a due proportion of long and short syllables, metre is sufficient. But one language cannot communicate its rules to another: where metre is scanty and imperfect, some help is necessary. The musick of the English heroic line strikes the ear so faintly, that it is easily lost, unless all the syllables of every line co-operate together; this co-operation can be only obtained by the preservation of every verse unmingled with another as a distinct system of sounds; and this distinctness is obtained and preserved by the artifice of rhyme. The variety of pauses, so much boasted by the lovers of blank verse, changes the measures of an English poet to the periods of a declaimer; and there are only a few happy readers of Milton, who enable their audience to perceive where the lines end or begin. *Blank verse,* said an ingenious critick, *seems to be verse only to the eye.*

Poetry may subsist without rhyme, but English poetry will not often please; nor can rhyme ever be safely spared but where the subject is able to support itself. Blank verse makes some approach to that which is called the *lapidary style;* has neither the easiness of prose, nor the melody of numbers, and therefore tires by long continuance. Of the Italian writers without rhyme, whom Milton alleges as precedents, not one is popular; what reason could urge in its defence has been confuted by the ear.

But, whatever be the advantage of rhyme, I cannot prevail on myself to wish that Milton had been a rhymer; for I cannot wish his work to be other than it is; yet, like other heroes, he is to be admired rather than imitated. He that thinks himself capable of astonishing may write blank verse; but those that hope only to please must condescend to rhyme.

The highest praise of genius is original invention. Milton cannot be said to have contrived the structure of an epic poem, and therefore owes reverence to that vigour and amplitude of mind to which all generations must be indebted for the art of poetical narration, for the texture of the fable, the variation of incidents, the interposition of dialogue, and all the stratagems that surprise and enchain attention. But, of all the borrowers from Homer, Milton is perhaps the least indebted. He was naturally a thinker for himself, confident of his own abilities, and disdainful of help or hindrance: he did not refuse admission to the thoughts or images of his predecessors, but he did not seek them. From his contemporaries he neither courted nor received support; there is in his writings nothing by which the pride of other authors might be gratified, or favour gained; no exchange of praise, nor solicitation of support. His great works were performed under discountenance, and in blindness; but difficulties vanished at his touch; he was born for whatever is arduous; and his work is not the greatest of heroick poems, only because it is not the first.